HEALTH CARE ISSUES, COSTS AND ACCESS

MAJOR HEALTH INSURANCE ISSUES AND PROPOSALS

HEALTH CARE ISSUES, COSTS AND ACCESS

Additional books in this series can be found on Nova's website under the Series tab.

Additional E-books in this series can be found on Nova's website under the E-books tab.

HEALTH CARE ISSUES, COSTS AND ACCESS

MAJOR HEALTH INSURANCE ISSUES AND PROPOSALS

ELIZABETH I. SWANNE
EDITOR

Nova Science Publishers, Inc.
New York

For permission to use material from this book please contact us:
Telephone 631-231-7269; Fax 631-231-8175
Web Site: http://www.novapublishers.com

Library of Congress Cataloging-in-Publication Data

Major health insurance issues and proposals / editor, Elizabeth I. Swanne.
p. ; cm.
Includes index.
ISBN 978-1-60741-330-1 (hardcover)
1. Health insurance--United States. 2. Medical care--United States. 3.
Cost--United States. 4. Health care reform--United States. I. Swanne,
Elizabeth I.
HG9383.M135 2010
368.38'200973--dc22
2010012872

Published by Nova Science Publishers, Inc. ✣ New York

CONTENTS

PREFACE

Concerns about the number of people who lack health insurance and about the high and rising costs of health insurance and health care have led to proposals that would substantially modify the health insurance system in this country. Medicare already provides nearly universal coverage to the elderly, those proposals generally focus on options for providing coverage to and reducing costs for the nonelderly population. They could, for example, provide new federal subsidies to pay some portion of health insurance premiums; impose mandates for individuals to purchase coverage or for employers to offer it and others. This book describes some of the key assumptions that the Congressional Budget Office (CBO) would use in estimating the effects of key elements of such proposals on federal costs, insurance coverage, and other outcomes.

Chapter 1 - People buy insurance to protect themselves against the possibility of financial loss in the future. Such losses may be due to a motor vehicle collision, natural disaster, or other circumstance. For patients, financial losses may result from the use of health care services. Health insurance then provides protection against the possibility of financial loss due to high health care expenses. Also, people do not know ahead of time exactly what their health care expenses will be, so paying for health insurance on a regular basis helps smooth out their out-of-pocket spending.

While health coverage continues to be mostly a private enterprise in this country, government plays an increasingly significant role. Especially during the latter half of the 20th century, the government both initiated and responded to dynamics in medicine, the economy, and the workplace through legislation and public policies. For example, the Internal Revenue System clarified that employer contributions to employee health benefits are exempt from taxation, which encouraged the growth of employment-based health coverage. Given the frequent introduction of legislation aimed at modifying or building on the current health insurance system, understanding the potential impact of such proposals requires a working knowledge of how health insurance is designed, provided, purchased, and regulated. This chapter provides background information about these topics.

Individuals and families without health coverage are more likely than those with coverage to forgo needed health care, which often leads to worse health outcomes and the need for expensive medical treatment. Since uninsured persons are more likely to be poor than insured persons, the uninsured are less able to afford the health care they need. Uninsurance can lead to health care access problems for communities, such as overcrowding in emergency rooms. Taxpayers and the nation as a whole are affected through increased taxes and health care prices to cover the uncompensated care expenses of uninsured persons.

Americans obtain health insurance in different settings and through a variety of methods. People may get health coverage through the private sector, or from a publicly funded program. Consumers may purchase health insurance on their own, as part of an employee group, or through a trade or professional association. However, approximately 47 million Americans did not have health coverage for the entire year of 2006.

Health insurance benefits are delivered and financed under different systems. The factors that distinguish one delivery system from another are many, including how health care is financed, how much access to providers and services is controlled, and how much authority the enrollee has to design her/his health plan. To illustrate, managed care is characterized by predetermined restrictions on accessing services and providers, whereas individual decision-making regarding use of health benefits is a hallmark of consumer driven health care, such as health savings accounts. As economic conditions change, a specific delivery system may gain or lose the interest of affected parties.

Chapter 2 - Much of the health care provided in the United States confers tremendous benefits, extending and improving lives. But the high and rising costs for health care in this country impose an increasing burden on individuals, businesses, states, and the federal government, and a substantial number of people may have trouble paying for that care because they do not have health insurance. Those issues are related: Rising costs for health care make health insurance policies more expensive and thus more difficult to afford. Lack of insurance can limit access to care, but having insurance can increase spending by encouraging the use of services that provide limited health benefits. More generally, despite spending more per capita than other countries, the United States lags behind lower-spending countries on several metrics, including life expectancy and infant mortality. Indeed, evidence suggests that a substantial share of spending on health care contributes little if anything to the overall health of the nation, but finding ways to reduce such spending without also affecting services that improve health will be difficult.

In: Major Health Insurance Issues and Proposals
Editor: Elizabeth I. Swanne

ISBN: 978-1-60741-330-1

Chapter 1

HEALTH INSURANCE: A PRIMER

Bernadette Fernandez

SUMMARY

People buy insurance to protect themselves against the possibility of financial loss in the future. Such losses may be due to a motor vehicle collision, natural disaster, or other circumstance. For patients, financial losses may result from the use of health care services. Health insurance then provides protection against the possibility of financial loss due to high health care expenses. Also, people do not know ahead of time exactly what their health care expenses will be, so paying for health insurance on a regular basis helps smooth out their out-of-pocket spending.

While health coverage continues to be mostly a private enterprise in this country, government plays an increasingly significant role. Especially during the latter half of the 20th century, the government both initiated and responded to dynamics in medicine, the economy, and the workplace through legislation and public policies. For example, the Internal Revenue System clarified that employer contributions to employee health benefits are exempt from taxation, which encouraged the growth of employment-based health coverage. Given the frequent introduction of legislation aimed at modifying or building on the current health insurance system, understanding the potential impact of such proposals requires a working knowledge of how health insurance is designed, provided, purchased, and regulated. This chapter provides background information about these topics.

Individuals and families without health coverage are more likely than those with coverage to forgo needed health care, which often leads to worse health outcomes and the need for expensive medical treatment. Since uninsured persons are more likely to be poor than insured persons, the uninsured are less able to afford the health care they need. Uninsurance can lead to health care access problems for communities, such as overcrowding in emergency rooms. Taxpayers and the nation as a whole are affected through increased taxes and health care prices to cover the uncompensated care expenses of uninsured persons.

Americans obtain health insurance in different settings and through a variety of methods. People may get health coverage through the private sector, or from a publicly funded program. Consumers may purchase health insurance on their own, as part of an employee group, or through a trade or professional association. However, approximately 47 million Americans did not have health coverage for the entire year of 2006.

Health insurance benefits are delivered and financed under different systems. The factors that distinguish one delivery system from another are many, including how health care is financed, how much access to providers and services is controlled, and how much authority the enrollee has to design her/his health plan. To illustrate, managed care is characterized by predetermined restrictions on accessing services and providers, whereas individual decision-making regarding use of health benefits is a hallmark of consumer driven health care, such as health savings accounts. As economic conditions change, a specific delivery system may gain or lose the interest of affected parties.

INTRODUCTION

As health insurance coverage evolved from an uncommon benefit to a routine one, government's role in subsidizing and regulating that coverage also changed. Although health coverage continues to be mostly a private enterprise in this country, public entities play an increasingly significant role.

Government's involvement in health coverage expanded dramatically in the latter half of the 20th century:

- A long-standing rule issued by the Internal Revenue Service (IRS) stated that an employer's contributions to employment-based health insurance could not be included in an employee's gross income for tax purposes (Internal Revenue Code, Section 106). This ruling helped spur the growth of employer-sponsored health benefits. The IRS also stated separately that employers could deduct such contributions as part of business expenses.
- Advances in medicine led to escalating consumer demand for newer, better treatments. At the same time, the cost of some treatments increased, which was especially problematic for certain groups of consumers who lacked health coverage. This led to government efforts to assist health care consumers in paying for medical services through social insurance programs.[1]
- More and more employees began to work for more than one employer over their lifetimes. Government was called on to address a problem many workers faced: keeping health coverage as workers moved from job to job.

Given the frequent introduction of legislation aimed at modifying or building on the current health insurance system, understanding the potential impact of such proposals requires a working knowledge of how health insurance is designed, provided, purchased, and regulated. This chapter provides background information about these topics.

WHAT IS HEALTH INSURANCE?

Definitions and Principles

People buy insurance to protect themselves against the possibility of financial loss in the future. Such losses may be due to a motor vehicle collision, natural disaster, or other circumstance. For patients, financial losses may result from the use of health care services. Health insurance then provides protection against the possibility of financial loss due to high health care expenses. Also, people do not know ahead of time exactly what their health care expenses will be, so paying for health insurance on a regular basis helps smooth out their out-of-pocket spending.

The concept underlying insurance is "risk" (i.e., the likelihood and magnitude of financial loss). In any type of insurance arrangement, all parties seek to minimize their own risk. In health insurance, consumers and insurers approach the management of insurance risk differently. From the consumer's point of view, a person (or family) buys health insurance for protection against financial losses resulting from the future use of medical care. From the insurer's point of view, it employs a variety of methods to minimize the risk it takes on when providing health coverage to consumers, to assure that it operates a profitable business. One method is to cover only those expenses arising from a pre-defined set of services (generally called "covered" services). Another method for limiting risk is to encourage healthier people to obtain health coverage, presumably because healthier people would not need as many medical services as sicker people, leading to fewer claims that the insurer would have to cover.

While the methods employed by an insurer differ from those of a consumer, each has the same goal: to minimize risk in an uncertain future. It is this uncertainty of the future and risk of financial loss which form the context for insurance, and the strategies to make financial loss more predictable and manageable which drive insurance arrangements.

Uneven Distribution of Health Care Expenses

In health care, a minority of consumers are responsible for a majority of expenses. According to a longitudinal study conducted by the federal Agency for Healthcare Research and Quality, 5% of the population accounted for about half of all health expenditures in 2002, and 10% of the population accounted for nearly two-thirds of expenditures in the same year.[2] Given the unevenness of health care spending and the improbability of identifying all of the highest spenders before they use medical services, insurers employ various strategies in order to minimize the risk they take on.

Risk Pool and Rate Setting

A function of insurance is to spread risk across a group of people. This is achieved in health insurance when people contribute to a common pool ("risk pool") an amount at least equal to the *expected* cost resulting from use of covered services by the group as a whole. In this way, the *actual* costs of health services used by a few people are spread over the entire group. This is the reason why insuring larger groups is considered less risky — the more individuals participating in a risk pool, the less likely that the serious medical experiences of one or a few persons will result in catastrophic financial loss for the entire pool.

An insurer calculates and charges a rate (i.e., a "premium") in order to finance the health coverage it provides. The premium reflects several factors, including the expected cost of claims for health care use in a year, administrative expenses associated with running the plan, and a profit margin. If the insurer accurately estimates future costs and sets appropriate premium levels, then that risk pool has reached equilibrium where premiums paid by healthy persons in the risk pool help subsidize the higher-than-average costs of less-healthy persons in the pool.

Risk Pool Composition and Adverse Selection

As noted above, one of the ways insurers attempt to make future costs more predictable is by spreading the risk of a few high-cost individuals across many people. But the number of people in a risk pool is not the only significant factor. Equally as important, if not more so, is the composition of the group.

A consumer's decision to obtain health coverage is based on a variety of factors, such as individual health status, estimated need for future medical care, and disposable income. Consumers with different health conditions, as well as varying degrees of comfort towards risk-taking, will differ on whether they consider health insurance necessary. This is a circumstance that insurers will consider when estimating their expenses to cover future health care use. With this in mind, insurers generally will vary the premiums they charge and the health services they cover (subject to state and federal statues) in order to attract various segments of the population. This flexibility in rate setting and benefit determination is particularly important in a competitive insurance market where insurers try to provide the most attractive rates to increase their market share.

However, some risk pools do attract a disproportionate share of unhealthy individuals. In part, this is because individuals generally know more about their own health conditions than anyone else, including an insurer. Therefore, health care consumers have an advantage over insurers in terms of knowing the kind and amount of health services they will use, at least in the short- to mid-term. This "information asymmetry" between what consumers know compared to what insurers know gives consumers an advantage when looking for health coverage that will meet their future demand for health care. For example, if a consumer plans on obtaining orthodontic care in the near future, that consumer will look for a health plan with generous dental benefits. Information asymmetry is another source of uncertainty that insurers take into account when developing and pricing insurance products.

When a disproportionate share of unhealthy people make up a risk pool, a phenomenon known as "adverse selection," the cost for each person in the pool rises. The higher costs may encourage the departure of healthier members from the group, and discourage the entrance of other healthy people, since healthier people may be able to find cheaper coverage elsewhere or decide that coverage is too costly and become uninsured. In either situation, it leaves an even less healthy group of people in the risk pool, which again causes the cost to rise for the remaining participants. If there is no change in this dynamic, the group may experience a "death spiral" as it suffers substantial adverse selection leading to an increasingly expensive risk pool and possibly dissolution of the pool altogether. Therefore, despite the consumer's information advantage, it does not guarantee access to affordable and adequate health coverage.

Group Market, Nongroup Market, and Medical Underwriting

Health insurance can be provided to groups of people that are drawn together by an employer or other organization, such as a trade union. Such groups are generally formed for some purpose other than obtaining insurance, like employment. When insurance is provided to a group, it is referred to as "group coverage" or "group insurance." In the group market, the entity that purchases health insurance on behalf of a group is referred to as the plan "sponsor."

Consumers who are not associated with a group can obtain health coverage by purchasing it directly from an insurer in the individual (or nongroup) insurance market. Insurance carriers in the nongroup market conduct an exhaustive analysis of each applicant's insurability. An applicant usually must provide the insurer with an extensive medical history and often undergo a physical exam. This information is used by carriers to assess the potential medical claims for each person by comparing characteristics of the applicant to the loss experience of others with similar characteristics. Once such an evaluation has been conducted, the carrier decides whether or not to provide health coverage and determines the terms for coverage. This evaluation and determination process is referred to as "medical underwriting."

Medical underwriting is standard practice in the individual insurance market, though a carrier's ability to reject applicants or vary the terms of coverage are restricted to some degree by federal and state requirements. In the group health insurance market, insurers forgo underwriting in the traditional sense (i.e., reviewing *each* person's demographics and medical history). Instead, an insurer looks at the characteristics of the collective group, such as its claims history, group demographics, and geographic location. The insurer then charges a premium based on the analysis of the group's characteristics. There are exceptions to this for very small groups. For example, when a firm with only a handful of employees applies for health coverage, the insurer may choose to review the health conditions of each person in order to establish a premium for the entire group. Or, the insurer may charge a larger premium due to the larger risk attributed to smaller groups, if permitted under law.[3]

Fully Insured vs. Self-Insured Plans

A common distinction made between types of health insurance products is whether they are fully insured or self- insured. A fully insured health plan is one in which the plan sponsor purchases health coverage from a state-licensed insurer. The carrier assumes the risk of providing health benefits to the sponsor's enrolled members. In contrast, organizations who self insure (or self fund) do *not* purchase health coverage from state-licensed insurers. Self-insured plans refer to health coverage that is provided directly by the organization seeking coverage for its members (e.g., a firm providing health benefits to its employees). Such organizations directly take on the risk for covering medical expenses, and such benefit plans are not subject to state insurance regulations. Firms that self fund typically contract with third-party administrators (TPAs) to handle administrative duties such as member services, premium collection, and utilization review. TPAs do not underwrite insurance risk.

Self-only vs. Family Coverage

Another common distinction made in health insurance is whether the policy covers one person or a family. Under self-only coverage, the holder of the insurance policy is the only person insured. (Self-only coverage is also called individual coverage. Individual coverage in this sense should not be confused with health coverage from the individual insurance market — see discussion above.) Family coverage applies to the policyholder, her/his spouse, and children.[4] Self-only and family policies may differ from each other in terms of the services they cover and the cost-sharing they impose.

Administrative Expenses

Costs for administrative functions encompass a wide range of operational activities. Administrative expenses include costs associated with contracting with providers, sales and marketing, enrollment and billing, customer service, utilization review, case management, and other functions. Because of economies of scale, administrative expenses in the group market are a smaller portion of overall costs, compared to those in the nongroup market.[5]

Tax Preference

Unlike most industrialized countries, the United States does not guarantee health coverage to all of its citizens. Instead, it relies on a patchwork approach that combines private and public means for providing health insurance and health care. One of the key pieces of this approach encouraged the growth of employment-based health coverage via the tax code.

Section 106 of the Internal Revenue Code states that employer contributions to employment-based health insurance are not included in workers' gross incomes for tax purposes. This tax preference encourages workers to sign up for ("take-up") health coverage within the work setting. A separate ruling by the Internal Revenue Service clarified that such employer contributions are business expenses and, therefore, deductible from employers' taxable income. Both parties benefit: employers use health insurance coverage as a means to recruit and retain workers, while workers typically get access to more services at better rates (see discussion below). However, workers generally receive reduced wages to compensate for richer benefits.

The tax exclusion of health benefits is one of the primary reasons why health insurance coverage is provided mainly through the workplace in the United States. Approximately two out of three nonelderly (under 65) Americans have employer- sponsored insurance. Moreover, of nonelderly persons with private health coverage, approximately nine out of 10 obtain it through the workplace.[6]

Health Insurance Regulation

Health insurance regulation addresses a wide variety of issues: the benefits that must be offered, the individuals to whom the insurance is made available, and the responsibilities insurers have to plan enrollees, to name a few. One of the most contentious issues regarding health insurance regulation is whether it is the responsibility of individual states or the federal government. This distinction is important because federal and state laws governing health plans differ on issues such as patient compensation in courts, consumer access to care, and mandated coverage for certain benefits.

Responsibility of the States

The regulation of insurance traditionally has been a state responsibility, as clarified by the 1945 McCarran-Ferguson Act. However, overlapping federal requirements complicate the matter with respect to health insurance. Individual states have established standards and regulations overseeing the "business of insurance," including requirements related to the finances, management, and business practices of an insurer. For example, all states have laws that require state-licensed insurance carriers to offer coverage for specified health care services (known as "mandated benefits"). Because fully insured plans are subject to state-established requirements, those plans must offer those mandated benefits. On the other hand, self-insured plans are not subject to state insurance regulations so they are exempt from such requirements.

Key Federal Statutes

Regardless of whether health plans are fully-insured or self-funded, they all are subject to a number of federal laws. Two of these federal laws, the Employee Retirement Income Security Act of 1974 (ERISA, P.L. 93-406) and the Health Insurance Portability and Accountability Act of 1996 (HIPAA, P.L. 104-191), have significant impact on how health insurance is provided.

ERISA outlines minimum federal standards for private-sector employer- sponsored benefits. (Public employee benefits and plans sponsored by churches are exempt from ERISA). Passed in response to abuses in the private pension system, the act was developed with a focus on pensions but the law applies to a long list of "welfare benefits" including health insurance. The act requires that funds be handled prudently and in the best interest of beneficiaries, participants be informed of their rights, and there be adequate disclosure of a plan's financial activities. ERISA preempts state laws that "relate to" employee benefit plans. (In other words, the federal law overrides state laws affecting private-sector employee benefits). This portion of ERISA was designed to ensure that plans would be subject to the same benefit laws across all states, partly in consideration of firms that operate in multiple states. However, state laws still apply for issues which involve the "business of insurance." The delineation of issues attributable to the phrases "relate to" and "business of insurance" is not clear, and have led to longstanding debates and active litigation over the scope of ERISA preemption.[7]

The core motivation behind the Health Insurance Portability and Accountability Act of 1996 (HIPAA) is to address the concern that insured persons have about losing their coverage if they switch jobs or change health plans ("portability" of health coverage). The act's health insurance provisions established federal requirements on private and public employer-sponsored health plans and insurers. It ensures the availability and renewability of coverage for certain employees and other persons under specified circumstances. HIPAA limits the amount of time that coverage for pre-existing medical conditions can be excluded, and prohibits discrimination on the basis of health status-related factors. The act also includes tax provisions designed to encourage the expansion of health coverage through several mechanisms, such as authorizing tax-advantaged medical savings accounts and a graduated increase of the portion of premiums self-employed persons may deduct from their federal income tax calculations. Another set of HIPAA provisions addresses the electronic transmission of health information and the privacy of personally identifiable medical information (administrative simplification and privacy provisions, respectively).[8]

Health Insurance Premiums

The most current, publicly available data on employer health benefits found that the average annual premium for self-only coverage was $4,479 in 2007. The average premium for a family of four was $12, 106.[9] Together, these premiums represent a 6.1% increase in the cost for employer-sponsored health benefits compared to last year's average premiums. While this signals a reprieve from double-digit increases in recent years,[10] the premium growth rate nonetheless outpaces both wage gains and the growth in prices for all goods and services. For 2007, the average growth rate for health insurance premiums was twice as much as the growth rate for overall inflation (2.6%), and one and a half times as much as the growth rate for workers' earnings (3.7%).[11]

WHY IS HEALTH INSURANCE CONSIDERED IMPORTANT?

While health insurance coverage is not necessary to obtain health care, it is a useful mechanism for accessing services in an environment of increasingly expensive health care. As health care costs continue to rise, more people need greater assistance with covering medical expenses. Health insurance provides some measure of protection for consumers, especially those who have limited means or greater-thanaverage need for medical care.

Health insurance is considered important also because of the well-documented, far-reaching consequences of uninsurance. For instance, uninsured persons are more likely to forgo needed health care than people with health coverage. This includes forgoing services for preventable or chronic conditions which often leads to worse health outcomes.[12] Uninsured persons also are less likely to have a "usual source of care," that is, a person or place identified as the source to which the patient *usually* goes for health services or medical advice (not including emergency rooms). Having a usual source is important because people who establish ongoing relationships with health care providers or facilities are more likely to access preventive health services and have regular visits with a physician, compared with individuals without a usual source.[13] Therefore, to the extent that health insurance coverage facilitates access to basic medical services, people without coverage face substantial barriers in the pursuit of the health care they need. For 2003-04, almost 10% of nonelderly adults with private health insurance identified no usual source of care, compared with around 49% of uninsured, nonelderly adults who reported no usual source.[14]

The negative consequences of uninsurance extends beyond the persons directly involved. The Institute of Medicine found that the insurance status of parents affects the amount of health care their children receive.[15] In locations with crowded emergency rooms, rising uninsurance rates can exacerbate that problem, since uninsured persons have fewer places from which they can get medical services compared to people with health coverage. Overcrowding in emergency departments, in turn, leads to longer waits for all patients seeking emergency care. Moreover, many uninsured persons forgo preventive health care and end up developing more serious conditions requiring complex, expensive medical services. Since health coverage is positively related to income, uninsured persons are less likely to be able to afford this level of care. In cases where patients are unable to cover the costs associated with receiving health services, the facilities that provided those services must take it as a financial loss (i.e., uncompensated care). These losses can be staggering. For example, one study estimated that health care providers would provide nearly $41 billion worth of uncompensated care to the uninsured in 2004.[16]

Ultimately, though, the costs for caring for the uninsured are "passed down to all taxpayers and consumers of health care in the form of higher taxes and higher prices for services and insurance."[17] Taxpayers are affected because the federal government makes payments to hospitals, which take into account the share of poor people treated. The assumption is that facilities that treat a larger proportion of poor people have a greater problem with uninsurance and uncompensated care. The federal government also provides grants to many health centers and other facilities that serve poor communities. In addition, states and localities fund local health programs, public hospitals, and clinics — facilities that generally serve an uninsured or medically underserved population. Health care consumers are affected by uninsurance because in order for physician practices and hospitals to survive financially they have to make-up the losses they sustain. Hospitals and physicians may raise rates for certain services or discontinue unprofitable programs in order to recoup those losses, thereby affecting consumers' pocketbooks and access to services. Uninsurance, then, has negative health and financial consequences for uninsured persons, their families, communities, and the nation as a whole.

WHERE DO PEOPLE GET HEALTH INSURANCE?

Americans obtain health insurance in different settings and through a variety of methods (see **Table 1**). People may get it through the private sector, or from a publicly funded social insurance program. Consumers may purchase health coverage on their own, as part of an employee group, or through a trade or professional association. A small minority of employees get health insurance at no up-front cost because their employer pays the total premium. However, approximately 47 million Americans did not have health insurance coverage for the entire year of 2006; that is, nearly 16% of the total population were uninsured.[18]

Employer-Sponsored Insurance

Even though examples of health insurance in this country stretch back more than 200 years, most Americans did not have health coverage until the latter half of the 20th century.[19] The demand for more workers during World War II and a wage freeze imposed by the National War Labor Board generated great interest in employer- sponsored insurance (ESI) as a worker recruitment and retention tool.[20] Buoyed by legislation and court rulings declaring the tax exemption of fringe benefits, and support from unions for work-based coverage, health insurance became a pervasive employment benefit.

Table 1. Health Insurance Coverage for All Persons, by Type of Insurance, 2006

	Population (millions)	Coverage Distribution
Total Population	296.8	100.0%
Employment Based	177.2	59.7%
Nongroup	27.1	9.1%
Medicare	40.3	13.6%
Medicaid/SCHIP/State Programs	38.3	12.9%
Military/Veterans Coverage	10.5	3.6%
No Health Insurance	47.0	15.8%

Source: U.S. Census Bureau, Current Population Survey, 2007 Annual Social and Economic Supplement, Table HI05, at [http://pubdb3.census.gov/macro/032007/health

Note: Columns do not add to totals because persons may receive insurance coverage from more than one source.

Note: The most current national data on health insurance coverage for an entire year is for 2006.

In employer-sponsored insurance, risk pools may be comprised of active workers, dependents, and retirees. Insurers use a number of strategies to increase the likelihood that each risk pool includes a good proportion of healthy individuals, thus avoiding adverse selection. For instance, insurers may restrict employees' opportunities to take-up health coverage or switch health plans by designating a specific time frame each year for such activities ("open enrollment period"). This strategy decreases the likelihood that people will "game" the system by taking up coverage only when they plan on using health services (e.g., for pregnancy and birth), and dropping coverage when they no longer plan to access care. Insurers also may require the employer to enroll a certain proportion of the firm's eligible population. Assuming that the eligible population consists of a good percentage of healthy people, requiring a certain proportion of all eligibles to enroll leads to an enrollee population which contains at least some healthy people. Employers also use strategies to encourage insurance take-up by healthy people. For example, employers usually pay part (or, in very few instances, all) of the total premium. This practice makes health coverage a more attractive benefit, even to those who do not plan to use medical services on a regular basis.

Advantages

ESI plans retain enrollees better than the individual health insurance market. As previously mentioned, health benefits provided at the workplace are exempt from income and employment taxes, encouraging the growth and continuity of employer-sponsored health insurance. Large risk pools with a good proportion of healthy enrollees tend to be more stable than small pools or those with a higher proportion of unhealthy enrollees. Given the strategies discussed above to discourage adverse selection, insurers assume that ESI pools — particularly large, diverse ones — are relatively stable. Generally, this translates into less volatile costs and better premiums overall in the group market compared to the nongroup market. Also, large ESI groups can use their size to negotiate for better benefits and lower cost-sharing, in contrast to individual applicants in the nongroup market. Plan sponsors negotiate and interact with insurers on behalf of all of their insured members, unlike in the individual market where each consumer must deal with the insurance carrier directly in order to apply for and purchase coverage. In addition, there are economies of scale for enrollees in the group market compared to the nongroup market for administrative functions such as sales, billing, and customer service. For these reasons, workers and their families benefit from receiving coverage through the workplace. For plan sponsors, the main advantage is to use health benefits for recruitment and retention of workers. This is particularly appealing in a growing economy — such as during most of the 1990s — when there may be high demand for workers.

Disadvantages

While there are many advantages to obtaining ESI coverage, there are challenges as well. From the vantage point of the enrollee, one of the biggest disadvantages is the general lack of portability. Because ESI coverage is tied to the job and not the person, any change in employment (such as going from full- time to part-time status, or changing jobs) may alter the health care providers or services to which the worker has access, or disrupt health coverage altogether. Also, in firms that offer health coverage, there is a trade off made between wages and benefits. For workers who do not take up health insurance from those firms, they end up accepting lower wages for a set of benefits they do not use. From the perspective of the sponsor, an underlying challenge is the lack of enrollee awareness of the true costs of health care. Because the sponsor contributes to the cost of the premium, enrollees do not bear the full cost of obtaining health coverage. Also, enrollees generally do not have to cover the entire cost of the services they use, since sponsors negotiate for lower rates and better cost-sharing arrangements from insurers. Consumers enrolled in managed care plans particularly are shielded from health care's true costs. Some observers contend that this lack of cost awareness gives little incentive to consumers to utilize medical services prudently, which leads to greater use of services and greater overall health care expenditures. In addition, sponsors' efforts to constrain their health care spending — by increasing the employee share of the premium or cost-sharing — are made even more difficult to justify or implement. Finally, from the perspective of the federal budget, the tax exclusion of employer-sponsored health insurance represents a lost source for Treasury funds. (The Joint Committee on Taxation estimated the FY2007 income tax exclusion for employer-paid insurance to be almost $100 billion.)[21]

Large vs. Small Groups

The group insurance market often is thought of as consisting of large and small groups. The underlying reason for this distinction is rooted in the inverse relationship between insurance risk and group size (i.e., the risk associated with a group grows as the size of the group shrinks). This concept affects employers' offers of health benefits. For instance, a very large employer often is able to offer multiple health plan options to its members (e.g., the Federal Employee Health Benefit Program (FEHBP)). A large business can leverage its size to get a more comprehensive set of benefits. In contrast, small employers are less able to provide health coverage at all because of the greater risk associated with small groups. Even when small employers do offer coverage, the benefits are often limited. Small employers also are much less likely to self-fund health coverage, since there is a smaller pool for spreading risk and protecting against catastrophic loss. Furthermore, such firms generally do not have the necessary administrative capacity to negotiate with multiple provider groups and handle all the day-to-day operational functions. It is conditions such as these which prompt legislators to develop proposals for expanding small group participation in health insurance; for example, by establishing association health plans, and opening up FEHBP to the small group market.

Association health plans are just one example among the spectrum of entities which bring groups of people together for the purpose of buying health insurance. These entities include trade and professional associations that offer health coverage to their members ("association-sponsored plans"), and small firms that band together to purchase coverage as a group ("health insurance purchasing cooperatives"). The premise behind group purchasing arrangements is to decrease the administrative burden on and increase the negotiating capacity of participants who cannot afford to offer or purchase coverage on their own. Around one-third of small firms buy health coverage through some type of purchasing pool.[22]

Public Programs

While most Americans with health insurance obtain it through the private- sector, tens of millions of people get their health care covered through public programs. Below are descriptions of selected federal and state programs which provide payments on behalf of many persons who, due to low incomes or high health care expenses, could not afford health care otherwise.

Medicare

The Medicare program was established in 1965, and is a federal program for persons age 65 and older and certain persons with disabilities. Medicare consists of four parts: Part A, Hospital Insurance; Part B, Supplementary Medical Insurance; Part C, Medicare Advantage (replaced the Medicare+Choice program with the passage of the Medicare, Prescription Drug, and Modernization Act of 2003 (MMA, P.L. 108-173); and Part D, the prescription drug benefit also added by MMA. The Medicare program provides coverage for a wide range of medical services, such as care provided in hospitals and skilled nursing facilities, hospice care, home health care, physician services, physical and occupational therapy, outpatient prescription drug benefits, and other services. Since its creation in the mid-1960s, Medicare has provided health coverage to tens of millions of American. In 2005, the program had approximately 40 million enrollees. Medicare has been so successful in covering the elderly that the problem of uninsurance usually is described in terms of the under-65 population.[23]

Medicaid and the State Children's Health Insurance Program (SCHIP)

Medicaid is the main health insurance program for low-income Americans. It is a means-tested program, and applicants must meet financial and other criteria in order to be eligible for program services. Everyone who meets the eligibility criteria is entitled to Medicaid benefits available in their state of residence. Medicaid provides coverage for health care and long-term-care services to certain adults (generally parents and pregnant women), children, the elderly, and persons with disabilities. It is jointly funded by federal and state governments, and is administered by the states within federally set guidelines. State Medicaid programs provide a comprehensive set of services, reflecting its diverse enrollee population. These programs must provide a set of federally specified benefits, such as hospital services (both inpatient and outpatient), physician services, nursing home care for ages 21 and over, home health care for those entitled to services from nursing facilities, and certain services for children. States may also cover additional optional services. Some states have used waiver authority under Medicaid to extend coverage to uninsured persons who do not meet the program's categorical (e.g., childless adult with no disability) and/or financial tests.[24]

The State Children's Health Insurance Program was established in 1997 to allow states to cover uninsured low-income children who are ineligible for Medicaid. In designing their programs, states can choose among three options: expand Medicaid, create a new "separate state" insurance program, or devise a combination of both approaches. States that choose to expand Medicaid to SCHIP eligibles must provide the full range of mandatory Medicaid benefits, as well as all optional services specified in their state Medicaid plans. States that establish SCHIP programs that are separate from Medicaid choose one of three benefit options. All 50 states, the District of Columbia, and five territories have established some type of SCHIP program. SCHIP's eligibility rules target uninsured children under 19 years of age whose families' incomes are above Medicaid eligibility levels. States may raise the upper income level for low-income children up to 200% of the federal poverty level, or higher under certain circumstances.[25]

Individual Health Insurance

The individual insurance ("nongroup") market is often referred to as a "residual" market. The reason is because this market provides coverage to persons who cannot obtain health insurance through the workplace and do not qualify for public programs such as Medicare, Medicaid, or SCHIP. Consequently, the enrollee population for this private health insurance market is small.

The residual nature of the nongroup market is evident in the demographic makeup of those who purchase coverage from it. The market is over-represented by the near elderly (55-64 years old); a group that has relatively weak attachments to the workplace. The individual market disproportionately consists of part-time workers, part-year workers, and the self-employed, groups unlikely to have access to ESI coverage.[26] Also, some people use the nongroup market as a temporary source of coverage, such as those in-between jobs or early retirees who are not yet eligible for Medicare.

Applicants to the individual insurance market must go through robust underwriting. Insurance carriers in most states conduct an exhaustive analysis of each applicant's insurability. An applicant usually must provide her/his medical history, and often undergo a physical exam. This information is used by carriers to assess the potential medical claims for each person. Federal and state requirements restrict somewhat insurers' ability to reject applications or design coverage based on health factors (such as benefit exclusions for certain pre-existing health conditions). Nonetheless, some applicants are rejected from the nongroup market altogether, and others who are approved may receive limited benefits or are charged premiums that are higher than those in the group market for similar coverage.[27] Rigorous underwriting results in an enrollee population that is fairly healthy (three out of four enrollees report that their health is excellent or very good[28]), thereby excluding persons with moderate to severe health problems from the private nongroup insurance market.

State High Risk Pools

A majority of states have established high risk health insurance pools. These programs target individuals who cannot obtain or afford health insurance in the private market, primarily because of pre-existing health conditions. If such individuals are not eligible for public programs (e.g., their incomes may exceed the financial eligibility requirements), they have very few options for obtaining coverage. In general, high risk pools tend to be small and enroll a small percentage of the uninsured. As of the first half of 2006, 34 states had high risk pools with participation of nearly 193,000 enrollees.[29] While health benefits vary across states and plans, they generally reflect coverage that is available in the private insurance market, with required cost-sharing for enrollees. The majority of high risk pools cap premiums between 125% to 200% of market rates, and pools often are subsidized through assessments imposed on insurance companies, general revenue, or other funding mechanisms.[30]

The Uninsured

Despite the multiple private and public sources of health insurance, millions of Americans are without health coverage. In 2006, nearly 47 million people were without health insurance coverage for the entire year. For the vast majority of the uninsured, they lack coverage because they cannot *access* coverage (e.g., their employer does not offer health insurance as an employment benefit) or they cannot *afford* it.

Uninsurance is characterized as a problem of the under-65 population, given near-universal coverage of seniors through Medicare. The nonelderly uninsured population differs from the insured population on a number of key demographic factors. One of the most striking characteristics of persons who lack coverage is that a significant proportion are in low-income families. For instance, among all uninsured persons under age 65, more than half were in poor or near poor families in 2006.[31] Moreover, among nonelderly persons who are poor, 34% lacked health coverage. This proportion is almost triple the share of nonelderly individuals with moderate/high incomes who had no health insurance (12%).

A defining characteristic of the nonelderly uninsured population is that 82% are persons with ties to the paid labor force, or dependents of such persons. Even more surprising is that 57% of the nonelderly uninsured were workers with full-time, full- year status, or the dependents of those workers. While such findings may be counterintuitive, there are multiple reasons why employed persons and their families may lack health coverage. For example, a worker may be offered health insurance by his/her employer, but declines it because he/she thinks it is too expensive. An employee may work for a small firm which is less likely than a large firm to offer health insurance as a benefit. A low-wage employee, even working full time, is less likely to be offered health insurance at work and less likely to be able to afford it than higher-wage workers in the same firm. Finally, a healthy worker may be willing to take on the risk of being uninsured and choose not to purchase insurance at all. So despite the dominance of employer-sponsored health insurance, the dynamics of work, insurance risk, and financial resources intersect to impede the coverage of all workers and their families.

The problem of the uninsured is an ongoing concern to many policymakers and legislators. One of the topics of ongoing debate is the overall number of uninsured individuals and the direction of the uninsurance rate. These issues have generated some controversy over dueling analyses which show slightly different (and sometimes, moderately different) findings.[32] But despite the forceful discussions regarding trends in uninsurance, the year-to-year changes in the uninsurance rate actually are small. For example, from 1987 to 2006, the change in the uninsurance rate from year to year has been less than 1%.[33] Nonetheless, tens of millions of Americans were without coverage during that time period. Such circumstances beg the questions: why does pervasive uninsurance persist (even during the robust economy of the mid-1990s), and what are the implications for legislation and public policies to expand health coverage?

How Are Private Health Benefits Delivered and Financed?

Given the complexity of the health care system overall, it is no surprise that health benefits are delivered and financed through different arrangements. Those arrangements vary due to numerous factors such as: how health care is financed, how much access to providers and services are controlled, and how much authority the enrollee has to design her/his health plan. While delivery systems may share certain characteristics, general distinctions can be made based on payment, access, and other critical variables.

Indemnity (Traditional) Insurance

Under indemnity insurance, the insured person decides when and from whom to seek health services. If the services the enrollee receives are covered under his/her insurance, the enrollee or the enrollee's provider files a claim with the insurer. Thus, insurers make payments *retrospectively* (i.e., after the health services have been rendered), up to the maximum amounts specified for each covered service. In this model of health care delivery, the financing of health services and the obtaining of those services are kept separate.

This bifurcated arrangement was unquestioned for a time. But as medical costs began to rise, sometimes faster than other sectors of the national economy, many observers criticized this delivery model as contributing to increasing expenses. Because providers were compensated on a fee-for-service basis, some argued that providers were not given incentives to provide efficient health care. In fact, some critics accused health care practitioners and institutions of providing an overabundance of health care in order to generate greater revenue. By the early 1970s, legislators, analysts, and others expressed considerable interest in alternative models, such as managed care models, with cost control as a key feature.

Managed Care

While managed care means different things to different people, several key characteristics set it apart from traditional (indemnity) insurance. One of the main differences is that the service delivery and financing functions are integrated under managed care. Managed care organizations (MCOs) employ various techniques to control costs and manage health service use *prospectively*. Among those techniques are restricting enrollee access to certain providers ("in-network" providers); requiring primary-care-physician approval for access to specialty care ("gatekeeping"); coordinating care for persons with certain conditions ("disease management" or "case management"); and requiring prior authorization for routine hospital inpatient care ("pre-certification"). MCOs may offer different types of health plans that vary in the degree to which cost and medical decision-making is controlled. As a consequence, enrollee cost-sharing also varies. Generally, the more tightly managed a plan is, the less the premium charged. Other distinguishing features of the managed care approach include an emphasis on preventive health care and implementation of quality assurance processes.

Managed care was touted as the antidote to rapidly rising health care costs. Starting with the passage of federal legislation in the 1970s which supported the growth of managed care (specifically in the form of health maintenance organizations (HMOs)), the number of MCOs grew quickly. Increased market competition among these organizations led to decreases in premiums, in order to gain market share. With high medical inflation in the 1980s and early 1990s, enrollees flocked to these less-costly managed care plans. By the mid-1990s, more insured workers were enrolled in HMOs than any other health plan type, and health insurance premiums had stabilized.

But in the latter half of the 1990s, a "backlash" of sorts against managed care grew.[34] Some enrollees had grown weary of provider and service restrictions. Many MCOs that had increased market share through artificially-low premiums began to raise them in order to increase revenue.[35] Consumers and others accused the managed care industry of caring more about controlling costs than providing health care. Some providers resented the role managed care played in medical decision- making. Many enrollees began to leave HMOs. The industry responded by developing insurance products that were less-tightly managed, but more costly. Some traditional HMOs widened their provider networks and eliminated the gatekeeping function, while employers began to offer plan types that were less tightly managed, such as preferred provider organizations (PPOs). In fact, by the end of the 1990s, more people with work-based health coverage were enrolled in PPOs than in HMOs.[36]

As the influence of managed care waned and health care costs began to rise at an increasing pace during the late 1990s, the impact on consumers began to be felt. For example, in the employment setting, employers absorbed the extra costs at first in order to recruit and retain workers during the booming economy of the mid to late 1990s.[37] But as the economy soured, employers began to pass these expenses along to enrollees in the form of greater cost-sharing.[38]

Consumer Driven Health Care

By the end of the 1990s, large increases in health costs again became commonplace. With the belief by some observers that the age of managed care was over, they began to search for alternatives. Consumer driven (or consumer-directed) health care have been offered as one such option.

Consumer driven health care refers to a broad spectrum of approaches that give incentives to consumers to control their use of health services and/or ration their own health benefits. In the workplace, at one extreme employers may choose to provide an array of insurance products from which workers can choose, while at the other end an employer could increase wages but not offer any health coverage allowing workers to decide how to spend that extra money to meet their health care needs. Within those two endpoints, the consumer directed approach varies in the degree to which consumers are responsible for health care decision-making.[39]

For example, one health benefits option that is at the heart of discussions about consumer driven care is the health savings account (HSA). Under this approach, the consumer is responsible for management of the account. HSAs are investment accounts in which contributions earn interest tax free. Consumers, their employers, or both may make contributions to HSAs. Consumers withdraw funds on a tax-free basis to cover medical expenses not covered by health insurance. Unused contributions roll over to the next year. HSAs must be paired with high-deductible health plans. If the HSA funds are exhausted and the deductible level has not been reached, the consumer is responsible for covering that gap. Once the consumer's spending reaches the deductible level, then coverage from the high-deductible plan takes effect. HSAs received a legislative boost when they were authorized in November 2003 by the Medicare Prescription Drug, Improvement, and Modernization Act of 2003 (P.L. 108-173).[40]

While consumer driven health care can take on many forms, the premise common to all of the approaches is that by making enrollees more responsible for their own health care, it creates incentives for people to use services prudently. The expectation is that greater cost-consciousness on the part of consumers will result in lower overall health costs. In essence, the service and cost control functions administered by MCOs and providers under managed care shifts to enrollees under the consumer driven health care scenario.

Proponents of consumer directed plans assert the merit in having people take increased responsibility for their own health care use and expenses. They predict that this approach will lead to better-informed consumers, more appropriate use of health services, and lower overall spending on health care. Opponents express concern that this approach does not recognize the possible range of health conditions in an enrolled population. They argue that these plans benefit the young and healthy who use relatively few services, and, therefore, would not need to expend a great deal of time and energy making these health care decisions. However, these plans impose a greater burden on individuals with moderate to severe health conditions because of their greater-than-average use of medical services.

End Notes

[1] Publicly funded health programs generally either provide funding for direct medical services or assist consumers in paying for health care. The latter are included in a broad category of programs based on "social insurance" principles. Social insurance refers to publicly funded insurance programs that are statutorily mandated for certain groups of people, such as low-income individuals.

[2] Mark W. Stanton, "The High Concentration of U. S. Health Care Expenditures," *Research In Action*, Issue #19, June 2006, at [http://www.meps.ahrq.gov/mepsweb/data_files/ publications/ra1 9/ra1 9.pdf].

[3] G. Claxton, "How Private Insurance Works: A Primer," Kaiser Family Foundation (KFF) website, April 2002, at [http://www.kff.org/insurance security/getfile.cfm&PageID=14053].

[4] Policies vary on the requirements children must meet (e.g., age, martial status, etc.) in order to become eligible for or stay on a family policy.

[5] Given that insurers monitor administrative costs as part of managing their businesses, such information is considered proprietary. Therefore, there are no reliable national estimates of the portion of insurers' expenses attributable to administrative functions.

[6] Paul Fronstin, "Sources of Health Insurance and Characteristics of the Uninsured: Analysis of the March 2006 Current Population Survey," EBRI Issue Brief No. 2897, October 2006, at [http://www.ebri.org/pdf/briefspdf/EBRI_IB_10a-20061 .pdf].

[7] For more information about ERISA preemption, see "ERISA Preemption Primer," State Coverage Initiatives website, [http://statecoverage.net/pdf/primer2000.pdf].

[8] For more information about HIPAA, see CRS Report RL3 1634, *The Health Insurance Portability and Accountability Act (HIPAA) of 1996: Overview and Guidance on Frequently Asked Questions*, by Hinda Chaikind, Jean Hearne, Bob Lyke, and Stephen Redhead.

[9] The Kaiser Family Foundation and Health Research and Educational Trust, *Employer Health Benefits 2007 Annual Survey*, at [http://www.kff.org/insurance. (Hereafter cited as *Employer Health Benefits Survey*.) These averages include both the employer and employee shares of the total premium.

[10] Other sources of premium data show a comparable trend in declining growth rates for health insurance costs. For example, see Mercer press release online, "U.S. employers' health benefit cost continues to rise at twice inflation rate, Mercer survey finds," November 19, 2007, at [http://www.mercer.com/referencecontent.jhtml?idContent=1287790].

[11] *Employer Health Benefits Survey*, p.19.

[12] Kaiser Commission on Medicaid and the Uninsured, "The Uninsured and Their Access to Health Care," November 2005 at [http://www.kff.org/uninsured

[13] J.E. DeVoe, et al., "Receipt of Preventive Care Among Adults: Insurance Status and Usual Source of Care," *American Journal of Public Health*, May 2003.

[14] National Center for Health Statistics, *Health, United States, 2006*, Table 77, at [http://www.cdc.gov/nchs/data/hus/hus06.pdf#executivesummary].

[15] Institute of Medicine, Committee on the Consequences of Uninsurance, *Coverage Matters: Insurance and Health Care*, 2001.

[16] J. Hadley and J. Holahan, "The Cost of Care for the Uninsured: What Do We Spend, Who Pays, and What Would Full Coverage Add to Medical Spending?," *Issue Update*, 2004, at [http://www.kff.org/uninsured

[17] Institute of Medicine, Committee on the Consequences of Uninsurance, *A Shared Destiny*, 2003, p 122.

[18] U.S. Census Bureau, *Income, Poverty, and Health Insurance Coverage in the United States: 2006*, August 2007, p. 18 at [http://www.census.gov/prod/2007pubs/p60-233 .pdf].

[19] See timeline from Employee Benefit Research Institute's "History of Health Insurance Benefits," March 2002, at [http://www.ebri.org/publications/facts/james/dis_0302fact.cfm].

[20] Health Insurance Association of America, *Fundamentals of Health Insurance*, 1997.

[21] For additional information on the tax treatment of health benefits, see CRS Report RL33 505, *Tax Benefits for Health Insurance and Expenses: Overview of Current Law and Legislation*, by Bob Lyke.

[22] For additional information, see CRS Report RL3 1963, *Association Sponsored Health Plans: Legislation in the 109th Congress*, by Jean Hearne.

[23] For additional information about Medicare, see CRS Report RL337 12, *Medicare: A Primer*, by Jennifer O'Sullivan.

[24] For additional information about Medicaid, see CRS Report RL33202, *Medicaid: A Primer*, by Elicia Herz.

[25] For additional information about SCHIP, see CRS Report RL30473, *State Children's Health Insurance Program (SCHIP): A Brief Overview*, by Elicia J. Herz and Chris L. Peterson.

[26] D. J. Chollet, "Consumers, Insurers, and Market Behavior," *Journal of Health Politics, Policy and Law*, February 2000.

[27] M. V. Pauly and A.M. Percy, "Cost and Performance: A Comparison of the Individual and Group Health Insurance Markets," *Journal of Health Politics, Policy and Law*, February 2000.

[28] General Accounting Office, "Private Health Insurance: Millions Relying on Individual Market Face Cost and Coverage Trade-Offs," November 1996.

[29] States with high risk pools: AL, AK, AR, CA, CO, CT, FL, ID, IL, IN, IA, KS, KY, LA, MD, MN, MS, MO, MT, NE, NH, NM, ND, OK, OR, SC, SD, TN, TX, UT, WA, WI, WV and WY.

[30] For additional information about state high risk pools, see CRS Report RL3 1745, *Health Insurance: State High Risk Pools*, by Bernadette Fernandez.

[31] The poverty level for a family of four was an annual income of $20,614 (weighted average) in 2006; see [http://www.census.gov/hhes/www/poverty/threshld/thresh06.html].

[32] For a discussion of the various sources of data on health insurance coverage, see CRS Report RL3 1275, *Health Insurance: Federal Data Sources for Analyses of the Uninsured*, by Chris Peterson and Christine Devere.

[33] Data available at [http://www.census.gov/hhes/www/hlthins/historic/hihisttl .html].

[34] Richard Kronick, "Waiting for Godot: Wishes and Worries in Managed Care," *Journal of Health Politics, Policy and Law*, vol. 24, no. 5 (October 1999), pp. 1099-1106.

[35] Jon Gabel, et al., "Job-Based Health Insurance in 2001: Inflation Hits Double Digits, Managed Care Retreats," *Health Affairs*, vol. 20, no. 5 (September/October 2001), pp. 180- 186.

[36] American Association of Health Plans, "Health Plans and Employer-Sponsored Plans," October 1999. Available at [http://www.ahip.org/content/default.aspx?bc=4 1|331|366].

[37] Jon B. Christianson and Sally Trude, "Managing Costs, Managing Benefits: Employer Decisions in Local Health Care Markets," *Health Services Research*, pt. II, vol. 38, no. 1, (February 2003), pp. 357-373.

[38] Jon Gabel, et al., "Job-Based Health Benefits in 2002: Some Important Trends," *Health Affairs*, vol. 21, no. 5 (September/October 2002), pp. 143-151.

[39] P. Fronstin, ed., Employee Benefit Research Institute, *Consumer-Driven Health Benefits: A Continuing Evolution?* 2002.

[40] For more information about HSAs, see CRS Report RL33257, *Health Savings Accounts: Overview of Rules for 2007*, by Bob Lyke.

In: Major Health Insurance Issues and Proposals
Editor: Elizabeth I. Swanne

ISBN: 978-1-60741-330-1

Chapter 2

KEY ISSUES IN ANALYZING MAJOR HEALTH INSURANCE PROPOSALS

Congressional Budget Office

SUMMARY

Much of the health care provided in the United States confers tremendous benefits, extending and improving lives. But the high and rising costs for health care in this country impose an increasing burden on individuals, businesses, states, and the federal government, and a substantial number of people may have trouble paying for that care because they do not have health insurance. Those issues are related: Rising costs for health care make health insurance policies more expensive and thus more difficult to afford. Lack of insurance can limit access to care, but having insurance can increase spending by encouraging the use of services that provide limited health benefits. More generally, despite spending more per capita than other countries, the United States lags behind lower-spending countries on several metrics, including life expectancy and infant mortality. Indeed, evidence suggests that a substantial share of spending on health care contributes little if anything to the overall health of the nation, but finding ways to reduce such spending without also affecting services that improve health will be difficult.

Main Conclusions

Concerns about the number of people who are uninsured and about the rising costs of health insurance and health care have given rise to proposals that would substantially modify the U.S. health insurance system. The complexities of the health insurance and health care systems pose a major challenge for the design of such proposals and inevitably raise questions about their likely impact. To assist the Congress in its upcoming deliberations, this chapter seeks to provide useful background information as well as insights into how the Congressional Budget Office (CBO) would estimate the effects of such proposals on the federal budget, the number of people who have health insurance coverage, and spending for health care. Some of its main conclusions are as follows:

- The rising costs of health care and health insurance pose a serious threat to the future fiscal condition of the United States. Under current policies, CBO projects that federal spending on Medicare and Medicaid will increase from about 4 percent of gross domestic product (GDP) in 2009 to nearly 6 percent in 2019 and 12 percent by 2050. Most of that increase will result from growth in per capita costs rather than from the aging of the population.
- Without changes in policy, a substantial and growing number of nonelderly people (those younger than 65) are likely to be without health insurance. CBO estimates that the average number of nonelderly people who are uninsured will rise from at least 45 million in 2009 to about 54 million in 2019.
- Those problems cannot be solved without making major changes in the financing or provision of health insurance and health care. In considering such changes, policymakers face difficult trade-offs between the objectives of expanding insurance coverage and controlling both federal and total costs for health care.
- By themselves, premium subsidies or mandates to obtain health insurance would not achieve universal coverage. Proposals could, however, achieve near- universal coverage using a combination of approaches.
    - One option would establish an enforceable mandate for individuals to obtain insurance and would provide subsidies for lower-income households to help them pay their required premiums.
    - Another option, under a voluntary system, would provide subsidies that cover a very large share of the expected costs of insurance for every enrollee and establish a process to facilitate enrollment (as is done in Medicare).

  Other policies could achieve substantial reductions in the number of people who are uninsured at a lower budgetary cost.
- Serious concerns exist about the efficiency of the health care system, but no simple solutions are available to reduce the level or control the growth of health care costs. Steps to restructure the insurance market and to encourage people to purchase less extensive coverage could reduce the use of treatments that provide minimal benefits, but enrollees would face higher cost sharing or tighter management of their care.
- Other approaches—such as the wider adoption of health information technology or greater use of preventive medical care—could improve people's health but would probably generate either modest reductions in the overall costs of health care or increases in such spending within a 10-year budgetary time frame.
- In many cases, the current health care system does not give doctors, hospitals, and other providers of health care incentives to control costs. Significantly reducing the level or slowing the growth of health care spending would require substantial changes in those incentives.

Scope and Focus of This Chapter

In the near future, the Congress is expected to consider major proposals to modify the health insurance system. This chapter describes the assumptions that CBO would use in estimating the effects of key elements of such proposals on federal costs, insurance coverage, and other outcomes; the evidence upon which those assumptions are based; and, if the evidence points to a range of possible effects rather than a precise prediction, the factors that would influence where a proposal falls within those ranges.

This document does not provide a comprehensive analysis of any specific proposal; rather, it identifies and examines many of the critical factors that would affect estimates of a variety of proposals. In particular, it considers the types of issues that would arise in estimating the effects of proposals to:

- Provide tax credits or other types of subsidies to make insurance less expensive to the purchaser.
- Require individuals to purchase health insurance, typically paired with a new system of government subsidies.
- Require firms to offer health insurance to their workers or pay into a fund that subsidizes insurance purchases.
- Replace employment-based coverage with new purchasing arrangements or provide strong incentives for people to shift toward individually purchased coverage.
- Provide individuals with coverage under, or access to, existing insurance plans such as the Medicare program, either as an additional option or under a "Medicare-for-all" single-payer arrangement.

Wherever possible, the analysis presented here describes in quantitative terms how CBO would estimate the budgetary and other effects of such proposals. In other cases, it describes the components that a proposal would have to specify in order to permit estimation of its effects on federal spending or other outcomes. This chapter reflects the current state of CBO's analysis of and judgments about the likely response of individuals, employers, insurers, and providers to changes in the health insurance and health care systems. The details of particular policy specifications and the way in which they are combined, as well as new evidence or analysis related to the issues discussed here, could affect future CBO estimates of the effects of large-scale health insurance proposals.

Because such proposals could incorporate a number of the elements that are discussed in this chapter, they could have interactions that are difficult to predict. Those proposals could also affect both tax revenues and outlays. Estimates of the impact on revenues of proposals to change the federal tax code are prepared by the staff of the Joint Committee on Taxation (JCT) and would be incorporated into any formal CBO estimate of a proposal's effects on the federal budget. In preparing this chapter, CBO consulted with the JCT staff about the behavioral considerations that are incorporated into both agencies' estimates.

The question of whether and how any net increases in federal spending for health care and health insurance would be financed by policy changes outside the health sector is beyond the scope of this chapter. Whether a proposal would make health insurance more affordable for a given individual or family would depend not only on its impact on the health insurance premiums that they face but also on the effect that its financing mechanisms would have on the household's budget. To the extent that such proposals would be financed by policy changes that fall outside the health sector—through tax increases or reductions in spending for other federal programs—those effects are not addressed here.

Background on Spending and Coverage

Health care costs are an important issue, not just for individuals and families seeking insurance coverage but also for the federal budget and the economy as a whole. Spending on health care and related activities will account for about 17 percent of gross domestic product in 2009—an expected total of $2.6 trillion—and under current law that share is projected to reach nearly 20 percent by 2017. Annual health expenditures per capita are projected to rise from about $8,300 to about $13,000 over that period. Federal spending accounts for about one-third of those totals, and federal outlays for the Medicare and Medicaid programs are projected to grow from $720 billion in 2009 to about $1.4 trillion in 2019.

Over the longer term, rising costs for health care represent the single greatest challenge to balancing the federal budget. The number of uninsured individuals is also expected to increase because health insurance premiums are likely to continue rising much faster than income, which will make insurance more difficult to afford.

Employment-Based Insurance

For several reasons, most nonelderly individuals obtain their insurance through an employer, and employment-based plans now cover about 160 million people, including spouses and dependents (see Summary Table 1). One fundamental reason such plans are popular is that they are subsidized through the tax code—because nearly all payments for employment-based insurance are excluded from taxable compensation and thus avoid income and payroll taxes. Another factor is the economies of scale that larger group purchasers enjoy, which reduce the average amount of administrative costs that are embedded in policy premiums; partly as a result, large employers are more likely than small employers to offer insurance to their workers. Overall, about three-fourths of workers are offered employment-based insurance and are eligible to enroll in it.

Another commonly cited reason for the popularity of employment-based policies is that employers offering coverage usually pay most of the premium—a step they take partly to encourage broad enrollment in those plans, which helps keep average costs stable. Ultimately, however, the costs of those employers' payments are passed on to employees as a group, mainly in the form of lower wages.

Other Sources of Coverage

Other significant sources of coverage include the individual insurance market and various public programs. Roughly 10 million people are covered by individually purchased plans, which have some advantages for enrollees; for example, they may be portable from job to job, unlike employment-based insurance. Even so, individually purchased policies generally do not receive favorable tax treatment; in most states, premiums may vary to reflect an applicant's age or health status, and applicants with particularly high expected costs are generally denied coverage.

Another major source of coverage is the federal/state Medicaid program and the related but smaller State Children's Health Insurance Program (S CHIP). Both programs provide free or low-priced coverage for children in low-income families and (to a more limited degree) their parents; Medicaid also covers poor individuals who are blind or disabled. On average, Medicaid and SCHIP are expected to cover about 43 million nonelderly people in 2009 (and there are also many people eligible for those programs who have not enrolled in them). Medicare also covers about 7 million people younger than 65 who are disabled or have severe kidney disease. About 12 million people have insurance coverage from various other sources, including federal health programs for military personnel. The total number of nonelderly people with health insurance at any given point in 2009 is expected to be about 216 million.

Approaches for Reducing the Number of Uninsured People

Concerns about the large number of people who lack health insurance have generated proposals that seek to increase coverage rates substantially or achieve universal or near-universal coverage. Two basic approaches could be used:

- Subsidizing health insurance premiums, either through the tax system or spending programs, which would make insurance less expensive for people who are eligible; or
- Establishing a mandate for health insurance, either by requiring individuals to obtain coverage or by requiring employers to offer health insurance to their workers.

By themselves, premium subsidies or mandates to obtain health insurance would not achieve universal coverage. Those approaches could be combined and could be implemented along with provisions to facilitate enrollment in ways that could achieve near-universal coverage.

Subsidizing Premiums

Whether new subsidies are delivered through the tax system or a spending program, several common issues arise. Trade-offs exist between the share of the premium that is subsidized, the number of people who enroll in insurance as a result of the subsidies, and the total costs of the subsidies. As the subsidy rate increases, more people will be inclined to take advantage of them, but the higher subsidy payments will also benefit those who would have decided to obtain insurance anyway. Beyond a certain point, therefore, the cost per newly insured person can grow sharply because a large share of the additional subsidy payments is going to otherwise insured individuals.

To hold down the costs of subsidies, the government could limit eligibility for subsidy payments to individuals who are currently uninsured. That restriction, however, would create incentives for insured individuals to drop their coverage. Some proposals might try to distinguish between people who become uninsured in response to subsidies and those who would have been uninsured in the absence of a government program (for example, by imposing waiting periods for individuals who were previously enrolled in an employment-based plan), but such proposals could be very difficult to administer. In addition, providing benefits only to the uninsured might be viewed as unfair by people with similar income and family responsibilities who purchase health insurance and are therefore ineligible for the subsidies.

Another approach to limiting costs would target subsidies toward the lower-income groups, who are most likely to be uninsured otherwise, but such approaches can also have unintended consequences that affect the costs of a proposal. If eligibility was limited to people with income below a certain level, then those with income just above the threshold would have strong incentives to work less or hide income in order to qualify for the subsidies or maintain their eligibility. Phasing out subsidies gradually as income rises would reduce those incentives, but it would increase the amount of subsidy payments that go to individuals and families who would have had insurance in any event.

Restructuring the Existing Tax Subsidies

Tax subsidies could be restructured to expand coverage in several ways. For example, the current tax exclusion for employment- based health insurance could be replaced with a deduction or tax credit to offset the costs of insurance, and tax subsidies could be extended to include policies purchased in the individual insurance market. That step would sever the link between employment and tax subsidies for private health insurance and could give similar people the same subsidy whether or not they were offered an employment-based health plan.

Summary Table 1. Sources of Insurance Coverage and Insurance Status of the Nonelderly Population, 2009

	Number (Millions)	Percent
	Source of Coverage	
Employment-Based[a]	160	61
Individually Purchased	10	4
Medicare	7	3
Medicaid[b]	43	17
Other[c]	12	4
	Insurance Status	
Insured, Any Source[d]	216	83
Uninsured	45	17

Source: Congressional Budget Office's health insurance simulation model.

Note: The nonelderly population (those younger than 65) excludes people in institutions and residents of U.S. territories.

a. Includes coverage obtained through local, state, and federal employers.

b. Includes the State Children's Health Insurance Program.

c. Includes military and other sources of coverage.

d. The sum of people by their sources of coverage exceeds the total number who are insured because about 14.5 million people are covered by more than one source at a time.

Deductions and credits differ, however, in their effectiveness at reaching the uninsured. An income tax deduction might provide limited benefits to low-income individuals because, like the existing exclusion, its value is less for those in lower tax brackets. In contrast, tax credits can be designed to provide lower- and moderate-income taxpayers with larger benefits than they would receive from tax deductions or exclusions. An important question regarding tax credits—particularly for lower-income people who pay relatively little in income taxes and are also more likely to be uninsured—is whether the credits would be refundable and therefore fully available to individuals with little or no income tax liability.

For the same budgetary costs, a refundable tax credit might be more effective at increasing insurance coverage, both because it can be designed to provide a larger benefit to people who have low income than they receive under current law and because those recipients might be more responsive to a given subsidy than are people with higher income. Still, the effect on coverage rates might be limited if people do not receive refundable tax credits before their premium payments are due.

Providing Subsidies through Spending Programs

The government could seek to increase coverage rates by spending funds to subsidize insurance premiums. New subsidies could be provided implicitly by expanding eligibility for Medicare, Medicaid, or SCHIP or explicitly by creating a new program. To hold costs down, benefits could be targeted on the basis of income, assets, family responsibilities, and insurance status. Targeting benefits, however, would require program administrators to certify eligibility and enforce the program's rules, which would affect coverage and the program's costs.

The Effects of Subsidy Proposals

Proposals to subsidize insurance coverage would affect decisions by both employers and individuals. Employers' decisions to offer insurance to their workers reflect the preferences of their workers, the cost of the insurance that they can provide, and the costs of alternative sources of coverage that workers would have. Smaller firms appear to be more sensitive to changes in the cost of insurance than are larger employers. Subsidies that reduce the cost of insurance offered outside the workplace would cause some firms to drop coverage or reduce their contributions. When deciding whether to enroll in employment-based plans, workers would consider the share of the premium that they pay as well as the price and attractiveness of alternatives. The available evidence indicates that a small share of the population would be reluctant to purchase insurance even if subsidies covered nearly all of the costs.

Mandating Coverage

In an effort to increase the number of people who have health insurance or to achieve universal or near-universal coverage, the government could require individuals to obtain health insurance or employers to offer insurance plans. Employer mandates could include a requirement that employers contribute a certain percentage of the premium, which would encourage their workers to purchase coverage. To the extent that the required contributions exceeded the amounts that employers would have paid under current law, offsetting reductions would ultimately be made in wages and other forms of compensation.

The impact of a mandate on the number of people covered by insurance would depend on its scope, the extent of enforcement, and the incentives to comply, as well as the benefits that enrollees would receive. Individual mandates, for example, could be applied broadly to the entire population of the United States or to a specific group, such as children; employer mandates might vary by the size of the firm.

Penalties would generally increase individuals' incentives to comply with mandates, but when deciding whether to obtain insurance, people would also consider the likelihood of being caught if they did not comply. Data from the tax system and from other government programs, where overall rates of compliance range from roughly 60 percent to 90 percent, indicate that mandates alone would not achieve universal coverage, largely because some people would still be unwilling or unable to purchase insurance.

Facilitating Enrollment

Simplifying the process of enrolling in health insurance plans or applying for subsidies could yield higher coverage rates and could also increase compliance with a mandate to obtain coverage. One approach would be to enroll eligible individuals in health insurance plans automatically, giving them the option to refuse that coverage or to switch to a different plan. Automatic enrollment procedures have been found to increase participation rates in retirement plans and government benefit programs. Automatic enrollment requires the government, an employer, or some other entity to determine the specific plan into which people will be enrolled, however, and those choices may not always be appropriate for every-one.

Factors Affecting Insurance Premiums

Premiums for employment-based plans are expected to average about $5,000 per year for single coverage and about $13,000 per year for family coverage in 2009. Premiums for policies purchased in the individual insurance market are, on average, much lower—about one-third lower for single coverage and one-half lower for family policies. Those differences largely reflect the fact that policies purchased in the individual market generally cover a smaller share of enrollees' health care costs, which also encourages enrollees to use fewer services. An offsetting factor is that average administrative costs are much higher for individually purchased policies. The remainder of the difference in premiums probably arises because people who purchase individual coverage have lower expected costs for health care to begin with.

The federal costs of providing premium subsidies, or the effects of those subsidies on the number of people who are insured, would depend heavily on the premiums charged. Premiums reflect the average cost that any insurer—public or private—incurs, and those costs are a function of several factors:

- The scope of the benefits the coverage includes and its cost-sharing requirements;
- The degree of benefit management that is conducted;
- The administrative costs the insurer incurs; and
- The health status of the individuals who enroll.

Insurers' costs also depend on the mechanisms and rates used to pay providers and on other forces affecting the supply of health care services. Proposals could affect many of those factors directly or indirectly. For example, the government might specify a minimum level of benefits that the coverage must provide in order to qualify for a subsidy or fulfill a mandate; such a requirement could have substantial effects on the proposal's costs or its impact on coverage rates.

Design of Benefits and Cost Sharing

Health insurance plans purchased in the private market tend to vary only modestly in the scope of their benefits—with virtually all plans covering hospital care, physicians' services, and prescription drugs—but they vary more substantially in their cost-sharing requirements. A useful summary statistic for comparing plans with differing designs is their "actuarial value," which essentially measures the share of health care spending for a given population that each plan would cover. Actuarial values for employment-based plans typically range between 65 percent and 95 percent, with an average value between 80 percent and 85 percent. Cost-sharing requirements for enrollees tend to be greater for policies purchased in the individual insurance market, where actuarial values generally range from 40 percent to 80 percent, with an average value between 55 percent and 60 percent.

Public programs also vary in the extent of the coverage they provide. Medicaid requires only limited cost sharing (reflecting the low income of its enrollees); cost sharing under SCHIP may be higher but is capped as a share of family income. Medicare's cost sharing varies substantially by the type of service provided; for example, home health care is free to enrollees, but most hospital admissions incur a deductible of about $1,000. In addition, the program does not cap the out-of-pocket costs that enrollees can incur. Overall, the actuarial value of Medicare's benefits for the nonelderly population is about 15 percent lower than that of a typical employment-based plan. Those considerations would affect CBO's analysis of proposals to expand enrollment in public programs.

In general, the more comprehensive the coverage a health plan provided, the higher would be the premium or cost per enrollee. Indeed, an increase in a health plan's actuarial value would also lead enrollees to use more health care services. Reflecting the available evidence, CBO estimates that a 10 percent decrease in the out-of-pocket costs that enrollees have to pay would generally cause their use of health care to increase by about 1 percent to 2 percent. A similar analysis would be applied to proposals that included subsidies to reduce the cost-sharing requirements that lower-income enrollees face.

Management of Benefits

Another factor affecting health insurance premiums and thus the costs or effects of legislative proposals is the degree of benefit and cost management that insurers apply. Nearly all Americans with private health insurance are enrolled in some type of "managed care" plan, but the extent to which specific management techniques are used varies widely. Common techniques used to constrain costs include negotiating lower fees with a network of providers, requiring that certain services be authorized in advance, monitoring the care of hospitalized patients, and varying cost-sharing requirements to encourage the use of less expensive prescription drugs. Overall, CBO estimates that premiums for plans making extensive use of such cost-management techniques would be 5 percent to 10 percent lower than for plans using minimal management Conversely, proposals that restricted plans' use of such management tools would result in higher health care spending than proposals that did not impose such restrictions.

Administrative Costs

Some proposals would affect the price of health insurance by changing insurers' administrative costs. Some types of administrative costs (such as those for customer service and claims processing) vary in proportion to the number of enrollees in a health plan, but others (such as those for sales and marketing efforts) are more fixed; that is, those costs are similar whether a policy covers 100 enrollees or 100,000. As a result of those economies of scale, the average share of the policy premium that covers administrative costs varies considerably—from about 7 percent for employment-based plans with 1,000 or more enrollees to nearly 30 percent for policies purchased by very small firms (those with fewer than 25 employees) and by individuals.

Some administrative costs would be incurred under any system of health insurance, but proposals that shifted enrollment away from the small-group and individual markets could avoid at least a portion of the added administrative costs per enrollee that are observed in those markets. In general, however, substantial reductions in administrative costs would probably require the role of insurance agents and brokers in marketing and selling policies to be sharply curtailed and the services they provide to be rendered unnecessary.

Spending by Previously Uninsured People

The impact that the mix of enrollees has on health insurance premiums is also an important consideration, particularly for proposals that would reduce the number of people who are uninsured. The reason is that the use of health care by the previously uninsured will generally increase when they gain coverage. On average, CBO estimates, the uninsured currently use about 60 percent as much care as the insured population, after adjusting for differences in demographic characteristics and health status between the two groups.

On the basis of the research literature and an analysis of survey data, CBO estimates that enrolling all people who are currently uninsured in a typical employment-based plan would increase their use of services by 25 percent to 60 percent; that is, they would use between 75 percent and 95 percent as many services as a similar group of insured people. The remaining gap in the use of services reflects the expectation that, on average, people who are uninsured have a lower propensity to use health care, a tendency that would persist even after they gained coverage. For more incremental increases in coverage rates, CBO would expect that people who chose to enroll in a new program would be more likely to use medical care than those who decided not to enroll.

In addition, recent estimates indicate that about a third of the care that the uninsured receive is either uncompensated or undercompensated—that is, they either pay nothing for it or pay less than the amount that a provider would receive for treating an insured patient. To the extent that such care became compensated under a proposal to expand coverage, health care spending for the uninsured would increase, regardless of whether their use of care also rose.

Proposals Affecting the Choice of an Insurance Plan

The government could affect the options available to individuals when choosing a health insurance plan—and the incentives they face when making that choice—in a number of ways. In particular, proposals could establish or alter regulations governing insurance markets, seek to reveal more fully the relative costs of different health insurance plans, or have the federal government offer new health insurance options.

The effects of proposals on insurance markets would depend on more than the impact they have on the premiums charged or on the share of the premium that enrollees have to pay; those effects would also reflect the market dynamics that arise as individuals shift among coverage options and as policy premiums adjust to those shifts. In particular, the risk that some plans would experience "adverse selection"—that is, that their enrollees will have above-average or higher-than-expected costs for health care—has important implications for the operation of insurance markets and for proposals that would regulate those markets or introduce new insurance options.

Insurance Market Regulations

Proposals could seek to establish or alter regulations governing the range of premiums that insurers may charge or the terms under which individuals and groups purchase coverage. Purchases in the individual insurance market and most policies for small employers are governed primarily by state regulations. Those regulations differ in the extent to which they limit variation in premiums, require insurers to offer coverage to applicants, permit exclusions for preexisting health conditions, or mandate coverage of certain benefits. Roughly 20 percent of applicants for coverage in the individual market have health problems that raise their expected costs for health care substantially, and in most states they may be charged a higher premium or have their application denied; as a result, premiums are correspondingly lower in those states for the majority of applicants.

Proposals may seek to modify the regulation of health insurance markets in order to make insurance more affordable for people with health problems or to give consumers more choices, but those goals may conflict with one another. For example, limiting the extent to which premiums for people in poor health can exceed those for people in better health (as some states currently do) would reduce premiums for those who have higher expected costs for health care, but it would also raise premiums for healthier individuals and thus could reduce their coverage rates. Other proposals might counteract such limits on variations in premiums—for example, by allowing people to buy insurance in other states. That approach would enable younger and relatively healthy individuals living in states with tight limits to purchase a cheaper policy in another state. Older and less healthy residents who continued to purchase individual coverage in the tightly regulated states, however, would probably face higher premiums as a result.

By themselves, changes in the regulation of the individual and small-group insurance markets would generally have modest effects on the federal budget and on the total number of people who are insured. Those budgetary effects would primarily reflect modest shifts into or out of Medicaid, SCHIP, or employment-based coverage as those options became more or less attractive relative to coverage in the individual market. Proposals to require insurers to cover all applicants or to guarantee coverage of preexisting health conditions would benefit people whose health care would not be covered otherwise, but insurers would generally raise premiums to reflect the added costs.

Another approach that has attracted attention recently involves so-called high-risk pools. Most states have established such pools to subsidize insurance for people who have high expected medical costs and have either been denied coverage in the individual insurance market or been quoted a very high premium. Overall participation in high-risk pools is limited—there are currently about 200,000 enrollees nationwide—but proposals could seek to expand the use of those pools by providing new federal subsidies. The costs of such subsidies would depend primarily on the average health care costs of enrollees, the share of those costs covered by the pool, and the number of people who enrolled as a result.

Steps to Reveal Relative Costs

Some proposals would seek to restructure the choices that individuals face—and expose more clearly the relative costs of their health insurance options—either by reducing or eliminating the current tax subsidy for employment-based insurance or by encouraging or requiring the establishment of managed competition systems. Both approaches would provide stronger incentives for enrollees to weigh the expected benefits and costs of policies when making decisions about purchasing insurance. As a result, many enrollees would choose health insurance policies that were less extensive, more tightly managed, or both, compared with the choices made under current law.

The current tax exclusion for the premiums of employment-based health plans provides a subsidy of about 30 percent, on average, taking into account both the income and payroll taxes that are avoided. Eliminating that exclusion, or replacing it with a fixed-dollar tax credit or deduction, would effectively require employees to pay a larger share of the added costs of joining a more expensive plan; conversely, employees would capture more of the savings from choosing a cheaper plan. As a result, CBO estimates that people would ultimately select plans with premiums that are between 15 percent and 20 percent lower than the premiums they would pay under current law. Less extensive changes, such as capping the amount that may be excluded at a certain dollar value, would have proportionally smaller effects on average premiums.

The key features of a managed competition system involve a sponsor, such as an employer or government agency, offering a structured choice of health plans and making a fixed-dollar contribution toward the cost of that insurance. Enrollees would thus bear the cost of any difference in premiums across plans. CBO estimates that a proposal requiring that approach would yield average premiums for health insurance that are about 5 percent lower than those chosen under current law. Proposals that also adopted other features of managed competition, such as standardization of benefits across plans and adjustments of sponsors' payments to those plans to reflect the health risk of each enrollee, might yield more intense competition among plans and help avoid problems of adverse selection.

Federally Administered Options

Under some proposals, the federal government would make available additional insurance options—for example, by providing access to the private health plans that are offered through the Federal Employees Health Benefits (FEHB) program. The effects of that approach would depend critically on how the premiums for nonfederal enrollees were set. If insurers could charge different premiums to different applicants on the basis of their expected costs for health care, the option would resemble the current individual and small-group markets and thus would have little impact. Alternatively, if new enrollees were all charged the same premium, the FEHB plans would be most attractive to people who expected to have above-average costs for health care. If no subsidies were provided, the total premiums charged to nonfederal enrollees would probably be much higher than those observed in the program today—so the number of new enrollees would probably be limited. Depending on the specific features of such proposals, providing access to FEHB plans might not prove to be financially viable because of adverse selection into those plans.

The government could also design an insurance option based on Medicare that would be made more broadly available, on a voluntary basis, to the nonelderly population. The federal costs per enrollee would depend primarily on the benefits that system provided; the rates used to pay doctors, hospitals, and other providers of health care; and the extent of any premium subsidies that were offered to enrollees—all of which could differ from Medicare's current design. As for whether such a plan would be more or less costly than a private health insurance plan that provides the same benefits to a representative group of enrollees, the answer would vary geographically. Assuming that Medicare's current rules applied, those costs would be comparable in many urban areas, but in other areas the cost of the government-run plan would be lower (as is evident in the current program through which Medicare beneficiaries may enroll in a private health plan). At the same time, because Medicare currently provides broad access to doctors and hospitals and employs little benefit management, a Medicare-based option might attract relatively unhealthy enrollees, which could drive up its premiums, federal costs, or both.

Many of the same considerations would arise in designing a single-payer, Medicare-for-all system, but that approach might raise some unique issues as well—and the scale of its impact on federal costs could obviously be much larger if nearly all of the population was covered. Enrollees could be offered a choice of plans under a single-payer system (as happens in Medicare). If, instead, only one design option was offered and all residents were required to enroll in it, then concerns about adverse selection would not arise. That approach could also reduce the administrative costs that doctors and hospitals currently incur when dealing with multiple insurers. The lack of alternatives with which to compare that program, however, could make it more difficult to assess the system's performance. More generally, that approach would raise important questions about the role of the government in managing the delivery of health care.

Factors Affecting the Supply and Prices of Health Care Services

The ultimate effects of proposals on the use of and spending for health care depend not only on factors that affect the demand for health care services, such as the number of people who are insured and the scope of their coverage, but also on factors that affect the supply and prices of those services. The various methods used for setting prices and paying for services, and the resulting payment rates, affect the supply of health care services by influencing the decisions that doctors, hospitals, and other providers of care make about how many patients to serve and which treatments their patients will receive. Average payment rates for Medicare,

Medicaid, and private insurers also differ, which would affect the budgetary impact of proposals that shifted enrollees—and their costs— from one source of coverage to another. Changes in payment rates for public programs or in the amount of uncompensated care provided to the uninsured could also affect private payment rates.

Payment Methods and Providers' Incentives

Most care provided by physicians in the United States is paid for on a fee-for-service basis, meaning that a separate payment is made for each procedure, each office visit, and each ancillary service (such as a laboratory test). Hospitals are generally paid a fixed amount per admission (a bundled payment to cover all of the services that the hospital provides during a stay) or an amount per day. Such payments may encourage doctors and hospitals to limit their own costs when delivering a given service or bundle, but they can also create an incentive to provide more services or more expensive bundles if the additional payments exceed the added costs.

Other arrangements, such as salaries for doctors or periodic capitation payments (fixed amounts per patient), do not provide financial incentives to deliver additional services. Those approaches raise concerns, however, about providers' incentives to stint on care or avoid treating sicker patients. One study randomly assigned enrollees to different health plans and found that those in an integrated plan (which owns the hospitals used by enrollees and pays providers a salary) used 30 percent fewer services than enrollees in a fee-for-service plan, but whether those results could be replicated more broadly is unclear.

Proposals could seek to change payment methods either indirectly or directly. They could change the payment methods used by private health plans indirectly by encouraging shifts in enrollment toward plans that have lower-cost payment systems. For public programs, such as Medicare and Medicaid, federal policymakers could directly change payment methods. In either case, making those changes could prove to be very difficult.

Payment Rates

The financial incentives created by different payment systems—and the spending amounts they yield—also depend on the level at which payment rates or prices are set. Those rates depend partly on the methods that are used to set them. Private-sector payment rates are set by negotiation, reflecting the underlying costs of the services and the relative bargaining power of providers and health plans; in turn, bargaining power depends on factors such as the number of competing providers or provider groups within a local market area. Fee-for-service payment rates in Medicare and Medicaid are generally set administratively. That method poses a number of challenges, including how to determine providers' costs—particularly for services that require substantial training or that become cheaper to provide when they are performed more frequently. Additional issues that arise include how to account for the quality of those services and their value to patients, and what impact rate setting might have on the development of new medical technology.

On average, payment rates under Medicare and Medicaid are lower than private payment rates. Specifically, Medicare's payment rates for physicians in 2006 were nearly 20 percent lower than private rates, on average, and its payment rates for hospitals were as much as 30 percent lower. As for Medicaid, recent studies indicate that its payment rates for physicians and hospitals were about 40 percent and 35 percent lower, respectively, than private rates.

Within Medicare, and probably within Medicaid as well, those differentials vary geographically and tend to be larger in rural areas and smaller in urban areas (where competition among providers is generally greater). Given those differences, proposals that shifted enrollment between private and public plans could have a large impact on payments to providers and on spending for health care. Depending on how providers responded to those changes, enrollees' access to care could be affected.

Responses to Changes in Demand or Payment Rates

Changes in payment rates could also have an indirect effect on spending by altering the number of services that providers would be willing to supply. Similarly, the budgetary effects of covering previously uninsured individuals would depend not only on the resulting increase in their demand for care but also on how that increase affected the supply and prices of services. Within a 10-year budgetary time frame, the number of U.S.- trained physicians is largely fixed, so adjustments would have to occur in other areas—which could include changes in the number of hours doctors worked or in their productivity, inflows of foreign-trained physicians, or changes in doctors' fees and patients' waiting times.

Whether and to what extent the supply of physicians would become constrained also depends on the size of the increase in demand for their services and the amount of time available for adjustments to occur. CB O's analysis indicates that providing the uninsured population with coverage that is similar to a typical employment-based plan would increase total demand for physicians' services and hospital care by between 2 percent and 5 percent. If payment rates rose in response to that increase in demand, the impact on spending could be larger. Spending on behalf of previously uninsured people would also increase to the extent that the uncompensated care they had received became compensated.

Uncompensated Care and Cost Shifting

Another issue that arises when analyzing payment rates is whether relatively low rates for public programs or the costs of providing uncompensated or undercompensated care to the uninsured lead to higher payment rates for private insurers—a process known as cost shifting. To the extent that such cost shifting occurs now, proposals that reduced the uninsured population or that switched enrollees from public to private insurance plans could affect private payment rates and thus alter insurance premiums. For that to occur, however, doctors and hospitals would have to lower the fees they charged private health plans in response to a decline in uncompensated care or an increase in their revenues from insured patients.

Overall, the effect of uncompensated care on private- sector payment rates appears to be limited. According to one recent set of estimates, hospitals have provided about $35 billion in uncompensated care in 2008, representing roughly 5 percent of their total revenues. Roughly half of those costs may be offset, however, by payments under Medicare and Medicaid to hospitals that treat a disproportionate share of low-income patients. Estimates of uncompensated care provided by doctors are considerably smaller, amounting to a few billion dollars, so the costs of providing such care do not appear to have a substantial effect on private payment rates for physicians.

Whether and to what extent payments to hospitals under Medicare and Medicaid fall below the costs of treating those patients is more difficult to determine. Recent studies indicate, however, that when payment rates change under those programs, hospitals shift only a small share of the savings or costs to private insurers (the same logic would apply for uncompensated care). Instead, lower payment rates from public programs or large amounts of uncompensated care may lead hospitals to reduce their costs, possibly by providing care that is less intensive or of lower quality than would have been offered had payments per patient been larger.

Administrative Issues and Effects on Other Programs

The extent to which proposals would affect health insurance coverage or federal budgetary costs, and the timing of those effects, would depend partly on the administrative responsibilities and costs that those proposals entailed and partly on their interactions with other government programs. Other factors would affect coverage and cost, including the impact of any maintenance-ofeffort provisions that might be applied to states or employers and the treatment of various segments of the population, including people who are ineligible for current government health programs and those who— although eligible—are generally difficult to reach and enroll.

Administrative Issues

Proposals could require both federal and state governments to assume new administrative responsibilities and could allocate those responsibilities to new or existing agencies. How well agencies fulfilled new missions—and how long it would take them to do so—would depend on their scope and funding. Even with adequate funding, implementing a major initiative might take several years, as illustrated by the experience with the new Medicare drug benefit. Another way to ease the implementation of a new federal program would be to build on existing programs; SCHIP, for example, was implemented relatively rapidly because it largely built on the existing infrastructure of the state-operated Medicaid program.

Maintenance-of-Effort Requirements

A proposal that created new subsidies for health insurance could lead employers or states to scale back the coverage that they sponsor, particularly if a new federally funded program provided similar or more generous benefits. To prevent such responses or offset their effects on federal spending, proposals could include maintenanceof-effort provisions. Monitoring and enforcing such requirements for private firms would be difficult, however, unless proposals specified effective reporting mechanisms and sufficient penalties for violations.

States' maintenance-of-effort provisions are generally structured in two ways: requiring states to maintain existing programs at historical eligibility or benefit levels (as is done under SCHIP); or requiring states to continue spending funds at certain historical or projected levels or to return some of their savings to the federal government (as is done for the Medicare drug benefit). The effectiveness of such requirements would depend on how they were defined, the enforcement mechanisms that were specified, and the incentives for states to comply. The provisions for SCHIP and the Medicare drug benefit are examples of effective approaches.

Effects on Other Federal Programs

Proposals could also have unintended effects on eligibility for other federal programs that are not directly related to health care. New subsidies for health insurance may be counted as income or assets when determining eligibility for benefits in means-tested programs (such as the Supplemental Nutrition Assistance Program, formerly known as the Food Stamp program) unless explicitly excluded by law. Proposals that changed the employment-based health insurance system could shift compensation between wages and fringe benefits, thus affecting eligibility for government benefits (including Social Security) or tax credits (such as the earned income tax credit) that are based on cash earnings. Temporary or aggregate adjustments could be made to benefit formulas in order to minimize any adverse effects, but some recipients might still be made worse off.

Treatment of Certain Populations

The treatment of certain populations would present various administrative challenges for proposals to expand coverage. Some individuals, including military personnel and veterans, already receive health insurance from the federal government, and issues might arise regarding the coordination of their current benefits with new federal subsidies. In other cases, federal health programs currently deny benefits to certain populations, such as unauthorized immigrants or prison inmates, and proposals would have to specify whether and how those restrictions would apply to new programs. Other populations, such as the homeless, face challenges enrolling in existing programs, and similar issues might arise in designing new subsidies for health insurance. Those considerations would affect both the costs of proposals and their overall impact on rates of insurance coverage.

Changes in Health Habits and Medical Practices

In addition to any broader changes they make in the health insurance and payment systems, proposals may include specific elements designed to induce individuals to improve their own health or to encourage changes in how diseases are treated. Through a combination of approaches, proposals could try to change the behavior of both patients and providers by:

- Promoting healthy behavior, including measures aimed at reducing rates of obesity and smoking;
- Expanding the use of preventive medical care, which can either impede the development or spread of a disease or detect its presence at an early stage;
- Establishing a "medical home" for each enrollee, typically involving a primary care physician who would coordinate all of his or her care;
- Adopting "disease management" programs that seek to coordinate care for and apply evidence-based treatments to certain diseases, such as diabetes or coronary artery disease;
- Funding research comparing the effectiveness of different treatment options, the results of which could help discourage the use of less clinically effective or less cost-effective treatments;

- Expanding the use of health information technology, such as electronic medical records, which would make it easier to share information about patients' conditions and treatments; and
- Modifying the system for determining and penalizing medical malpractice.

Some of those initiatives could improve individuals' health or enhance the quality of the care that they receive, but it is not clear that they also would reduce overall health care spending or federal costs. In its analysis of such initiatives, CBO considers the available studies that have been done to assess particular approaches. In many cases, those studies do not support claims of reductions in health care spending or budgetary savings.

For several reasons, it may be difficult to generate reductions in health care spending from such initiatives. In some cases, the problem is largely one of identifying and targeting the people whose participation would cause health care spending to decline. Broad programs aimed at preventive medical care and disease management could reduce the need for expensive care for a portion of the recipients but could also provide additional services—and incur added costs—for many individuals who would not have needed costly treatments anyway. To generate net reductions in spending, the savings that such interventions generated for people who would have needed expensive care would therefore have to be large enough to offset the costs of serving much larger populations.

A related issue is that many individuals or health plans might already be taking the steps involved (or will in the future) even in the absence of a new requirement or incentive. The effect of any proposal would have to be measured against that trend, and a large share of any subsidies involved might go to people who (or health plans that) would have taken those steps even if there were no requirements or incentives to do so. For example, some doctors and hospitals are already using electronic medical records, and more will adopt that technology in the future under current law, so any subsidy payments those providers might receive under a proposal would add to its costs but would not affect adoption rates.

In other cases, the effect on health care spending depends crucially on whether doctors and patients have incentives to change their use of health care services. For example, studies may find that a given treatment has fewer clinical benefits or is less cost-effective (meaning that added costs are high relative to the incremental health benefits) for certain types of patients. But those results may not have a substantial effect on the use of that treatment unless the financial incentives facing doctors (through their payments) or patients (through their cost sharing) are aligned with the findings. Similarly, proposals to establish a medical home may have little impact on spending if the primary care physicians who would coordinate care were not given financial incentives to limit their patients' use of specialists.

Other types of initiatives might ultimately yield substantial long-term health benefits but might not generate much savings, at least in the short term. Even if successful, measures to reduce smoking and obesity—two factors linked to the development of chronic and acute health problems—might not have a substantial impact on health care spending for some time. In the long term, spending on diseases caused by poor health habits could decline substantially, but the impact on federal costs would also have to account for people living longer and receiving more in Medicare benefits (for the treatment of other diseases and age-related ailments) as well as other government benefits that are not directly related to health care (including Social Security benefits). Similarly, investments in health information technology might require substantial start-up costs that would be difficult to recapture in the typical 5- and 10-year budgetary time frames used to evaluate legislative proposals.

Demonstrating savings might also be difficult because of data limitations and methodological concerns. For example, studies have found that tort limits, by reducing malpractice awards, cause premiums for malpractice insurance to fall and thus could have a very modest impact on doctors' fees and health care spending. Some observers argue that tort limits would yield larger reductions in that spending because doctors would stop ordering unnecessary tests and taking other steps to reduce the risk of being sued. CBO has not found consistent evidence of such broader effects, but that may reflect the difficulty of disentangling the impact of changes to the medical malpractice system from other factors affecting medical costs.

Effects on Total Health Care Spending, the Scope of the Federal Budget, and the Economy

Proposals that would substantially change the health insurance market could have an effect on total spending on health care, the flow of payments between various sectors of the economy, and the operation of the U.S. economy. CBO will consider those effects in its analysis of major health care proposals.

Effects on Total Spending and the Scope of the Federal Budget

Many health insurance proposals would have an impact on total spending for health care, and some might contain provisions that explicitly limit the level of or rate of growth in health care spending; such proposals might impose a global budget or budgetary cap on all or a part of that spending. The effectiveness of such strategies would depend on several factors, including the scope of the global budget, the targets selected for different categories of spending, and the mechanisms used to enforce the caps.

In addition to their overall effects on federal spending and revenues, proposals that made substantial changes to the health insurance system or its financing methods could raise a number of budgetary issues. Such proposals could have substantial effects on the flows of payments among households, employers, and federal and state governments—even if the proposals were budget neutral from a federal perspective. Some proposals might assign the federal government a more active role in the health insurance market; for example, the government could be required to disburse subsidies covering the cost of health insurance, collect health insurance premiums from policyholders, or make payments to insurers. Any of those changes might raise questions regarding who—the government, the insured, or the insurer—would bear financial responsibility for any shortfalls in payments that might occur.

Other proposals might require that individuals or businesses make payments directly to nongovernmental entities. Depending on the specific provisions of such proposals, CBO might judge that payments resulting from federal mandates should be recorded as part of the federal budget even if the funds did not flow through the Treasury. The extent of federal control and compulsion is a critical element in determining budgetary treatment. In general, CBO believes that federally mandated payments—those resulting from the exercise of sovereign power—and the disbursement of those payments should be recorded in the budget as federal transactions.

Effects on the Economy

Proposals that made large-scale changes affecting the provision and financing of health insurance could also have an impact on the broader economy. Because most health insurance is currently provided through employers, proposals could affect labor markets by changing individuals' decisions about whether and how much to work and employers' decisions to hire workers. Such effects could arise in several ways:

- Proposals that decreased the return from an additional hour of work, by imposing new taxes or phasing out subsidies or credits for health insurance as earnings rise, could cause some people to work fewer hours or leave the labor force.
- Proposals that made health insurance less dependent on employment status could induce some people to retire earlier and others to change jobs more often.
- Proposals that treated firms differently on the basis of such characteristics as the number of employees or average wages could affect the allocation of workers among firms.
- Proposals that required employers to provide health insurance could adversely affect the hiring of employees earning at or near the minimum wage, because the total compensation of those workers could exceed their value to the firm.

Some observers have asserted that domestic firms providing health insurance to their workers incur higher costs for compensation than do competitors based in countries where insurance is not employment based and that fundamental changes to the health insurance system could reduce or eliminate that disadvantage. Although U.S. employers may appear to pay most of the costs of their workers' health insurance, economists generally agree that workers ultimately bear those costs. That is, when firms provide health insurance, wages and other forms of compensation are lower (by a corresponding amount) than they otherwise would be. As a result, the costs of providing health insurance to their workers are not a source of competitive disadvantage for U.S.-based firms.

In addition to their effects on the labor market, proposals could also affect the size of the nation's stock of productive capital, especially through their effects on government budgets. Those effects would depend partly on how the costs of any insurance expansions or other changes are financed, which is beyond the scope of this chapter. The net effect on the economy of a broad proposal to restructure the health insurance system would, not surprisingly, depend crucially on the details.

1. Introduction and Background

The health care provided in the United States can confer tremendous benefits, extending and improving lives. But the high and rising costs for health care in this country impose an increasing burden on individuals, businesses, states, and the federal government, and a substantial number of people may have trouble paying for that care because they do not have health insurance. Those issues are related: People seek insurance to protect themselves against the risk of experiencing financial hardship when they need expensive medical care, and yet rising costs for health care also make health insurance policies more expensive and thus more difficult to afford.

Lack of insurance can limit access to care, but having insurance can increase spending by encouraging the use of services that have relatively low clinical value. More generally, despite spending more per capita than other countries, the United States lags behind lower-spending countries on several metrics, including life expectancy and infant mortality. Indeed, evidence suggests that a substantial share of spending on health care contributes little if anything to the overall health of the nation, but finding ways to reduce such spending without also affecting services that improve health will be difficult.

Spending on health care services and related activities accounts for about 17 percent of gross domestic product (GDP)—an expected total of about $2.6 trillion in 2009—and under current law that share is projected to reach nearly 20 percent by 2017 (according to the Centers for Medicare and Medicaid Services). Correspondingly, annual health expenditures per capita are projected to rise from about $8,300 to about $13,000 in nominal (current-dollar) terms over that period. Federal spending accounts for about one-third of those totals, and federal outlays for the Medicare and Medicaid programs are projected to reach about $720 billion in 2009.

Over the longer term, rising health care costs represent the single greatest challenge to balancing the federal budget. The Congressional Budget Office (CBO) projects that under current law, federal spending on Medicare and Medicaid alone will grow from about 4 percent of GDP in 2009 to about 12 percent of GDP by 2050.

The number of people who lack health insurance is also on the rise. Recent estimates indicate that about one in four nonelderly residents (those age 64 or younger) is uninsured at some point during the year, and at any given point in 2009 at least 45 million residents are expected to lack insurance—a figure that has grown rather steadily over time and that CBO projects to reach about 54 million by 2019.[1] The nonelderly population will also increase, so the share of that population projected to be uninsured at a given point during the year will grow more slowly, from about 17 percent in 2009 to about 19 percent in 2019. (Those estimates for 2009 do not reflect the recent deterioration in economic conditions, which could result in a larger uninsured population.) The number of uninsured individuals is expected to increase because health insurance premiums are likely to continue rising considerably faster than income, which will make insurance more difficult to afford.

Scope and Focus of This Chapter

The challenge of seeking to increase the number of people who have health insurance while attempting to constrain the high and rising costs of health care has led to proposals that would substantially modify the health insurance system in this country. Because the Medicare program already provides nearly universal coverage to the elderly, those proposals generally focus on options for providing coverage to and reducing costs for the nonelderly population; even so, options that would reduce Medicare spending could be used to offset the government's costs for insurance expansions and could have broad effects on spending for health care.

This chapter describes the assumptions that CBO would use in estimating the effects of key elements of such proposals on federal costs, insurance coverage, and other outcomes; the evidence on which those assumptions are based; and, if the evidence points to a range of possible effects rather than a precise prediction, the factors that would influence where a proposal falls within those ranges. (A companion report—*Budget Options, Volume 1: Health Care*—describes CBO's estimates of the effects on the federal budget of numerous specific options related to health care and health insurance.)

This document does not provide a comprehensive analysis of any specific proposal; rather, it identifies and discusses many of the critical factors that would affect estimates of various proposals. In particular, it considers the types of issues that would arise in estimating the budgetary effects of proposals to:

- Provide tax credits or other types of subsidies to make insurance less expensive to the purchaser.
- Require individuals to purchase health insurance, typically paired with a new system of government subsidies.[2]
- Require firms to offer health insurance to their workers or pay into a fund that subsidizes insurance purchases.
- Replace employment-based coverage with new purchasing arrangements or provide strong incentives for people to shift toward individually purchased coverage.
- Provide all citizens or residents with coverage under, or access to, existing insurance plans such as the Federal Employees Health Benefits program or the Medicare program (or modified versions of such plans), either as an additional option or under a "Medicare-for-all" single-payer arrangement.

Wherever possible, the analysis presented here describes in quantitative terms how CBO would estimate the budgetary and other effects of such proposals. In other cases, it describes the components that a proposal would have to specify in order to permit estimation of its effects on federal spending or other outcomes. This chapter reflects the current state of CBO's analysis of and judgments about the likely response of individuals, employers, insurers, and providers to changes in the health insurance and health care systems. The details of particular policy specifications and the way in which they are combined, as well as new evidence or analysis related to the issues discussed here, could affect future CBO estimates of the effects of large-scale health insurance proposals.

Because such proposals could incorporate a number of the elements that are discussed in this chapter, they could have interactions that are difficult to predict. Those proposals could also affect both tax revenues and outlays. Estimates of the impact on revenues of proposals to change the federal tax code are prepared by the staff of the Joint Committee on Taxation (JCT) and would be incorporated into any formal CBO estimate of a proposal's effects on the federal budget. In preparing this chapter, CBO consulted with the JCT staff on the behavioral considerations that are incorporated into both agencies' estimates.

CBO's analysis of whether people obtain insurance focuses on the scope of the coverage that the available policies provide and the cost to them. All else being equal, more comprehensive coverage will be more expensive. The cost of an insurance policy also depends on who enrolls in the plan; how much health care they seek; and how much doctors, hospitals, and other providers of care are paid for their services. Although those considerations are closely related, this chapter analyzes the following questions:

- For insurance policies with the same scope and total cost, how does the share of that cost that individuals have to pay affect whether they purchase insurance? How would various types of subsidies that reduce the cost to them directly or indirectly—or mandates to offer or purchase coverage—affect the rates and sources of insurance coverage?
- How does the cost of an insurance policy vary with the scope of its coverage, insurers' use of various cost- management techniques, and the types of people it covers? How would health care spending and average policy premiums be affected by extending coverage to people who are now uninsured?
- Taking the demand for insurance overall and the premiums charged for various options as given, how are individuals' decisions about which policy to choose affected by the laws and regulations governing those choices? How would consumers respond to changes in the structure of or incentives governing the insurance market?
- What impact do factors affecting the supply of health care services and the level and mechanism of payments to providers have on the costs of health care and insurance premiums? How would changes in those supply factors interact with demand to determine future spending on health care?

Proposals to modify the health insurance system that include subsidies would probably have the most immediate and direct impact on the federal budget. Their costs would depend primarily on the nature and extent of those subsidies, the number of people who take advantage of them, and the scope of insurance coverage that is purchased or provided as a result. This chapter also considers other effects, including any federal administrative costs and challenges that might be involved in implementing a proposal; the effects on eligibility for and spending under other federal programs; the impact of provisions that seek to reduce spending on health care by encouraging consumers to make healthier choices and providers to change some of the ways in which they practice medicine; and other macroeconomic effects or budgetary implications that a proposal might have.

The question of whether and how any net increases in federal spending for health care and health insurance would be financed by policy changes outside the health sector is beyond the scope of this chapter. Whether a proposal makes health insurance more affordable for a given individual or family would depend not only on its impact on the health insurance premiums that they face but also on the effect that its financing mechanisms have on the household's budget. To the extent that such proposals are financed by provisions that fall outside the health sector—through increases in tax revenues or reductions in spending for other federal programs—those effects are not addressed in this chapter.

As background for the discussion of the broad policy options presented in subsequent chapters of this book, the remainder of this chapter describes the primary sources of health insurance coverage, the reasons that people lack coverage, the extent and nature of the coverage that is currently purchased, and the main components and drivers of health care spending.

Health Insurance Coverage

The primary purpose of health insurance is to protect individuals against the risk of financial hardship when they need expensive medical care. In principle, most people would be willing to pay an insurance premium that was somewhat higher than their own expected costs for health care in order to avoid that risk, but in practice many people with low income or high expected costs might consider the premiums they would face to be unaffordable.

Over the years, various policies have been adopted that subsidize insurance coverage for certain groups. Medicare provides highly subsidized coverage to the elderly and also insures several million people under the age of 65 who are disabled—two groups that have relatively high costs for health care. The Medicaid program and related initiatives offer free or low-priced coverage to many children and (to a more limited degree) their parents; Medicaid also covers many elderly and disabled individuals who have low income and few assets (and thus would have difficulty paying for insurance). Most employers offer health insurance to their workers and most workers enroll in a plan, motivated in part by a tax subsidy for employment-based insurance. People may also be able to purchase coverage in the individual insurance market, but that coverage is not generally subsidized. Those sources of coverage also vary in the ease of enrollment, which affects their attractiveness.

Because health insurance provides more benefits to people who incur relatively high costs for health care, health insurance coverage generally—or specific health insurance plans—may attract enrollees with above-average costs, a phenomenon known as "adverse selection." Conversely, people with low expected costs for health care may be reluctant to pay an insurance premium that reflects the average costs of all enrollees, or they might prefer to wait until they develop a health problem to sign up for coverage. To the extent that such adverse selection occurs, average insurance premiums (or the costs of government subsidies for insurance) would tend to rise to reflect the higher spending per enrollee. The potential for adverse selection exists with almost any health insurance plan, but the manner in which it arises and the mechanisms used to address it differ across insurance markets.

The availability of health insurance affects not only who enrolls but also how much health care people consume. People who are insured are likely to use more health care than they would if they had to pay the full costs of those services—a phenomenon economists call "moral hazard." To offset that tendency toward increased use, health insurance policies typically feature some degree of cost sharing by enrollees. Health plans may also seek to control their costs and premiums by using various methods of managing care and by varying the range of benefits offered. Of course, those features also affect the premiums for health insurance policies and the attractiveness of the coverage to enrollees.

Sources of Insurance Coverage

In the United States, most people obtain health insurance coverage from either public or private sources, but about 17 percent of the nonelderly population will be uninsured in 2009 (see Table 1-1).[3] Insurance obtained through an individual's employment is the primary source of coverage for the nonelderly.

Table 1-1. Sources of Insurance Coverage and Insurance Status of the Nonelderly Population, 2009

	Number (Millions)	Percent
	Source of Coverage	
Employment-Based[a]	160	61
Individually Purchased	10	4
Medicare	7	3
Medicaid[b]	43	17
Other[c]	12	4
	Insurance Status	
Insured, Any Source[d]	216	83
Uninsured	45	17

Source: Congressional Budget Office's health insurance simulation model.

Note: The nonelderly population excludes people in institutions and residents of U.S. territories.

a. Includes coverage obtained through local, state, and federal employers.

b. Includes the State Children's Health Insurance Program.

c. Includes military and other sources of coverage.

d. The sum of people by their sources of coverage exceeds the total number who are insured because about 14.5 million people are covered by more than one source at a time.

Employment-Based Insurance

In 2009, roughly 160 million people under the age of 65—or about three out of every five nonelderly Americans—are expected to have health insurance that is provided through an employer or other job-related arrangement, such as a plan offered through a labor union. That figure includes active workers, spouses and dependents who are covered by family policies, and nonelderly retirees.

One prominent feature of employment-based insurance is that employers generally contribute a large share of the total premium; that is, the amount that is directly and visibly deducted from workers' paychecks for health insurance (called the employees' contribution) usually represents a relatively small share of the average cost per enrollee. According to a survey of firms conducted in 2008, employers contribute 73 percent of the cost of a family policy for their workers and 84 percent of the cost of single coverage, on average.[4] One reason employers make those contributions is to encourage broad participation by their employees, so as to limit the potential for adverse selection.

Although employers may appear to pay most of the costs of their workers' health insurance, economists generally agree that workers ultimately bear those costs. Employers' contributions are simply a form of compensation, and if labor markets are competitive (which is generally the case), an employee's total compensation should equal his or her contribution to the revenue of the firm. Thus, when an employer offers to pay for health insurance, it pays less in wages and other forms of compensation than it otherwise would, keeping total compensation about the same.[5]

That relationship can be difficult to observe and may not hold perfectly for every worker at every instant. In particular, workers who turned down an employer's offer of subsidized health insurance generally would not see an immediate or corresponding increase in their wages. Moreover, firms offering health insurance actually tend to pay higher wages than firms that do not do so, but those differences in total compensation reflect disparities in the skill and productivity of the workers, not a failure to pass on the costs of providing insurance. For their part, many employers behave as though they do bear the costs of the insurance plans they offer (as reflected in their efforts to control those costs). Nevertheless, the available evidence indicates that employees as a group ultimately bear the costs of any payments an employer makes for health insurance.[6]

How the costs of employers' contributions are allocated among different types of workers and how quickly wages would adjust to changes in those contributions is less clear. In principle, workers who would obtain more benefits from health insurance coverage—such as older workers, who have higher average costs for health care—would be willing to accept a greater reduction in their wages than other workers would accept in return for that coverage. The extent to which that phenomenon occurs in practice, however, is uncertain.[7] Similarly, it could take labor markets several years to adjust to unexpected changes in employers' costs for health care. For purposes of estimating the impact of proposed legislation, however, CBO makes the simplifying assumption that total compensation is fixed and that changes in the costs of health insurance translate immediately into offsetting changes in wages and other forms of compensation; the JCT staff makes the same assumption when estimating the effects of proposals on revenue collections.

Compared with the individual insurance market, employment-based coverage offers several advantages, particularly for employees of larger firms. Unlike wages, the employer's costs for providing that coverage are excluded from the enrollee's taxable income. As a result, that portion of employees' compensation is not subject to individual income and payroll taxes. In addition, most employees are also able to exclude the portion of the premium that they pay. For a typical worker, that favorable tax treatment provides a subsidy from the government that reduces the net cost of employment-based health insurance by about 30 percent.

That tax subsidy provides an incentive for workers to obtain insurance through their employer and for their employer to provide it. Because out-of-pocket costs for health care do not generally receive a tax subsidy, workers also have an incentive to secure more extensive coverage, thereby increasing the share of spending for health care that is covered and decreasing the share that they pay out of pocket. The value of the exclusion from taxation is generally somewhat larger for workers with higher income because they face higher income tax rates (although they may also face lower rates of payroll taxation).

Box 1-1. Regulation of Health Insurance and the Employee Retirement Income Security Act

In the United States, some forms of private health insurance are subject to both state and federal regulation, but others are exempt from state regulation. That distinction, which is a common source of confusion, stems from the treatment of employment- based health plans under the Employee Retirement Income Security Act of 1974 (ERISA). Under that act, employers that bear the financial risk of covering their workers' health insurance claims—and thus effectively serve as the insurer—are exempt from state insurance laws and regulations. If, instead, an employer contracts with an insurance company to provide coverage and that company bears the associated financial risk, then state insurance laws and oversight apply.

The main practical effect of the difference in treatment is that employers who serve as the insurer for their employees are exempt from the benefit mandates and other insurance regulations that many states impose (such as requirements to cover certain treatments, procedures, or types of providers). A rationale for that arrangement is that an employer with operations in several states would otherwise be unable to offer the same coverage to all of its employees, given the variation in state mandates and regulations; similarly, complying with the differing requirements in each state might be cumbersome for such an employer.

Of the roughly 160 million people whose primary insurance will come from an employment-based plan in 2009, the Congressional Budget Office estimates that about 88 million will have coverage from an employer that bears the financial risk of providing it and that 72 million will have coverage from an insurer that is subject to state regulation. (Policies covering another 10 million enrollees that are bought in the individual insurance market are also regulated by the states.) Large firms are more likely to bear insurance risk for their workers; according to one survey, 86 percent of workers at firms with 5,000 or more employees were in such plans in 2007, compared with 12 percent of workers at firms with fewer than 200 employees.[1]

Confusion about the implications of ERISA may stem in part from the terminology that is used to describe its provisions and from subtle distinctions about the roles of employers and insurers. Employers that bear insurance risk are referred to as having "self-insured" or "self-funded" plans, whereas employers that contract with an insurer are said to have "insured" or "fully insured" plans. Many employers that bear insurance risk still use insurers to carry out some functions, such as developing networks of providers, negotiating payment rates, processing claims, and so forth. In those cases, the insurance company is called a third-party administrator. Further, employers may qualify for ERISA's exemptions even if they purchase a separate insurance policy (known as reinsurance or "stop loss" coverage) to protect themselves against unusually high claims, so long as the employer continues to bear sufficient financial risk.

[1] William Pierron and Paul Fronstin, *ERISA Pre-emption: Implications for Health Reform and Coverage,* Issue Brief No. 314 (Washington, D.C.: Employee Benefit Research Institute, February 2008), www.ebri.org.

Table 1-2. Share of Employees Offered Health Insurance, by Size of Firm, 2009

Size of Firm (Number of employees)	Total Employees		Health Insurance Employees Offered	
	Number (Millions)	Percent	Number (Millions)	Percent
Fewer than 25	31.0	22	14.9	48
25 to 99	17.6	13	12.7	72
100 to 999	27.2	19	21.0	77
1,000 or More	63.9	46	54.9	86
All	139.7	100	103.5	74

Source: Congressional Budget Office's health insurance simulation model.

Employment-based insurance offers a number of other advantages. For example, because sales and marketing costs for insurers are relatively fixed, as the number of enrollees covered by an employer's policy increases, those fixed costs can be spread over a larger number of enrollees. As a result, the average premium needed to purchase a given amount of coverage is lower for employees of larger firms. Some analysts have suggested that employers also act as employees' agents, using their power to bargain for lower premiums, sorting out the employees' options, and making it easier for them to choose an insurance plan.[8] In particular, employers may take steps that substantially simplify the process of enrolling in a health insurance plan, and the use of automatic payroll deduction to pay for employees' premiums may also encourage participation.

Another important feature of employment-based insurance is that policies offered by firms of all sizes are subject to certain federal requirements, but most policies offered by larger firms are exempt from state insurance laws and regulations. That distinction stems from the provisions of the Employee Retirement Income Security Act, which are described in Box 1-1. As a result, policies offered by smaller employers generally must comply with requirements that vary by state regarding the benefits they cover, the premiums that insurers may charge, and other terms of purchase. (Those regulations are discussed further in Chapter 4.) Policies provided in the large-group market, by contrast, generally face few legal constraints regarding their benefits and premiums. One exception is that, among workers who are similarly situated (that is, workers who are in the same class of employment and work in the same geographic location), employers may not vary employees' contributions to premiums on the basis of their health.

Whether employers offer coverage largely reflects the aggregate preferences of their workers, but for several reasons smaller firms are less likely to offer insurance than larger firms. Overall, about half of the workers at very small firms (those that have fewer than 25 employees) are offered coverage and are eligible for it, compared with 77 percent of the workers at firms with 100 to 999 employees and 86 percent of the workers at firms with 1,000 or more employees (see Table 1-2).[9] One reason is that households with lower income find it more difficult to accept lower wages in return for health insurance, and smaller firms are more likely to employ low-wage workers. Another reason is that policies purchased by smaller firms incur higher administrative costs per enrollee, so the share of the policy premium that covers medical costs is lower, reducing the attractiveness of such policies. Because employees of larger firms constitute most of the total workforce, the percentage of all workers who are offered coverage—about three out of four—is closer to the proportion for larger firms.

The share of workers who are enrolled in employment- based coverage has varied somewhat over time, partly reflecting changes in the mix of employment and partly tracking fluctuations in the business cycle. According to recent surveys of employers, that share rose from 62 percent in 1999 to 65 percent in 2001 but has fallen since then and stands at 60 percent in 2008.[10] The coverage rate has been somewhat more volatile for smaller firms (those with fewer than 200 workers); that rate was 52 percent in 1996, rose to 58 percent in 2001, and fell back to 52 percent in 2008. Studies have attributed the recent decline in enrollment to a combination of modest reductions in the number of employers offering insurance, shifts in employment toward firms and industries that are less likely to offer health insurance coverage, and a reduction in enrollment rates among workers who are offered coverage. The estimated impact of each of those factors varies, however, depending on the specific years examined, the data used, and the methodology employed.

One source of employment-based health insurance that has received considerable attention is the Federal Employees Health Benefits (FEHB) program, which provides coverage to about 8 million active and retired federal employees in 2008. Under that program, several private health insurance plans are available nationwide, and in most regions employees have a range of local plans available to them as well. The federal government covers 75 percent of the cost of each participating plan up to a limit set at 72 percent of the national average premium; to purchase a policy more expensive than that, the enrollee has to pay the added costs (although those payments may also be excluded from taxable income).[11] Like employees of private firms that offer a choice of insurance plans, federal workers may generally sign up for coverage or change plans only during an annual open-enrollment season—a rule that limits their opportunities to wait until they develop a health problem to enroll or to switch plans for health reasons and thus limits the degree of adverse selection that can occur.

Although employment-based insurance has certain advantages, the central role of employers in sponsoring coverage also has disadvantages. Unlike federal workers, many employees are not offered a choice of insurance plans, and others may have only a few plans from which to select, so the plan in which they enroll might not fit their preferences. Furthermore, employees and their dependents typically have to change plans when changing jobs and could become uninsured if their new employer does not offer coverage—potentially making them reluctant to switch jobs in the first place (a phenomenon known as "job lock").[12] In addition, employees who become disabled or too sick to keep their job may eventually lose their employment-based coverage.

Individually Purchased Insurance

Overall, CBO estimates that about 10 million nonelderly individuals will be covered by a policy purchased in the individual insurance market in 2009. In principle, anyone may purchase coverage in that market—to cover only themselves or their family as well—but in practice that option may be more attractive to some people than to others. (Such coverage is sometimes called "nongroup" insurance to distinguish it from group coverage, which is primarily employment based.)

The potential for adverse selection may be stronger in the individual market than in the employment-based market, partly because people can apply for individual insurance at any time and may therefore wait until a health problem arises before seeking coverage and partly because applicants do not have to be healthy enough to work. To address those possibilities, insurers usually "underwrite" the policy—a process by which they assess the health risk of applicants. Although most applicants end up being quoted a standard premium rate (which usually varies by age), underwriting can result in adjustments to premiums, adjustments to benefits (for example, to exclude coverage of known health conditions), or denials of coverage. As a result, individuals who have more health problems may face higher premiums when they apply for coverage. Some states, however, prohibit or limit those practices—which generally has the effect of reducing premiums charged to older or less healthy applicants and raising premiums for younger and healthier applicants (as discussed further in Chapter 4).

Individual insurance products have some other advantages and disadvantages compared with employment- based coverage. Some applicants may be able to obtain basic insurance protection (such as "catastrophic coverage" plans) in the individual market at a relatively low cost. That market generally offers consumers a greater choice of plans, and the coverage may be portable from one job to another. Insurers incur greater administrative costs for policies sold in the individual market, however, and those costs are built into the policy premiums. Compared with the enrollment process for an employment- based plan, the effort required of applicants to search for a policy and sign up for coverage in the individual market can be considerably greater. In general, individually purchased coverage does not receive favorable tax treatment, which also makes its effective price higher.[13]

Reflecting those disadvantages, participation in the individual insurance market is relatively low. Only about 1 percent of nonelderly adults who are offered employment-based coverage (either by their own employer or through a spouse) elect to purchase individual coverage. Even among people who lack other coverage options, only about 20 percent elect to purchase a policy in the individual market; the rest are uninsured. In many cases, individually purchased policies are held for relatively short periods of time—serving to cover individuals between jobs, for a short period following college (a point at which children may become ineligible for coverage under their parents' plan), or between retirement and age 65 (the age of eligibility for Medicare).

Medicare

Medicare provides coverage for about 37 million people who are age 65 or older, and it also covers about 7 million nonelderly people who are disabled (and generally become eligible after a two-year waiting period) or have severe kidney disease.[14] In 2008, about 80 percent of Medicare's beneficiaries are insured through the traditional fee-for-service program, which pays providers for services directly using prices set administratively; the rest have chosen to receive coverage through private insurers that contract with Medicare to provide program benefits in return for a fixed monthly payment per enrollee (known as the Medicare Advantage option). About 3 percent of people under age 65 are covered by Medicare (see Table 1-1 on page 4), but their average costs to the program are substantial—more than $35,000 per person in 2007 for those with kidney failure and roughly $8,000 per person for other disabled enrollees.

When it was created, Medicare had two primary components Part A, which generally covers hospital care and other services provided by institutions; and Part B, which generally covers physicians' services and various forms of outpatient care. Enrollment in Part A is free of charge and essentially automatic for individuals (and their spouses) who have sufficient earnings subject to payroll taxes to qualify for Social Security benefits; certain others may enroll but must pay a monthly premium. To participate in Part B, enrollees must pay a monthly premium that covers about 25 percent of the program's average costs. Although participation is voluntary, seniors who choose not to participate in Part B when they are first eligible are subject to penalties if they decide to enroll at a later date—penalties that are intended to discourage eligible individuals from waiting to develop a health problem before they enroll. As a result of those provisions, nearly 95 percent of individuals who are eligible to enroll in Part B do so. Many of those who do not enroll have retiree coverage from a former employer that limits the benefits they would receive from enrolling in Part B (and may also exempt them from the late-enrollment penalty).

A voluntary outpatient prescription drug benefit— known as Part D—was added to Medicare in 2006; its premium subsidy and penalty for late enrollment are similar to Part B's.

About 70 percent of the people who are eligible to participate in Part D have chosen to do so.[15] Analysis by the Centers for Medicare and Medicaid Services (CMS) indicates that a majority of those non- enrollees have drug coverage from another source that is at least as comprehensive as the Medicare benefit, but about 10 percent of the Medicare population appears to lack substantial drug coverage.

Medicaid and the State Children's Health Insurance Program

Medicaid is the main source of health insurance coverage for Americans who have very low income, and the smaller State Children's Health Insurance Program (S CHIP) provides coverage for children in families that have somewhat higher income. Unlike the Medicare program, which does not take into account income or assets when determining eligibility and is federally financed, Medicaid and SCHIP are needs-based assistance programs that are jointly financed by the federal government and state governments.

CBO estimates that at any given point in 2009, roughly 64 million nonelderly individuals will be eligible for Medicaid or SCHIP coverage and that about 43 million will be enrolled.[16] Eligibility for Medicaid was originally limited to very low income families with dependent children and to poor elderly or disabled individuals. Over the past two decades, coverage has been extended to children in families with somewhat higher income and to pregnant women. Nonelderly, nondisabled adults who have no children are generally ineligible for the program. Able- bodied parents and children represent about three- fourths of all Medicaid enrollees, but about 70 percent of the program's spending is for the remaining enrollees who are either elderly or disabled and have low income and few assets.

Subject to broad federal requirements governing eligibility and benefits, the Medicaid program is largely administered by the states, and thus its specific features may vary considerably from state to state. On average, the federal government covers about 57 percent of the costs of the health care services received by enrollees (the share varies among states and is higher for states with relatively low per capita income). State Medicaid programs cover a comprehensive set of services, including hospital care (both inpatient and outpatient), physicians' services, nursing home care, home health care, and certain additional services for children. States have the authority to cover other services and populations and have used that authority extensively.[17] They may also apply to the federal government for waivers from various federal Medicaid rules.

SCHIP was established in 1997 to provide coverage to children whose family income is above the eligibility levels for Medicaid. States generally cover children in families that have income up to 200 percent of the federal poverty level (or about $44,000 for a family of four in 2009), but some states have higher income limits and some cover parents as well as their children. Like Medicaid, SCHIP is jointly funded by the federal government and the states, but the federal share of costs is higher for SCHIP—covering 70 percent of health care claims, on average. States have a fair amount of discretion in designing and implementing their programs: They may expand Medicaid, create a new state system specifically for SCHIP, or use some combination of the two approaches.[18]

SCHIP is currently authorized in law through March 2009. Consistent with statutory guidelines, CBO assumes in its baseline spending projections that federal funding for the program in later years will continue at $5.0 billion, the base amount provided for the first half of fiscal year 2009. In fiscal year 2008, the program's budget authority was $6 billion and its outlays were about $7 billion. Because average costs per enrollee are expected to rise, CBO projects that average enrollment would decline from a peak of about 5.3 million in 2008 to about 2 million in 2018 under that assumption about future funding. (References to Medicaid in the remainder of this chapter also include SCHIP.)

Other Sources of Coverage

A significant number of people obtain insurance coverage from various other sources including the military, universities (for students), and other organizations. CBO estimates that roughly 12 million people will be covered under such arrangements in 2009. Although military coverage could be considered a form of employment-based insurance, it is typically counted separately. The Department of Veterans Affairs provides some health care to military veterans, but its programs are not considered a comprehensive health insurance plan; similarly, the Indian Health Service provides some care to Native Americans and Alaska natives but is not counted as a source of health insurance (such programs are discussed more extensively in Chapter 6).

The Uninsured Population

About 45 million people, or about 15 percent of the total U.S. population, will be uninsured at any given point in 2009, by CBO's most recent estimates. Because the elderly have near-universal coverage from Medicare, many analyses of the uninsured focus on the nonelderly population, about 17 percent of which is expected to lack coverage in 2009. Those estimates for 2009 do not reflect the recent deterioration in economic conditions, which could result in a larger uninsured population.

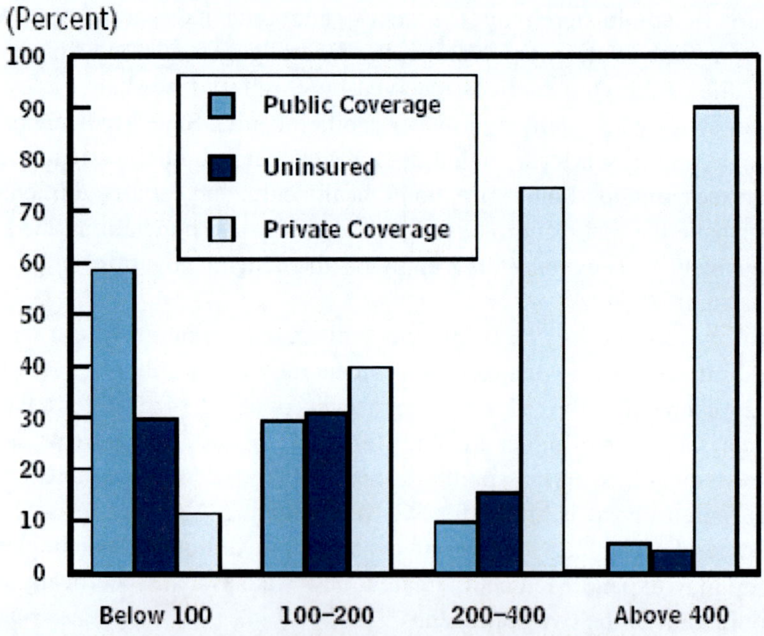

Source: Congressional Budget Office's health insurance simulation model.

Figure 1-1. Patterns of Health Insurance Coverage for Nonelderly People, by Family Income Relative to the Federal Poverty Level, 2009

In many cases, people's insurance status varies over the course of a year. For example, CBO's analysis of survey data showed that between 57 million and 59 million people—or roughly one-fourth of the nonelderly n population—were uninsured at some point during 1998. The average number of people who were uninsured at a give point in 1998 was smaller—between 39 million and 44 million, of which 21 million to 31 million were uninsured for all of that year.[19] CBO also found that for those who became uninsured at some point between July 1996 and June 1997, nearly half had spells of uninsurance lasting four months or less and about one in six had spells lasting two years or more.

According to CBO's projections, the average number of people who are uninsured at any one time will rise to about 54 million, or about 19 percent of the nonelderly population, by 2019. The number of uninsured individuals is expected to increase because health insurance premiums are likely to rise considerably faster than income, which will make insurance more difficult to afford.

Characteristics of the Uninsured

The purchase of health insurance in the United States is voluntary, so the main reason that people are uninsured is that they are unwilling or unable to purchase coverage. Several characteristics are associated with insurance status—including income, age, being offered insurance at work, or being eligible for public coverage—but whether they are a causal factor or are merely correlated with coverage rates is not always clear.

Because the costs of health insurance can represent a substantial share of income for lower-income individuals and families who are not eligible for subsidized public coverage, it is not surprising that coverage patterns are strongly correlated with income. In particular, as income rises, the share of nonelderly people who are uninsured or have public coverage declines and the share with private coverage rises (see Figure 1-1). In 2009, the highest rates of uninsurance—about 30 percent—will be found among people whose family income is below 200 percent of the federal poverty level. For people in that group that have insurance, those with family income below the poverty line will be much more likely to have public coverage, whereas those with income above the poverty line will be more likely to have private insurance. Only about 12 percent of people below the poverty line will have private coverage; that rate rises to 40 percent for those between 100 percent and 200 percent of the poverty level. For people whose income is between 200 percent and 400 percent of the poverty level, by contrast, 74 percent have private coverage and 16 percent are uninsured. For people with income above 400 percent of the poverty level, 90 percent have private coverage and 4 percent are uninsured.

Another characteristic that is associated with the lack of health insurance, at least among adults, is age. Younger adults are particularly likely to be uninsured—about 27 percent of those ages 18 to 34 lacked coverage, compared with about 14 percent of those ages 45 to 64 in 2007—possibly reflecting a lower perceived need for using health care services (younger people are generally healthier) as well as lower average income and assets.[20] Those younger adults make up about one-fourth of the nonelderly population but represent about 40 percent of the uninsured. Children under the age of 18 account for about the same share of that population but are much less likely to be uninsured.

Not surprisingly, rates of coverage are also associated with whether an individual (or a close family member) is offered insurance at work. In part that correlation probably reflects differences in income—firms with more low-wage workers are less likely to offer coverage—

but even within a given income range, workers in relatively small firms (which are less likely to offer coverage) are much more likely to be uninsured than workers in larger firms (see Figure 1-2). For example, among full-time workers whose income is between 100 percent and 200 percent of the federal poverty level, CBO projects that 56 percent of those employed by very small firms (fewer than 25 employees) will be uninsured in 2009, compared with 30 percent for those employed by larger firms (those with 100 or more workers). Determining cause and effect is difficult, however, because workers with less of a desire for insurance or who consider coverage unaffordable would be more likely to join firms that do not offer coverage and pay those workers higher wages instead.

Looking at income levels and insurance options simultaneously may provide additional insights about the uninsured population. For example, CBO projects that among the uninsured in 2009, 17 percent will have family income above 300 percent of the poverty level (about $65,000 for a family of four); 18 percent will be eligible for but not enrolled in Medicaid; and 30 percent will be offered, but will decline, coverage from an employer (see Figure 1-3). Some people will be in more than one of those categories at the same time—so overall, about half of the uninsured will meet at least one of those three criteria. Conversely, the rest of the uninsured are projected to have relatively low income and to lack both an offer of employment-based coverage and eligibility for public coverage.

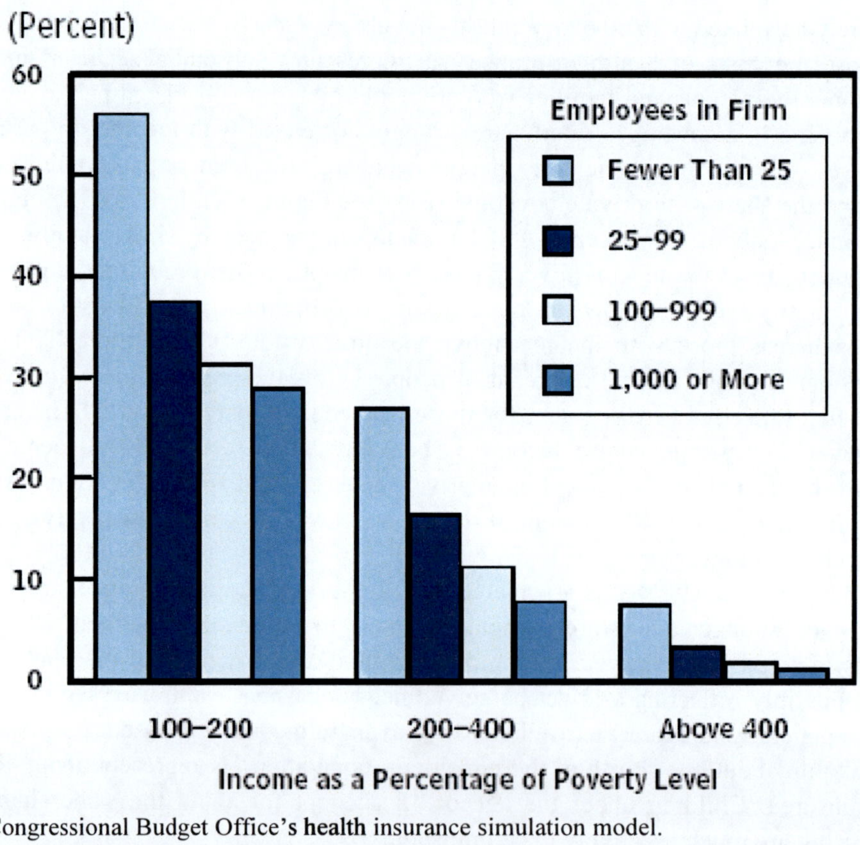

Source: Congressional Budget Office's **health** insurance simulation model.

Figure 1-2. Uninsurance Rates of Full-Time Workers, by Size of Firm and Family Income Relative to the Poverty Level, 2009

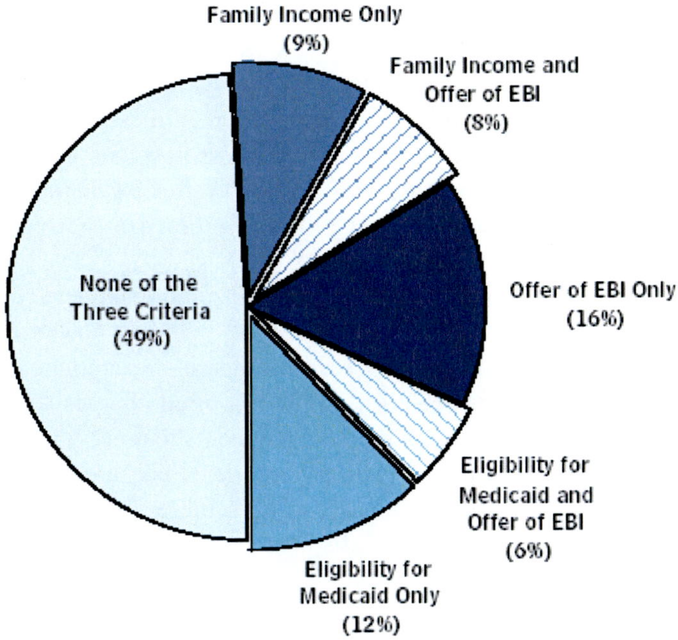

Source: Congressional Budget Office.

Note: This analysis categorizes uninsured nonelderly people according to whether they will meet any of the following criteria in 2009: Their family income will be above 300 percent of the federal poverty level; they will have an offer of employment-based insurance (EBI); or they will be eligible for Medicaid or the State Children's Health Insurance Program (SCHIP). The Congressional Budget Office estimates that a very small number of people will have family income above 300 percent of the federal poverty level and will be eligible for Medicaid or SCHIP.

Figure 1-3. Projected Distribution of the Uninsured Nonelderly Population, by Selected Characteristics, 2009

The reasons people remain uninsured even though they are offered employment-based coverage or are eligible for Medicaid are not always clear. In the case of employment- based coverage, the share of the premium that the employee must pay may be relatively high, or the employee may simply place a low value on having insurance. As for Medicaid, studies indicate a mixture of reasons for failing to enroll. Some people may not be aware that they are eligible; others may be deterred by the application process or see some stigma associated with a program for low-income families. An additional factor is that people who are eligible for Medicaid may be enrolled when they are hospitalized and then may gain retroactive coverage for recent medical expenses; thus, eligibility— even without enrollment—gives them some degree of protection against high medical costs and may reduce the incentive to enroll sooner.

Use of Health Care by the Uninsured

How the uninsured obtain health care affects both their incentives to seek insurance coverage and the impact that policies designed to reduce the number of uninsured have on spending and health. Many of the uninsured receive care from free clinics and other community health centers, which are funded by a combination of federal and state sources and private donations. Others may use traditional health care providers—hospitals as well as physicians in private practice—and pay all charges for the services they receive.

In many cases, however, people who are uninsured receive treatments from traditional providers for which they either do not pay or pay very little, which is known as "uncompensated care." Hospitals that participate in Medicare and offer emergency services are required by law to stabilize any patient who arrives, regardless of whether he or she has insurance or is able to pay for that care. In addition, most hospitals are nonprofit organizations and thus have some obligation to provide care for free or for a minimal charge to members of their community who could not afford it otherwise. For-profit hospitals also provide such charity or reduced-price care.[21]

Estimates of how much uncompensated care the uninsured receive vary depending on the data sources and methods used and the categories of spending that are included in the analysis. Some measures of uncompensated care compare the amount that providers are actually paid for their services with their list prices or posted charges for those services. A more useful comparison, however, is with the total payments that providers would receive for the same service when treating a privately insured patient, because that amount (which is generally much lower than the list price) more closely resembles their costs.

A recent study by Hadley and others, which used that analytic approach, examined a sample of medical claims for uninsured individuals and projected that they would receive about $28 billion in uncompensated care in 2008.[22] That study also examined reports by doctors and hospitals and derived a higher estimate: Their gross costs of providing uncompensated care would be about $43 billion in 2008, of which $8 billion would come from doctors and $35 billion would come from hospitals. But as the study noted, at least a portion of those costs could be offset by added payments under Medicare and Medicaid to hospitals that treat a disproportionate share of low-income patients (and by similar dedicated payments made under other federal and state programs). Another recent study found that, as a group, office-based physicians roughly "broke even" when treating uninsured patients because some of those patients paid more than the doctors would have received for treating a privately insured patient.[23] (The issue of whether and to what extent the net costs of providing uncompensated care are shifted to other payers in the health sector is discussed in Chapter 5.)

The uninsured generally use fewer health care services than people who have insurance, although estimates regarding the magnitude of the difference also vary. The study by Hadley and others estimated that an individual who is uninsured for all of 2008 will use about $1,700 worth of care—including about $540 in uncompensated care—or less than half as much as someone who is privately insured all year would use (see Table 1-3). The disparity in the amount spent for care is even larger; subtracting uncompensated care yields an estimate that spending incurred by and on behalf of people who are uninsured for the entire year (about $1,160) is about 30 percent of the amount spent for people who are privately insured all year (about $3,900). Spending by and for those who are insured for part of the year (about $3,000) falls between those two points. According to those estimates, average out-of-pocket payments are similar for each group, although those payments cover a higher share of total spending for the uninsured.

Reflecting a range of other findings on that topic, CBO estimates a somewhat smaller disparity in the use of health care services than the study by Hadley and others would indicate.[24] According to several other studies and CBO's own analysis of data for the nonelderly population, the uninsured do use fewer health care services than the insured, but the difference is generally in the range of 30 percent to 50 percent. (See Chapter 3 for a more extensive discussion of those estimates.) Studies comparing the insured and uninsured populations usually account for any differences that are observed in the demographic characteristics and health status of those populations, which would affect their use of health care.

Thus, CBO would expect an uninsured person to use 30 percent to 50 percent fewer health care services, on average, than a person who is similar in other respects but has typical private insurance coverage. Among people who have similar demographic characteristics and health status, there are two possible reasons why those who are uninsured would use fewer services than those who are insured: First, some of the uninsured may simply be less inclined to seek health care, resulting in less use of services; and second, the prospect of having to pay the full cost of the services they receive gives them an incentive to use less medical care or less expensive services.

A related consideration is whether the lack of insurance has adverse effects on health. Some studies examining the treatment of serious health conditions have found relatively clear links between insurance coverage and health outcomes.[25] For example, uninsured individuals who develop cancer generally have poorer outcomes and die more quickly than cancer patients who have private health insurance. That difference is attributed partly to later diagnosis for the uninsured; broader analyses of the uninsured population have found that they are less likely to receive screening tests, such as mammograms. Similarly, uninsured individuals who have heart disease are less likely to receive expensive treatments for it and also have higher rates of mortality than those who have heart disease but are privately insured.

Table 1-3. Health Care Expenditures in 2008, by Insurance Status

Insurance Status	**Out-of-Pocket Spending**	**Third-Party Payments**		**Uncompensated Care**	**Total**
		Insurance	**Other[a]**		
	Dollars of Spending				
Uninsured for Full Year	583	0	567	536	1,686
Insured for Part of the Year	550	2,030	260	145	2,983
Privately Insured for Full Year	681	3,018	215	0	3,915
Insured for Full Year	654	3,563	246	0	4,463
	Shares of Spending (Percent)				
Uninsured for Full Year	35	0	34	32	100
Insured for Part of the Year	18	68	9	5	100
Privately Insured for Full Year	17	77	5	0	100
Insured for Full Year	15	80	6	0	100

Source: Congressional Budget Office based on data from Jack Hadley and others, "Covering the Uninsured in 2008: Current Costs, Sources of Payment, and Incremental Costs," *Health Affairs*, Web Exclusive (August 25, 2008), pp. W399–W415. The authors used data from the Medical Expenditure Panel Survey, 2002–2004, and adjusted the data to 2008.

a. Includes workers' compensation, veterans' benefits, and other payments not counted as health insurance.

For more routine care, however, disentangling the effects on health of being uninsured from the impact of other factors that are associated with lack of insurance is more difficult. One recent and comprehensive review of the literature noted that most studies of such effects on health simply compare insured and uninsured individuals and thus do not account for underlying differences between those populations.[26] Some studies with a better design have examined the effects of expanding eligibility for public insurance programs and have found specific health benefits for the targeted populations, but broad health improvements stemming from insurance coverage have been difficult to identify. For example, one recent study found that the creation of Medicare had no discernible effect on the mortality rates of the elderly during the first 10 years of the program's operation.[27] Of course, reduced mortality is a relatively crude measure of the benefits conferred by medical care, but the ability to analyze other outcomes, such as quality of life, is constrained because those effects are more difficult to measure.

Nature and Extent of Coverage

In addition to differences in the sources of and financing for health insurance and health care, coverage varies by the type of health plan providing it, the scope of services that are covered, and the cost-sharing requirements and limits that apply. That variation largely reflects different approaches to controlling costs for insured individuals and can have substantial effects on the premiums charged for an insurance policy (as discussed in Chapter 3).

Types of Plans

Through the 1 980s, private health insurance coverage in the United States typically took the form of an **"indemnity" policy**, which reimbursed enrollees for their incurred costs, left it to them and their doctors to determine what care to provide, and largely allowed doctors and hospitals to set the prices for those services. As health care costs grew rapidly in the 1980s, however, private insurance coverage began to shift from indemnity policies toward other types of health plans, involving various degrees of managed care (as described below) and negotiated pricing.

One form of managed care plan that emerged was a **preferred provider organization** (PPO). PPOs establish lists or networks of preferred doctors and hospitals and—to give enrollees an incentive to use those providers—charge more for care received outside the plan's network. The preferred providers thus gain a higher volume of patients and, in return, usually accept lower negotiated payment rates for each service from the health plan. According to a major survey of employers conducted by the Kaiser Family Foundation, PPOs are the most common type of managed care plan, accounting for about 58 percent of enrollees in employment-based plans in 2008.[28] (That survey is the primary source of statistics about coverage and benefits cited in this subsection.)

At the same time, more stringent forms of managed care, such as **health maintenance organizations** (HMOs), also grew in prominence. Like PPOs, those plans establish networks of providers; unlike PPOs, they offer no coverage for services received outside their networks (except for emergencies). HMOs have also instituted various measures to limit the use of certain services, such as requiring patients to get a referral from a primary care physician in order to see a specialist or to obtain prior authorization from the plan before using some types of specialty care. Some HMOs are fully integrated; the plan owns the hospitals, and doctors work on salary. A more common arrangement, however, is to have a network of independent hospitals and physicians' practices in which providers either receive a fixed payment per patient (in the case of some primary care physicians) or are paid negotiated rates on a fee-for-service basis. As a share of enrollment in employment-based plans, HMOs peaked at roughly 30 percent in the mid-1990s and then fell, reaching about 20 percent in 2008.

Point-of-service (POS) plans have emerged as a kind of middle ground between PPOs and HMOs. Like PPOs they allow enrollees to go outside a plan's network for care (albeit at a higher charge), but like HMOs they typically require enrollees to secure referrals for specialty care from a primary care physician within the plan's network. More common among small firms, they accounted for 1 2 percent of enrollment in employment-based plans in 2008.

Another design option that has arisen in recent years is a **consumer-directed health plan**, which combines a high- deductible insurance policy with an account that enrollees can use to finance their out-of-pocket payments on a tax-preferred basis. (In other respects, those plans are usually similar to PPOs.) As of 2008, those plans account for about 8 percent of enrollment in employment-based coverage; one form of consumer-directed plan (known as a **health savings account**) can also be purchased in the individual insurance market.[29]

Scope of Covered Services. Both public and private health insurance plans generally cover hospitalizations, visits to doctors and other outpatient care, tests and imaging services (such as X-rays), and prescription drugs. Coverage varies to a greater extent for dental care and vision-related services, particularly when care is discretionary (for example, laser surgery to correct vision problems is typically not covered). According to a 2004 survey of employers, about 20 percent offered vision benefits and two-thirds offered dental benefits (although nearly all firms with more than 500 employees offered dental benefits and about half of those firms offered vision benefits).[30] Another source of variation is government requirements to cover certain types of benefits (such as infertility treatments) or the services of specific providers (such as chiropractors), which some states impose and others do not. Those mandates generally affect policies offered in the individual market and by small employers.

Cost-Sharing Requirements. A more significant way in which health insurance plans vary, even among the broad categories of plans noted above, is their cost-sharing structure. Most plans include one or more of the following provisions:

- An annual deductible (expenses that enrollees must pay out of pocket before the insurer begins paying for services),
- Coinsurance (a specified percentage) or copayments (a specified amount) that enrollees pay out of pocket to providers after satisfying any deductible, and
- An out-of-pocket maximum (a cap on the total amount that an individual or family pays out of pocket in a given year).

Those features not only affect the share of health care costs covered by the insurance policy but also influence total spending for health care.

Cost-sharing requirements typically differ by type of plan. According to the 2008 Kaiser/HRET survey of employment-based health insurance plans, almost 20 percent of HMO enrollees face a deductible in 2008, compared with about 68 percent of PPO enrollees. Among PPO enrollees, deductibles for care received within the plan's provider network average about $560 for single coverage and about $1,300 for family coverage in 2008. For hospital care, some enrollees face separate deductibles, and most (about 69 percent) are subject to coinsurance or copayments.

Most HMO and PPO plans that have a deductible exempt visits to a physician's office for care received within the network. Enrollees typically have a fixed copayment of around $20 for seeing a primary care physician and around $25 for seeing a specialist physician within their network. For visits outside the network, PPO enrollees who have met the deductible typically pay coinsurance in the range of 30 percent to 35 percent (thus encouraging enrollees to use network providers and also limiting the plan's liability for those costs). Most people who have employment-based insurance must also pay a portion of the costs for advanced diagnostic tests and outpatient surgery (coinsurance is more common) and for emergency room and urgent care visits (copayments are more common).

Most plans also limit total out-of-pocket spending that enrollees might incur in a given year. For PPO plans, median levels of the out-of-pocket maximum are roughly $2,000 for single coverage and $4,000 for family coverage in 2008, although those limits vary considerably across plans. Nearly half of HMOs do not have an out- of-pocket limit, but those plans typically have no deductible and relatively low cost sharing for individual services, so enrollees would be unlikely to incur very high out-of- pocket costs in the aggregate.

Many plans vary the amount of coinsurance by the type of service or exempt some services from the general deductible in an attempt to create differing incentives for enrollees to use certain types of care. For example, preventive services may have little or no cost sharing, either because insurers want to encourage their use or because those benefits are attractive to enrollees. Similarly, plans typically exempt prescription drugs from their general deductible and require relatively low copayments for less expensive generic drugs. Conversely, plans that cover dental and vision services may charge a separate deductible for them, require higher rates of cost sharing, or limit the maximum annual benefits that enrollees can receive.

Cost-sharing requirements tend to be higher in the individual insurance market, reflecting not only insurers' efforts to control the health care spending of their enrollees but also enrollees' desire for lower premiums (because those policies are generally not subsidized through the tax code). One survey of policies purchased in the individual market in late 2006 and early 2007 found that about 70 percent of single policies had deductibles of more than $1,000 and about two-thirds of family policies had deductibles of more than $2,000.[31] Largely because they cover a smaller share of enrollees' health care costs, the premiums for those policies are generally lower than the average premiums observed for employment-based insurance (even though the premiums for individually purchased policies include higher administrative costs per policy).

Cost-sharing requirements in the Medicaid program tend to be much lower than those in employment-based or individually purchased plans—typically $1 to $3 for a doctor's visit or $2 to $3 for a brand-name drug prescription—reflecting the limited income of Medicaid recipients. Cost-sharing requirements may be more substantial under SCHIP but are generally limited to about 5 percent of enrollees' family income.

Cost sharing under the Medicare program varies widely by service. In 2009, enrollees will face a deductible of about $135 for physicians' services and will be charged 20 percent coinsurance beyond that point. Some services, such as lab tests and home health care, are free to the enrollee. Most hospital admissions require a deductible of about $1,070, however, and the effective coinsurance rates for some skilled nursing care and outpatient hospital services may exceed 30 percent. In addition, the program does not cap annual out-of-pocket costs. To limit their financial exposure, most Medicare enrollees have some form of supplemental insurance that covers most or all of their cost-sharing obligations. That supplemental coverage typically comes from a former employer, the Medicaid program, a Medicare Advantage plan, or an individually purchased medigap policy.

Health Care Spending

Both the amount and rate of growth of spending for health care have important implications for proposals that would seek to expand insurance coverage, reduce that spending, or do both simultaneously. The budgetary impact of subsidizing insurance coverage depends in part on the health care costs that would be covered, and the effects of efforts to control costs depend on how those efforts influence the factors that cause cost growth. Other key aspects of health care spending include its concentration (a relatively small share of individuals account for the bulk of expenditures in any given year), how much an individual's health care costs vary from year to year, and the substantial variation in average spending that is observed from one region of the country to another.

Amount and Growth of Spending

For 2009, the Centers for Medicare and Medicaid Services projects that national health expenditures will total $2.6 trillion. The bulk of that spending—about five out of every six dollars spent in the health sector—is for personal health expenditures. That category includes such services and supplies as hospital care, physicians' and clinical services, and prescription drugs, among others. The remaining expenditures are for broad categories of spending that support but do not provide health care, including the administrative costs of private and public insurers; the outlays of public health departments and related activities; and investments in medical research, equipment, and structures.

Data on national health expenditures can be broken down in two basic ways: by the sources of payment and by the types of services provided (see Table 1-4). Private spending will account for about 54 percent of the total in 2009, and public outlays—primarily for the Medicare and Medicaid programs—will account for the remaining 46 percent.[32] About 65 percent of private health care costs are covered by insurance, and the rest are paid out of pocket or from other sources (including philanthropy). As for the types of services provided, hospital care and physicians' services combined will account for about half of all health care expenditures, outpatient prescription drugs for 10 percent, and the administrative costs of public and private insurers for about 7 percent. (Administrative costs borne by doctors, hospitals, and other providers are financed through the payments they receive for their services.) The remainder of personal health care expenditures is primarily for dental and other professional care, home health and nursing home care, and medical equipment.

Table 1-4. National Health Expenditures, by Source of Payment and Type of Service, 2009

(Billions of dollars)											
	Private				Public					Total, NHE	
						Medicaid[b]					
	Insured	Out-of-Pocket	Other[a]	Subtotal	Medicare[b]	Federal	State	Other[c]	Subtotal	Billions of Dollars	Percentage
	Personal Health Care Expenditures										
Hospital Care	291	27	36	355	230	79	61	75	445	800	31
Physicians' and Clinical Services	264	55	34	353	108	22	16	34	180	533	21
Dental and Other Professional Care	79	65	3	148	15	6	4	4	29	177	7
Prescription Drugs	113	56	0	170	52	14	10	19	95	264	10
Home Health and Nursing Home Care	17	43	6	67	51	48	39	6	144	210	8
Medical Equipment and Other Personal Care	3	51	7	61	10	34	27	14	85	146	6
Subtotal, Personal Health Care	**767**	**298**	**87**	**1,152**	**467**	**203**	**156**	**152**	**978**	**2,131**	**83**
	Other Expenditures										
Administration and Net Cost of Private Insurance	112	0	2	113	28[d]	16[d]	13[d]	14	71	184	7
Public Health Activity	0	0	0	0	0	0	0	72	72	72	3
Research, Equipment, and Structures	0	0	104	104	0	0	0	65	65	169	7
Subtotal, Other	**112**	**0**	**105**	**217**	**28**	**16**	**13**	**151**	**207**	**424**	**17**
Total, NHE											
Billions of dollars	879	298	193	1,369	495	219	169	303	1,186	2,555	100
Percentage	34	12	8	54	19	9	7	12	46	100	

Source: Centers for Medicare and Medicaid Services.

Note: NHE = national health expenditures.

a. Includes private philanthropy.

b. Figures for Medicare and Medicaid differ from the Congressional Budget Office's projections.

c. Includes payments for workers' compensation programs and for health care provided by the Departments of Defense and Veterans Affairs.

d. Administrative costs for Medicare and Medicaid include costs incurred by private health plans to deliver their benefits.

Compared with other developed countries, the United States devotes a substantially larger share of its economy to health care and related expenditures. That share was about 16 percent of gross domestic product in 2006—up from about 8 percent in 1975. Under current law, that share is projected to reach nearly 20 percent by 2017 (the last year of the current CMS projections). By contrast, spending for health care among the other countries that belong to the Organisation for Economic Co-operation and Development (OECD) averaged about 9 percent of GDP in 2006.[33]

Comparisons of growth rates for health care spending across countries can be sensitive to the time period used and to other factors included in the analysis (such as age, average income, or overall rates of economic growth). Some comparisons indicate that real (inflation-adjusted) growth rates have been similar across developed countries, which might suggest that common forces are causing spending to rise despite substantial differences in their health care systems; other studies conclude, however, that the United States has experienced faster growth in the share of GDP spent on health care than have other, comparable nations.[34]

Within the United States, growth rates in health care spending have varied over time but have generally outpaced those in the overall economy. An exception was the period between 1993 and 2000, when the share of GDP spent on health care held nearly constant at about 14 percent, but spending growth has accelerated since then. Over extended periods, the annual growth rate of health care spending per capita in the United States has typically exceeded the growth rate of GDP per capita by 2 percentage points or more, accounting for the substantially larger share of the economy that spending for health care now represents. CBO projects that as the share of family and state budgets devoted to health care grows even larger, growth in health care expenditures will eventually moderate even in the absence of changes in federal law. By CBO's estimates, spending per capita will nevertheless continue to grow more quickly than the economy as a whole—about 1.7 percentage points faster, on average—and total health care spending will reach nearly 40 percent of GDP by 2050.[35]

Over the past 30 years, federal spending on Medicare and Medicaid has nearly tripled as a share of GDP, rising from about 1.5 percent in 1975 to about 4.0 percent in 2007. According to CBO's projections, such spending will reach about 12 percent of GDP by 2050 under current policies, but substantial uncertainty surrounds that estimate. If spending per enrollee continued growing over the next four decades as quickly as it has over the past four—about 2.5 percentage points faster than per capita GDP—then federal spending on those programs would reach about 17 percent of the economy. If, instead, spending per enrollee grew at the same rate as GDP per capita, demographic changes alone would push those federal expenditures to about 6 percent of GDP in 2050.

As those figures suggest, the rate at which health care spending grows relative to the economy is the most important determinant of the country's long-term fiscal balance; it exerts a significantly larger influence on the budget over the long term than other commonly cited factors, such as the coming retirement of the baby-boom generation.[36] Rising health care spending represents a challenge not only for the federal government but also for private payers. Indeed, trends in both sectors reflect many of the same underlying forces, so controlling federal outlays over the long term will be difficult without addressing the forces that are also causing private spending for health care to rise.

Sources of Spending Growth

The effects of proposals to reduce spending on health care depend in part on how they affect the factors that are driving the growth of that spending. The factor with the greatest impact on spending growth is probably the development and diffusion of medical technology (broadly defined). Other influences include the aging of the population; reductions in the share of costs paid out of pocket; growth in the relative prices of health care services; and the growing prevalence of chronic health problems. (A recent CBO report analyzed several of those factors and provides additional information about the studies used to estimate their effects.[37]) In addition, the manner in which health care services are financed probably has an effect on the amount of spending and could also affect its growth rate.

Advances in Medical Technology

Many analysts attribute the bulk of the growth in health care spending to the development and diffusion of new medical "technology"—a term that is defined broadly to include new procedures and treatments as well as new medicines and devices. Some breakthrough developments permit the treatment of previously untreatable conditions; such innovations can confer substantial benefits, but they also add new sources of spending. Other advances may simply improve medical outcomes (compared with those provided by older treatments) but at added costs. In some cases, however, new procedures and treatments—or broader application of existing ones to new types of patients—could add to spending without yielding better outcomes. Whatever the magnitude of the health benefits may be, studies indicate that about half of the growth in health care spending over the past several decades reflects changes in medical care made possible by the development of new treatments and procedures.

Improvements in medical technology do not have to increase costs; technological innovation could reduce the unit cost of treating a given health problem and could also reduce total spending. Under current arrangements, however, the nature of technological advances in medicine and the changes in clinical practice that have ensued in the United States have tended to raise total spending— because the treatments themselves are expensive, because the number of people receiving them grows rapidly, or for both reasons. In the aggregate, that tendency may well reflect the willingness of individuals to pay for the added spending through higher insurance premiums; as some observers have noted, the demand for health plans offering "1960s medicine at 1960s prices" appears to be low.[38] Decisions about whether to cover new technologies, however, are ultimately made by public and private insurers, and the benefits and costs of those technologies may not be carefully evaluated in each case, in part because the information needed to do so is lacking in many situations.[39]

In assessing the role of medical technology, analysts also considered other sources of past spending growth (including increases in income and rising administrative costs for insurers, as well as those listed above). Yet each of those factors individually has accounted for a relatively small share of that growth, and collectively they can account for about half of total spending growth—even using estimated effects toward the upper end of the range for each factor. Analysts have thus attributed the large residual effect to technology because it is the one remaining force that could be responsible for cost growth (and because the effects of technology on spending are hard to measure directly).[40] Even if that conclusion is correct, it still leaves open the question of what underlying forces are causing technological changes to be adopted or why those changes tend to yield net increases in spending.

Aging of the Population

One noteworthy finding from studies that have analyzed past spending growth is that the impact of aging has been relatively small. The elderly do use more health care than the nonelderly, and the share of the population that is elderly increased by about 30 percent between 1965 and 2005—from 9.5 percent to 12.4 percent. By itself, however, that change would cause total spending on health care to rise by about 16 percent and thus accounts for only about 3 percent of the total cost growth over that period. (After adjusting for general price inflation using the GDP implicit price deflator, per capita spending on health care grew by more than 500 percent between 1965 and 2005.)

Aging has had a larger effect on federal spending for health care, however, primarily because nearly all residents become eligible for Medicare once they turn 65. In particular, the impending eligibility of the baby-boom generation will have a substantial effect on the share of GDP devoted to Medicare as a result of the increase in enrollment, but that effect pales in comparison with the likely impact of continued increases in health care spending per enrollee. According to CBO's analysis, future demographic changes will account for somewhere between one-fifth and one-third of the increase in federal spending on Medicare and Medicaid over the next 25 to 75 years, and rising outlays per enrollee (over and above demographic effects) will account for the remainder.[41]

Reductions in the Share of Costs Paid for Out of Pocket

Another important factor that both reflects and has contributed to rising health care expenditures is the declining proportion of those costs that are paid out of pocket—and the corresponding increase in the share covered by insurance. According to the estimates of national health expenditures produced by CMS, out-of-pocket payments accounted for 33 percent of all personal health care expenditures in 1975; by 2000, that share had fallen to 17 percent, and it declined to 15 percent in 2006.

Reducing the share of costs that patients have to pay generally increases their demand for care, and studies have concluded that more extensive insurance coverage is responsible for about 10 percent of historical spending growth. But that estimate does not account for the effect that expanded insurance coverage has on the diffusion of medical technology. By contrast, a recent study that examined the effects of Medicare's introduction found that a broad expansion of insurance coverage had much larger effects on spending. It attributed part of the impact to more rapid and widespread adoption of existing treatment methods (such as those provided by cardiac intensive care units), although some questions remain about the precise magnitude of those effects.[42]

Out-of-pocket payments have continued to decline slightly as a share of health care spending in recent years, despite recent increases in cost-sharing levels. For example, the average deductible for single coverage in an employment-based PPO plan tripled between 2000 and 2008 (rising from $187 to $560).[43] However, total out- of-pocket payments have not increased as quickly, and spending covered by insurance has also risen substantially, roughly keeping pace with the increases in out-of-pocket costs. Indeed, the overall rise in health care spending and the decline in the share paid out of pocket have had roughly offsetting effects on the share of GDP accounted for by out-of-pocket costs, which has held steady over the past three decades at about 2 percent. Even so, such increases in cost-sharing requirements have raised concerns that some people who have insurance coverage may be underinsured. For example, a recent study estimated that about 25 million insured adults faced relatively high out-of-pocket costs (as a share of their income) in 2007, up from about 16 million in 2003.[44]

Financing of Health Care Services

The way in which health care services are financed also affects the amount of health care spending and could affect its growth rate as well. With the exception of some HMOs, most health care provided by doctors in the United States is currently paid for on a fee-for-service basis. In some cases (such as hospital stays under Medicare), a fixed payment is made for a bundle of related services. Such payments encourage doctors and hospitals to deliver a given service or bundle efficiently, but they can also create an incentive to provide additional services or more expensive bundles if the payments exceed the costs of providing care.

Fee-for-service payments may yield a higher quantity or a greater intensity of services at any given time, but whether that type of payment contributes to the rate of spending growth is less clear. Because that method of financing has been in place for many years, it could have affected the amount of spending in a constant way without changing the growth rate of spending. Consistent with that view, an older study found that growth rates of spending in HMOs and fee-for-service plans did not differ substantially.[45] Compared with other payment systems, fee-for-service payment could encourage or at least facilitate the adoption of newer, more costly services, but whether that happens depends on how quickly fees are established for new treatments and on the level at which those fees are set. (See Chapter 5 for additional discussion of fee-setting mechanisms.)

Growth in the Relative Prices of Health Care Services

Growth in payment rates that exceeds general price inflation has probably contributed to the increase in the share of GDP devoted to health care. Between 1975 and 2005, the increase in the medical component of the consumer price index was nearly twice as large as the increase in prices overall—which might suggest that price increases for health care have played a large role in cost growth.

Measuring price inflation in the health sector can be difficult, however, both because it is hard to control for changes over time in the quality or type of the products being compared (which can make historical price comparisons misleading) and because discounts negotiated by private insurers are typically confidential. Such problems can arise with any price index but may be particularly acute for health care because of the relatively large role played by technological advances and because the prevalence of insurance obscures the price of many transactions. Despite those challenges, some observers have suggested that prices for health care, when properly measured, have actually grown at rates comparable with or lower than general inflation and that prices have not played a substantial role in the growth of U.S. health care spending over time. But other analyses (which are also cited in CBO's January 2008 paper on the growth of health care spending) suggest that rising relative prices for medical care may have accounted for as much as 10 percent to 20 percent of past spending growth.

Whether or not they have contributed to the growth in spending, price levels affect total spending, so the methods used to set those levels can also play an important role. In some cases, private insurers may have difficulty negotiating low prices for health care items and services, whereas public purchasers have sometimes intervened to obtain relatively low prices. Limited competition among doctors and hospitals in some parts of the country hampers the ability of private insurers to negotiate lower payment rates for their services. In the case of prescription drugs, public policy (through patents) gives manufacturers monopoly power, which leads to higher prices when drugs are introduced but also encourages those drugs to be developed in the first place. Federal and state purchasers have established payment systems that yield lower prices for drugs (under Medicaid and the health program for military veterans) and for doctors and hospitals (under Medicare and Medicaid), although many doctors are unwilling to accept Medicaid's payment rates. (See Chapter 5 for additional discussion.)

Rising Prevalence of Health Problems

Spending on health care would also be expected to grow if Americans were developing more health problems or were becoming more likely to contract diseases, but the evidence on those points is mixed. Perhaps the most alarming trend has been the growth in obesity over the past several decades. According to one set of surveys, the share of the adult population that is obese grew from about 23 percent in 1988 to about 34 percent in 2004, and the share that is either obese or overweight increased from 56 percent to 67 percent over that period.[46] CBO's analysis indicates that the share of spending growth attributable to rising weight over a similar period is between 4 percent and 12 percent, depending on the methodology used.[47]

More generally, determining whether spending on health care is rising because Americans are getting sicker is difficult. Trends in the incidence and prevalence of chronic and acute health problems have varied—some rates have increased, some have decreased, and some have held steady. For example, cancer is a leading cause of death and a major source of health care spending, but the incidence of cancers has declined slightly since 1990. In other cases, the analysis is complicated by the fact that reported rates of disease prevalence may rise when new treatments for the disease become available. Moreover, increases in the intensity of treatment may also increase the likelihood of diagnosing a disease (even if the true prevalence of the disease has not changed).

For example, obesity is associated with many serious medical conditions, including diabetes, heart disease, and high blood pressure. According to one government survey, the share of adults with diabetes grew by about 2 percentage points between 1988 and 2004, from about 8 percent to about 10 percent.[48] The share of the population being treated for diabetes grew even faster—by more than 50 percent among those with private insurance, according to one study—partly because the probability that someone with diabetes would be diagnosed also increased by about 10 percent.[49] Over that same period, however, the fraction of adults who have high blood pressure held constant at about 18 percent (in part because an increasing share of patients were taking medications to lower their blood pressure). Meanwhile, the percentage of adults with high cholesterol has fallen steadily and is now about half what it was in the early 1 960s, partly because of the development and use of cholesterol-lowering drugs. Overall, it is not clear what role changes in the prevalence of disease—as opposed to increases in the rate at which existing diseases are diagnosed and in the intensity of their treatment—are playing in the growth of health care spending.

Individual and Regional Variation in Health Care Spending

In addition to the overall level and growth of health care costs, three other significant aspects of spending for health care are the concentration and the persistence of individuals' spending and the substantial geographic variation in average spending levels across the United States. In any given year, the vast majority of spending on health care is generated by the relatively small share of individuals who use extensive or expensive services. Furthermore, people with high health care costs in one year tend to have above-average costs the next year; below-average costs for health care are also likely to persist.

In addition to individual variation, average health care spending varies sharply from one region of the country to another in ways that are not explained by regional differences in age or measures of sickness and that do not appear to yield better health overall in the high-spending regions. Reducing those differences in spending without harming health would improve the efficiency of the health sector, but steps to achieve that goal would undoubtedly prove quite challenging and complex to implement.

Concentration and Persistence of Individuals' Health Care Spending

The concentration of annual health care spending among a relatively small share of the population has been well documented, both among the nonelderly and in the Medicare program. For example, CBO analyzed spending by nonelderly individuals who had health insurance and found that 13 percent of them used more than $5,000 worth of care in 2004. That high- spending subgroup (with average costs of about $15,000) accounted for about 68 percent of the health care costs for that population. If the threshold is lowered to $2,000 worth of care, the share of nonelderly insured people with higher spending increases to 30 percent, and the share of health care spending attributable to those individuals rises to 86 percent. By contrast, about 55 percent of that population used less than $1,000 worth of care in 2004, and their collective spending amounted to only 6 percent of the total (with average spending of about $300). Among the Medicare population, similar degrees of concentration are observed. In 2001, the most expensive 5 percent of enrollees accounted for about 43 percent of program spending in one year, and the top 25 percent accounted for 85 percent of spending.[50]

Protecting themselves against the relatively low risk of incurring substantial costs is the main reason most people seek health insurance, and the uncertainty about those costs is large enough that most people who can afford to purchase insurance do so. Even so, a predictable element of health care spending also affects the type and extent of insurance coverage that people seek. CBO's analysis found that nonelderly insured individuals who used less than $1,000 worth of care in 2003 had a 78 percent chance of using less than $1,000 worth of care in 2004 but only a 5 percent chance of using more than $5,000; their average costs in 2004 were about $1,200 (see Table 1-5). By contrast, individuals who used more than $5,000 worth of care in 2003 had a 37 percent chance of using more than $5,000 worth of care in 2004 and only a 24 percent chance of using less than $1,000 worth; their average costs in 2004 were about $7,800. In some cases, those correlations are an artifact of the calendar year and simply reflect treatments begun in late 2003 that continued into early 2004. But in other cases, those raw year-to- year correlations may understate the extent to which individuals can anticipate their likely needs for health care in the near future; even if they have similar spending initially, people who have had health problems that are unlikely to recur and those who have conditions that are more chronically costly can use that information in choosing a health insurance plan.

As more time passes, the difference in average spending between those who initially had high expenditures and those who initially had low expenditures would tend to decline further, reflecting a common statistical phenomenon known as "regression to the mean." People with very high initial spending were probably hospitalized, which is unlikely to happen year after year (even though they may have an above-average chance of being hospitalized again). Conversely, some of those who had low initial spending may develop a chronic or acute health problem that generates higher costs. As a result, when examined over longer periods of time, health spending appears to be less concentrated. For example, looking at Medicare spending over a five-year period (from 1997 to 2001), CBO found that the most expensive 5 percent of Medicare beneficiaries accounted for 27 percent of total Medicare spending (compared with 43 percent in 2001 alone) and that the top 25 percent of beneficiaries accounted for 68 percent of total five-year spending (compared with 85 percent in 2001). Analysis of younger populations has been limited by lack of data, but one study simulated expenditure patterns for workers from age 25 to age 60 and suggested that the most expensive 25 percent of employees would account for roughly half of expenditures over that 35-year period.[51]

Geographic Variation in Health Care Spending

Spending on health care varies not only from person to person (because of differences in their health and in the treatments they receive) but also from region to region in the United States. In particular, per capita health care spending varies widely within the Medicare program, and yet that variation is not correlated with measures of the quality of care that beneficiaries receive or with available metrics of overall health outcomes. In 2004, for example, Medicare spending per beneficiary ranged from about $5,600 in South Dakota to about $8,700 in Louisiana. Yet a comparison of composite quality scores for medical centers and average Medicare spending per beneficiary shows that facilities in states with high average spending are no more likely to provide recommended care for some common health problems than are facilities in states with lower spending (see Figure 1-4). Health care spending per capita also varies widely when examined for the entire population—ranging from roughly $4,000 in Utah to $6,700 in Massachusetts in 2004—but the connection between that variation and health outcomes has not been examined as closely. Medicaid spending per enrollee also varies considerably among states (partly reflecting differences in the population covered and benefits provided).

The observed variations in Medicare spending per enrollee are even greater when examined by the area in which enrollees generally receive their hospital care, but a link between higher spending and better health in that population is still hard to discern. In 2005, average costs ranged from about $5,200 in the regions with the lowest spending to nearly $14,000 in those with the highest spending (those averages were adjusted to account for differences in the age, sex, and race of Medicare beneficiaries in the various regions). According to one study, higher- spending regions did not have lower mortality rates than lower-spending regions, even after adjustments were made to control for different rates of illness among patients and across regions.[52] That study also found that higher spending did not slow the rate at which the elderly developed functional limitations (a measure of their difficulties in taking care of themselves).

Table 1-5. Persistence of Health Care Spending

Total 2003 Spending Range (Dollars)	Percentage of Population in Range	Percentage of 2003 Subgroup with Total 2004 Spending in Range				Spending in 2004 (Dollars)	
		0 to $1,000	$1,000 to $5,000	$5,000 or More	All Ranges	Mean	Median
Zero to 1,000	50	78	17	5	100	1,214	279
1,000 to 5,000	35	41	47	13	100	2,597	1,313
5,000 or More	15	24	39	37	100	7,765	3,316

Source: Congressional Budget Office based on merged data for 2003 and 2004 from the Medical Expenditure Panel Survey conducted by the Department of Health and Human Services, Agency for Healthcare Research and Quality.

Notes: The figures include only individuals who were under the age of 65 in 2003 and were privately insured for all of that year.

CBO increased total health care spending for 2003 to 2004 dollars by using the growth in health care spending per capita as estimated from the national health expenditures compiled by the Department of Health and Human Services.

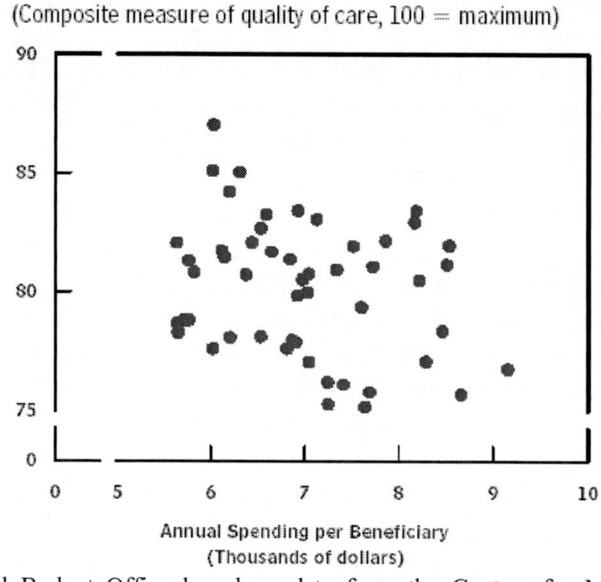

Source: Congressional Budget Office based on data from the Centers for Medicare and Medicaid Services and from the Department of Health and Human Services, Agency for Healthcare Research and Quality, *National Healthcare Quality Report, 2005* (December 2005), Data Tables Appendix, www.ahrq.gov/qual/nhqr05/index.html.

Notes: The composite measure of the quality of care, based on Medicare beneficiaries in the fee-for-service program who were hospitalized in 2004, conveys the percentage who received recommended care for myocardial infarction, heart failure, or pneumonia.

Spending figures convey average amounts by state.

Figure 1-4. The Relationship Between Quality of Care and Medicare Spending, by State, 2004

Other studies of spending variation reach somewhat different conclusions, even though they also suggest opportunities to improve the efficiency of the health sector. Some research suggests that health overall might not suffer if medical practice in higher-spending regions changed to match that of lower-spending regions. Patients who would benefit most from more expensive treatments, however, might be made worse off as a result, whereas patients who would do better with less expensive treatments would gain. Other, older studies of geographic variation indicate that there may be room to reduce spending without harming health in both high-use and low-use regions of the country, because a large share of certain surgeries were performed in both types of regions even though they were found to be clinically inappropriate or of equivocal value.

What factors contribute to geographic variation? Some of the differences in spending reflect varying rates of illness as well as differences in the prices that Medicare pays for the same service (those prices are adjusted on the basis of local costs for labor and equipment in the health sector). But according to researchers at Dartmouth, differences in illness rates account for less than 30 percent of the variation in spending among areas, and differences in prices can explain another 10 percent—indicating that more than 60 percent of the variation is due to other factors.[53] Differences in income or the preferences of individuals for specific types of care appear to explain little of the variation in spending. Unmeasured differences in the demand for care could be important, but some of the variation in medical practice probably is attributable to regional differences in the supply of medical resources (specialist physicians or health care facilities, for example) and the propensity to take advantage of the financial incentives provided by Medicare or other payers in developing and using those resources. Overall, patterns of treatment in high-spending areas tend to be more intensive than those in low-spending areas; that is, in high-spending areas, a broader array of patients will receive more costly treatments.[54]

In sum, the evidence about variation in spending suggests that efficiency gains in the health care system are possible: Expenditures in high-spending regions could probably be lowered without producing worse outcomes, on average, or reducing the overall quality of care. But if policies that reduced expenditures in high-spending areas did not successfully target ineffective or harmful treatments—a challenging task—they might not lead to increased efficiency and could result in worse health outcomes.

2. Approaches for Reducing the Number of Uninsured People

About one in six nonelderly people in the United States will be without health insurance at any given time during 2009. Those without insurance will include nearly 10 million children, over 14 million adults living in families with children, and another 21 million adults who do not reside with children. Nearly two-thirds of the uninsured are in families whose income is less than 200 percent of the federal poverty level.

Concerns about the number of people who lack health insurance have generated proposals that seek to increase coverage rates substantially or to achieve universal or near-universal coverage. Coverage could be expanded by:

- Subsidizing health insurance premiums, either through the tax system or spending programs, which would make insurance less expensive for people who are eligible.
- Mandating health insurance coverage, either by requiring individuals to obtain coverage or by requiring employers to offer health insurance to their workers. If effective penalties were imposed on those who did not comply, a mandate would increase insurance coverage by making it more costly for individuals to be uninsured and for employers not to offer coverage to their employees.
- Automatically enrolling individuals in health plans, giving them the option to refuse coverage or switch plans. Recent studies suggest that automatic enrollment in plans that subsidize savings for retirement substantially increases participation rates, especially among young and low-income workers.

The three approaches could also be used in combination to reduce the number of people who are uninsured. At the federal level, **subsidies** for health insurance premiums have been provided through spending programs and tax provisions. Millions of low-income children and their parents receive subsidized health insurance coverage through Medicaid and the State Children's Health Insurance Program; tax subsidies, such as the exemption of employer-paid premiums from taxation, encourage middle- and higher-income taxpayers to purchase private health insurance (primarily through their employer). Those subsidies, however, are distributed unevenly. Some low-income adults—particularly those who are under the age of 65, childless, and able-bodied—are generally not eligible for Medicaid or SCHIP. Taxpayers who do not work for a firm that offers coverage may not receive any tax subsidies for purchasing private health insurance.

Coverage could be expanded by restructuring tax subsidies, spending programs, or both. However, redesigning existing subsidies or creating new benefits raises several issues. First, the form of the subsidy can determine who would benefit. Tax preferences, such as the current-law exclusion or a tax deduction, reduce taxes but do not provide benefits to those who do not have any income tax liability. A refundable tax credit would provide full benefits to individuals, regardless of whether they have any income tax liability, but might require some people to file returns solely to obtain the subsidy. A second consideration is costs, which could be high depending on the numbers of uninsured receiving the subsidies and the amounts necessary to encourage them to enroll in health plans. Targeting benefits toward specific segments of the population would reduce costs but could also add to the burden of administering a program. A third consideration is the impact of the subsidies on people who already have coverage; although subsidies would probably increase coverage on net, some subsidies would go to people who would have coverage anyway, and the availability of subsidies might cause some people to lose coverage because firms might drop existing plans if their workers could obtain comparable health insurance elsewhere at equal or lower cost.

Because subsidies may not be sufficient to achieve universal coverage, some analysts have suggested imposing a **mandate** on individuals to obtain health insurance or on employers to offer plans. The effectiveness of a mandate in expanding coverage would depend on its scope, the incentives to comply, and the ease of enforcement. Many factors affect compliance with a mandate, and the Congressional Budget Office will consider the specifics of each proposal requiring individuals or employers to purchase health insurance in determining the proposal's effect on coverage.

Coverage could also be increased by **automatically enrolling** individuals in health insurance plans, giving them the option to refuse coverage. Automatic enrollment has increased participation in employer-sponsored 401(k) plans and certain government programs. Firms that offer health insurance might be encouraged or required to automatically enroll employees in a basic plan, unless the employees chose to opt out of coverage or signed up for a more comprehensive plan. Automatic enrollment, however, might be more difficult to implement in settings other than the workplace or public programs because of the complexities of determining eligibility, collecting premium payments, and other factors.

All three approaches to expanding coverage could affect participation in employment-based health plans. To the extent that employers' payments for health insurance increased as a consequence, firms would respond over the long term by paying lower wages and providing fewer fringe benefits than they otherwise would in order to maintain the same level of compensation. Because employers' contributions for health insurance (unlike wages) are exempt from income and payroll taxes, such changes could have substantial effects on the federal budget.

Methods of Subsidizing Premiums

Proposals that are designed to increase substantially the number of people who have health insurance typically include federal subsidies to cover some portion of the premium for that coverage.[55] In addition, proposals may set eligibility for subsidies or the size of the subsidy payment on the basis of income, family structure, availability of insurance, or other factors. By lowering the costs of health insurance to enrollees, subsidies encourage uninsured individuals to obtain coverage. The design of the subsidies, however, may involve trade-offs with other policy goals that could affect their costs.

A basic set of trade-offs arises between the share of the premium that is subsidized, the number of people who enroll in an insurance plan as a result, and the total costs of the subsidies. As the rate of the subsidies increases, more people will be inclined to take advantage of them, but the higher subsidy payments also go to those who would have purchased insurance anyway. Beyond a certain point, therefore, the cost per newly insured person can grow sharply because a large share of the additional subsidy payments is going to individuals who are otherwise uninsured.

To hold down the costs of subsidies, proposals could seek to limit eligibility for subsidy payments to individuals who are currently uninsured. That restriction, however, increases incentives for people who have insurance to drop their coverage (or for their employers to stop offering coverage) in order to qualify for the new subsidies. Some proposals may try to distinguish between people who become uninsured in response to subsidies and those who would have been uninsured in the absence of a government program, but such proposals raise significant administrative challenges. In addition, providing benefits only to the uninsured may be viewed as unfair by people with similar income and family responsibilities who purchase health insurance and are therefore ineligible for the subsidies.

Table 2-1. Distribution of the Nonelderly Population, by Insurance Status, Family Income, and Family Structure, 2009

(Millions)								
Family Income Relative to Poverty Level (Percent)	Children		Adults				Total	
			With Children		Without Children			
	Insured	Uninsured	Insured	Uninsured	Insured	Uninsured	Insured	Uninsured
Below 100	17.2	2.7	6.5	3.5	7.3	6.9	30.9	13.1
100 to 200	15.5	3.4	10.8	5.8	9.1	6.6	35.3	15.8
200 to 300	11.9	1.8	12.9	2.9	10.9	3.6	35.7	8.3
300 to 400	9.6	0.9	12.3	1.3	10.3	2.0	32.2	4.2
Above 400	17.2	0.8	28.9	1.0	36.1	1.9	82.2	3.7
Total	**71.3**	**9.6**	**71.3**	**14.5**	**73.7**	**20.9**	**216.3**	**45.1**

Source: Congressional Budget Office's health insurance simulation model.
Note: Children are age 22 or younger.

Another way to limit costs would be to target subsidies toward lower-income groups, who are most likely to be uninsured otherwise, but such approaches can also have unintended consequences that affect the costs of the proposal. If eligibility was limited to people with income below a certain level, then those with income just above the threshold would have strong incentives to work less or hide income in order to qualify for the subsidies or to maintain their eligibility. Phasing out subsidies gradually as income increases would reduce, but would not eliminate, those incentives. At the same time, the more gradually the subsidies were phased out, the greater the number of people who would be eligible for them—and the more likely that subsidy payments would go to those who would have had insurance in any event. The number of uninsured—regardless of the individual's age or the presence of children in his or her home—gradually declines as family income rises above 200 percent of the federal poverty level. Still, nearly 4 million uninsured individuals have family income that is greater than 400 percent of the federal poverty level; however, over 80 million insured individuals have income that exceeds that level (see Table 2-1).

Whatever eligibility rules are applied, subsidy systems generally need to establish methods for determining who is eligible, how much of a subsidy each person receives, and how the subsidy will be delivered. In particular, basing subsidies on income reqires a system for measuring and verifying income, and trade-offs can arise between the timeliness and accuracy of that information. Verifying eligibility could impose costs not only on the agencies that administer the programs but also on the individuals applying for subsidies who might choose to forgo benefits rather than bother with administrative hassles and the perceived stigma of participating in such programs. Subsidy payments could go directly to individuals or could instead be channeled through insurers, employers, state governments, or other intermediaries.

The design issues raised by various subsidy systems and their implications for the federal budget can be illustrated by examining more closely the two largest subsidies currently provided to the nonelderly population: the tax exclusion for employment-based insurance and the Medicaid program (along with the smaller SCHIP program). Both the tax exclusion and Medicaid also illustrate the many challenges involved in providing subsidies to lower-income individuals and families, who typically have limited tax liabilities—and thus might derive little benefit from certain types of tax-based subsidies—but may find it burdensome to apply for programs like Medicaid or S CHIP or may be ineligible for those two programs under current rules.

Subsidizing Premiums Through the Tax System

Most workers receive a subsidy through the tax system when they purchase private health insurance through their employer. Employers' payments for health insurance are a form of compensation, but those payments are exempt from income and payroll taxes (as are most employees' payments for their share of health insurance premiums). Changes to those subsidies could have substantial effects on coverage rates and the federal budget.

Current Tax-Based Subsidies

The favorable tax treatment currently provided for health insurance purchased through an employer represents the largest single source of federal premium subsidies for the nonelderly population. Employers may compensate their employees by paying health insurance premiums in lieu of cash wages, but the two types of compensation receive very different tax treatment.[56] Employers may deduct the costs of providing that coverage as a business expense— just as they deduct employees' wages and other forms of compensation—and thus those payments are not subject to corporate income taxes. But unlike wages, the costs that employers pay for health insurance are also excluded from the taxable income and earnings of the covered employees. That portion of employees' compensation is therefore exempt from individual income and payroll taxes.

Partly as a result of that favorable tax treatment, employers that offer health insurance to their workers typically pay a substantial share of the premium for that coverage; that is, the amount that employees pay directly usually covers a relatively small fraction of the total premium. Many firms also offer their workers a "cafeteria plan," which allows employees to choose cash or other taxable benefits in lieu of receiving nontaxable benefits. (Such plans are referred to as Section 125 plans, after the section of the tax code that authorizes them.) Under that arrangement, employees are able to exclude the portion of the health insurance premium that they pay from their taxable income—so for most workers, the full cost of the employer-sponsored plan receives favorable tax treatment.[57]

The subsidy provided by the current tax exclusion shows up as a reduction in taxes (commonly referred to as a tax expenditure) rather than as an overt payment. The manner in which the tax exclusion subsidizes health insurance can be seen by comparing the tax liabilities of two otherwise identical workers employed at different firms. Both workers receive $40,000 in compensation from their respective employers in 2009, but that compensation— which is a combination of wages, employers' contributions for payroll taxes, and fringe benefits—takes different forms at the two firms:

- Employee A works for a firm that does not offer health insurance. He receives about $37,160 in cash wages, and his employer pays the remaining compensation— about $2,840—to the government in the form of payroll taxes. Employee A pays $5,000 for a health insurance plan in the individual market.
- Employee B works for a firm that offers health insurance. She receives about $32,500 in wages, and her employer pays nearly $2,500 in payroll taxes on her wages. In addition, she has an employment-based health insurance plan valued at $5,000 per enrollee.

For simplicity, assume that both workers have no other sources of income and are in the 15 percent income tax bracket; that the employee's and the employer's portions of the Social Security and Medicare payroll taxes (which have a combined rate of 15.3 percent) are ultimately paid by the workers; and that the costs of the second firm's health plan are borne evenly across its workforce.[58]

Although the two workers receive the same total compensation and have comparable health insurance coverage, their tax liabilities differ. Employee A, who purchases health insurance in the individual market, pays $9,439 in income and payroll taxes, or $1,407 more than the worker who receives part of her compensation in the form of health insurance premiums. For Employee B, federal taxes have effectively reduced the cost of insurance by more than 28 percent, to $3,593 (see Table 2-2). The effective subsidy rate increases by several percentage points if the employee lives in one of the 41 states (or the District of Columbia) that have an individual income tax; those states generally follow federal definitions of earnings and other income and thus exclude employers' contributions for health insurance from their calculation of taxable income.[59]

The aggregate effects of that exclusion on the federal budget are large, exceeding federal spending on Medicaid. The Joint Committee on Taxation has estimated that the total federal tax expenditure associated with the exclusion for employment-based health insurance was $246 billion in 2007, consisting of $145 billion in individual income taxes and $101 billion in payroll taxes.[60] (By comparison, the federal government spent over $195 billion on Medicaid in 2007.) In addition, the federal government incurs an additional tax expenditure of about $5 billion annually by allowing self-employed individuals to deduct the costs of health insurance from their taxable income (but health insurance costs for the self-employed are not deductible for purposes of payroll taxes). However, the magnitude of the estimated tax expenditures is not the same as the increase in revenues that would result from repealing the current exclusion or the deduction for the self-employed, because the calculation of the tax expenditures does not account for any changes in taxpayers' behavior that would result if the exclusion was repealed. (The revenue gain from repeal would be less than the estimated tax expenditures because some individuals would find other ways to reduce their tax liabilities if the exclusion was repealed; some individuals, for example, might claim their health insurance premiums as an itemized deduction.)

The current tax treatment of health insurance premiums encourages employers to offer health insurance to their employees and encourages employees to enroll in those plans, but it has also raised several concerns. In particular, the exclusion does not provide benefits for health insurance evenly. Individuals with the same income and similar family responsibilities can receive very different tax benefits for medical costs. Employees who can exclude premiums for employment-based insurance from payroll taxation, as well as from individual income taxes, typically receive more generous tax subsidies than do self- employed individuals. Employees who work for firms that do not offer insurance do not benefit from the exclusion.

In addition, the current system provides different tax subsidies to people at different income levels. Because the rate structure of the income tax is progressive—that is, as income rises, each additional dollar of income may be taxed at a higher rate—the value of the exclusion generally grows as income increases. If, in the example above, the single employee with an employer-sponsored health insurance policy worth $5,000 had earned $70,000 in total compensation instead of $40,000, that individual would probably be in the 25 percent rate bracket; being in that higher bracket would increase the total tax savings by $465 (from $1,407 to $1,872) and raise the federal tax subsidy to over 37 percent. The share of the premiums that the federal exclusion offsets can be somewhat lower at higher levels of income if taxpayers reach the wage ceiling for Social Security payroll taxes ($106,800 in 2009). The value of the exclusion represents a larger *percentage* of income for middle-income households than for high- income households, however, largely because average premiums for health insurance do not vary substantially with income and therefore decline as a share of income as income rises.

Although the exclusion of employer-paid premiums is by far the largest tax expenditure related to health care, two others worth noting are the itemized deduction for medical expenses and the health coverage tax credit that is available for workers displaced from their jobs by international trade. (For a general discussion of the key differences between tax exclusions, tax deductions, and tax credits, see Box 2-1.)

Taxpayers who **itemize deductions** on their income tax return may deduct unreimbursed medical expenses, including any premiums and out-of-pocket expenses that they paid out of after-tax income. The deduction is generally limited to expenses in excess of 7.5 percent of adjusted gross income; for example, a taxpayer with $50,000 in adjusted gross income could deduct medical costs in excess of $3,750. Furthermore, the total amount of itemized deductions is gradually reduced for taxpayers with adjusted gross income above $166,800 in 2009. In 2007, the tax expenditure for the itemized deduction for medical expenses was about $9 billion.

The **health coverage tax credit** covers up to 65 percent of the cost of health insurance for certain dislocated workers. Because the credit is refundable, individuals can claim the full benefit even if its value exceeds their income tax liabilities. To be eligible, individuals must be receiving either trade adjustment assistance or payments from the Pension Benefit Guaranty Corporation (which pays at least a portion of the pension benefit promised to retired workers if their company goes out of business or otherwise defaults on its obligations). The credit is not available to people receiving certain other government health benefits, including Medicare. In 2007, the tax expenditure for the credit was about $100 million.[61]

Options to Modify Tax Subsidies for Health Insurance

Tax subsidies could be redesigned in several ways to expand coverage. One option would be to replace the current exclusion of premiums for employment-based health insurance with a tax deduction or a tax credit. Another option would be to provide new subsidies to employers, in the form of tax credits, to encourage them to offer health insurance and to pay a portion of their employees' premiums. (Such an option could replace or supplement the current-law exclusion or be combined with new credits or deductions for individuals.)

Table 2-2. Illustrative Tax Subsidy for Employment-Based Health Insurance for a Single Worker Who Receives $40,000 in Total Compensation, 2009

(Dollars)	Employee A: Pays $5,000 for Individual Health Insurance	Employee B: Receives $5,000 of Employment-Based Health Insurance	Difference
Compensation			
Cash wages	37,157	32,513	4,644
Premiums for employment-based health insurance	0	5,000	-5,000
Employers' contribution for payroll taxes	2,843		
Total compensation	**40,000**	**40,000**	**0**
Premiums for Health Insurance in Individual Market	5,000	0	5,000
Income Tax			
Adjusted gross income	37,157	32,513	4,644
Minus personal exemption	3,650	3,650	0
Minus standard deduction	5,700	5,700	0
Taxable income	**27,807**	**23,163**	**4,644**
Income tax	3,754	3,057	697
Payroll Tax			
Employee's contribution at 7.65 percent	2,843	2,487	355
Employer's contribution at 7.65 percent	2,843	2,487	355
Total payroll tax	**5,685**	**4,974**	**711**
Total Income and Payroll Taxes	9,439	8,031	1,407
After-Tax Cost of Health Insurance	5,000	3,593	1,407
Subsidy as a Percentage of Costs of Health Insurance	0	28	-28

Source: Congressional Budget Office.

Note: To simplify the example, both workers are assumed to be unmarried, to have no dependents, to receive $40,000 in total compensation, and to have no sources of income other than wages and salaries.

Replacing the Exclusion with a Tax Deduction or a Tax Credit

The exclusion of premiums for employment- based insurance could be replaced with a deduction or a tax credit that is designed to encourage coverage. In addition, eligibility for those tax deductions or credits could be extended to all taxpayers who purchase health insurance, including those who purchase policies in the individual market. Providing tax preferences for individually purchased health insurance, however, could cause some employers to drop plans because they realize their workers have alternative tax-preferred options. In response, some of those workers may switch to individually purchased insurance, and others may become uninsured. (The likely magnitudes of those responses are discussed later in this chapter.)

Table 2-3. Effects on a Single Worker of Repealing the Tax Exclusion and Replacing It with an Above-the-Line Deduction, 2009

(Dollars)					
		Change from Current Law			
Type of Tax	Current-Law Taxes	Effect of Repealing Exclusion for Employment-Based Health Insurance	Effect of Above-the-Line Deduction for All Health Insurance	Combined Effect	Taxes After Change
	Employee A: Pays $5,000 for Individual Health Insurance				
Individual	3,754	0	-750	-750	3,004
Payroll	5,685	0	0	0	5,685
Total taxes	**9,439**	**0**	**-750**	**-750**	**8,689**
	Employee B: Receives $5,000 of Employment-Based Health Insurance				
Individual	3,057	697	-750	-53	3,004
Payroll	4,974	711	0	711	5,685
Total taxes	**8,031**	**1,407**	**-750**	**657**	**8,689**

Source: Congressional Budget Office.

Notes: To simplify the example, both workers are assumed to be unmarried, to have no dependents, to receive $40,000 in total compensation, and to have no sources of income other than wages and salaries. For Employee B, repealing the exclusion causes the employer's contributions for payroll taxes to rise by $355 and cash wages to fall by an offsetting amount.

An above-the-line deduction is subtracted from total income to derive adjusted gross income. Taxpayers can claim both an above-the-line deduction and the standard deduction.

The different structure of tax deductions and tax credits affects not only the value that various types of individuals and families will derive from them but also the impact that those subsidies will have on insurance purchases. Like the current exclusion for health insurance premiums, a deduction reduces taxable income, causing the value of the deduction to increase as income and marginal tax rates rise. A deduction is subtracted from total income solely for purposes of computing the income tax and thus may have no impact on payroll taxes—unlike the existing exclusion.[62] In some cases (as with the current itemized deduction for medical expenses), taxpayers can claim the deduction only if they itemize instead of claiming the standard deduction. In contrast, taxpayers can claim "above-the-line" deductions along with their standard deduction.

Consider, again, the two single workers who each earn $40,000 in total compensation but one receives health insurance at work and the other purchases a comparable policy in the individual market. Employee A, who purchases a health insurance policy for $5,000 in the individual market and does not itemize deductions, receives no tax benefit for his or her premiums under current law; an above-the-line deduction for the costs of health insurance would lower that worker's taxes by $750 (see Table 2-3). That same proposal would increase taxes by $657 for Employee B, who receives $5,000 in employment-based health insurance;

that worker's taxes would rise because the amount spent on employment-based health insurance would no longer be exempt from payroll taxes. In contrast to current law, both workers would pay the same total amount of taxes—$8,689—if the above-the-line deduction replaced the current exclusion.

BOX 2-1. TAX EXCLUSIONS, TAX DEDUCTIONS, AND TAX CREDITS

Several types of subsidies for health care costs are embedded in the current structure of the individual income tax. Proposed tax subsidies can take the form of exclusions, deductions, or credits, each of which has a different structure and different effects on individual income tax liabilities. Briefly,

- A tax exclusion reduces the amount that tax filers report as their total, or gross, income.
- A tax deduction is an expense that is subtracted from total income when calculating taxable income. It reduces tax liability in proportion to an individual's tax bracket.
- A tax credit is the direct dollar-for-dollar reduction of an individual's tax liability. If the tax credit is refundable, individuals can receive its full amount even if they do not have any income tax to offset.

Tax Exclusions

Certain forms of compensation are excluded from taxable income, effectively providing a subsidy for the excluded amount. Some types of income are excluded because they are difficult to measure. Other types of income are excluded to reflect policy choices to encourage taxpayers to engage in a particular activity. For example, employers' contributions to 401(k) retirement savings plans are not counted as income for employees, and employees' contributions are subtracted from their earnings when determining the amount that is reported as taxable. (Contributions to 401(k) plans are still subject to payroll taxes, however.) Similarly, the amounts that employers pay for employees' health insurance are not counted as taxable income for employees, thus subsidizing the purchase of employment-based health insurance.

Tax Deductions

There are several types of income tax deductions. All taxpayers may subtract certain types of income or expenses—commonly referred to as **above-the-line deductions**—from total income to derive their adjusted gross income. Those deductions may try to adjust for differences among taxpayers in terms of family or other personal characteristics or to meet other goals of tax and social policy. For example, people who move more than a specified distance may deduct their moving expenses, and contributions to individual retirement accounts may also qualify (up to an annual limit) for an above-the-line deduction. Similarly, self-employed individuals may deduct the full cost of their health insurance. (However, the self- employed are not allowed to exclude health insurance premiums from their income for purposes of payroll taxes.)

Starting from adjusted gross income, taxable income is computed by subtracting personal exemptions and either a standard deduction amount or the total amount of **itemized deductions**, and it is generally to taxpayers' advantage to subtract the larger of the two. In 2009, the standard deduction ranges from $5,700 for single filers to $11,400 for married couples filing jointly. Expenses that are allowed as itemized deductions include property taxes and mortgage interest, state and local income taxes, and charitable contributions; medical expenses not covered by insurance are also allowed, but only to the extent that those expenses exceed 7.5 percent of adjusted gross income. The value to taxpayers of allowing itemized deductions for certain expenses thus depends in part on what other expenses they have that can be itemized and how those expenses compare with their standard deduction. In general, higher-income households are more likely to itemize their deductions, although the total amount of itemized deductions that can be taken is gradually reduced for taxpayers whose adjusted gross income exceeds $166,800.

Tax liabilities are next determined by applying the statutory tax rates, currently ranging from 10 percent to 35 percent, to taxable income. The value of tax exclusions and deductions generally depends on an individual's marginal tax rate—the rate that applies to the last dollar of income. For example, a self- employed person who is in the 25 percent tax bracket and deducts the cost of a $5,000 health insurance policy reduces his or her taxes by $1,250; in the 35 percent bracket, the tax savings is $1,750.

Tax Credits

Tax liabilities can be reduced by tax credits. For example, a portion of the costs that working parents incur for child care can be taken as a tax credit. An important distinction between tax credits, on the one hand, and exclusions and deductions, on the other, is that a tax credit can be designed so that its dollar value does not depend on one's tax bracket.

Most tax credits are **nonrefundable**, however, meaning that the actual credit that taxpayers receive cannot exceed their income tax liability. Because lower-income individuals and families generally owe less in income taxes than those with higher income, they are less likely to benefit from nonrefundable tax credits.

Some tax credits are **refundable**, however, allowing individuals to receive the entire credit amount regardless of their income tax liability. The only example of a tax credit related to health care is a refundable one for workers who lost their job as a result of international trade and are receiving trade adjustment assistance (certain other workers are also eligible); they may be eligible for a tax credit for 65 percent of the costs of their health insurance.

In contrast, tax credits can be designed to provide lower- and moderate-income taxpayers with larger subsidies than they would receive from tax deductions or exclusions. A credit could reduce income tax liabilities by a fixed amount, or it could have a progressive rate schedule, thereby reducing the dollar value of the tax credit as income rises.

An important issue with tax credits—particularly for lower-income individuals and couples that pay relatively little in income taxes and are more likely to be uninsured—is whether the credits are refundable. If they are not, the value of the credit may not exceed a taxpayer's income tax liability. Compare two workers who each purchase a health insurance policy in the individual market that costs $2,000; however, one worker earns $40,000 and the second earns $20,000. Under current law, the worker who earns $40,000 pays $4,180 in income taxes. Because that worker has more than $2,000 of income tax liability, he or she would be entitled to the full $2,000 tax credit; the credit thus effectively reduces the costs of health insurance to zero. In contrast, the worker with lower earnings owes $1,180 in income taxes. The value of the tax credit would be limited by the amount of the second worker's income tax liability, effectively reducing the costs of his or her health insurance by $1,180 (to $820). If, instead, the credit was made refundable, the second worker would receive the full amount of the tax credit—providing the lower-earning worker with the same subsidy for health insurance as the higher earner.

Recent expansions in child-related tax credits have increased the amount of income a taxpayer with children must have before he or she owes any individual income tax, making it more difficult to target assistance toward lower-income families through the tax system unless credits are made refundable. In 2009, a married couple with two children may not owe any income taxes unless their adjusted gross income is about 200 percent of the federal poverty level (approximately $44,000 for a family of four); in contrast, for workers without children, the threshold for owing income taxes is close to the poverty level. In 2009, over 20 percent of the people who are projected to be uninsured at any given time either do not have any income tax liability or are claimed as a dependent by others who do not owe any income taxes. Nearly half as many are in the 10 percent income tax bracket and thus may not have sufficient income tax liability to receive the full benefit of a nonrefundable tax credit (see Figure 2-1).

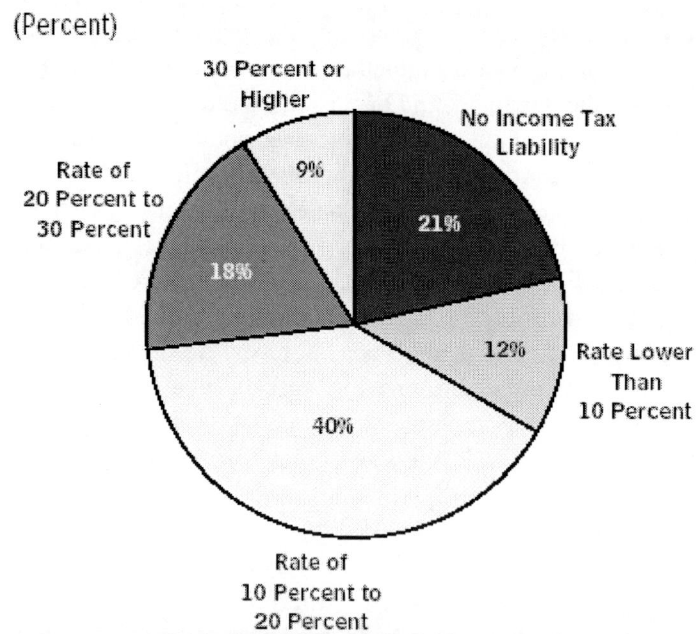

Source: Congressional Budget Office's health insurance simulation model.

Note: A dependent is assigned the marginal tax rate for the taxpayer who claims him or her as a dependent.

Figure 2-1. Distribution of Marginal Tax Rates on Income for the Nonelderly Uninsured Population, 2009

Because low-income individuals are also more likely to be uninsured, a refundable tax credit could be more effective in increasing health insurance coverage than other forms of tax-based subsidies for the same budgetary costs. The effectiveness of a tax credit, however, could be lessened if low-income individuals with limited resources had to wait until they filed tax returns to claim the benefit or if it was difficult to reach eligible individuals because they do not file tax returns. For those reasons, some proposals would make tax credits payable in advance as well as refundable, but doing so would raise a number of additional administrative issues (see Box 2-2).

Providing Tax Credits for Employers

To encourage firms to offer health insurance to their employees, some proposals would provide subsidies to businesses that contribute toward their employees' health insurance, with the expectation that those subsidies would ultimately benefit workers. Employers could receive a tax credit to cover a specified percentage of the per-worker cost of health insurance or a fixed-dollar amount per worker. As with tax credits for individuals, tax credits for businesses can be designed so that their value does not depend on the business's marginal tax rates. In a competitive labor market, such subsidies would be passed on to employees in the form of higher wages or lower premiums for health insurance.

Providing subsidies to businesses entails many of the same issues and trade-offs that arise in providing subsidies to individuals. Small firms are less likely to offer health insurance to their workers, particularly if a large share of those workers has low income. Thus, in firms with fewer than 25 employees, more than half of full-time workers who have income between 100 percent and 200 percent of the federal poverty level lack insurance (see Figure 1-2). Partly as a result, small businesses are more likely to respond to a subsidy for insurance than are larger firms. To reflect those relationships, proposals might target tax credits toward smaller firms or to firms that do not currently offer health insurance.

Such targeting strategies could reduce the cost of a subsidy proposal but would also lead some employers to respond in ways that would diminish the budgetary benefits of targeting. Basing subsidies on the size of a firm's workforce might discourage some businesses from expanding and encourage others to reorganize into smaller entities in order to take advantage of the subsidies. Phasing out subsidies as the size of firms increases would reduce those incentives but would also make more firms eligible for the subsidies than would a strict cutoff based on size. As with subsidies provided directly to individuals, requiring that recipients had not previously offered insurance to their workers could raise concerns about equitable treatment of similar firms—some of whom had already offered coverage—and would also create an incentive for firms to drop coverage in order to qualify.

Proposals to provide tax credits to employers would also need to address the issue of whether the credits are refundable or payable in advance. As is the case with tax credits for individuals, some employers—particularly smaller employers—may not have sufficient income tax liability to take full advantage of a credit. Similarly, smaller employers may have liquidity problems, making it difficult for them to cover the costs of an insurance policy if they have to wait until they file their tax return to receive a tax credit for health insurance. Those considerations would affect whether firms took advantage of the subsidies that they are offered.

Trying to target subsidies according to the size of a firm and the characteristics of workers would also raise administrative challenges. For example, the Internal Revenue

Service currently does not have sufficient information to target subsidies on the basis of the size of a business's workforce. Quarterly and annual reports on withholding taxes contain some information on the number of employees, although those reports do not specify whether employees work full or part time or on a temporary or permanent basis. Tax subsidies could, instead, be targeted toward businesses on the basis of gross receipts (as reported to the IRS), but some small firms might not qualify as a consequence. Basing subsidies on workers' characteristics (such as their earnings or the number of hours they work each week) would raise additional complexities.

Subsidizing Premiums through Spending Programs

Proposals designed to increase coverage rates may use spending programs rather than tax provisions to subsidize insurance premiums. One reason for taking that approach is the difficulty of reaching many uninsured individuals through the income or payroll tax systems in a timely fashion. Subsidies provided through spending programs could take the form of direct payments to individuals for purchasing health insurance. Alternatively, individuals could receive the subsidy indirectly through reductions (or elimination) of premiums, with the insurer receiving payments from the government for the difference between the average cost of providing coverage and the premium (if any) that enrollees are charged. The primary determinants of a proposal's cost would be the amount of the subsidy per enrollee and the number of participants.

Many of the factors that would affect eligibility for and participation in a publicly funded program—and thus the federal costs involved—can be illustrated by examining the current rules for Medicaid and SCHIP. Whether new subsidies would be provided by expanding those programs or creating a new program, similar design issues would arise. In particular, CBO's estimates of program participation and costs would depend heavily on such factors as:

- Whether and how family and personal characteristics affect eligibility,
- Whether and how income is counted and used to determine eligibility or the size of the subsidy (or both),
- Whether and how asset holdings will be taken into account,
- Whether and how eligibility will be targeted toward individuals who are otherwise uninsured,
- The process for determining and recertifying eligibility, and
- The incentives for states to participate if some state financing is required.

Family and Personal Characteristics

As with tax-based subsidies, spending programs that are designed to provide subsidies to or coverage for families or children need to define rules for determining who counts as a family member and who is responsible for the health care of children. In many cases, those relationships will be straightforward, but a variety of challenges may arise. For example, determining who may claim a dependent for a benefit can be difficult, particularly when children live with a divorced parent or in an extended family. One option is to provide the benefit to the custodial parent, who is generally the recipient of other child-related benefits. In many instances, however, health insurance is obtained by noncustodial parents (who, in fact, may be required to do so under provisions for child support). In the Medicaid program, custodial parents may apply for benefits for themselves and their children, but the state is authorized to take cost-effective measures to determine the legal liability of noncustodial parents to contribute toward the costs of the children's benefits.

Box 2-2. Issues with Refundable Tax Credits

The value of a tax credit to people who owe little or no income tax depends crucially on whether the credit is refundable, because the value of a nonrefundable credit cannot exceed the recipient's income tax liability. Implementing refundable tax credits in a way that helps low-income households purchase health insurance, however, presents at least two challenges:

- Reaching all eligible individuals, many of whom may not file income tax returns; and
- Making the funds available in a timely manner—that is, before the premium payments are due.

Reaching Eligible Individuals, Including Nonfilers

Making tax credits refundable allows people who have little or no income tax liability to receive a benefit, but many may have to file forms with the Internal Revenue Service (IRS) solely for the purpose of obtaining the subsidy. Filing behavior differs among those who have no income tax liability, largely depending on whether they work or not. In early 2008, the Joint Committee on Taxation (JCT) estimated that more than 66 million potential tax filing units (primarily individuals or married couples) did not have any income tax liability.[1] Of those, more than half were expected to file a tax return for 2007. Many were required to file because their income was above the IRS filing threshold or they owed self-employment taxes. Others may have filed to obtain a refund of overwithheld amounts or to claim a refundable tax credit like the earned income tax credit (EITC). Nearly all of those "nontaxable filers" were employed. In contrast, nearly all individuals with legitimate reasons for not filing a return had low income and little or no attachment to the workforce.

For the estimated 28 million nonfilers with no income tax liabilities, obtaining subsidies through the income tax system could require them to file a return. Experience with the recent economic stimulus package illustrates that many such individuals may not file, even though they would gain financially by doing so. In 2008, individuals were eligible for stimulus payments if they had at least $3,000 of income from earnings, Social Security, or veterans' benefits, even if they had no income tax liabilities. As of September 2008, however, about 4.2 million retirees and disabled veterans who normally do not file a tax return but were eligible for the stimulus payments had not yet claimed the one-time benefit. (Individuals who were induced to file a return by the stimulus package were not included in JCT's analysis cited above, which was prepared before the enactment of that legislation.)

Paying Credits in a Timely Manner

A tax benefit meant to encourage the purchase of health insurance is less effective if beneficiaries must wait a long time to receive the subsidy. Some low- income individuals will lack the resources to purchase health insurance until they receive the subsidy. Several studies have found that individuals procrastinate when faced with large up-front costs and complicated choices.[2] Long lags between the premium's due dates and the receipt of tax subsidies may result in low enrollment rates.

Generally, however, taxpayers do not claim tax credits until they file their tax return at the end of the year, so they might not receive any benefit from reduced tax payments or larger refunds until after their insurance premiums are due. In principle, individuals can adjust the amount of taxes withheld from their paychecks in order to accelerate the receipt of tax benefits, but many low-income individuals have little or no income tax withholdings to adjust and cannot reduce their withholding below zero.

Tax credits could also be paid in advance. For example, eligible individuals can claim advance payments of the EITC and the health coverage tax credit. One challenge of providing advance payments of tax credits is verifying eligibility before the end of the tax year—particularly if eligibility or payment amounts depend on total income received during the year. Workers may claim advance payments of the EITC by giving a form to their employer, who then provides them with a prorated amount of the credit in their paycheck based on their projected earnings. A change in circumstances during the year (for example, a spouse's entering the workforce) could cause the couple's income to rise, reducing the amount of the EITC to which they are entitled for the tax year. As a consequence, they would be required to repay the overpayment when they filed their tax return. Some analysts believe that the risk of such overpayment discourages eligible individuals from claiming the EITC in advance. One recent study found that only 3 percent of eligible taxpayers claim the EITC in advance, and that among those who do claim advance payments, erroneous payments are prevalent and difficult to recapture.[3]

[1] Joint Committee on Taxation, *Overview of Past Tax Legislation Providing Fiscal Stimulus and Issues in Designing and Delivering a Cash Rebate to Individuals,* JCX-4-08R (February 13, 2008).

[2] See, for example, Janet Currie, *The Take-Up of Social Benefits* (paper prepared for the Conference in Honor of Eugene Smolensky, Berkeley, Calif., December 2003; revised June 2004).

[3] Government Accountability Office, *Advance Earned Income Tax Credit: Low Use and Small Dollars Paid Impede IRS's Efforts to Reduce High Noncompliance*, GAO-07-1 110 (August 2007).

Eligibility could be narrowed on the basis of other factors, including age, disability, or participation in another public assistance program. For example, Medicaid eligibility is limited to individuals who are elderly, disabled, or pregnant and to families with children; able-bodied adults who do not have children are generally ineligible. Individuals are presumed to be eligible for Medicaid in most states if they receive Supplemental Security Income (SSI) benefits (which go to elderly and disabled individuals) or would have met the eligibility criteria for Aid to Families with Dependent Children (AFDC) that were in effect when welfare reform was enacted in 1996. SCHIP primarily covers children under the age of 19. Medicaid and SCHIP both provide mechanisms for states to extend eligibility to other groups by requesting waivers of existing rules from the Department of Health and Human Services. For example, some states have been granted waivers to cover able-bodied individuals who have no dependents under Medicaid or to cover parents of eligible children under SCHIP.

Income

Subsidies can be targeted toward lower-income individuals and families by reducing or eliminating the subsidy as income rises. Medicaid covers pregnant women and children under age 6 whose family income is below 133 percent of the federal poverty level. Older children (younger than 19) are covered if their family income is below 100 percent of the poverty level. Elderly and disabled enrollees must generally have low income as well. SCHIP covers children in families with income up to 200 percent of the poverty level, although some states use higher income limits. Those income cutoffs provide incentives for potential enrollees to reduce or hide their income in order to maintain their eligibility. Those incentives may be reduced (but not eliminated) by phasing out subsidies more gradually as income rises—for example, by charging premiums to enrollees on a sliding scale— but that approach tends to increase the number of people who are eligible and thus raises the program's costs.

Tying subsidies to income requires rules for determining how to count the income of individuals and families.

That requirement raises several issues: whose income to include, what types of income to include, and the period over which to measure income.

Whose Income to Include

Eligibility for Medicaid and SCHIP is based on family income, including income received by the head of a family, his or her spouse, and possibly their children. States, however, have some discretion in defining whose income to include in the family unit.

What Types of Income to Include

Some sources of income may be excluded because they are difficult to measure. Public programs such as Medicaid or S CHIP generally reduce gross income by deducting the amount of the costs that individuals incur in earning income; such "income disregards" include costs for child care and other work-related expenses. In addition, individuals with higher income may qualify for the program if they incur high medical expenses, which may be deducted from their income so that they "spend down" to become eligible. Not surprisingly, broader measures of income would tend to reduce the number of people who could meet a given income standard, whereas greater use of income disregards would tend to expand eligibility.

Choosing a Period over Which to Measure Income

Current income best reflects a potential beneficiary's ability to pay for health insurance, but income may fluctuate and may be more difficult to measure accurately. Many federal programs use relatively short accounting periods to measure income (for example, the current month). For any given income standard, using shorter accounting periods is likely to increase eligibility because monthly income tends to vary more than annual income. The income tax system bases eligibility for tax subsidies on all income received during a year, but that information is not available until the following year, and data from a previous year's tax return may overstate or understate current resources.

Assets

Proposals may further target subsidies through asset tests. Such tests measure the value of certain investments that families could liquidate to pay for their needs (in this case, health insurance) in order to determine eligibility. Some types of assets may be excluded because they are difficult to sell or are viewed as a necessity. For example, to be eligible for the Supplemental Security Income program, applicants' assets must be worth less than $2,000 for individuals or $3,000 for couples, but the program does not include the value of a person's home, burial sites, or, in most cases, car. Asset tests, however, can be difficult to administer and may discourage saving. Beneficiaries and program administrators may have to assess the value of property and other investments for which complete and reliable information may not be available. Asset tests also create incentives for individuals to divest themselves of current investments and avoid accumulating new assets in order to qualify for assistance.[63]

Under current law, states may restrict eligibility for Medicaid or SCHIP on the basis of assets but are not required to do so. As of January 2008, 45 states plus the District of Columbia did not consider assets when determining whether children qualify for Medicaid or S CHIP; 21 states and the District of Columbia disregarded assets for determining parents' eligibility for those programs. For disabled and elderly enrollees, however, eligibility for Medicaid can be linked to SSI, so the same asset tests may apply.

Insurance Status

One of the more vexing issues that arise when providing assistance for health insurance is whether applicants have to be currently uninsured to receive a subsidy. On the one hand, it may be considered inequitable to subsidize uninsured individuals and families while providing no assistance to those with similar income and family responsibilities who have incurred the costs of purchasing health insurance. On the other hand, offering subsidies to those who are already covered by insurance—referred to as "buying out the base"—can substantially increase a program's costs. As a result, many policy proposals, particularly those that would expand Medicaid or SCHIP, seek to contain federal costs by targeting subsidies toward the uninsured alone. However, determining who is uninsured and thus qualified for subsidies raises a number of policy and administrative concerns that could affect a program 's costs.

One concern is that determining who is uninsured can be difficult because of the dynamic nature of insurance status. Many people are uninsured for short periods of time—for example, they may lose coverage for a few months while between jobs. During the period that they are uninsured, they may qualify for subsidies; however, unless program administrators can certify eligibility continuously—which would raise administrative costs substantially—they may continue to receive the subsidies for some time after they start their new job and health plan.

Another concern is that public programs that are targeted toward the uninsured increase incentives for individuals (or their employers) to drop their current coverage and switch to the new subsidized program.[64] To the extent that such crowd-out occurs—with public insurance replacing private insurance—program costs rise without reducing the number of people who are uninsured. Determining whether applicants were previously uninsured may not be difficult; most private insurance is provided through employers, and program administrators can check with them about an applicant and do not have to rely on self-reporting. Yet program administrators cannot easily determine the reason an applicant is uninsured or distinguish between applicants who would have been uninsured in the absence of the subsidized program and those who lack insurance because of incentives to drop coverage.[65]

States' experiences with SCHIP provide some insight into the challenges of minimizing crowd-out. One common approach has been to impose a waiting period, specifying the length of time that previously insured children must be uninsured before they are permitted to enroll in the program. As of July 2007, 37 states imposed a waiting period (usually three to six months). Although that approach discourages privately insured individuals from dropping their coverage, it also imposes a hardship on affected applicants by making them wait longer to receive coverage.

The trade-off between strict policies to prevent crowd-out and efforts to encourage maximum enrollment among the targeted population has led many states to allow exceptions to waiting periods (for example, if a family loses insurance coverage because of a job loss). However, states' strategies to prevent crowd-out have apparently met with limited success. A number of studies analyzing crowd-out in the Medicaid and SCHIP programs have varied widely in their methodologies and in their findings. On the basis of a review of that empirical literature, CBO has estimated that for every 100 children who gain coverage as a result of S CHIP, there is a corresponding reduction in private coverage of between 25 and 50 children.[66] The extent to which that finding would apply to new proposals is difficult to predict, but as a general matter the probability of crowd-out increases as eligibility for a public program is extended to people at higher income levels, simply because a greater share of the population already has private insurance. Because incomes, the costs of health insurance, and coverage rates vary geographically, the extent of crowd-out under a given subsidy schedule is also likely to vary from region to region.

Crowd-out may occur even if eligibility for a public program is not limited to the uninsured. If a new public program provides a larger effective subsidy than the one that privately insured individuals receive, those individuals will have a financial incentive to shift to the public program. That incentive can be blunted if the subsidies are actively extended to privately insured individuals who would otherwise qualify, as was done for the Medicare drug benefit. Extending new subsidies to individuals who already have private insurance tends to increase total program costs, however, and also generates crowd-out of another type—substituting public spending for private spending without changing the source of insurance for those individuals.

Certifying and Verifying Eligibility

Targeted benefits require that program administrators certify eligibility and enforce the program's rules. Benefit programs differ in their approaches toward certification and enforcement, and those differences have effects on coverage and program costs. Two common approaches are the self-assessment model (generally with third-party verification) and the caseworker model, each of which has different implications for accuracy rates and for administrative burdens on the programs and applicants. A related issue is the time between recertifications of eligibility for enrollees, which raises the same trade-offs between accuracy and administrative burdens.

Self-Assessment Model

Under this model, individuals assert their eligibility on an application form, and agencies try to verify at least some applicants' statements with information from reliable third parties. That approach is used to verify eligibility for many tax subsidies, including the earned income tax credit, as well as some spending programs (such as the school lunch program).

The self-assessment model appears to work best when third-party information is readily available and can be matched to the applications (or tax returns) automatically—and worst in the opposite case. For example, studies of compliance with the EITC have shown errors to be most prevalent for family-related eligibility criteria (for example, the taxpayer's marital status or whether a child claimed as a dependent actually resides in the taxpayer's home), for which the IRS has lacked administrative data.[67] Conversely, rates of misreported income are generally lower because the IRS receives information on most earnings from employers. For other administering agencies, which have different monitoring capabilities, the sources of error may be reversed. For example, misreported income constitutes the largest source of error in the school lunch program; schools generally rely on parents' reports of income to certify eligibility for subsidies.[68] Schools may be in a stronger position to monitor a child's living arrangements than to monitor his or her family income.

Caseworker Model

This model is typically used to determine eligibility for the Supplemental Nutrition Assistance Program (SNAP), which was formerly known as the Food Stamp program, and for the Temporary Assistance for Needy Families (TANF) program. The case-worker model uses in-office visits, up-front requests for documentation (such as pay stubs), and phone calls to third parties to validate nearly all statements made by every applicant. As a result, the application process may be time-consuming for program administrators and for applicants. That factor, and any stigma that applicants may associate with being in the program, tends to reduce participation.

The differences in the verification processes used by various programs affect participation, compliance with the programs' stated rules, and administrative costs. For example, when some EITC claimants were asked to obtain and submit documentation showing that they met the credit's child residency requirements, compliance improved but the number of claims by eligible taxpayers dropped and administrative costs increased. Studies of Medicaid and federal nutrition programs also find that participation decreases as the complexity of the application process increases.[69] In response to those concerns, most states have eliminated face-to-face interviews for determining eligibility for families with children under Medicaid and SCHIP and have simplified their application processes.

Exceptions for Retroactive and Presumptive Eligibility

Another issue concerns the timing of enrollment in a public program. Some people may be eligible to participate in a public program but do not apply for benefits until the onset of a medical emergency. Some programs would deem those individuals covered—at least for a short period before their application for benefits. Medicaid coverage, for example, may be retroactive: Once an application is approved, the plan may cover costs incurred in any or all of the three months before application.[70]

Another way that a public plan may provide coverage to those who have not completed the application process is through presumptive eligibility. States have the option of allowing qualified entities—including Medicaid providers and certain other programs serving low-income children (for example, Head Start)—to deem that a child is temporarily eligible for Medicaid; if the child's parent or guardian does not submit a completed application during the time period established by the state, the child's presumptive eligibility ends. States can also extend presumptive eligibility to women who are pregnant or who need treatment for breast or cervical cancer.

Time between Recertifications

The length of time between certification periods affects participation, coverage, and program costs. Basing eligibility on current resources provides the best measure of ability to pay, but continuously monitoring eligibility is costly. Beneficiaries also may be more likely to drop out of a program if they are frequently asked to recertify their eligibility. Most states have a 12-month renewal period for SCHIP, which enables children to remain enrolled unless their family reports a change in income or other circumstances— something they may be reluctant to do if it would cause them to lose eligibility. For SNAP, states have the option to allow households with earned income to retain the same benefits for six months even if their income fluctuates over that certification period, as long as their total income remains below 130 percent of the federal poverty level.

Providing Incentives for States

The effects of any proposal that requires action by the states—and, in particular, funding from them—depends on the incentives states have to participate. States currently have substantial latitude to expand Medicaid; indeed, over half of current Medicaid spending is for coverage of populations or benefits beyond those required by federal law. States could expand their programs even more (with approval from the Department of Health and Human Services), but the fact that they have not pursued substantial further expansions of Medicaid suggests that the current federal matching rate—which averages 57 percent for medical costs—is not a sufficient inducement to do so. Indeed, states' budgetary pressures sometimes lead them to limit eligibility or benefits, but those changes have generally been modest. Proposals that would expand insurance coverage by, in effect, subsidizing states' efforts would probably require a higher federal subsidy rate to generate a substantial response. At the same time, increases in the share of costs borne by the federal government not only raise federal spending but also reduce the incentives that states have to manage those funds in a prudent manner.

Effects of Premium Subsidies on Rates and Sources of Insurance Coverage

Because of the central role played by employment-based insurance, the effects of any proposal to offer new premium subsidies or to modify existing ones depend not only on how individuals respond to those provisions but also on how firms respond in their decisions about offering coverage to their employees and about subsidizing that coverage. To capture those complex interactions, CBO has developed a microsimulation model to estimate how rates of coverage and sources of insurance would change from those currently projected as a result of proposals that alter the subsidies for—and thus the net cost of—various insurance options. That model is based on survey data and includes a wide range of information about a representative sample of individuals and families, including their income, employment, health status, and health insurance coverage. This section discusses some of the key parameters and assumptions that CBO uses to estimate coverage rates and sources of insurance.[71]

Employers' Decisions to Offer Health Insurance

Most nonelderly Americans obtain health insurance through their employers, but before individuals can enroll in such private group coverage, employers must offer it to their employees. In general, businesses compete for workers by offering wage and benefit packages that will attract and retain employees. Employers offer health insurance (and other benefits) if they believe their employees want such coverage enough, in effect, to trade cash wages for it. Consequently, an employer's response to a policy will be a function of how that policy affects its workforce, on average. Those effects could arise from proposals that would change the subsidies for employment-based health insurance, but they could also stem from changes to employees' other health insurance options—either in the individual insurance market or from a public program such as Medicaid.

Changes in Subsidies for Employment-Based Insurance

For several reasons, large employers are more likely than small employers to offer health insurance. Reflecting that fact, the response of firms to changes in the subsidies for employment-based insurance would depend not only on the impact of those changes on the net price of insurance but also on the size of their workforce. To estimate the likelihood that firms would offer (or drop) health insurance in response to a change in price, CBO multiplies the average change in price for a firm's employees by an "elasticity of offer"—a factor that measures how employers' offers of insurance respond to changes in price. The elasticity of offer varies with the size of the firm and is based on estimates from several studies (see Table 2-4).[72] For example, for firms with between 25 and 99 employees, CBO estimates the elasticity of offer to be -0.38; thus, a 10 percent increase in the premiums for firms of that size would cause a 4 percent decline in the number of employees offered coverage. Consistent with the available evidence, the relevant "price" in that calculation is the total cost of insurance to the employer and employee combined—net of any federal (or state) subsidies—not just the portion that the employer pays directly.

Consider, for example, how firms of different sizes would respond to a subsidy proposal that reduced the net price of employment-based insurance by 20 percent. CBO anticipates that such a subsidy would increase the availability of health insurance at very small firms (those with fewer than 25 employees) by about 23 percent (the 20 percent reduction in price multiplied by -1.14, the elasticity of offer). The share of employees at such firms that are currently offered insurance is estimated to be 48 percent, so the proposal would be expected to increase that share by 23 percent, to 59 percent, or a gain of 3.4 million workers. Larger firms would be less responsive to the subsidy, and analogous calculations for all firms would yield an overall increase in the offer rate of about 6 percent (an average elasticity of offer of -0.28 times -20 percent); that translates into an increase of about 6 million in the number of workers offered coverage, roughly half of whom would have been uninsured before receiving the new offer.[73]

Changes in Employees' Other Insurance Options

Employers' decisions about offering coverage are also affected by changes in the relative attractiveness of their employees' other insurance options, such as individually purchased plans or Medicaid coverage. For example, legislation that expanded eligibility for Medicaid could make some of a firm's employees (or their dependents) eligible for that program; alternatively, a proposal could provide a new tax credit for policies that are purchased in the individual market. Other factors held equal, a firm would be less likely to offer coverage if the relative attractiveness of its employees' other options increased.[74] The magnitude of that effect is estimated to be roughly one-third as large as the direct effect of changes in the price of employment-based insurance; that is, a proposal that provided a 10 percent subsidy for policies purchased in the individual insurance market would have about the same effect on employers' offers as a proposal that increased the net price of insurance purchased through an employer by 3 percent to 4 percent. (Both proposals would increase the *relative* attractiveness of individually purchased insurance.)

In addition to a firm's size, the other factors that would affect whether employers drop coverage include the average tax rate its employees face (lower rates mean that employees obtain less of a benefit from the current exclusion for employment-based insurance) and the relative value of the alternative insurance. Some firms that continue to offer coverage may also change the amount they contribute toward premiums in response to changes in the attractiveness of outside insurance options. On the basis of the limited evidence that is available, CBO estimates that firms would increase the share of the total premium employees pay by about 2 to 3 percentage points if the share of their workers eligible for Medicaid increased from 20 percent to 40 percent.[75]

Table 2-4. Effects of a Premium Subsidy on Offer Rates for Employment-Based Coverage, by Size of Firm, 2009

Size of Firm (Number of employees)	Employees (Millions)	Employees Offered and Eligible for Coverage		Elasticity of Offer[a]
		Number (Millions)	Percent	
Fewer Than 25	30.6	14.7	48.0	-1.14
25 to 99	17.4	12.5	72.0	-0.38
100 to 999	26.9	20.8	77.2	-0.15
1,000 or More	62.9	54.0	85.7	-0.07
All	137.8	102.0	74.0	-0.28

Source: Congressional Budget Office's health insurance simulation model.

a. Elasticity of offer is a factor that measures how employers' offers of health insurance respond to changes in price. It is based on estimates from several studies: Jonathan Gruber and Michael Lettau, "How Elastic Is the Firm's Demand for Health Insurance?" *Journal of Public Economics*, vol. 88, nos. 7–8 (July 2004), pp. 1273–1293; Jack Hadley and James D. Reschovsky, "Small Firms' Demand for Health Insurance: The Decision to Offer Insurance," *Inquiry*, vol. 39, no. 2 (2002), pp. 118–137; and Len Nichols and Linda J. Blumberg, "Estimating Employer Elasticity of Demand for Health Insurance" (paper presented at Academy Health Annual Research Meeting, Washington, D.C., 1999).

Individuals' Decisions to Enroll in an Insurance Plan

Individuals' decisions to enroll in a plan are affected by the price of insurance, their income, and the options available to them. In the private market, those options may include enrolling in an employment-based plan (if they work for a firm that offers insurance) and purchasing insurance in the individual market. Individuals' decisions to enroll in a private plan will also be affected by whether they are eligible to participate in a public program.

Purchasing Employment-Based Insurance

After firms make their decisions about offering and subsidizing insurance—reflecting the average effects of the policy proposal on their workers and the aggregate cost of insurance—workers choose whether to enroll and where to obtain their coverage. As with employers' decisions to offer health insurance, the choice to enroll in a plan will depend on the price of employment-based health insurance and alternative options. In this case, however, the key factor affecting enrollment rates is the premium that employees themselves pay, not the total cost to the employer and employee combined. Even though workers ultimately "pay" for employers' contributions toward their health insurance, primarily through reduced wages, studies have found that employees' decisions about enrollment are not sensitive to the amount the employer pays. That finding reflects the fact that once an individual has decided to work for an employer that offers insurance, it is generally infeasible for that worker to recoup the employer's contribution by declining coverage.

Several studies have attempted to estimate employees' responses to changes in the amount they have to pay for employment-based insurance by comparing the behavior of workers who face lower insurance premiums with that of workers who face higher premiums.[76] The results of those studies can be illustrated by examining what would happen to enrollment in employment-based plans as the share of the premium that the employee pays is reduced from current levels to zero; for simplicity, the illustration focuses on the 149 million nonelderly individuals, including workers and their dependents, who work for employers that offer health insurance but who are not eligible for public coverage.

According to a survey of employers conducted by the Kaiser Family Foundation, employees' premiums currently average about 16 percent of the cost of single coverage and about 27 percent of the cost of family coverage, and at those subsidy rates approximately 137 million people are covered through an employment-based plan in 2009. Another 1 million choose to purchase insurance in the individual market. Of the 11 million who are not covered, CBO estimates that about 3 million would obtain coverage if their contribution was cut in half, and about 4 million more would do so if that contribution was reduced to zero. In other words, even if they were offered insurance for free, the remaining 4 million—or 3 percent of the individuals who could be covered through their employer—would decline that coverage and remain uninsured.

Those enrollment rates are average measures of the expected response by employees to a change in the price of insurance, but other factors would also play a role. For example, the probability of uninsured individuals' enrolling in their firm's plan is affected by their income and by the availability and attractiveness of other coverage options. Workers with higher income tend to have higher enrollment rates than those with lower income, although those rates would be expected to converge as subsidies approached 100 percent. By contrast, individuals with access to Medicaid or other public coverage or whose children have public coverage would be less likely to enroll in family coverage offered by an employer, and the likelihood would be reduced in proportion to the percentage of children covered by a public program.

Purchasing Insurance in the Individual Market

Proposals could seek to expand coverage through the individual insurance market—for example, by equalizing the tax treatment of employment-based and individually purchased coverage or by subsidizing individually purchased insurance through new tax credits and tax deductions. As with their choices regarding employment-based coverage, individuals' decisions about whether to purchase coverage in the individual market are affected by its price, their income, and the availability of other insurance options.

Estimates of the response to changes in the price of individually purchased insurance are most reliable if subsidy rates are low, because that situation is similar to current experience. The available studies suggest that a new 25 percent subsidy for individually purchased coverage would cause 2 percent to 6 percent of the uninsured population to buy that coverage. The academic literature is not very informative, however, when prices are close to zero (that is, when subsidies approach 100 percent), because that situation is currently not observed in the individual market. CBO therefore estimates the effects of high subsidies using evidence about participation rates in existing public programs (which are, in general, highly subsidized).

On the basis of that evidence, CBO estimates that people would gradually become more responsive to changes in the price of individually purchased insurance as subsidy rates increased; moreover, they would become increasingly likely to obtain coverage when subsidy rates exceeded 70 percent (see Figure 2-2). Of the roughly 45 million nonelderly individuals who do not work for employers that offer health insurance or who are not eligible for public coverage, about 20 percent are covered by an individually purchased policy in 2009; the current subsidy rate is close to zero. Adding a 25 percent subsidy for individually purchased coverage would increase the participation rate for that population by 3 percentage points, to 23 percent, CBO estimates, reducing the uninsured by about 1.4 million people. Increasing the subsidy rate to 50 percent would roughly double the impact, but increasing the participation rates above 50 percent would require the subsidy rate to exceed 80 percent (holding other factors equal). Such subsidies, moreover, would make insurance in the individual market more attractive relative to employment-based plans, causing some employers to decide not to offer coverage to their employees.

Impact of Eligibility for Public Programs

People who are eligible to participate in public programs, such as Medicaid and S CHIP, will also be affected by proposals that lower the costs of employment-based or individually purchased plans. Their response will be influenced by many of the same factors that affect the decisions of those who are not eligible for public programs to purchase health insurance in the private market—the price of health insurance, their income, and the availability of other insurance options.

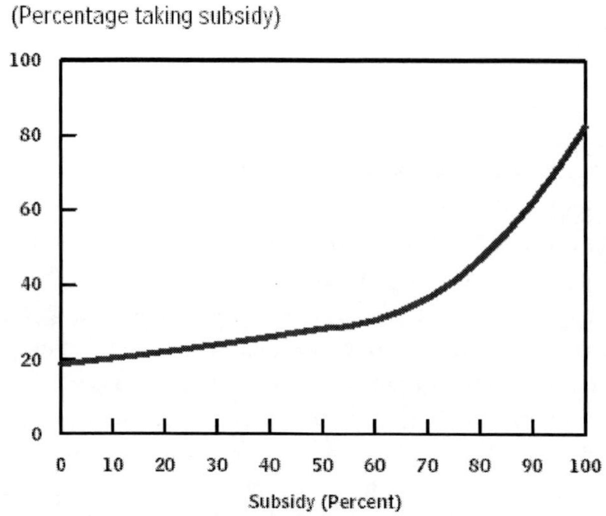

Source: Congressional Budget Office's health insurance simulation model.

Note: Roughly 45 million nonelderly U.S. residents lack access to an offer of employment-based insurance and are ineligible for Medicaid or the State Children's Health Insurance Program. The curve displays the estimated probability of that population enrolling in an individually purchased insurance plan as a function of a subsidy set at a percentage of the insurance premium.

Figure 2-2. Probability of Enrolling in an Individually Purchased Insurance Plan with a Subsidy

In addition, other nonmonetary factors appear to affect whether an individual who is eligible for a public plan purchases private insurance—and, more generally, whether that person instead enrolls in a public plan or does not obtain any coverage. Applying for a public program may impose burdens that people do not encounter when they apply for private health insurance. Those burdens include learning about the program and its eligibility rules, the additional expenses incurred when applying for benefits (for example, the amount of time it takes to complete an application, collect documentation proving eligibility, and—if required—visit a government office for an interview); and concerns that enrolling in a public program will somehow stigmatize the participant. Retroactive and presumptive eligibility rules may also affect the timing of a decision to enroll, by allowing people to delay applying for a public program until the onset of a medical emergency.

Those factors may help explain why many people who are eligible for Medicaid or SCHIP purchase coverage in the private market. In 2009, about 23 percent of nonelderly people who are eligible for Medicaid or SCHIP will have employment-based insurance coverage and about 2 percent will have individually purchased coverage. Reflecting that evidence, CBO models the purchase of private coverage among people who are eligible for or enrolled in Medicaid in a manner that is similar to enrollment rates among the uninsured but is reduced by a factor (generally more than half) to reflect that those people would be giving up free or low-cost public coverage to take private coverage.

Decisions to Switch or Drop Coverage

Changes in the relative attractiveness of health insurance options could affect whether individuals who already have insurance would remain in their current plans. A proposal to expand coverage could cause some people to switch from one type of plan to another and still others to become uninsured, even though the proposal would, on net, result in an increase in coverage.

A proposal, for example, might increase the attractiveness of individually purchased coverage through a deduction or tax credit for health insurance premiums. Because their employees could receive tax benefits for purchasing health insurance elsewhere, some employers would drop existing plans. In response, some of their workers would obtain coverage in the individual market; others might (if able) obtain employment-based insurance through a spouse's job, enroll (if eligible) in Medicaid, or become uninsured. A number of workers at firms that continued to provide coverage might switch to an individually purchased plan. Workers in relatively good health would be the most likely to prefer individually purchased insurance because they might pay lower premiums in that market (in which premiums usually vary to reflect enrollees' age and health status) than in the employment-based insurance market (in which healthier workers are pooled with less healthy coworkers).

Suppose, for example, that a subsidy for individually purchased insurance was provided to low-income individuals and families in the amounts of $1,500 for single coverage and $3,000 for a family policy. Under that scenario, CBO estimates that about 2.3 million people who would have been uninsured would instead use the voucher to obtain coverage. In addition, 100,000 people who would have otherwise had employment-based insurance would be covered in the individual market; roughly half of them would no longer be offered insurance by their employer as a result of the new policy, and half of them would have individually purchased coverage despite being offered coverage by their employer. About 100,000 people would become uninsured because their employer elected not to offer coverage and they neither purchased an individual plan nor enrolled in a public program.[77]

Individual and Employer Mandates

Premium subsidies would increase the number of people with insurance but would not be sufficient to achieve universal coverage, even if the subsidies covered a very large share of policy premiums. To increase coverage rates further, policymakers could impose a mandate that individuals obtain insurance or that employers offer coverage. Individual mandates can be applied broadly (to the entire population of the United States) or to a specific group (for example, children). Employer mandates target a more specific subpopulation of the uninsured: workers without insurance and, depending on the scope of the mandate, their spouses and dependents. Under an employer mandate, firms could be required to provide health insurance for their workers or contribute to a fund—an approach commonly referred to as "play or pay." If effective penalties were imposed on individuals and firms that did not comply, mandates would increase coverage rates by raising the cost of remaining uninsured or of not offering coverage—that is, by using a stick rather than a carrot. However, the ultimate impact of a mandate would depend largely on its scope, the extent of its enforcement provisions, and the resulting incentives to comply.

An important distinction between the two types of mandates is that individual mandates generally require people to *have* insurance coverage, whereas employer mandates generally require employers to *offer* coverage. Employer mandates could also require that employers subsidize a certain percentage of the premium, which would encourage their workers to purchase coverage, but the ultimate effect on coverage rates would depend on how those workers responded to the subsidies (and to the ensuing offsetting changes in other aspects of their compensation). As a result, determining the degree of employers' compliance with mandates is only the first step in estimating the impact of the mandate on rates of insurance coverage.

Experience with Mandates

The federal government does not have any experience administering a health insurance mandate, but Hawaii and Massachusetts, which have enacted such requirements, provide some insights. In addition, it is useful to examine the impact of other mandates that may be analogous, such as requirements to pay taxes, purchase automobile insurance, and vaccinate children.

Existing State Mandates for Health Insurance

Since 1974, Hawaii has required employers to provide health insurance for their full-time, permanent employees. Employers also must pay at least half of the premium for single coverage for each eligible employee (with the exception of part-time employees, government employees, and seasonal workers).

In 2007, Massachusetts began phasing in a mandate that all adult residents have health insurance. By 2009, all adults must have a policy that covers a basic set of benefits or they will have to pay a penalty—for each month not covered—equal to half the premium for the cheapest health insurance plan that provides the minimum benefit package. Penalties are waived, however, for people who are deemed unable to afford insurance. Massachusetts also requires all but the smallest employers to provide health insurance for their workers or pay $295 per year for each uncovered worker to a state fund. (For additional details about the mandates in each state, see Box 2-3.)

Several studies have examined the effects of the employer mandate in Hawaii. Although Hawaii has relatively high rates of insurance coverage compared with other states, determining how much of that difference is due to the mandate itself and how much reflects other factors, such as population characteristics, is a challenge. One study found that the number of uninsured fell by roughly 1 percentage point—from about 11 percent to about 10 percent—after Hawaii implemented the mandate, attributing that relatively small effect to the exclusion of dependents and certain classes of workers as well as limited enforcement.[78] Other studies have examined the effects of the mandate on exempted sectors, particularly part-time workers. Although part-time employment in Hawaii increased after the mandate relative to part-time employment in the rest of the country, the evidence is mixed regarding the mandate's effects on rates of insurance coverage in the exempt sectors.[79]

Although it is still too soon to evaluate the full effect of the mandates in Massachusetts, preliminary data suggest that the number of uninsured has fallen substantially since the state implemented its health reform plan. According to one recent study, the share of nonelderly adults who were uninsured declined from 13 percent in the fall of 2006 to 7 percent in the fall of 2007.[80] However, the study did not attempt to isolate the effects of the coverage mandates from other aspects of the state's initiative, which included reforms in the insurance market and new premium subsidies for lower-income individuals and families.

Other Types of Mandates

Although the U.S. experience with enforcing health insurance mandates is limited, some lessons can be drawn from other types of mandates. For example, both federal and state governments require individuals and businesses to pay taxes; many states have imposed mandates for drivers to have auto insurance and to wear seat belts; and many school districts require children to be immunized in order to attend public schools. For those mandates, national compliance rates range from 63 percent to 86 percent (see Table 2-5). Those rates, however, do not clearly identify the effect of the mandate itself because they include people who might have acted in the desired manner even if there were no legal requirements—which may reflect the intrinsic value of a mandated item (such as auto insurance), subsidies (such as free or low-cost vaccinations), or social norms (such as a perceived obligation to pay taxes). For example, studies indicate that about 77 percent of young children were vaccinated against chicken pox in states without immunization requirements and that mandates increased vaccination rates by about 8 percentage points (to 85 percent).

Factors Affecting Compliance with Mandates

The observed variation in compliance with existing mandates reflects the fact that their impact depends largely on their scope and on the expected costs of noncompliance for people who are subject to them. In the case of a mandate to have health insurance, individuals would generally weigh the benefits of that coverage against those expected costs when determining whether to comply.

Scope of a Mandate

An individual mandate could apply to the entire population or be limited to certain subpopulations. Requiring all residents to have health insurance coverage would encompass the largest number of uninsured but could be more difficult to implement quickly than a more narrowly targeted mandate. For example, it might take government agencies longer to develop the administrative apparatus necessary to enforce mandates covering the entire population. Alternatively, a mandate could be limited, at least initially, to adults, children, or another subpopulation; that approach would allow insurers, providers, and government administrators to adapt more gradually to new responsibilities but could potentially reduce or slow the impact on the uninsured population.

Proposals could also limit the scope of individual mandates by allowing for certain exemptions. In particular, individuals who are not able to afford health insurance could be exempted from the mandate. In Massachusetts, for example, uninsured individuals whose income is below 150 percent of the federal poverty level are not penalized if they fail to obtain health insurance.[81]

Establishing such exemptions would involve defining a standard for affordability—and, depending on the definition, such provisions could vary in their ease of administration. Massachusetts also allows exemptions for religious beliefs and personal hardships; verifying whether hardship exemptions are valid would require developing review and appeals procedures, adding to administrative costs.

Box 2-3. Health Insurance Mandates in Hawaii and Massachusetts

Both Hawaii and Massachusetts have enacted health insurance mandates. In Hawaii, the mandate is imposed on employers, requiring them to offer coverage to most of their workers and to subsidize the premium; in Massachusetts, both adults and employers are subject to mandates.

Hawaii

The state's Prepaid Health Care system, as it is known, was enacted in 1974 and requires all employers in Hawaii to offer employees a health insurance plan that covers at least a minimum set of specified benefits. Most employers with at least one employee are subject to the requirement, but they do not have to offer coverage to employees who work less than 20 hours a week or whose monthly wages fall below a specified amount (about $600 in 2008). In addition, the mandate can be waived for employees covered by Medicare, Medicaid, or their own (or their parents') health plan and for members of certain religious groups.

Employers must generally pay at least half of the premium for individual coverage, subject to limits on how much the employee must pay. Employers may demonstrate compliance with the mandate by purchasing an approved plan from an insurer or by obtaining certification for their own health care plan.[1] The minimum penalty for failure to comply with the employer mandate is $25, or $1 per employee for each day of noncompliance, whichever is greater. The business may be closed if the employer fails to provide health insurance for more than 30 days. Additional penalties are imposed for willful noncompliance. The mandate is administered by the state's Department of Labor and Industrial Relations.

Massachusetts

As a result of a law enacted in 2006, every Massachusetts resident who is age 18 or older is now required to have health insurance. (New subsidies were also offered to encourage families to obtain coverage, but insurance is not mandatory for children.) The state's individual mandate is being phased in over three years. By the end of 2007, individuals had to have health insurance or they would be subject to income tax penalties. In 2008, they must have coverage each month. In 2009, they must have coverage under a health plan containing specified benefits.

Beginning in 2008, the penalty for noncompliance equals half of the premium for the minimum affordable health insurance plan (a fixed amount determined by Massachusetts officials at the beginning of each year) for each month not covered. Subsidies are provided to lower-income households to help them pay for insurance, and individuals with income under 150 percent of the federal poverty level are exempted from the mandate (and those with somewhat higher income may also be exempt if they cannot find affordable insurance). Individuals may also apply for exemptions on the basis of religious beliefs or personal hardship. The individual mandate is administered by the state's Department of

Revenue; residents receive a form from their insurer that they must submit along with their tax return to verify that they have qualified coverage, and insurers and state agencies also report health insurance coverage to that agency.

Employers with 11 or more full-time-equivalent employees must offer health insurance to their workers and must also establish a "cafeteria plan" that allows employees to exclude payments for their portion of the premium from income and payroll taxes. The state has also established an insurance "connector" agency through which small businesses (as well as individuals) may purchase qualified insurance plans. In addition, employers must either make a "fair and reasonable contribution" to their employees' health insurance or pay the state up to $295 per employee. Employers are also subject to a surcharge if employees and their dependents use more than $50,000 of care a year from a state-funded pool that has been established to finance free care for the uninsured. The amount of the surcharge varies with such factors as the number of employees and the amount of free care used.

[1] Shortly after Hawaii enacted the Prepaid Health Care Act, the Congress passed the Employee Retirement Income Security Act (ERISA), which exempts many employers from state health insurance mandates and other regulations. (For a discussion of ERISA, see Box 1-1.) The Supreme Court ruled in 1981 that ERISA preempted Hawaii's legislation, but in 1983 the Congress granted Hawaii a waiver from the ERISA provisions.

Exemptions and subsidies could reduce the costs of complying with an employer mandate for certain types of employers, such as small businesses. Massachusetts exempts employers with 10 or fewer employees from its play-or-pay requirements. In addition, employers that have 50 or fewer employees receive subsidies for each employee whose family income is at or below 300 percent of the federal poverty level. Definitions of a "small" business vary, however, in terms of the threshold for determining who counts as an employee and the number of employees involved. A small business could be defined on the basis of the number of full-time permanent employees, although the administering agency might find it difficult to determine who meets those qualifications without on-site visits (an administratively burdensome and costly activity). Depending on the definition used, businesses might find it advantageous to reorganize to avoid mandates or to qualify for subsidies on the basis of the number of employees.

Expected Penalty for Noncompliance

An individual's decision to purchase health insurance or an employer's choice to offer health insurance will largely depend on the costs of policies and the availability of subsidized alternatives (such as Medicaid). Mandates could affect those decisions by imposing penalties on individuals who remain uninsured or on employers who fail to offer health insurance.

As is the case with other legal requirements, individuals and employers will generally comply with mandates when the costs of noncompliance exceed the net costs of compliance. Thus, a mandate can become more effective in expanding coverage by either increasing the penalties for noncompliance or raising the probability of being "caught"—either of which would raise the expected value of the penalty.

Health insurance mandates differ from many other requirements, such as payment of taxes, because individuals receive a tangible item that has some value in exchange for their compliance. Thus, individuals' responsiveness to mandates would depend, in part, on the amount of the penalty relative to the net value of insurance. For example, the penalty for noncompliance with the individual mandate in Massachusetts is equal to half the cost of the lowest-cost qualifying plan. Although that penalty represents a significant portion of the insurance premium, it is still less than the cost of paying for coverage—at least for higher-income individuals who do not receive premium subsidies—and individuals who place a small value on insurance coverage may not be induced to purchase it. For such individuals, the lower-cost option is to simply pay the penalty. For others, however, the value of the insurance coverage gained plus the penalty avoided by complying may be sufficient to induce enrollment.

The degree to which individuals who are subject to a mandate believe that their noncompliance would be detected, and that fines would be levied as a result, also greatly affects a mandate's impact on coverage. The probability of detection is higher when enforcement agencies have access to accurate and timely information regarding individuals' coverage status and have sufficient resources to use the information collected to identify noncompliance.

Evidence from the individual income tax system illustrates how compliance can vary with the likelihood of detection and enforcement. Taxpayers are generally subject to the same penalties for misreported income and deductions, regardless of the source of the error. However, compliance rates vary substantially across income types, reflecting differences in the IRS's ability to detect reporting errors. Tax compliance is relatively high when the agency can match information in reports from third parties (such as employers and financial institutions) to income tax returns and send notices to taxpayers when discrepancies are found. The net misreporting rate for income subject to third-party reporting was about 5 percent in 2001 (see Table 2-6). In contrast, the IRS in many cases cannot verify individuals' reports of their self-employment income (including net income from both nonfarm proprietors and farms) on tax returns because third-party data are not independently reported to the IRS and resources for audits are limited.[82] Largely as a consequence, the net misreporting rate for self-employment income and other forms of income that are not subject to third-party reporting exceeded 50 percent in 2001.

Although compliance generally improves as penalties increase, there may be diminishing returns beyond a certain point. As penalties increase, some individuals may respond by taking more aggressive action to avoid detection; at the same time, program administrators may be reluctant to impose penalties that seem excessive.[83] Another issue is that penalties are not costless to impose. If penalties are increased, administering agencies may devote more resources to ensure that their determinations are correct, and individuals may be more vigorous in defending themselves against the charge of noncompliance so that they can avoid the penalty.[84]

Table 2-5. U.S. Experience with Enforcing Mandates

Mandate	Administering Agency	Availability of Data	Methods of Verification	Penalties	Evidence of Compliance
Individual Mandate					
Immunization	School districts	Parents must provide proof of immunization.	School officials review documentation provided by parents.	Exclusion from schools.	Immunization rates for chicken pox among child-ren ages 19 to 35 months range from 76.8 percent in states without mandates to 84.9 percent in states with mandates.[a]
Auto Insurance	State Depar-tments of Motor Vehicles	Self-reporting; some states receive Infor-mation from insurers.	Vary by states.	Vary by states, ranging from none to $50 to $5,000.	85.4 percent of drivers were insured in 2004, but rates range from 74 percent in Mississippi to 96 per-cent in Maine;[b] compliance is better in states with third- party reporting.[c]
Seat Belts	State and local law Enforcement agencies	None.	Vary by states; 26 states and the District of Columbia allow police to stop cars solely to check if seat belts are worn.	Citations, with cash penalties.	Seat belt use was 82 percent in 2007, but rates vary by states with scope and enforcement, ranging from 63.8 percent in New Hampshire (where adults are not required to wear seat belts) to 97.6 percent in Hawaii.[d]
Income Taxes	Internal Revenue Service	Self-reporting; third-party data for many (but not all) types of income.	Matching; audits.	Back amount due plus inte-rest; civil and criminal penalties.	86.3 percent of tax liabil-ities was collected in tax year 2001.[e]
Employer Mandate					
Minimum Wage	Department of Labor (DOL)	Complaints filed by workers.	DOL's inve-stigations and employees' lawsuits.	Back pay; criminal prosecution and fines if there is evidence of egregious abuse.	63 percent to 75 percent in 1973.[f]

Source: Congressional Budget Office based on data from sources listed below.

a. Matthew M. Davis and Michael A. Gaglia, "Associations of Daycare and School Entry Vaccination Requirements with Varicella Immunization Rates," Vaccine, vol. 23, no. 23 (2005), pp. 3053–3060.

b. Insurance Research Council, *Uninsured Motorists, 2006 Edition* (Malvern, Pa.: Insurance Research Council, June 2006). The IRC computes the uninsurance rate as the probability that an at-fault driver in an accident was uninsured or unable to meet the liability for someone else's injury caused by the accident. The estimate is derived from insurance claims for 11 insurers (representing 58 percent of premiums for private passenger auto liability insurance in the United States). The insurance rate is equal to one minus the uninsurance rate.

c. Yu-Luen Ma and Joan T. Schmit, "Factors Affecting the Relative Incidence of Uninsured Motorists Claims," *Journal of Risk and Insurance*, vol. 67, no. 2 (2000), pp. 281–294.

d. Department of Transportation, National Highway Transportation Safety Administration, National Center for Statistics and Analysis, *Seat Belt Use in 2007—Use Rates in the States and Territories*, DOT HS 810 949 (May 2008).

e. Internal Revenue Service, *Reducing the Federal Tax Gap: A Report on Improving Voluntary Compliance*, IR-2007-137 (August 2, 2007).

f. Orley Ashenfelter and Robert S. Smith, "Compliance with the Minimum Wage Law," *Journal of Political Economy*, vol. 87, no. 2 (1979), pp. 333–350.

Table 2-6. Impact of Third-Party Data and Enforcement Methods on Income Tax Compliance, 2001

Income or Tax Preference	Third-Party Data	Enforcement	Net Misreporting Rate[a] (Percent)
Wages and salaries	Employers file W-2s with IRS.	W-2s are matched to tax returns, generating notices to taxpayers when discrepancies are detected.	1
Interest, dividends, Social Security benefits, pensions, and unemployment compensation	Payers file 1099s with IRS.	1099s are matched to tax returns, generating notices to taxpayers when iscrepancies are detected.	5
Partnerships, S corporations, deductions, exemptions, capital gains, and alimony	Some, but not complete, Information from third parties.	Some matching, but largely audits.	9
Nonfarm proprietor income, farm income, other income, rents and royalties, Form 4797 income, and adjustments	None.	Audits.	54

Source: Congressional Budget Office based on data from Internal Revenue Service, *Reducing the Federal Tax Gap: A Report on Improving Voluntary Compliance,* IR-2007-137 (August 2, 2007).

Note: IRS = Internal Revenue Service.

a. The net misreporting rate is the ratio of the amount misreported (including errors in both the taxpayers' and government's favor) to the amount that taxpayers should have reported. The estimates do not include amounts that should have been reported by individuals who failed to file an individual income tax return.

Personal Values and Social Norms

Economic models that focus solely on monetary benefits and costs would probably overstate noncompliance with a mandate. In a number of areas, program administrators and the judicial system lack complete information to monitor every individual's compliance with government rules and regulations. Yet some compliance is generally observed, even when there is little or no enforcement of mandates.

Compliance, then, is probably affected by an individual's personal values and by social norms. Many individuals and employers would comply with a mandate, even in the absence of penalties, because they believe in abiding by the nation's laws. However, such compliance may also be moderated by perceptions of fairness; individuals may comply more readily if they believe that a mandate is fair and is consistently enforced. If enforcement efforts appear to be unevenly applied, compliance may diminish.[85] Social psychologists find that compliance could be affected not only by personal values but also by individuals' perceptions of how others will act. Such studies find that many people want to take the popular—as well as the moral—course of action.[86]

Finally, a small number of individuals may refuse to comply with mandates on religious or philosophical grounds. Thus, even in the face of strict penalties and rigorous detection and enforcement mechanisms, it is unlikely that everyone targeted by mandates would comply.

Automatic Enrollment Provisions

Some experts have suggested that proposals to facilitate automatic enrollment in health insurance plans could achieve coverage goals similar to those of a mandate but without requiring a complicated administrative system. Under those proposals, individuals would be automatically enrolled in insurance plans for which they qualify, but they could "opt out" if they chose to refuse coverage. A person could begin receiving health insurance benefits without completing any additional forms, simply by virtue of his or her participation in another public program or employment with a firm offering coverage. People who chose to opt out of insurance coverage would be required to initiate action and complete the necessary forms.

Evidence of Effects

Some evidence indicates that provisions for automatic enrollment encourage higher participation in public programs (Medicare and welfare programs, for example) and in employment-based benefits such as 401(k) plans.

Public Programs

Most eligible individuals are enrolled automatically in Part B of Medicare (which covers physician and outpatient services) when they turn 65; although they have the option of declining that coverage, they must send in a form to do so. Enrollees also receive a substantial premium subsidy—covering about 75 percent of average program costs—and face a penalty for late enrollment, both of which encourage prompt sign-up for Part B. Nearly 95 percent of those eligible are enrolled in Part B, and many of those who are eligible but are not enrolled have other coverage that substantially reduces the benefits of enrolling in Part B.

By contrast, the new Medicare prescription drug benefit (known as Part D) features a similar premium subsidy and late-enrollment penalty but does not feature automatic enrollment (except in the case of some low-income enrollees). Overall, roughly 70 percent of eligible individuals are now enrolled in the Medicare drug benefit program in some way, including those receiving subsidized coverage through a former employer. Although many individuals who are eligible for Part D have not enrolled because they have other qualified drug coverage, recent estimates indicate that about 10 percent of the Medicare population has not enrolled and does not have other insurance for their drugs, even though it would generally be financially beneficial for them to enroll.

Although the differences in participation rates between Part B and Part D suggest that automatic enrollment strategies increase participation, other differences between the two programs may also have played a role. Both programs provide relatively high premium subsidies and conduct extensive outreach campaigns; automatic enrollment could have a larger effect if combined with less generous subsidies or less extensive outreach.

Another example of the impact of automatic enrollment stems from recent changes to federal welfare programs.

Until 1996, recipients of Aid to Families with Dependent Children were automatically enrolled in Medicaid and the Food Stamp program. After the enactment of welfare legislation, which replaced AFDC with a new program called Temporary Assistance for Needy Families, some former AFDC recipients did not qualify for TANF but still retained eligibility for

Medicaid and the Food Stamp program. Nonetheless, participation in the two programs fell among those families, and studies largely attribute that effect to the fact that the families were no longer enrolled automatically.[87]

Employment-Based Plans

Other recent studies of automatic enrollment have focused on decisions about saving, especially the choice to participate in 401(k) plans offered by employers. Those plans allow workers to defer payment of income taxes on money they save for retirement (and on the interest accumulated on those savings); in many cases, employers also contribute to their employees' accounts, so workers who do not participate are leaving some money "on the table." Until recently, the vast majority of employers who offered 401(k) plans required their workers to take action to enroll; that is, the default option was to not participate in the plan. With such "opt-in" arrangements, participation in 401(k) plans tends to be low for newly hired workers, although it increases substantially with tenure at a firm.

Several case studies have found that participation in 401(k) plans increases substantially, particularly among new hires, as a consequence of automatic enrollment— that is, when the default case is to participate in the plan, with the choice to opt out. A study of one Fortune 500 company found that participation in a 401(k) plan increased from 37 percent to 86 percent among employees with 3 to 15 months of tenure with the firm after the plan switched to automatic enrollment. The effects of automatic enrollment are greatest among workers who are least likely to participate under opt-in systems, including younger and lower-income workers.[88] Three years later, participation in plans with automatic enrollment was higher than in plans requiring active enrollment; about half of the participants who were automatically enrolled also continued to accept both the default contribution rate and the choice of investment fund.[89] Reflecting those findings, many firms have switched to automatic enrollment for their 401(k) plans in the past few years.

Implications for Enrollment Rates

The results from public and private programs suggest that inertia is a factor in decisionmaking and that the framing of choices affects behavior—aspects that have been a focus of recent research on behavioral economics. Many individuals are likely to remain with the default option, even when they can choose a better option with little effort. The studies of retirement savings also suggest reasons for such inertia. It may be a response to complexity; that is, faced with complicated choices, people may opt for the path of least resistance. Or they may procrastinate if the costs associated with a decision are certain and immediate and the benefits do not accrue for some time or depend on the outcome of an uncertain event. People may also stay with the default option because they view the choice as "endorsed" by their employer or the firm's benefit advisers.[90]

Decisions regarding health insurance share some features with choices about retirement saving. Retirement plans may vary considerably in the riskiness of their investments, their expected returns, and their fees. Similarly, health insurance plans may differ in their selection of benefits, provider networks, and costs. In both cases, an individual's decision to participate involves trade-offs that may be difficult to weigh.

The two decisions differ, however, in some important ways. For example, the timing and nature of the costs and benefits surrounding the two decisions are not identical. The benefits of saving for retirement may seem remote, particularly for younger or newly hired workers, but contributions can be withdrawn at any time if the worker is willing to pay income taxes and a 10 percent penalty on the withdrawal. For younger workers in good health, having health insurance may not provide immediate financial returns, but enrollees gain protection against unpredictable risks right away. At the same time, premium payments (or forgone wages) cannot be recouped at a later date by withdrawing past contributions, so enrollees might see their payments as wasted if they do not end up needing expensive care.

Options for Implementing Automatic Enrollment

As with mandates, the effectiveness of an automatic enrollment provision would depend partly on its scope. Employers, for example, could be encouraged or required to provide a "default" health insurance plan for their employees if they offer insurance. Employees' shares of premiums for a default plan, as with other employment- based plans, would be collected through payroll deductions. However, unless employers were also required to provide health insurance, the effects of an automatic enrollment provision would extend only to uninsured workers at firms offering insurance. On the basis of recent studies, CBO estimates that about 30 percent of the uninsured are workers (and their dependents) who turn down insurance offered by their employers (see Chapter 1). Whether or not they would simply opt out again if automatically enrolled would depend heavily on what premiums they would have to pay (net of any subsidies). If automatic enrollment requirements increased participation in employment-based health plans, wages or employers' contributions toward health insurance premiums might be lower than they otherwise would be, so that the total amount of compensation paid to workers would not change as a result.

Another approach might be to automatically enroll individuals in health plans if they participate in any public assistance program. Under current law, individuals receiving Supplemental Security Income are automatically enrolled in Medicaid in most states. Similarly, individuals who are dually eligible for full benefits under the Medicare and Medicaid programs are enrolled by default in one of the lower-cost drug plans available to them (for which they pay no premiums) if they do not select a plan. Automatic enrollment could be extended to participants in other needs-based programs such as TANF or SNAP or to programs like unemployment compensation. The effects of such a strategy would depend, in large part, on the number of individuals who are uninsured and participating in those programs. In contexts other than the workplace or public programs, automatic enrollment provisions might be more difficult to implement— depending on the complexities involved in determining eligibility, collecting premium payments, or other factors.

3. Factors Affecting Insurance Premiums

The effect of proposals to increase coverage would depend in part on the premiums charged and the value of the coverage provided. In particular, the costs of a subsidy that covers a specified percentage of policy premiums would be affected by the amount of those premiums, whereas the impact of a fixed-dollar subsidy on coverage rates would depend on the share of the premiums it covers. Thus, the factors that determine premiums also affect the impact that a proposal has on insurance coverage and the federal budget.

In general, the premium charged for a private health insurance policy is equal to the sum of two components: the average amount that an insurer expects to pay for services covered under the plan; and a loading factor that reflects the insurer's costs of operating the plan (including administrative expenses and a return on investment). An insurer's costs for covered services in turn reflect the scope of benefits that are included, the plan's cost-sharing requirements, and the health status of the plan's enrollees.

The aggregate effects of those factors are illustrated by examining current premium levels. Reflecting the choices that individuals and families currently make, premiums for employment-based plans are expected to average about $5,000 per year for single coverage and about $13,000 per year for family coverage in 2009. Premiums for policies purchased in the individual insurance market are much lower—about one-third lower for single coverage and half that level for family policies.[91] In large part, those differences reflect the fact that policies purchased in the individual market cover a lower share of enrollees' health care costs, on average, which also encourages enrollees to use somewhat fewer services. At the same time, average administrative costs are higher for individually purchased policies. The remainder of the difference in premiums probably arises because people who purchase individual coverage have lower expected costs for health care to begin with. In other words, if both employment-based and individually purchased policies covered the same enrollees, the difference in their premiums would be smaller.

Those premiums could change under proposals that would modify the health insurance market or extend coverage to individuals who are currently uninsured. Some proposals could affect premiums by requiring that individuals enroll in plans that meet certain design specifications in order to qualify for subsidies or comply with a mandate. For example, proposals could require that plans cover certain services, limit the amount of cost sharing that would be required of enrollees, or be "actuarially equivalent" to an existing plan.[92] The more comprehensive the insurance coverage, the higher the premium would be. Because of the resulting increase in the use of health care services, total spending also would be greater under proposals that reduced cost sharing. CBO has concluded that a 10 percent decrease in enrollees' out-of- pocket costs would typically cause average spending on health care to increase by 1 percent to 2 percent.

In addition, premiums could be affected by proposals that changed insurers' management of covered benefits. Most people who have private health insurance are enrolled in some form of managed care plan. Those plans use various techniques to contain health care spending, including negotiating lower fees with a network of providers, requiring that certain services be authorized in advance by the plan or by the patient's primary care physician, monitoring the care of hospitalized patients, and varying cost-sharing requirements to encourage the use of less expensive prescription drugs. Proposals that restricted plans' use of such management tools would tend to yield higher premiums and health care spending.

Another factor affecting the level of premiums is the cost of administering a health plan. Some administrative costs (such as those for customer service) vary with the number of enrollees in a plan, but others (such as those for sales and marketing efforts) are more fixed—that is, those costs are similar whether a policy covers 100 enrollees or 100,000. As a result of those economies of scale, the average share of the policy premium that covers administrative costs varies from about 7 percent for employment- based plans with 1,000 or more enrollees to nearly 30 percent for policies purchased by very small firms and by individuals. Some administrative costs are unavoidable, but proposals that shift enrollment away from the small-group and individual markets have the potential to avoid the added administrative costs per enrollee that are observed in those markets. In other cases, however, tradeoffs may arise between reducing administrative costs and limiting overall health costs and insurance policy premiums because some administrative costs are incurred when using management tools designed to limit health care spending.

Proposals could change the types of coverage in which many people are enrolled as well as expand coverage to include people who would have otherwise been uninsured. The greatest effects on health care spending are likely to be for the latter group because their use of health care services could increase substantially once they became insured. After accounting for differences in the demographic characteristics and health status of the two populations, CBO estimates that the uninsured use about 60 percent as much care as similar people who are insured.

On the basis of a review of the research literature and original data analysis, CBO concludes that if all people who are currently uninsured were enrolled in health insurance coverage that is similar in design to a typical employment-based plan, they would use between 75 percent and 95 percent as much care as the previously insured. The remaining gap reflects CBO's assessment that, on average, people without insurance have a somewhat lower propensity to use health care services—a tendency that would persist if they became covered under a new program. Providing all uninsured people with such coverage would thus cause total demand for health care services to increase by 2 percent to 5 percent.

Those estimates are sensitive to the effects of proposals on the extent of coverage that people receive, however; that is, more extensive coverage would have a larger effect. In addition, how proposals that do not achieve universal or near-universal coverage would affect people's health care spending depends on the extent to which the uninsured would be covered under a plan and on assumptions about the underlying demand for health care among people who would become insured. For more incremental increases in insurance coverage rates, CBO would assume that people who enrolled under a new program would have a greater propensity to use medical care than those who did not enroll. Depending on the design of such a proposal, those newly covered individuals might use health care services at a rate comparable with—or even greater than—that of people with similar demographic characteristics and health status who are currently insured.

In addition, studies indicate that about one-third of the services the uninsured population uses either are provided for free or yield lower total payments to providers than if the same services were provided to privately insured individuals. To the extent that uncompensated care became compensated, spending for the currently uninsured population would rise even if they did not use more services.

Design of Benefits and Cost Sharing

A health insurance plan is essentially a contract between an insurer and an enrollee. In exchange for premium payments, the insurer agrees to cover certain medical services that are specified in the plan. The plan also details the share of costs that both the insurer and the enrollee will bear for each of those services. Thus, two key design elements of a health insurance plan are its scope of covered benefits and its cost-sharing requirements.

Covered Benefits

Nearly all health insurance policies cover hospitalization, physicians' services, and prescription drugs—the three largest categories of spending on health care—but greater variation in coverage exists for dental care and more specialized medical services (such as infertility treatments). Legislative proposals to increase the number of insured people could require that health insurance plans cover certain types of medical services. Under such proposals, individuals (or their employers) might not qualify for subsidies or fulfill a mandate unless they were covered by plans that included those benefits.

Benefit mandates ensure that enrollees who may need those services will have coverage for them, but they also tend to raise insurance premiums in order to cover the added costs of the services. The extent of the premium increase resulting from a mandate would depend not only on the costs of the services involved and the likelihood they would be used by enrollees but also on whether health insurance policies would have covered those services in the absence of a mandate. Moreover, because many states already require coverage of various benefits, the impact of any federal mandates would depend on their scope relative to those existing state requirements and their applicability to plans that fall outside the purview of state regulation.

Empirical evidence on the effect of benefit mandates on premiums and coverage is limited. A recent study sponsored by the state of Maryland found that the total cost of services covered by the state's benefit mandates equaled 15 percent of all covered claims.[93] That figure overstates the extent to which benefit mandates raise health insurance premiums nationally, for two reasons: first, because Maryland mandates more benefits than most other states; and second, because some insurers would have covered the mandated benefits even if they had not been required to do so (a factor noted in the study). On the basis of data on mandated benefits in other states and evidence on the extent to which insurers cover such benefits in the absence of mandates, CBO assumes that, averaged across the country as a whole, existing state benefit mandates increase premiums in the individual and small-group markets by approximately 2 percent to 3 percent.[94]

Cost Sharing

Cost-sharing requirements—the amount that consumers are required to pay out of pocket when they use health care services—can take the form of deductibles, coinsurance, or copayments. Deductibles are the amount of spending an enrollee must incur before coverage begins; coinsurance and copayments are a portion of spending an enrollee pays at the time of service. Most private insurance plans also limit enrollees' financial exposure through an annual cap on out-of-pocket spending. (See Chapter 1 for additional discussion of cost-sharing requirements.)

A proposal to increase health care coverage could specify either minimum or maximum levels of cost sharing that would be allowed in order for an insurance policy to qualify for a subsidy or fulfill a mandate. For example, in order to contribute to a health savings account (which allows enrollees to pay many of their out-of-pocket costs using tax-preferred funds), an individual must be enrolled in a health insurance policy that in 2009 has an annual deductible of at least $1,150 for single coverage or $2,300 for family coverage and has an annual limit on out-of- pocket spending that does not exceed $5,800 or $11,600, respectively.

Some proposals might also include additional subsidies to reduce or eliminate cost sharing for lower-income individuals and families—to reflect their more limited ability to pay for services. The Medicaid program fills that role for low-income Medicare enrollees by offering to cover their cost-sharing requirements under Part A and Part B of that program. About 12 million Medicare enrollees with low income and few assets are entitled to subsidies that reduce or eliminate the deductible or other cost- sharing requirements under the Medicare drug benefit. Such subsidies would also raise many of the same issues about identifying and enrolling eligible individuals that arise in designing and implementing premium subsidies. (See Chapter 2 for a discussion of the issues that arise in targeting such assistance toward lower-income individuals.)

Changes in cost-sharing requirements primarily affect premiums by shifting the share of spending that is covered by the policy between the insurer and the enrollee. Those changes can also affect premiums, however, by causing total health care spending to increase or decrease. The best available evidence about the effects of cost sharing on spending for health care comes from the RAND Health Insurance Experiment, a large-scale study that was conducted between 1974 and 1 982.[95] The RAND study measured the effects of cost sharing on the use of services, expenditures for health care, and health outcomes by randomly assigning nonelderly people to several different types of health insurance plans and tracking their experience over time. A major advantage of using random assignment is that differences in outcomes across plans can be attributed to the design features of each of the plans rather than to the characteristics of the people who were enrolled in them.

The RAND study found that, compared with a plan in which all care was free, a plan with no deductible and a coinsurance rate of 25 percent reduced spending on covered services by about 20 percent; with a coinsurance rate of 95 percent, spending fell by about 30 percent.[96] (The differences in health care costs that would be covered by the plan were even larger; compared with the free-care plan, covered costs were about 40 percent lower with 25 percent coinsurance and about two-thirds lower with 95 percent coinsurance.) The RAND study also found that the effect of cost-sharing requirements varied with the type of services provided. Overall, though, cost- sharing requirements resulted in less use of health care services. Compared with study participants who received free care, those with cost-sharing requirements made, on average, one to two fewer visits to their doctors and had 20 percent fewer hospitalizations during a year. The reduction in the use of health care services that resulted from cost-sharing requirements did not have a substantial impact on health outcomes for the general population, although some adverse effects were observed for low- income people in poor health.

Even though the RAND study was conducted more than 25 years ago, its findings continue to be widely used by analysts because of the strength of its experimental design and the limited availability of more recent evidence. Although the provision of health care and the design of insurance plans have changed considerably since the study was conducted, the implications of those changes for the impact of cost sharing are not obvious. Most of the plans examined in the RAND experiment were indemnity plans, which essentially reimbursed enrollees for the health care costs that they incurred; since that time, the spread of managed care has provided insurers with tools to contain health care spending. To try to capture those effects in its analysis, CBO supplements the results from the RAND study with more recent findings and advice from experts in the health care industry.

Based on its review of the literature and discussions with outside experts, CBO assumes that a 10 percent decrease in enrollees' out-of-pocket costs will generally cause the total spending on their health care to increase by 1 percent to 2 percent. CBO uses that assumption for all types of plans and applies an additional factor to account for the effect of benefit management on spending. The effect of cost sharing on spending varies by type of service. For example, the use of hospital care is less sensitive to cost- sharing requirements than is the use of prescription drugs. A similar analysis would be applied to proposals that provided subsidies to reduce cost sharing for lower- income enrollees.

Actuarially Equivalent Plans

One useful way to compare health insurance plans with different design features is by examining their actuarial value. That summary statistic measures the share of health care spending for a given population that would be covered by each plan and thus reflects both covered services and cost-sharing requirements (see Box 3-1). Although actuarial value provides one measure of the comprehensiveness of benefits offered by an insurance plan, it does not capture all features of a plan—such as the utilization controls and size of the provider network—that affect the benefits that are delivered. Because of differences in those and other features, such as plans' administrative costs and the populations they cover, plans with the same actuarial value may charge different premiums.

The actuarial values of current insurance plans vary across employers and between the group market and the individual market. For employment-based plans, actuarial values—expressed as the share of a given population's medical claims that would be covered by the plan—are typically between 65 percent and 95 percent, with an average value that is between 80 percent and 85 percent. Deductibles and other cost-sharing requirements are typically larger for policies purchased in the individual insurance market, where actuarial values generally range from 40 percent to 80 percent, with an average value that is between 55 percent and 60 percent.

Actuarial-value calculations could be incorporated into legislative proposals in various ways. Proposals that specified a particular benefit design could allow plans to deviate from that design so long as they provided actuarially equivalent benefits. For example, the Medicare drug benefit specifies a standard benefit with a specific deductible, coinsurance rate, and catastrophic threshold (above which enrollees pay about 5 percent of their drug costs).[97] But drug plans are allowed to reduce the deductible, vary the coinsurance rate, or use tiered copayments for different types of drugs so long as the plan's overall actuarial value remains the same and certain other actuarial tests are met. Drug plans are not, however, allowed to increase the deductible or change the catastrophic threshold.

In a similar manner, proposals could require that a qualified plan be actuarially equivalent to an existing plan. For example, the standard Blue Cross and Blue Shield plan available in the Federal Employees Health Benefits program could be used as a model. The impact of that approach would depend partly on the extent to which the model plan differed from the insurance plans that individuals currently have. According to CBO's analysis, the standard Blue Cross and Blue Shield plan has an actuarial value that is slightly above the national average for employment-based plans. In evaluating a proposal that established the actuarial value of that plan as the minimum requirement for all qualified plans, CBO would account for the increased spending that would result as lower-value plans were enhanced to meet that higher standard.

Update Factors

Whether a required level of coverage was defined using the actuarial value of a benchmark plan or with reference to specific cost-sharing requirements, the way in which those values were updated over time would have important implications for a proposal's effects on the federal budget and on coverage rates. If a requirement regarding the actuarial value of plans was fixed in nominal dollars (that is, not adjusted for inflation), plans would cover a declining share of health care costs as those costs rose. Alternatively, if plans were required to cover a specified percentage of health care costs, their actuarial value in dollar terms would rise along with those costs. Similar issues would arise if requirements were imposed on cost sharing. If deductibles or other cost-sharing requirements were fixed in nominal dollars, the share of costs covered by an insurance plan would increase over time as health care costs rose—making the coverage more valuable but also increasing its premium. (An example is the deductible under Part B of Medicare, which remained at $100 from 1991 to 2004.)

Those issues can be addressed by indexing a plan's parameters, but the choice of index can significantly affect the cost of a new program and the scope of coverage provided. If the required actuarial value of plans was specified in dollar terms and updated using a general inflation index (such as the consumer price index) rather than a health-specific index (such as growth in per capita health expenditures), that value would probably decline in future years relative to the cost of health care because health care spending is expected to grow more rapidly than general price levels.

Management of Benefits

Over the past 30 years, private insurance coverage in the United States has largely shifted away from indemnity policies and toward managed care plans. Such plans vary considerably, but all use management techniques to try to contain health care spending. Provisions that would restrict plans' use of such techniques would probably increase premiums and health care spending, although the amount of the increase would depend on the details of the provisions.

Most people who have private health insurance are enrolled in some type of managed care plan. Among workers covered by employment-based insurance, about 58 percent are enrolled in preferred provider organizations, about 20 percent are enrolled in health maintenance organizations, and about 12 percent are covered by point-of-service plans.[98] Those plans vary in their use of provider networks, authorization requirements for more expensive treatments, and other features. About 8 percent of workers are enrolled in policies known as consumer- directed health plans, which combine a high deductible with an account that enrollees can use to help finance their out-of-pocket costs. Those plans generally feature provider networks and other requirements that are similar to PPO plans but are not included in the count of PPO enrollees.

BOX 3-1. WHAT IS ACTUARIAL VALUE?

Actuarial values provide a useful yardstick for comparing insurance plans with different benefit designs. Actuarial values may be calculated holding medical claims constant, or they may take into account the effects of different designs on enrollees' use of services. Because those two methods can affect the comparisons of plans, it may be important for policy proposals that incorporate actuarial-value tests to specify which method to use.

Illustrative Calculation of Actuarial Values

(Dollars)		Plan A			Plan B		
	Total Spending for Health Care	Out-of-Pocket Costs	Covered Costs	Share Covered (Percent)	Out-of-Pocket Costs	Covered Costs	Share Covered (Percent)
Enrollee 1	600	450	150	25	600	0	0
Enrollee 2	1,000	550	450	45	720	280	28
Enrollee 3	1,500	675	825	55	820	680	45
Enrollee 4	3,700	1,225	2,475	67	1,260	2,440	66
Enrollee 5	18,200	2,500	15,700	86	2,000	16,200	89
Average	5,000	1,080	3,920	78	1,080	3,920	78

Source: Congressional Budget Office.

Note: The actuarial value of both plans is $3,920, or 78 percent of enrollees' average spending on health care.

The calculation of actuarial values is easiest to illustrate if enrollees' medical claims are taken as constant. In a simplified example, suppose Plan A has a $400 deductible and charges a 25 percent coinsurance rate beyond that point, up to an annual limit on out-of- pocket costs of $2,500, whereas Plan B has a $650 deductible, a 20 percent coinsurance rate, and a $2,000 limit on out-of-pocket costs. An analysis of those plans' actuarial values would simply take the same set of claims, apply the two benefit designs, and determine the average amount of spending covered by each policy (see the table for a stylized analysis in which the actuarial values of those two plans are constructed to be equal). Actuarial values are sometimes expressed as the percentage of health claims that an insurance plan will cover and sometimes as the average dollar value of covered claims; if the universe of claims is held constant, then those two measures are interchangeable.

Those calculations of actuarial value provide a simple metric by which to compare differing benefit designs—but by holding medical claims fixed, they do not take into account how enrollees might respond to those different designs. The lower deductible in Plan A could lead some enrollees to use more medical services, whereas the higher coinsurance rate in that plan could have the opposite effect. If the aggregate effects of those behavioral responses to cost- sharing requirements differed, the two plans would have different expected costs and would be expected to charge different premiums as a result.

If, instead, the calculation of actuarial value considers those behavioral responses to cost-sharing requirements, then the comparison of plans could be affected. For example, suppose Plan B yielded lower overall spending on health care and thus had lower covered costs. If that effect was taken into account, the plan would have to reduce its cost-sharing requirements (perhaps by lowering its coinsurance rate or out-of-pocket limit) in order to have the same actuarial value as Plan A.

Regardless of whether calculations of actuarial values account for enrollees' responses to cost sharing, there are several other reasons that health insurance plans with the same actuarial value might charge different premiums:

- The total price paid for each service may differ. Calculations of actuarial value hold the prices of services constant, but in practice, one plan may negotiate lower payment rates for its providers.
- The degree to which benefits are managed may differ. One plan might use more utilization controls, such as requirements to receive authorization for certain surgeries, or may contract with doctors and hospitals that have less expensive patterns of practice.
- Administrative costs may differ. Comparisons of actuarial value look only at covered benefits under each plan, but insurance premiums also reflect the administrative costs that insurers incur.
- The enrollees in each plan may differ. Calculations of actuarial values use a broadly representative population, but plans that attract enrollees who use above-average amounts of health care will tend to charge higher premiums. (Correspondingly, the actuarial value of a given benefit design would differ if provided to an elderly population rather than a younger population, simply because the elderly tend to use more health care and may use a different mix of services.)

An additional consideration arises when evaluating the actuarial value of consumer-directed health plans. Such plans generally combine a high-deductible health insurance policy with an account that enrollees may use to help finance their out-of-pocket costs (and which may accumulate balances over time). By design, the high-deductible insurance policy will generally have a lower actuarial value than conventional insurance policies. But the actuarial value of consumer-directed plans would include the expected value of any contributions that an insurer or employer sponsoring the plan would make to an **enrollee's account**—so that contribution could be set to make the overall actuarial value of the consumer- directed plan equal to the value of a conventional health plan.

Average premiums for those plans also vary (see Figure 3-1); that variation reflects not only differences in benefit design and management but also differences in administrative costs the populations covered by the plans, and the geographic areas that those plans serve. Consequently, those premiums do not measure the average costs of different types of plans in delivering a particular benefit package to a particular enrolled population.

Use of Provider Networks

One important way that managed care plans seek to control costs is by developing networks of providers—including hospitals, physicians, and laboratories—and negotiating discounts within those networks. Many providers are willing to charge lower fees to a plan's enrollees in the expectation that the plan will direct patients to them (and to avoid the loss of patients that could occur if the provider was excluded from a plan's network). Despite those efforts, the rates that health plans pay hospitals have risen substantially in many market areas in recent years, as hospitals have achieved stronger bargaining positions in their dealings with plans. The enhanced bargaining position of hospitals has been attributed in part to consolidation among hospitals and also to strong consumer preferences that hospitals not be excluded from a plan's network.[99]

Managed care plans differ in their coverage for services that enrollees receive from providers who are not in a plan's network. That coverage affects plans' costs directly as well as their leverage in negotiations with providers. PPOs cover services received from any licensed provider, but they encourage enrollees to receive care from providers in their network by charging them less for such care. HMOs do not provide any coverage for services received outside their provider network (except in emergencies). POS plans offer a middle ground: They cover services received outside a plan's network (usually for a higher charge), but they typically apply some of the same management tools that HMOs use to limit costs within the network.

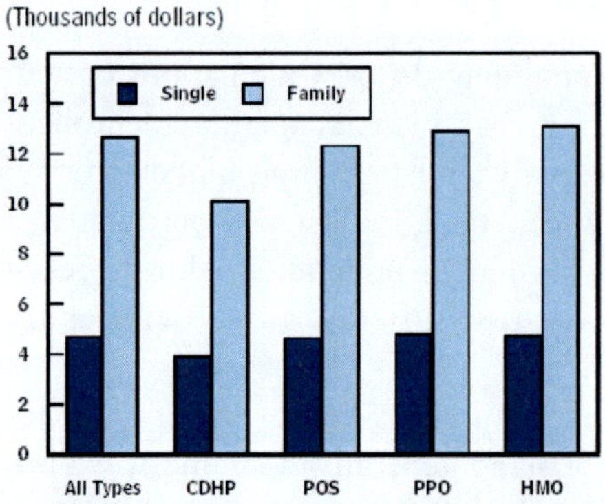

Source: Congressional Budget Office based on data from Kaiser Family Foundation and Health Research and Educational Trust, *Employer Health Benefits: 2008 Annual Survey* (Washington, D.C.: Kaiser/HRET, September 2008).

Note: CDHP = consumer-directed health plan; POS = point-of-service plan; PPO = preferred provider organization; HMO = health maintenance organization.

Figure 3-1. Average Annual Premiums for Covered Workers for Single and Family Coverage, by Plan Type, 2008

The differences between PPOs and HMOs have generally narrowed in recent years. In the past, HMOs typically had smaller provider networks than PPOs. In response to consumer demand for broader networks, however, HMOs have generally increased the size of their networks, and many are now similar to PPOs in that respect; indeed, some insurance carriers use the same provider network for their HMO and PPO products.

Use of Other Cost-Containment Practices

Health plans use a variety of other practices to contain health care costs. One approach is to manage access to expensive medical benefits by requiring prior authorization before the services will be covered. A second approach is to use price signals—that is, variations in cost-sharing requirements—to encourage enrollees to use less expensive medical care. Managed care plans also may use evaluations of providers on both price and quality terms to give feedback to those providers or to structure the information and incentives given to enrollees.

Managing Access and Use

Controlling enrollees' access to more specialized (and expensive) medical services can help health plans manage their costs. Many plans require prior authorization for nonemergency hospital admissions and other selected services. To limit access to expensive drugs, many plans use "step therapy"—a process in which patients are required to begin treatment with less expensive alternatives (such as generic drugs) and then switch to a more expensive drug only if necessary. Enrollees in some HMO and POS plans must select a primary care physician who is responsible for approving referrals to specialists, but that approach is less common than in the past. More generally, differences between HMOs and PPOs have diminished as many managed care plans eliminated or relaxed some of their cost-control procedures in response to widespread complaints in the late 1 990s from consumers and providers. However, some of those cost-containment procedures were subsequently reinstated or replaced by new procedures to limit spending.[100]

Some managed care plans also seek to monitor the performance of providers and the use of services more actively. To limit the length of hospital stays, plans may conduct "concurrent reviews" of the care and medical condition of hospitalized patients; that is, the insurer may review the medical necessity of a treatment upon or shortly after a patient's hospital admission and continue to monitor the services provided during the course of his or her treatment. Some insurers also apply such reviews to patients receiving other types of care, such as rehabilitation and skilled nursing care.[101] Insurers sometimes use information from medical claims to obtain detailed information about the care furnished by individual providers (a procedure known as provider profiling). That information is then used to give feedback to providers on how their practice patterns compare with those of their peers and to identify providers who are furnishing inappropriate or excessive care (and who might be removed from the plan's network as a result).

Varying Cost Sharing

Plans encourage enrollees to use providers within their network by requiring lower cost sharing for in-network care. In some cases, plans also use differences in cost-sharing requirements or other techniques to influence consumers' choices within their approved networks or range of covered treatments and services. For example, plans generally establish a drug formulary or list of drugs that the plan covers (which is akin to a provider network). In addition, plans typically try to limit spending on prescription drugs by negotiating price discounts or rebates from drug manufacturers in return for giving their drugs preferred status on the formulary— and with it, lower copayments for enrollees. Plans also encourage enrollees to use lower-cost generic versions of drugs when they are available, by setting the lowest copayment amounts for those drugs.

More recently, some plans have begun using the information collected from provider profiling to designate a preferred "tier" of providers based on quality and cost standards. For example, an insurer might rank providers on the basis of the total cost per medical "episode," which accounts for complications, readmissions to the hospital, and other factors that go beyond a consideration of the provider's fees. In addition, enrollees may be given financial incentives—such as lower cost-sharing requirements—to receive their care from higher-tier providers.

Effects of Managed Care on Premiums and Spending

Determining the effects of the various cost-containment tools can be difficult because health plans use different combinations of them, and plans vary along a number of other dimensions. Consequently, much of the published research has focused on comparing HMOs (which have traditionally used more stringent cost-containment methods) with other types of plans. The evidence suggests that HMOs deliver a given package of benefits at a lower cost than PPOs and other plans. In particular, studies have found that HMOs reduce the use of hospital services and other expensive services.[102] Because those studies rely largely on data that are more than a decade old, however, they probably overstate the differences that exist today between HMOs and other types of plans. On the basis of the available evidence, CBO estimates that plans making more extensive use of benefit-management techniques would have premiums that are 5 percent to 10 percent lower than plans using minimal management techniques.

The slowdown in health care spending that occurred in the 1990s—as private insurance coverage shifted away from indemnity policies and toward various forms of managed care—provides additional evidence on the potential effects of managed care on spending. Before 1993, health care spending generally grew at a faster rate than gross domestic product. From 1993 to 2000, the share of workers with private health insurance who were enrolled in some kind of managed care plan rose from 54 percent to 92 percent. During that period, total spending for health care remained nearly constant as a share of the economy, at about 13.8 percent of GDP. Many analysts believe that the growth in managed care plans contributed significantly to the slowdown in the growth of health care spending during that period.

By the end of the 1990s, opposition to the restrictions imposed by managed care plans was growing among consumers and providers. The plans responded by relaxing those restrictions, and enrollment shifted to more loosely managed PPO plans. Health care spending also began to increase at a faster rate, rising to 16.0 percent of GDP in 2006. Other factors, however, have undoubtedly contributed to the growth in health care spending relative to the size of the economy since 2000; hospital mergers became more pervasive, for example, enhancing hospitals' leverage in negotiating with health plans.

Regulating the Operations of Health Plans

Proposals to change the health insurance market or to subsidize insurance purchases might include provisions affecting the management of health plans. During the past decade, for example, the Congress has considered several versions of legislative proposals—commonly referred to as a "Patients' Bill of Rights"—that would have restricted insurers' management of health benefits. Although lawmakers did not enact those proposals, some states adopted similar provisions restricting health insurers that operate in their jurisdiction. (As discussed in Chapter 1, plans purchased in the individual insurance market and most plans purchased by smaller employers are subject to state regulations, whereas the majority of plans offered by larger employers are exempt.) In modeling the effects of such proposals, CBO considers the nature of any provisions governing the plan's structure, utilization management, and provider networks and their interaction with existing state requirements.

Types of Provisions

Proposals like the Patients' Bill of Rights could change how health insurers interact with enrollees, in several ways. Under some proposals, insurers would be required to cover certain types of care, such as visits to specialists, without a referral from an enrollee's primary care physician. Past proposals also would have granted enrollees rights of redress, allowing those who had been denied coverage for a particular service to appeal the decision or pursue other remedies in civil courts. Transactions among insurers, providers, and enrollees are another area of concern, with legislative proposals addressing how information about a plan is presented to enrollees or specifying rules for the prompt payment of claims to providers.

Other provisions could also regulate insurers' networks of providers. Any-willing-provider laws require that health plans include in their network any provider who agrees to abide by the terms and conditions of the plan's contract. Many states enacted such laws in the 1990s, but those laws do not apply to employment-based plans that are exempt from state regulation. Network-adequacy requirements would establish rules about the number of different types of providers that plans must have in their network, and restrictions on provider profiling would limit plans' ability to use their analysis of medical claims and other factors to exclude providers from their networks or to develop tiered networks.

Effects on Health Insurance Premiums

In its previous analyses of proposals to create a Patients' Bill of Rights in 1999 and 2001, CBO generally determined that many of their provisions—which are similar to those described above—would increase spending on health care.[103] Since then, however, many health plans have dropped certain cost-containment procedures or replaced them with other techniques; to the extent that such changes were not anticipated, the magnitude of CB O's estimates of the effects of new proposals that affect plans' management techniques may differ from its previous findings.

For certain provisions that CBO analyzed, the effects today would most likely differ from what the agency previously estimated. For example, CBO estimated that a federal any-willing-provider law or federal network- adequacy requirements and proposals requiring plans to cover certain types of care—including visits to specialists without prior authorization, visits to an emergency room if a "prudent layperson" would have regarded the patient's condition as an emergency, and the routine costs of enrollment in approved clinical trials—would, in combination, have increased private health insurance premiums by amounts ranging from 1.2 percent to 1.7 percent. If reintroduced today, however, similar provisions would probably have a smaller impact on premiums; to an extent not anticipated in CBO's original estimates, many health plans have acceded to consumers' preferences for broader access to care by expanding the size of their provider networks and eliminating or reducing some of their restrictions on the use of covered services.

For other provisions, CBO's estimates of the effects would be similar to the agency's previous estimates. For instance, the effects of proposals to expand enrollees' access to the courts for pursuing civil remedies to settle disputes with insurers would probably be similar to the effects that were estimated in 2001 because the expectation in the original estimates that the legal environment would not change substantially has, so far, proved to be accurate. At that time, CBO estimated that the combined effect of various provisions creating new civil remedies and establishing grievance processes would have been to increase premiums by 1.1 percent to 1.7 percent.

Administrative Costs of Health Plans

Proposals to change the regulation of insurance markets—as well as many other types of proposals—could affect the costs of health insurance by changing the administrative costs of health plans (sometimes referred to as "administrative load"). In this discussion, administrative costs refer to any expenses insurers incur that are not payments for health care services, including the profits retained by private insurers and the taxes paid on those profits.

Table 3-1. Administrative Costs for Private Health Plans, by Category, 2006

(Billions of dollars)	Costs
Marketing Costs	
Sales and marketing	20
Customer service	3
Actuarial and underwriting services	1
Subtotal	24
Medical Activities	
Medical management	7
Claims processing	7
Regulatory compliance	*
Subtotal	14
General Administrative Costs	
General management and overhead	10
Information technology	12
Taxes	9
After-tax profits	21
Subtotal	52
Total Administrative Costs	**90**

Source: Congressional Budget Office based on Diana Farrell and others, *Accounting for the Cost of U.S. Health Care, 2008: A New Look at Why Americans Spend More* (San Francisco: McKinsey Global Institute, December 2008).

Note: * = between zero and $500 million.

Types of Administrative Costs

Administrative costs can be divided into three categories:

- **Marketing costs** include expenses for advertising, sales, enrollment processing, customer service, billing, and actuarial and underwriting activities. (Underwriting involves an assessment of an applicant's health and expected use of health care in order to determine what premium to charge.)
- Costs associated with **medical activities** include expenses for claims review and processing, medical management (such as utilization review, case management, quality assurance, and regulatory compliance), and provider and network management (contracting with doctors and hospitals and maintaining relations with providers).
- **General administrative costs** are difficult to allocate to a specific function; they include expenses for information technology, general management overhead, profits, and taxes.

According to a recent analysis, administrative costs for private health insurance totaled $90 billion in 2006 (see Table 3-1), of which about $24 billion was for marketing and related costs, roughly $14 billion was for medical activities, and about $52 billion was for general expenses (including $9 billion in tax payments and $21 billion in after-tax profits).[104] Overall, those costs accounted for about 12 percent of private insurance premiums.

A common metric that is used to assess an insurer's administrative costs is the ratio of claims payments to the total premium, referred to as the "medical loss ratio." (The difference between the medical loss ratio and 100 percent is the share of the premium devoted to administrative expenses.) When comparing two plans that are equivalent on other dimensions, such as the total premium and quality of service, a low loss ratio could indicate a plan that is run less efficiently. But a loss ratio is not always indicative of a plan's efficiency or value.[105] For example, a health plan that devotes more resources to managing the use of health care services might have a relatively low loss ratio but also a lower overall premium. In contrast, a more lightly managed plan might have a high loss ratio but a correspondingly higher overall premium and might be covering more services that provide limited health benefits. The former plan, despite its low loss ratio, may well be preferable because of its lower overall premium for the package of services that it provides. Thus, a loss ratio provides just one way of evaluating a health plan's administrative expenses.

Variation of Administrative Costs

Administrative costs typically vary not only by the type of insurance plan but also by the size and nature of the group being insured. Among employment-based plans, the share of the premium that pays for administrative costs varies significantly by the size of firms, from about 7 percent for firms with at least 1,000 employees to 26 percent for firms with 25 or fewer employees.[106] The latter loading factor is comparable with the one seen in the individual insurance market, where administrative costs account for nearly 30 percent of premiums.

To a large extent, the variation in administrative costs among private plans reflects economies of scale. Some types of administrative costs, such as sales and marketing expenses, are relatively fixed for the group being insured; thus, the larger the group, the smaller the cost per enrollee. In particular, plans that are sold to individuals and small groups are more likely to incur fees for insurance agents and brokers to handle the responsibilities that larger firms generally delegate to their human resources departments—such as finding plans and negotiating premiums, providing information about the selected plans, and processing enrollees. Because large firms can spread those costs over a greater number of enrollees, their average administrative costs per enrollee are lower.

Other factors appear to play a lesser role in the variation of average administrative costs across markets. One commonly cited difference is that underwriting is used in the individual and small-group markets, but those efforts appear to account for a relatively small share of insurers' administrative costs and thus seem unlikely to explain the higher administrative costs per enrollee that are observed in those markets. Plans sold in the individual and small-group markets are also generally subject to state taxes on the premiums they collect, whereas the plans offered by large employers are generally exempt from such requirements. Other expenses—such as the costs of responding to telephone calls from enrollees and providers with questions regarding coverage and payments—are roughly proportional to the number of enrollees (at least for broadly similar populations) and thus would probably constitute a similar share of the premiums for groups of different sizes.

Potential Effects of Proposals on Administrative Costs

Depending on their design, proposals could have a significant impact on the administrative costs involved in providing health insurance—which, in turn, could have a substantial effect on policy premiums. Administrative costs would probably be affected indirectly by proposals that altered the number of insurers, the size of purchasing pools, and insurers' responsibilities. Some proposals might seek to limit the amount spent on administrative costs by specifying a minimum loss ratio, but the net effect of such proposals on insurance premiums or health care spending is uncertain.

Trade-offs are likely to arise between the number of insurance plans that are offered to consumers and the total administrative costs incurred by all insurers. Because some administrative costs are largely fixed, duplication of functions would arise in proportion to the number of insurers participating in the market. Greater competition among insurers, however, would also tend to provide stronger incentives to control costs and thus could yield lower total premiums despite causing aggregate administrative costs to increase.

Proposals that would organize insurance purchasers into larger groups could avoid some of the high administrative costs observed in the individual and small-group markets. In the extreme, if a proposal established a purchasing system under which all insurers incurred administrative costs that were comparable with the costs of large employment-based plans, average policy premiums would be about 3 percent lower than they would be if administrative costs for individual and small-group purchasers remained at their current levels. Administrative savings, however, might be smaller if plans still had to rely on insurance agents and brokers to enroll workers who were not employed by large firms or if other entities had to perform similar functions.

Some proposals would try to directly limit administrative costs by mandating minimum loss ratios—that is, by specifying that the amounts spent on benefits should be at least some specified percentage of the premium. That strategy could be problematic, however, because a high loss ratio may not imply greater efficiency on the part of an insurer. Moreover, whether insurers serving the individual and small-group markets could increase their loss ratios simply because they were required to do so is not clear, so the effects of such requirements on those markets are hard to predict. If the requirement was set too high, insurers would probably exit the market.

Effects of Gaining Insurance Coverage on Health Care Use and Spending

Proposals that expand coverage to people who currently lack insurance would lead to an increase in their use of medical services, which in turn would affect the costs of those proposals and their impact on spending for health care. The extent to which the demand for care would increase depends partly on the number and characteristics of the newly enrolled individuals—including their health status and their preferences for medical care—and partly on the scope of the coverage that they obtain. Estimating that likely impact presents a number of challenges.

Based on a review of the research literature and original analysis, CBO concludes that if all people who are currently uninsured were enrolled in insurance coverage equivalent to a typical employment-based plan, they would use about 75 percent to 95 percent as much medical care as people who are currently insured (and also have the same demographic characteristics and health status). Those figures provide a benchmark for analyzing the impact of various coverage expansions. Depending on their design, proposals for more incremental coverage expansions could provide coverage to a group of people who would use at least as much health care as similar people who are currently insured.

Estimates of Demand for Health Care by the Uninsured

How much more care the uninsured would seek and the impact that such an increase would have on premiums and spending depend in part on how much care they now receive. According to several studies and CBO's own analysis of the nonelderly population, the uninsured use about 50 percent to 70 percent as many health care services as the insured.[107] A key challenge in estimating the impact of a coverage expansion is sorting out the extent to which that disparity stems from the uninsured's lack of coverage, how much reflects other observable differences between the insured and the uninsured, and what role is played by differences that researchers cannot easily observe.

Although there are substantial demographic differences between the insured and the uninsured, some of those differences have offsetting effects on their relative use of services. For example, younger adults are represented disproportionately in the uninsured population, whereas the insured population is more likely to contain children (who tend to use fewer health care services than average) and older adults (who have above-average use). As a result, differences in age do not appear to explain much of the overall disparity in use of services between the insured and the uninsured. Differences in health status may play a larger role. CB O's analysis of survey data indicates that the share of the nonelderly population reporting their health as fair or poor is higher among the uninsured (10 percent) than among the privately insured (5 percent).

A more difficult factor to assess is whether the uninsured differ from those with insurance in other less observable ways that affect their demand for health care services. Understanding the reasons that the uninsured currently do not have insurance could also provide some insight into how they would respond to an increase in coverage.

The uninsured are not a monolithic group, however, and there are many reasons that they lack coverage. Some uninsured individuals may have a strong preference for health insurance but lack coverage because of limited financial resources. If those financial constraints were relaxed, their use of health services might become comparable with that of otherwise similar people who have insurance. Other people may not purchase insurance because they place a relatively low value on health care or think they will not need to use it. Still others may be willing to accept more risk than those who enroll in health insurance plans or may believe that they will be able to obtain the care they need without insurance. Such individuals may not substantially increase their use of health care services even if they become insured.

Both because individuals' preferences for health care vary and those preferences are not easy to observe, estimating the impact of gaining health insurance coverage on the use of medical services is difficult. If individuals who are more likely to use health care are also more likely to have insurance, simple comparisons of the insured and uninsured populations would overstate the impact of becoming insured. An ideal research strategy would randomly assign individuals to an insured or uninsured group and see how much care they use—but people would be understandably reluctant to participate in such an experiment. Short of that, researchers have used three broad methodological approaches to examine the extent to which people who are uninsured would increase their use of services if they were provided with coverage:

- Simulations based on findings from the RAND Health Insurance Experiment, which randomly assigned individuals to different insurance plans;
- Analysis of so-called natural experiments, in which coverage under Medicaid or Medicare has been extended to individuals who previously lacked insurance; and
- Studies that have compared the use of services by people who are insured with that of people who are uninsured, taking into account various differences among the two populations.

None of those approaches resolves all of the methodological issues that arise when trying to estimate an uninsured individual's likely use of health care if provided with insurance. Reflecting the different strengths and weaknesses of the approaches—as well as their differing sources of data and analytic techniques—studies based on those approaches have yielded a wide range of estimates of those effects.

The studies also differ in what they examine. Some studies focus on people's use of services (primarily doctors' visits and hospitalizations), and others analyze spending. The impact that covering uninsured individuals has on spending for health care and health insurance premiums depends both on the quantity of services that they use and on the amount per service that is paid to the providers of their care. Analyzing those elements separately can be useful, however, because differences in payment rates can complicate comparisons between insured and uninsured individuals. In particular, a substantial minority of the care that the uninsured receive is uncompensated or undercompensated—that is, they either pay nothing for it or pay less than the amount that a provider would receive for treating an insured patient. To the extent that such care became compensated under a proposal to expand coverage, health care spending for the uninsured would increase, regardless of whether their use of care also rose. (Other factors that might affect the impact of an insurance expansion on spending, including any constraints on the supply of health care services and any effects on other payment rates from reductions in uncompensated care, are discussed in Chapter 5.)

Simulations Based on Experimental Evidence

One study used the results of the RAND Health Insurance Experiment to simulate spending for individuals enrolled in hypothetical insurance plans as well as for individuals with no insurance.[108] Although that study used older data, its results can be adjusted so that they reflect current levels of health care spending. The simulations indicate that, on average, people enrolled in a plan with a $400 deductible, 25 percent cost sharing, and a $4,000 maximum on out-of-pocket spending (a plan that is roughly equivalent to typical employment-based plans) would incur about 13 percent more in health care expenditures than similar people who are uninsured. Because the prices paid for services were standardized in that analysis, that difference in spending also reflects the projected differences in use of services.

Basing simulations on the findings from the RAND experiment builds on both the strengths and weaknesses of that study. Because random assignment ensured that enrollees in different plans were comparable, its design allowed researchers to isolate responses to variations in the extent of insurance coverage. Yet the RAND study did not include any individuals who were uninsured; the closest design resembled a high-deductible plan, which covered more than half of its enrollees' health care costs. The researchers therefore had to extrapolate from the RAND results to simulate spending among the uninsured. One concern with that approach is that uninsured individuals may be more reluctant to seek treatment than a comparison of enrollees in low-deductible and high- deductible plans would indicate. Extrapolating from those results may also fail to reflect certain constraints on the medical care available to the uninsured. For example, some physicians do not accept new patients who are uninsured. As a result, simulations based on the RAND study's results may underestimate the increased use of services that would occur if insurance coverage was extended to people who are uninsured.

Studies of Expansions in Medicaid and Medicare

Some studies have examined the change in service use that occurs when uninsured people become eligible for Medicaid or Medicare. The creation or expansion of such programs can provide useful insights, but only to the extent that people gain insurance coverage for reasons that are unrelated to their health or their preferences about health care. One study examined the impact of Medicaid expansions between 1984 and 1992, finding that children who became eligible for the program increased their likelihood of visiting a physician at least once during the year by about 10 percent and roughly doubled their probability of being hospitalized.[109] A more recent study on expanding eligibility for Medicaid found similar effects on visits to physicians.[110]

Two other studies examined health care use by previously uninsured individuals shortly before and after they became eligible for Medicare at age 65—a natural experiment that is similar in many respects to a proposal that yields near-universal coverage. One study, which focused on a subset of clinical services, found that the use of preventive care by the previously uninsured rose substantially once they were eligible for Medicare but remained below the levels seen for individuals who had been insured before age 65.[111] In addition, visits for arthritis treatments not only increased substantially among those who lacked insurance before becoming eligible for Medicare but also reached a higher level than was seen for the continuously insured. The other study compared overall numbers of physicians' visits and hospital admissions and found that, among the near elderly, use of care was about 15 percent lower for those who lacked insurance coverage compared with those who were insured.[112] Once they enrolled in Medicare, previously uninsured individuals increased their health care use by 30 percent to 40 percent and ended up with higher levels of use than were observed for Medicare enrollees who had been insured before becoming eligible for Medicare at age 65 (although the differences were not always statistically significant).

One advantage of the studies of Medicaid and Medicare is that they clearly isolate the effects of gaining insurance coverage; one limitation is that their results may not be applicable to the entire uninsured population. To some extent, those studies may reflect the responsiveness of people who are uninsured primarily because of financial constraints—and who are thus more likely to increase their use of health services once they receive coverage. More specifically, the findings related to Medicaid expansions may apply only to similar proposals. On the one hand, Medicaid coverage has relatively low cost sharing, so it could have stimulated demand for care to a greater extent than a typical insurance policy; on the other hand, the observed impact may have been dampened because some of the people who gained eligibility for Medicaid would have otherwise had private coverage and because some doctors do not accept Medicaid's relatively low payment rates.

Comparisons of Insured and Uninsured Populations

Other studies have used statistical methods to try to isolate the effects of insurance when comparing the use of medical services by people who are insured and those who are uninsured. Those studies attempt to identify and adjust for other differences between the two populations (such as income and health status) that would be expected to influence their use of services. To the extent that the insured and the uninsured differ in ways that are not observed in the data, however, those studies may not have isolated the effect of insurance on the use of medical services. The studies themselves also vary along several dimensions. Some studies examine the use of services, and others analyze spending; some look at a cross-section of insured and uninsured people, and others focus on changes in coverage over time. In addition, the studies may analyze different subsets of the nonelderly population. (Because a large number of studies have made such comparisons, this discussion highlights only a few of them.)

One recent example of a cross-sectional study compared spending on health care for the insured and uninsured populations and then sought to project what expenditures for the uninsured would be if they gained a typical level of coverage.[113] The study used data on the nonelderly population from the Medical Expenditure Panel Survey (MEPS), a large-scale survey that collects information on individuals' insurance coverage and use of health care services. The analysis controlled for differences in demographic, health, and socioeconomic characteristics between the insured and uninsured populations. To account for the fact that a large share of services received by the uninsured are uncompensated, the study also sought to adjust their spending figures upward so that they would reflect payment rates for the privately insured. The study estimated that spending on health care for the uninsured—and, by implication, their use of services—would increase by about 70 percent if they became continuously insured; the estimated impact was larger for individuals who had been uninsured all year and smaller for those who spent only part of the year uninsured. The resulting amount of spending per person was similar to that observed for privately insured individuals.

Other studies have tracked individuals from one year to the next to see what happens when they gain or lose insurance coverage. One recent study used MEPS data to analyze the health care expenditures of insured nonelderly adults.[114] It found that individuals who were also insured in the previous year had expenditures that were similar to those who had been previously uninsured—suggesting that spending for the uninsured will rise to the level seen for the insured once they gain coverage. That approach has the advantage of avoiding the need to estimate how much uncompensated care the uninsured receive. An important limitation of that approach, however, is that individuals who became insured in the second year may not be representative of the entire uninsured population; that is, they may have obtained coverage partly because of a greater preference for medical care (or a greater need for care) than those who remained uninsured in the second year. In particular, some people may have been enrolled in Medicaid when they were hospitalized or treated in an emergency room—in which case it was their higher health care spending that caused them to become insured rather than their insurance causing them to use more health care.

More generally, the results of such comparisons are sensitive to the methodologies used and to the types of people included in the analysis. To examine that sensitivity, CBO conducted its own analysis of MEPS data to track changes in insurance coverage from year to year. The analysis measured use of services rather than expenditures, included children and nonelderly adults, and excluded people who had public coverage.[115] CBO conducted the analysis separately for two groups of people— those who were insured for only part of the first year and those who were uninsured throughout the entire first year—and then compared the use of services in the following year by people in each group who were insured or uninsured during all of that year. Grouping people on the basis of their coverage in the first year was designed to limit the extent to which people gaining or losing coverage in the second year differed with respect to their attitudes toward health insurance and medical care. Comparing the use of services rather than expenditures holds aside any differences in the prices paid for the same services—and the challenges of measuring uncompensated care—that could affect the results.[116] One downside of that approach, however, is that it could miss differences in the types of services provided to insured and uninsured individuals during a given visit to a physician or a hospital stay.

Among people who were insured for only part of the first year, those who were insured for all of the second year used 26 percent more health care services during that year than those who were uninsured for all of the second year. More specifically, people in that group who were insured for all of the second year used 88 percent as much care in that year as those who were continuously insured in both years, whereas those who were uninsured for all of the second year used 70 percent as much care as the continuously insured. The possibility that some of those who became insured in the second year obtained coverage partly because of a greater preference for medical care (or a greater perceived need for care) than those who were uninsured in the second year also remains an issue with that analytic approach. To the extent that such sorting occurred, however, it would mean that the true effect of gaining insurance coverage was smaller than the 26 percent estimate.

Among people who were uninsured throughout the entire first year, CBO found that those who were insured during all of the second year used 29 percent more services during that year than people who were uninsured throughout the year. That is, those who gained coverage in the second year used 67 percent as much care as people who were continuously insured in both years, whereas those who remained uninsured in the second year used 52 percent as much care as the continuously insured. Thus, in both analyses, people who gained coverage in the second year increased their use of services, but they did not use the same amount of care as people who had been continuously insured in both years.

Synthesizing the Evidence

Although the wide range of estimates generated by different studies makes it difficult to be certain about the effects of gaining health insurance coverage on health care use and spending, some central tendencies can be observed. A 2005 review of the research literature in that area analyzed studies using the strongest methodologies and concluded that extending insurance coverage to the uninsured would increase the number of physicians' visits by 30 percent to 50 percent for children and by 60 percent to 100 percent for adults.[117] The studies that were reviewed obtained a broader range of estimates for the effects on children's use of inpatient hospital care; among adults, the estimated increases in hospital use ranged from about 40 percent to 80 percent. That review encompassed studies evaluating Medicaid expansions and research comparing insured and uninsured populations; it did not include the findings based on the RAND study or some of the more recent research on Medicare.

Examining the full range of studies also highlights the potential biases in each type of analysis. The findings based on the RAND experiment may have understated the dampening effect of being uninsured on expenditures and thus underestimated the increase that would result from gaining insurance coverage. Conversely, studies relying on comparisons of currently insured and uninsured people, or on changes in their insurance coverage from one year to the next, may overstate the true effect of gaining coverage because those studies may not fully account for differences between the two groups in their attitudes toward health care and health insurance. Studies using natural experiments resulting from policy changes often yield intermediate results, but those findings generally reflect how the target populations would respond and thus may not apply to proposals that would achieve near- universal coverage.

Based on its review of the literature and analysis of health care data, CBO has adopted an intermediate range of estimates. Specifically, the agency expects that providing all of the uninsured with health insurance coverage equivalent to a typical employment-based plan would increase their demand for medical services to a level that is between 75 percent and 95 percent of the level of similar people who are currently insured. (To the extent that the insured and uninsured populations differ in age and health status, CBO would make additional adjustments to account for the effects of those differences on health care use and spending.) Relative to current amounts of health care use by the uninsured—for which estimates average around 60 percent of the amount seen for insured individuals—those assumptions reflect an increase of between 25 percent and 60 percent that would result from gaining insurance coverage. Compared with currently projected levels of health care use for the population as a whole, that rise in the demand for services would constitute an increase that is between 2 percent and 5 percent.[118]

Those figures provide a framework for analysis, but the effects of specific proposals will depend in part on the extent of coverage that the uninsured receive; that is, more extensive coverage would have a larger effect on health care use and spending. In addition, the impact of proposals that did not achieve universal or near-universal coverage would depend on the extent to which the uninsured would be covered under a plan and on assumptions about the underlying demand for health care among those who would become insured. For more incremental increases in insurance coverage rates, CBO would assume that people who enrolled under a new program would have a greater propensity to use medical services than those who did not enroll. Depending on the design of such a proposal, those newly covered individuals might use health care services at a rate comparable with—or even greater than—that of people who have similar demographic characteristics and health status and are currently insured.

All else being equal, the increase in use of services by previously uninsured individuals would also yield a corresponding increase in health care spending. In addition, measured spending for the uninsured population would rise as uncompensated care that they had received was compensated by their insurance plan. Even so, the assessment that the entire pool of uninsured individuals would have somewhat lower use of services under a typical employment-based policy means that they would have somewhat lower total spending per person than those who are currently insured. The expected effect on spending also depends on several other factors, however; in particular, the rates used to pay providers are an important consideration, and limits on the ability and willingness of health care providers to meet an increase in demand could affect both utilization rates and payment rates (see Chapter 5 for more details).

4. Proposals Affecting the Choice of an Insurance Plan

Proposals could affect the options available to individuals when choosing a health insurance plan—and the incentives they face when making that choice—in a number of ways. For example, proposals could:

- Establish or alter regulations governing the range of premiums that may be charged or the terms under which insurers may sell or renew coverage.
- Reveal more fully the relative costs of different health insurance options by reducing or eliminating the current tax subsidy for employment-based insurance, encouraging or requiring the establishment of managed competition systems, or providing more readily accessible information about those costs.
- Have the federal government create additional insurance options, either by offering a new health insurance plan through the Medicare program or by providing access to the health plans that are available to federal employees.

The effects of those options would not just depend on the factors that affect the premium for a given insurance policy or on the share of the premium that enrollees have to pay; those effects would also reflect the market dynamics that arise as individuals shift among coverage options and as policy premiums adjust to those shifts. In particular, the risk that some plans would experience "adverse selection"—that is, that their enrollees will have above-average or higher-than-expected costs for health care—can have important implications for the operation of insurance markets and for proposals that would regulate those operations or introduce new insurance options. To the extent that proposals had an impact on average premiums, they would also affect the federal costs of any premium subsidies as well as coverage rates and spending on health care.

Many of the considerations that arise in designing a new option for individuals to enroll in Medicare would also affect the analysis of proposals to replace the current mix of private insurance and public programs for the nonelderly population with a single-payer, Medicare-for-all system.

Regulating Insurance Premiums and Sales

Proposals may seek to create, remove, or modify regulations governing health insurance markets in order to make insurance more affordable for people with chronic health problems or to provide consumers with more choices, but those goals may conflict with one another. For example, proposals could limit the extent to which premiums for people in poor health can exceed those for people in better health (as some states currently do). Such provisions would reduce premiums for individuals who have higher expected costs for health care, but they would also raise premiums for healthier individuals and thus could reduce their coverage rates. Other proposals might give people greater choice among insurance plans—for example, by allowing them to buy insurance across state lines. That approach would counteract tight limits on variations in premiums; that is, younger and relatively healthy individuals living in states with such limits could purchase a cheaper policy in another state that does not regulate premiums, but older and less healthy residents who continued to purchase individual coverage in the tightly regulated states would probably face higher premiums as a result. Those trade-offs stem from the proposals' differing effects on the composition of insurance pools.

As those examples suggest, federal efforts to alter the regulation of insurance markets would also have to take into account states' current regulatory practices. Although existing state regulations might limit the impact of any federal initiatives, they also provide insights about the manner and magnitude of effects that similar proposals at the federal level would have on both premiums and insurance coverage. The effects of existing regulations also indicate the likely impact of federal proposals that would override or restrict state-level provisions.[119]

Although federal legislation regulating insurance markets could have substantial consequences for the operation of those markets, by itself that legislation would tend to have a relatively small impact on the federal budget. An exception could arise with proposals to expand high-risk pools, which subsidize premiums for individuals who are denied insurance coverage or face very high premiums because of their health problems. The federal costs of such proposals would depend on the scope of those subsidies, the way they were financed, and the number of people who took advantage of them.

Background on Insurance Pooling Arrangements and Regulatory Structure

People purchase insurance policies to protect themselves financially against the risk of an expensive adverse event, such as a car accident, house fire, or serious health problem. Insurance markets that work well do not simply shift that financial risk from individuals to insurers, however; such markets actually reduce that risk by pooling policyholders together. Even if the cost of insuring a given individual may vary widely, the average cost of insuring a large group can be fairly stable and predictable—making it less risky (and thus less costly) to offer insurance. For example, if there are 100,000 subscribers to a given homeowners' insurance policy, only a few will submit claims in a given year; if the frequency of incidents that result in a claim remains stable, the growth in the average claim and the policy premium over time will reflect only the rising costs of repairing or replacing the lost, stolen, or damaged goods that are covered by the policy. Because homeowners are unlikely to know before purchasing insurance whether they will need to submit a major claim, the pool of policyholders is also likely to be stable, with each one willing to pay premiums to protect against the risk of an accident or other incident someday.

A challenge facing health insurance markets is that individuals have some ability to predict their future use of health care.[120] In particular, a substantial minority of people have at least one chronic health condition and are likely to incur higher health care costs year after year, whereas others can expect to have lower costs. According to one recent study, about 30 percent of people ages 18 to 64 have at least one of seven chronic health problems (including heart disease, high blood pressure, diabetes, and asthma).[121] Among that population, average health care costs also tend to rise with age, at least partly reflecting a higher prevalence of chronic conditions. In some cases, those conditions may have only a limited impact on the expected use of health care; for example, high blood pressure was the most common chronic condition examined in that study, and another recent study indicates that the average annual costs of treating that condition are relatively low.[122] Other chronic conditions such as diabetes and heart disease are more expensive to treat, however, and a smaller subset of the population has several conditions simultaneously. Determining what share of health care spending is truly predictable from one year to the next is difficult, but some experts suggest that the overall share probably exceeds 20 percent to 25 percent.[123]

The large share of health care spending that is unpredictable provides a strong incentive for most people to purchase health insurance. To the extent that health care spending varies in predictable ways, however, insurance coverage in general—or plans that offer more extensive benefits in particular—could attract enrollees with above- average costs for health care. Those who expect to have lower expenditures, meanwhile, might wait until they develop a health problem before purchasing coverage, or they might prefer a plan that offers less extensive coverage and lower premiums. If a health plan experiences such adverse selection, its costs may exceed the premiums it has charged; premiums could be raised, but that might encourage relatively healthy enrollees to switch to other plans. In extreme cases, adverse selection could trigger a spiral of rising premiums and declining enrollment that leads to the plan's demise.

In practice, such spirals are rarely observed—in part because insurers take steps to avoid them—but the potential problems caused by adverse selection are a more common concern. The available evidence suggests that roughly 20 percent of applicants for individually purchased health insurance have expected costs for health care that are substantially above the average for their age group. Similarly, employers seeking to offer insurance coverage to their workers may differ substantially in terms of those workers' average costs for health care, and they may be concerned that workers with above-average costs will be more likely to enroll. For applicants with higher expected costs, health insurers face competitive pressures to charge higher premiums, limit coverage of preexisting health problems, or deny coverage altogether to keep premiums down while remaining profitable.

To address concerns about the operations of markets for private health insurance or to achieve other policy goals, policymakers have adopted various laws and regulations governing those markets, and over time some important distinctions have arisen in that regulatory structure. State governments are generally responsible for regulating the business of insurance; as a result, any policy that individuals and firms buy from insurance companies is regulated at the state level. In some cases, however, federal legislation has established provisions that supersede or limit states' efforts. In particular, federal law exempts from state regulation any coverage that is offered by an employer who chooses to bear the financial risk of providing health insurance to its employees and their dependents; in those cases, the employer effectively serves as the insurer. (For additional discussion of the Employee Retirement Income Security Act, which established that exemption, see Box 1-1 on page 6.)

Though open to all employers, the option of bearing insurance risk is generally taken by larger firms—those with enough employees to form a more certain estimate of the cost per enrollee. As a result of that distinction, policies for individuals and most small employers must comply with requirements that vary by state regarding the benefits they cover, the premiums that insurers may charge, and other terms of purchase. Insurance coverage provided through larger firms, by contrast, typically faces few regulatory or legal constraints regarding its benefits and premiums.

One exception is that employers, regardless of size, cannot charge different premiums for similarly situated workers on the basis of health-related factors—that is, for workers who are in the same class of employment and work in the same geographic location, the employees' contribution for health insurance cannot vary on the basis of such factors as health status, medical condition, claims experience, or medical history. Reflecting a concern that having a uniform contribution could lead to adverse selection, however, insurers have typically required that a substantial share of employees participate in an employer's plan in order to help stabilize the average cost of providing that coverage. One way employers seek to achieve that goal is by contributing a large share of the total premium. In addition, employers typically allow their employees to sign up for health insurance only at selected times—when they are first hired or during an annual open-enrollment period—in order to mitigate selection pressures.

Types of Regulations

Many state and federal regulations have an impact on insurance premiums, either directly or indirectly. Some regulations affect premiums directly by restricting the amount by which they can vary or the factors that may be used to adjust them. (Many states require certain benefits to be covered by health insurance, which also affects insurance premiums.) Other regulations can affect the cost of health insurance indirectly, through their impact on the composition of the insured population. Some regulations aim to guarantee the offer or renewal of insurance policies, a step that primarily affects people who might not otherwise be offered coverage. In addition, provisions may limit or prohibit insurers from excluding coverage for preexisting medical conditions—health problems that are present at the time of application. Many states have also established high-risk pools, which offer subsidized insurance to people who have been denied coverage in the private market because of their health problems.[124]

Guaranteed Issue and Renewal

The federal government and many states have taken various steps to require that insurers offer coverage to applicants (a practice known as guaranteed issue) and that they renew policies that are not delinquent (guaranteed renewal). The existing provisions differ between the individual and small-group markets, however. The Health Insurance Portability and Accountability Act (HIPAA) requires insurers that offer coverage to small businesses (those who have fewer than 50 employees) to accept all applicants; before the enactment of that federal legislation in 1996, most states had the same or similar requirements.

By contrast, only a handful of states currently require insurers in the individual insurance market to offer policies to all individuals and families who apply for coverage, and federal legislation does not generally mandate that such offers be made. HIPAA prohibits insurers from failing to renew policies for health reasons, however, whether those policies are purchased in the individual market or by employers. Insurers may still terminate policies for fraud or failure to pay premiums, and they may also require that plans purchased by employers meet a participation requirement (for example, that a specified percentage of employees remain enrolled in the plan).

Federal legislation has addressed in a more limited way the question of guaranteed offers of coverage in the individual market and the related issue of whether new policies may exclude coverage for preexisting medical conditions—steps designed to increase the portability of insurance coverage. Specifically, HIPAA essentially requires insurers to offer coverage to anyone who had held insurance through a previous job but was losing or had recently lost that coverage (for example, because he or she changed jobs). The requirements differ somewhat depending on whether the new coverage is purchased in the individual market or comes through the new employer's group plan, but under most circumstances the new policy may not limit coverage for preexisting conditions. The law, however, does not restrict the premium that insurers may charge for new policies purchased in the individual market.

HIPAA allows states to take additional steps to regulate the portability of insurance, and many states have done so. For individuals who were not previously insured, however, states generally give insurers broad latitude to exclude certain benefits or services from coverage in the individual market. Currently, 38 states permit health care services that are related to preexisting conditions to be excluded from coverage permanently, and most states also allow insurers to determine whether a condition was in fact preexisting by examining more closely the medical history of enrollees when they submit a claim. Proposals that limit the ability of insurers to exclude high-risk individuals and preexisting conditions from coverage might benefit less healthy individuals, who might not be offered coverage otherwise, but the effects of those proposals on insurance premiums would depend on the rules that apply in each state.

Direct Regulation of Premiums

All insurers—whether they cover health care, property, automobiles and their drivers, or another type of risk—seek to set premiums so that the aggregate payments will at least cover the expected payouts for the policies they sell as well as the administrative and other costs they incur in providing insurance. Other things being equal, expected costs for health insurance are higher for older people and for people with more, or more serious, health problems. In theory, that relationship could yield premiums for individually purchased coverage that vary widely, with some enrollees paying many multiples of the average quote for a given policy to reflect their higher expected costs for health care.

In practice, however, premiums in the individual insurance market do not vary as widely as do individuals' expected costs for health care, for several reasons. First, insurers may find it difficult or costly to obtain information about each applicant's health status, so assessments of the applicant's expected costs (a practice known as "medical underwriting") are far from perfect. Second, to the extent that underwriting efforts are successful, insurers tend to limit coverage for or screen out applicants who have preexisting health problems that are costly to treat. According to a 2005 study, about 70 percent of applicants for individual coverage are quoted a standard rate based only on their age; about 20 percent are either charged a higher premium (generally not exceeding twice the standard rate for their age group) or are sold a modified package that does not cover treatments for their preexisting health conditions (at least for some period of time); and about 10 percent are denied coverage.[125] Some applicants are charged a premium that is only modestly higher than the standard rate, so the share of applicants that are either charged a substantially higher premium or denied coverage is probably on the order of 20 percent.

A third reason that premiums in the individual market vary less than do enrollees' expected health care costs is the states' regulation of those premiums, which takes various forms. Many states restrict premium "rating"—that is, they directly limit the extent to which premiums are allowed to vary according to the age or health status of enrollees. The specific restrictions vary widely, however, in ways that differ between the individual and small- group markets. According to one survey of states' practices in the individual insurance market, three states require **pure community rating** of premiums, meaning that insurers may vary premiums for a given policy only by the size of the enrolling family and their place of residence within the state.[126] Six other states allow **adjusted community rating**, meaning that health insurance premiums are allowed to vary by family size and residence as well as by age and sex—but not by health status. Twelve states apply **rating bands** that allow premiums to vary on the basis of age and sex but prohibit insurers from deviating from the standard rate by more than a specified percentage for reasons relating to health.

Regulations may also affect the extent to which premiums can be changed over time. In the individual market, states generally preclude the practice—sometimes called "re-underwriting" or experience rating—of adjusting a particular enrollee's premium on the basis of his or her insurance claims or changes in health status after purchasing the policy. Thus, premiums for a given policy would generally increase over time to reflect higher expected costs for health care on average, but they do not vary across individuals to reflect updated estimates of each one's expected health costs. Insurers could circumvent those restrictions, however, by raising premiums for all enrollees in an existing policy and simultaneously offering a new, cheaper product whose applicants would be subject to underwriting. That practice would tend to discourage individuals who had developed expensive health conditions after enrolling in the original policy from changing plans, so they would pay the new, higher premium for that policy. It is not clear how common that practice is, however.

Premiums charged to small employers may be somewhat less volatile than are premiums in the individual market, for several reasons. First, those premiums reflect the average costs of their enrollees, so high expected costs for one person would be spread across all enrollees. Second, insurance is regulated more extensively in the small-group market than in the individual market. According to a 2003 survey, 35 states employed rating bands in the small-group market, 10 used adjusted community rating, 2 used pure community rating, and only 3 states and the District of Columbia chose not to regulate rates offered to small firms.[127] Some states also limit the degree to which premiums for small employers can increase from one year to the next to reflect enrollees' costs or changes in their health status (for example, permitting no more than a 15 percent adjustment for those reasons). In other states, however, high health care costs for an employee or a dependent in one year can lead to substantial increases in the average premium charged to the employer in the following year, and lower-than-expected claims can lead to corresponding reductions in premiums.

The overall effect of those state regulations is generally to compress the range of premiums offered. Although insurers could comply with a rating band by reducing the premiums charged to the least healthy enrollees or groups, they could also satisfy those regulations by raising their standard rates. In practice, they appear to do some of both, and rating restrictions have been found to increase premiums for healthier enrollees, decrease them for sicker enrollees, and to raise average premiums (primarily because of the resulting increase in enrollment of predictably higher-cost individuals).[128] The net impact of regulation of premiums on the number of people who have insurance coverage is difficult to predict in the abstract because some people face increases in premiums and others face decreases.

High-Risk Pools

Another approach to reducing health insurance premiums is to separate people with the highest health risks from the rest of the pool and partially subsidize their coverage. High-risk pools, as they are called, are a mechanism employed in varied forms by more than 30 states, primarily to assist individuals who are unable to obtain health insurance for medical reasons. Typically, such individuals must apply for private insurance and be denied coverage or be quoted a high premium before they can enroll in the pool. Enrollees are then charged a premium that usually ranges between 125 percent and 150 percent of the standard rate for their age group.

Those premiums are generally insufficient to cover those enrollees' costs for health care, however, so high-risk pools require subsidies to remain solvent (typically averaging several thousand dollars per enrollee). To limit the cost of those subsidies, states may cap enrollment in high- risk pools. As of 2007, however, all states with pools but one (Florida) appeared to be accepting new applicants.[129] In many cases, the costs of subsidizing high-risk pools are financed by an assessment or tax on other health insurance policies sold in the state; in recent years, the federal government has also provided some financial assistance to defray the costs of starting and operating high-risk pools.

As of 2007, about 200,000 people were enrolled in high- risk pools nationwide—about half of that total came from five states—so those enrollees account for about 2 percent of the approximately 10 million nonelderly people who purchase health insurance in the individual market.

High-risk pools obviously reduce the health insurance premiums that their enrollees pay, but covering those high-cost individuals separately could also lower premiums for other purchasers because it would reduce the average costs of the remaining enrollees. The strength of that ripple effect on premiums depends on the extent to which premiums are allowed to vary within the state. At one extreme, if no rating restrictions were in place and all enrollees were charged a premium exactly in accordance with their own expected expenses—or if high-risk applicants had been denied coverage—then establishing a new pool for those with the highest expected costs would have no effect on the premiums of other policyholders. In a community-rated state, by contrast, separating high risks could reduce premiums for the remaining enrollees in rough proportion to the share of covered costs that high- risk enrollees had generated. In states with rating bands, the likely effect would fall between those extremes; reductions in the costs of covering high-risk enrollees could make the bands less constraining and thus could lead insurers to reduce their standard rates.

Effects of Proposals on Insurance Markets

Proposals to change the regulations governing insurance markets would generally have modest effects on the federal budget, and many of them would entail trade-offs between reducing average policy premiums and making insurance less expensive for individuals with health problems. Although generalizing about the precise effects of such proposals is difficult because their content might vary substantially, some indication of the likely magnitudes of budgetary effects and changes in insurance premiums and coverage can be gleaned from the Congressional Budget Office's recent analysis of legislative proposals to modify state regulations or to allow individuals to buy insurance across state lines. In addition, some quantitative or qualitative information can be provided to help illustrate the potential effects of or key considerations surrounding proposals for which CBO has not previously generated a cost estimate.

The Health Insurance Marketplace Modernization and Affordability Act of 2006 is one example of a proposal affecting the regulation of insurance markets that CBO has analyzed.[130] That legislation would have created a more uniform set of regulatory standards for the individual and small-group health insurance markets—standards that would have fallen somewhere between the strictest and most lenient state regulations currently in place. CBO estimated that those changes would decrease the average premium paid by policyholders in those markets by 2 percent to 3 percent, primarily by overriding some benefit mandates and reducing costs that insurers incur in complying with varying state rules. The legislation would have increased insurance coverage by about 600,000 people, on net, but it would have tended to increase premiums (and thus reduce coverage) for people with health problems.

CBO also estimated the budgetary impact of that legislation, concluding that it would increase federal revenues by about $3 billion over 10 years and would reduce federal spending for Medicaid by about $1 billion over that period. The increase in revenues would reflect a net reduction in spending on employment-based health insurance (stemming from the decline in average premiums). Reflecting CBO's assumption that total compensation would not change, that development would shift some compensation from a form that is tax-preferred (health insurance premiums) to a form that is taxable (wages and salaries). Because employment-based insurance would become somewhat less expensive under the proposal, some people who would be covered by Medicaid under current law would switch to private coverage and federal Medicaid spending would decline.

Alternatively, proposals could allow individuals to avoid the requirements set in their home state by purchasing insurance across state lines. In particular, that approach would allow individuals who are relatively healthy and live in states that regulate insurance more extensively to purchase a less expensive policy.[131] CBO analyzed one proposal to allow cross-state purchasing of insurance— the Health Care Choice Act of 2005—and concluded that over 10 years it would increase federal revenues by about $13 billion and federal spending for Medicaid by about $1 billion.[132] The increase in revenues would result largely from a reduction of about 1 million in the number of people who receive health insurance through employment-based plans, which would occur because individually purchased insurance would become relatively attractive (especially to people with lower expected health care costs). The increase in Medicaid spending would reflect the net impact of an increase in spending for people who would lose private coverage and a decrease in spending for those who would gain it. Overall, CBO estimated that the legislation would not have a substantial effect on the number of people who have health insurance because the number who would gain coverage (including previously uninsured people who would purchase coverage in the individual market) would roughly offset the number who lost it.

CBO's previous estimates of federal proposals to add new regulatory requirements also indicate the important influence that existing state practices have on those estimates. For example, the effect of the requirement under HIPAA to guarantee renewal of insurance policies was judged to be limited because nearly all states already had such a requirement in place. Similarly, CBO estimated that HIPAA's requirement for portability of insurance from group to individual coverage would have a relatively small effect on insurance premiums in the individual market. Although insurers would have to offer coverage to relatively unhealthy individuals who would otherwise have been turned down, CBO estimated that in most cases the premiums for those policies could be set to reflect the expected costs for health care for those enrollees and thus would not have a substantial effect on premiums for other enrollees.[133]

Rather than add or remove regulations, the federal government could seek to affect the operation of insurance markets by offering additional subsidies for high-risk pools. The costs of such proposals and their effects on coverage rates and premiums would depend primarily on the following factors:

- The number of individuals who would be eligible for and enrolled in those pools;
- The scope of the insurance coverage they would receive;
- The premiums they would have to pay themselves; and
- The mechanism used to subsidize the difference between enrollees' costs for covered health care services and those premium payments.

Because nearly all states with high-risk pools are accepting new applicants, there may not be substantial unmet demand in those states given the coverage and premiums they currently feature (although additional subsidies could encourage more active efforts by states to enroll eligible individuals). Lower premiums for enrollees and more extensive coverage would generate higher enrollment but would also increase subsidy payments and make it more likely that individuals who would have been insured otherwise would switch into the high-risk pool.

The financing of subsidies for high-risk pools raises a number of issues. Larger federal subsidies could lead more states to create high-risk pools and could encourage states to expand existing pools, but they could also cause some substitution of federal funds for existing state funds. Proposals might also address whether payments would be made to states that currently require guaranteed issue and use community rating or narrow rating bands in the individual market; residents of those states might never meet the eligibility terms for a high-risk pool. Payments could be made to those states in an effort to reduce premiums in the individual market, but doing so would raise the cost of the proposal. More generally, the impact of a proposal on the federal budget would depend on whether and to what extent the costs of the subsidy payments were shared between the federal and state governments; a higher federal share would encourage states to participate but would also reduce the incentive for them to control the pool's costs.

Revealing the Relative Costs of Health Plans

Most Americans with health insurance are shielded from—or may not be aware of—the price of their coverage, either in absolute terms or relative to other options. Many employers pay a large share of the premium for their workers; even though employees as a group ultimately bear that cost, they may not know its magnitude. Moreover, the tax code subsidizes employment-based health insurance by excluding the employer's contributions to the premium from the employee's taxable wages and income; in most cases, the employee's contribution is also excluded. Those features encourage people to have insurance coverage, but they also lead workers to buy more extensive insurance than they would if they faced the full price of their policy; those features also may limit the extent of price competition in the insurance market.

Some proposals would make consumers bear the cost of their health insurance more directly, either by paying the full cost themselves or by paying the added cost of more expensive policies. Proposals could achieve that goal by:

- Reducing or eliminating the current tax subsidy for employment-based insurance, perhaps replacing it with a tax credit or some other fixed-dollar subsidy (an approach discussed in Chapter 2); or
- Establishing a managed competition system, in which a range of plans is offered and the employer's or the government's contribution to the premium is a fixed amount—for example, the premium of the average plan or the least expensive plan available—thus requiring consumers to pay the additional cost of more expensive plans.

Those approaches—taken separately or in combination—would provide stronger incentives for enrollees to weigh the expected benefits and costs of policies when making their decisions about purchasing insurance. As a result, enrollees would generally choose health insurance policies that were less extensive, less expensive, or both, compared with the choices made under current law. A related option would be to give workers more readily accessible information about the full costs of their coverage, including the employer's contribution. Whether and how that information might affect their choice of a health plan is less clear, however.

Reducing or Eliminating the Tax Exclusion

The current tax treatment of health insurance premiums constitutes a relatively large subsidy—known as a tax expenditure—for the purchase of employment-based insurance, amounting to $145 billion in forgone federal income taxes and $101 billion in forgone federal payroll taxes in 2007.[134] Individuals living in states that have income taxes receive an additional subsidy because those states generally follow federal definitions of taxable income and thus exclude the costs of employment-based health insurance as well. The total tax subsidy averages about 30 percent and generally ranges from about 20 percent to 40 percent of the premium for most workers, depending on their tax bracket and state of residence.[135]

Although the subsidy provides an incentive to purchase insurance—and to do so through one's employer—it also encourages people to buy policies that are more extensive or more expensive than they would purchase otherwise. Reducing or eliminating that exclusion thus could have a large effect on insurance premiums and coverage because it could substantially increase the effective price of any given policy—by 25 percent for someone who had been receiving a 20 percent subsidy and by two-thirds for someone who had been receiving a 40 percent subsidy.[136] (The impact of such changes on whether people purchase insurance is discussed in Chapter 2.)

Relevant Studies

Several studies have attempted to quantify how removing or limiting the favorable tax treatment for employment-based insurance would affect insurance coverage, insurance premiums, and total spending on health care. Ideally, a study would compare systemwide outcomes with and without those tax preferences, holding all other factors equal. In practice, however, that type of comparison cannot be readily made because income and payroll tax rates are largely determined at the federal level—so the rules are similar across all states at any given time. Although federal tax rates have changed over time, many other aspects of the health care system and the national economy have simultaneously changed, making it difficult to separate cause and effect when comparing one period with another. As a consequence of those methodological challenges, the findings of older studies using aggregate data on tax rates and insurance premiums vary widely, depending on the period they examined and the assumptions they made.

Two recent studies have attempted to address those methodological issues more carefully, but some concerns remain about using their results to estimate the impact of eliminating the tax exclusion. A 2004 study by Gruber and Lettau examined how employers' spending on health insurance varied across states with different tax structures, exploiting the fact that state income tax rates changed at different times (and did so in ways that were not caused by trends in health insurance).[137] Extrapolating from those results, they estimated that eliminating the tax exclusion for health insurance premiums—which in the sample that they studied would increase the effective price of health insurance by 58 percent, on average— would yield a 29 percent reduction in health care spending by employers who continued to offer coverage. In other words, the reduction in those employers' contributions would be about half as large (in percentage terms) as the increase in the effective price facing enrollees.

Gruber and Lettau's paper improved substantially on earlier work by better isolating the effect of the net price of health insurance on premiums, but it still has limitations. In particular, their estimate is based on relatively small differences in state tax rates, and extrapolating the effects of those differences could overstate the impact of larger changes. One way that employers could reduce premiums would be to limit the extent of the coverage they offer (for example, by increasing cost-sharing requirements). But that approach would also heighten the variability of health costs for employees, and workers might become increasingly reluctant to accept higher levels of cost sharing as their degree of financial risk grew. At the same time, more rigorous management efforts by health plans (or shifts in enrollment toward more tightly managed plans) would yield somewhat lower premiums, but more substantial reductions might become increasingly difficult to achieve. In other words, existing differences in employers' contributions across states could largely reflect the use of cost-control options that represent the "low- hanging fruit."

Another limitation of the study is that it includes the impact of employers changing the share of the premium they pay in response to different tax rates. In that case, employees would see their contributions rise but the total premium for their coverage would not change. Even with that effect included, the impact of changes in tax rates that the study found barely meets the standard threshold for statistical significance—that is, the odds of getting their results by pure chance (assuming that the true effect of the tax exclusion was zero) were only slightly less than one in twenty. Gruber and Lettau estimated, on the basis of other studies, that reductions in the share of the premium that employers cover would account for about one-fourth of the effect on employers' spending that they report. But if that component was removed, the remaining effect they found might not meet a test of statistical significance.

A more recent study by Heim and Lurie avoided some of those methodological problems but was based on a relatively small segment of the population that may not be representative. The study analyzed spending on health insurance premiums for self-employed individuals, who were able to deduct a growing proportion of their premiums from their taxable income over time.[138] Their results, which were similar to Gruber and Lettau's estimate, imply that the reduction in premiums that would result from scaling back the tax exclusion for health insurance would be about half as large as the resulting price increase; that is, an increase of about 50 percent in the net price of health insurance would lead people to choose policies with premiums that were about 25 percent lower than otherwise. An advantage of their study is that it accounts for the full effect on insurance premiums rather than the impact on employers' contributions, because in their study the employer and the employee are the same person. The self-employed, however, may differ in both observable and unobservable ways from people who work in a firm; to the extent that their study did not fully account for those differences, caution must be used in extrapolating their results to a broader population.

CBO's Assessment

Reflecting the limitations of those two studies, CBO's assessment is that removing the tax preference would have a smaller effect on the level of premiums that individuals choose. Specifically, CBO estimates that a 50 percent increase in the price of health insurance, all else being equal, would lead people to select plans with premiums that are between 15 percent and 20 percent lower than the premiums they would pay under current law. Reaching that point would probably take several years, as health plans, employers, and enrollees adjusted their offerings and choices. A portion of that ultimate decrease in premiums would come from reductions in the extent of coverage that enrollees purchased (that is, fewer benefits covered or higher cost-sharing requirements), and the remainder would come from choosing plans that exercise tighter management over the use of health care (that is, plans might have more features typical of health maintenance organizations such as utilization review, restricted provider networks, or gatekeeper requirements).

The effect of a specific policy proposal would depend primarily on what changes it made in the tax treatment of health insurance. Removing the exclusion of premiums from income and payroll taxation would increase the after-tax price of health insurance by roughly 50 percent, on average, for people currently covered by employment-based insurance. Removing the exclusion only for income tax purposes (keeping the payroll tax exclusion in place) would raise the average price by roughly 30 percent, which would ultimately yield health insurance premiums that are 9 percent to 12 percent lower. In both cases, the reduction in overall spending on health care would be smaller than the reduction in premiums because some costs would be shifted from covered spending to out-of- pocket spending.

Alternatively, proposals could cap the amount of premium payments that may be excluded from workers' taxable income—the effects of which would depend critically on the level at which the cap was set. Workers whose premiums exceeded the cap by a substantial margin would have strong incentives to switch to a less expensive plan. Workers whose premiums fell below the cap, however, would not be affected, so the overall impact on premiums would generally be smaller. One objective of capping the exclusion might be to target employees who have relatively extensive insurance coverage and, as a result, above-average premiums. Workers who reside in areas with higher-than-average medical costs or whose firms have higher premiums because their covered workforce is older or in poorer health could also be affected by a fixed-dollar cap, however, even if the generosity of their health plan was not above average.

The effects of reducing, eliminating, or capping the exclusion for employment-based insurance would also depend on a number of issues relating to implementation. Insurers and employers would have to report to both employees and the Internal Revenue Service the amount of premiums subject to tax. However, calculating the average premium and allocating those costs among employees could be difficult, particularly for large employers whose plans cover employees' expenses for health care as they are incurred (in which case timely data may not be available). Limiting or eliminating the exclusion would also create incentives for employers to misrepresent benefits as company overhead or to reallocate costs among subsidiaries so as to reduce their employees' tax liability. (Those considerations would affect the proposal's impact on revenues as well as the incentives for workers to choose less expensive policies.)

Another source of uncertainty is whether the 41 states (and the District of Columbia) that have their own income tax would continue to follow the federal lead in the tax treatment of premiums for employment-based coverage. If, instead, some states took action to maintain the full exclusion of premiums from taxable income, the incentive for workers to choose a less expensive plan would be smaller. The extent of that difference would depend on the number of states that did not conform their tax systems to mirror the federal tax change and on the tax rate structure in those states.

Establishing a Managed Competition System

The term "managed competition" refers to a purchasing strategy that seeks to create stronger incentives for consumers to be cost-conscious in their choice of health plans and for plans to compete more intensely on the basis of premiums and quality of care.[139] Under that approach, a sponsor—such as an employer or government agency—would offer a choice of health plans and would make a fixed-dollar contribution toward the cost of insurance. Enrollees would thus bear the cost of any difference in premiums across plans (although that effect would be muted if enrollees could continue to exclude their own premium payments from taxation). Sponsors would give enrollees comparative information about their options. Some versions of managed competition would also involve standardizing the benefits offered—to a greater or lesser degree—in order to foster stronger price competition. In addition, sponsors could adjust payments to health plans to account for differences in the health status of their enrollees (in an effort to limit the impact of those differences on the plans' premiums).

Background

Most employers do not use the principles of managed competition to purchase health insurance benefits for their employees. Indeed, surveys indicate that most firms that offer health insurance do not give their employees a choice of health plans. That statistic is somewhat misleading, however, because most firms have few employees. Large firms are much more likely than small firms to offer a choice of plans, and they also account for the majority of workers. Consequently, about 57 percent of workers who are offered insurance have a choice of plans. In the case of firms that do not offer their workers a choice of plans, health plans still compete on the basis of their price and value but do so in an effort to be chosen by the employer. For small employers in particular, the administrative costs of offering several competing plans and the potential problems of adverse selection that could arise may outweigh the benefits of giving their employees more options.

Even among firms offering a choice of plans, fixed-dollar contributions to employees' insurance premiums— another key feature of managed competition—are less common than fixed-percentage contributions. A 2002 survey found that among Fortune 500 companies (which generally offer their employees a choice of plans), only about one-quarter took the fixed-dollar approach.[140] The following example illustrates the incentives created by each approach. Suppose that an employer makes two plans available—one with a total premium of $4,000 per year and one with a premium of $5,000. If that employer pays 80 percent of the total premium for each plan, an employee who chooses the more costly plan pays an additional $200 (20 percent of the $1,000 difference in premiums between the two plans). Under a managed competition system, however, the employer would contribute the same amount to both plans (for example, 80 percent of the *average* premium, or $3,600). Employees would face the full $1,000 price difference between the two plans and would therefore have a much stronger incentive to choose the lower-cost plan. Making employees pay the full difference in premiums could also stimulate greater competition among insurance plans to keep their premiums down. (Whether enrollees actually faced that full difference would also depend on whether their premium payments were tax-preferred.)

Some proposals that are based on the principles of managed competition would require health plans to offer a standard benefit package. In principle, standardizing benefits would promote competition among health plans by making it easier for consumers to compare their options; that step would also help prevent plans from structuring their benefit packages to attract enrollees who are less likely to use medical care (which could in turn reduce the plan's premiums and thus distort the comparison of plans). In practice, however, some aspects of health benefits are easier to standardize than others. For example, specifying uniform levels of cost sharing is relatively straightforward, but other aspects—such as definitions of covered services and utilization review procedures—can affect a consumer's ability to use certain benefits and are more to difficult to standardize.[141] Moreover, having standard benefits has two disadvantages. First, by limiting consumers' options, standardization would make some people worse off (specifically, those who would prefer a different design). Second, rigid standardization could prevent health plans from developing innovative designs that might lead to more efficient delivery of care.

Another important design issue is whether the sponsor's payments to insurers would vary to reflect differences in expected health care costs for different enrollees—a process known as risk adjustment. Under managed competition systems, all enrollees in a given health plan would typically pay the same premium—so if payments to plans were not adjusted, plans that attracted less healthy members would have higher premiums as a result.[142] Because enrollees would have strong financial incentives to switch out of those plans, the adoption of managed competition could trigger an "adverse selection spiral" for plans offering the most extensive coverage or doing little to manage benefits. In fact, some employers that implemented a managed competition system dropped such plans as their premiums skyrocketed and their enrollments plummeted.[143] (Health plans might also drop out of a managed competition system for other reasons that make them broadly unpopular with enrollees, such as being poorly run.)

In principle, adjusting the sponsors' payments to plans to account for expected differences in their enrollees' health care costs would limit the impact of adverse selection. If those adjustments worked well, the premiums that enrollees faced would vary across plans because of differences in the value of their benefits or the efficiency of their operation, but not because of differences in their mix of enrollees. Government programs currently use risk adjustment in cases in which private health plans compete against a government-administered option (as with Medicare Advantage plans or Medicaid HMOs) and against one another to deliver program benefits (as with the prescription drug plans in Medicare).

In practice, however, risk-adjustment methods are imprecise, so fully offsetting the effects of enrollees' characteristics on a plan's premium may not be feasible. Those methods do not need to account for all differences in health care spending across enrollees to be effective; indeed, comparisons of predicted spending using risk- adjustment models with actual spending will inevitably find some enrollees who used more care than was expected and some who used less. What matters is accounting for the predictable differences in spending that might affect an enrollee's choice of a health plan or a health plan's efforts to attract or discourage particular types of members. Some experts have indicated that at least 20 percent to 25 percent of health care spending may be predictable from one year to the next, yet studies show that existing risk-adjustment methods account for no more than half of that variation.[144] That degree of predictive power may be sufficient to prevent widespread problems from arising because of selection pressures. Even so, individual health plans could receive overpayments or underpayments relative to the true expected health care costs of their enrollees.

Relevant Studies

Limited evidence is available about the effects of managed competition on health care costs. A few studies have conducted in-depth analyses of particular employers that implemented that approach. Other studies have compared employers that make fixed-dollar contributions to their employees' insurance premiums with employers that use other contribution formulas. Both types of studies have limitations—employers who adopted managed competition (or their workers) may differ from firms that did not, and all of those studies have used data from the mid-1990s or earlier. A more recent example comes from the new Medicare drug benefit, which incorporates many elements of managed competition, but it has not been operating long enough to permit detailed analysis. In any event, comparisons with alternative designs for the drug benefit would be hypothetical because the same approach was adopted nationwide.

The available evidence indicates that, when compared with systems in which employers make a larger premium contribution for more expensive health plans, setting the employer contribution as a fixed-dollar amount reduces total health insurance premiums (the amount paid by employers and employees combined) by 5 percent to 10 percent.[145] Employers that have implemented managed competition have seen large numbers of their employees switch to lower-cost plans, which is an important source of the cost reductions. Some evidence indicates that adopting managed competition has also led insurance plans to lower their premiums; whether the plans did so because of changes in benefit design, tighter management of benefits, or reductions in profits or administrative costs is not clear. Studies of managed competition systems have generally not involved standardization of benefits or risk-adjustment of premium payments, however, so the effects of those features are more difficult to determine.

CBO's Assessment

The effects of specific proposals on average premiums would depend on how extensively they adopted the key features of a managed competition system; those proposals could vary along several dimensions. First, proposals would tend to have a larger impact if they gave sponsors clearly defined roles in overseeing the competition among health plans on the basis of price and quality. For example, sponsors could be responsible for enforcing the requirements that plans must satisfy to be included in the system; providing comparative information to consumers on the plans' premiums, benefits, and quality of care; and managing the enrollment process. Less structured systems that relied more on individual enrollees to gather that information would have less of an impact because the cost to enrollees of doing so would be greater and the pressure on insurers to demonstrate value would thus be less intense.

A second key consideration in determining the effects of a managed competition proposal is whether and to what extent enrollees would be required to pay the full additional cost of more expensive plans. The incentives for enrollees to choose lower-cost plans would be strongest if sponsors made a fixed-dollar contribution toward the premium. That contribution could be based on the premium for the lowest-cost plan that is available, the average premium, or some other fixed reference point. The key feature is that enrollees would be able to capture the savings from joining a less expensive plan, which could take the form of a rebate for joining a plan costing less than the employer's or the government's contribution.

CBO estimates that widespread adoption of a system involving those two key elements of managed competition—with a sponsor coordinating information about and enrollment in health plans and making a fixed contribution toward the premium—would yield average premiums that are about 5 percent lower than those typically seen in employment-based coverage today. That effect is at the lower end of the range observed in the studies of managed competition, for several reasons. First, some firms have already adopted those features of managed competition, so the incremental effect in those cases would be smaller. Second, and more important, the experience of those firms may not be representative of other firms or of today's competitive environment. Some of those studies involved enrollees switching out of a relatively high-cost indemnity insurance plan and into a relatively low-cost HMO plan. Today, indemnity plans are rare, HMO plans are not available in all areas, and the difference in their costs in areas where they are offered appears to have declined slightly. More generally, the fact that many employers have not adopted that approach suggests that savings might be somewhat more difficult to obtain on a broad scale than the available studies of particular firms would indicate.

Achieving widespread adoption of such purchasing strategies would also involve a number of challenges and trade-offs. In particular, smaller firms would have more difficulty implementing those strategies because the fixed administrative costs of setting up a system of managed competition would be divided over a much smaller number of enrollees. Achieving the effects of managed competition for plans offered by small employers would thus probably require establishing a purchasing cooperative or similar arrangement. Setting up such arrangements would involve addressing how premiums would be set for different employers and how policies would be marketed and sold.[146] More generally, trade-offs might arise in determining the rules for participation by insurers; limiting the number of insurers could reduce complexity for enrollees as they considered their options but could also have a substantial impact on insurers that were not chosen and thus could curtail competitive pressures in the future. The extent of those effects would depend on the number of insurers involved and the share of the market encompassed by the managed competition system.

Other features of managed competition could also yield lower average premiums, but their impact is more difficult to quantify. Average premiums would depend heavily on any standards or limits imposed on the scope of covered benefits and cost-sharing requirements for competing plans (as discussed in Chapter 3); for any given set of specifications, the average premium would probably be lower the more that those offerings were standardized. For example, all plans might be required to offer benefit packages that include the same set of covered services and have equal actuarial value.[147] Limiting variation in cost-sharing requirements could also generate stronger competition among health plans to offer a low premium.

A downside of greater standardization is that enrollees would have a narrower range of choices and might prefer a design that differs from the standard. In principle, that concern could be addressed by allowing plans to offer supplemental coverage—priced separately—that goes beyond the standard benefit package or reduces its cost- sharing requirements. In practice, the feasibility of that approach would depend on the extent to which adverse selection affected the additional premiums charged for the extra coverage; if that supplemental coverage was most attractive to individuals with higher expected health care costs, it would probably become expensive or difficult to obtain. Trade-offs thus arise in setting a minimum benefit standard; a relatively high standard would ensure that enrollees were offered that level of coverage, but more comprehensive coverage would also be more expensive.

Assuming that insurers had to charge all enrollees the same premium, a related issue is whether payments to plans would be risk-adjusted to account for differences in enrollees' expected health care costs. If those payments were risk-adjusted, the differences in premiums that enrollees face would be more likely to reflect differences in the efficiency of health plans (rather than differences in their mix of enrollees), which in turn would help foster more intense competition among plans on the basis of their value. The resulting reduction in selection pressures would also tend to limit (but would not eliminate) volatility in a plan's offerings from year to year. As with standard benefits, however, the likely impact of risk-adjusting payments on average premiums is difficult to quantify.

Informing Workers about the Full Cost of Their Health Insurance

Some research in the field of behavioral economics suggests that workers demand more health insurance than they would otherwise prefer because they are unaware of its true cost. Although employers usually pay a portion of their employees' health insurance costs, workers may not recognize that they have given up cash wages or other fringe benefits in exchange. Instead, once workers have joined a firm that offers health insurance, they appear to make decisions about whether to purchase coverage largely on the basis of their share of the premium's costs—ignoring the amount that employers pay on their behalf. To increase the transparency of the total cost of health insurance borne by workers, some experts have recommended that employers report their share of premiums to their employees either annually (for example, on workers' W-2 income tax forms) or on the pay stubs that workers receive periodically.[148]

Although researchers have not examined the effect of increased information about employers' contributions on employees' decisions to purchase health insurance, two recent studies provide some evidence about the impact that the "salience" of prices has on demand for other items. In one study, researchers went into grocery stores and added the sales tax to the price posted in the aisles for 750 different items.[149] As a result, customers could see the full after-tax cost of a grocery item before they decided whether to add it to their cart. Even though the amount that customers had to pay for those items did not change, sales dropped by about 8 percent as a result of the posting. Those researchers found similar results when comparing how alcohol sales are affected by excise taxes (which are included in posted prices) and sales taxes (which are added at checkout). A related study found that drivers were less responsive to changes in toll rates when states switched to electronic collection of tolls, in which payments are automatically deducted as the car drives through the toll plaza.[150]

Although the findings of those studies offer new insight into how people make choices about their spending, more research is needed to determine precisely how employees might respond to reports from their employer detailing the full cost of their health insurance. That response might be muted if the typical worker ignores such notices. Even if the notices are heeded, an individual worker's cash wages are unlikely to increase substantially because he or she chooses a less expensive health insurance plan; as a result, the financial incentive for an individual worker to act on that information will be limited.

Expanding Access to Federally Administered Plans

In addition to regulating the purchase of privately administered insurance plans, the federal government could be given a more active role in providing or contracting for health insurance in any of several ways:

- By offering enrollees an additional option, such as a plan delivered through the Medicare program, alongside privately administered plans;
- By setting up a new mechanism through which individuals could obtain private coverage, such as allowing them to purchase one of the plans offered to federal employees; or

- By providing a contingent option, or “fallback” plan, that would be available if an insufficient number of private insurers participated in a new purchasing system.

Such options would need to address several questions in order for their effects to be estimated. Depending on its design, a Medicare-based option could be less expensive than comparable private health plans—at least in many parts of the country—but it might also attract relatively unhealthy enrollees, which could drive up its premiums or federal costs. The effects of providing access to the Federal Employees Health Benefits program would also depend on how its premiums were set; if new enrollees had to pay a community-rated premium that fully covered their expected costs, the number of enrollees would probably be limited and the option might not prove to be viable in the market. As for provisions to offer fallback plans, the key question is what conditions would trigger their use.

Proposals could also seek to establish a single-payer system based on Medicare through which all U.S. residents could obtain their health insurance. The costs of that approach would depend on many of the same factors that affect the analysis of a new Medicare-based coverage option, but the scale of the impact would obviously be much larger if nearly all of the entire population was covered. Whether enrollees would still have a choice of health plans (paid through Medicare) or could purchase private insurance to supplement the government-run plan could have important implications for the system’s operation and costs.

Offering a Medicare-Based Option

The effects of having the federal government offer new insurance options depend on several factors that any such proposal would need to specify. Those factors may be easiest to illustrate under a proposal to add a Medicare-based option to the choices available to enrollees. Establishing such an option for the nonelderly population would involve defining the plan’s benefits, determining the rates used to pay providers, and setting the premium for enrollees and any government subsidy.[151]

Another factor affecting the cost of and premium for such an option is that Medicare’s administrative costs are lower than those of large private insurers, although the differences are smaller in dollar terms than they are as a percentage of the premium. If that option used Medicare’s current payment rates, which are relatively low, it could have lower premiums than comparable private health plans when serving the same population, at least in many parts of the country. However, the broad access that Medicare provides to doctors and hospitals and its very limited use of benefit-management techniques might also attract relatively unhealthy enrollees, which could drive up its premiums or federal costs.

Design and Management of Benefits

The design of a health insurance plan’s benefits plays a central role in determining its premium (see Chapter 3 for further discussion). Under current law, Medicare’s cost-sharing requirements vary substantially across types of health care services; CBO estimates that the program’s overall actuarial value for the nonelderly population is about 15 percent lower than that of typical employment-based insurance plans. Although Medicare covers care from home health agencies and skilled nursing facilities, which are used frequently by its enrollees, those benefits would generally not be used extensively by the younger population that has private health insurance and thus would not contribute to the actuarial value for that population. In addition, Medicare does not place an annual limit on out-of-pocket costs for enrollees, whereas most private insurance policies include such a limit. Another factor is that Medicare's drug benefit has a lower actuarial value than the drug benefits typically seen in employment- based plans.

Although those features would make Medicare coverage less attractive compared with an average employment- based plan, the difference between Medicare's actuarial value and that of plans purchased in the individual insurance market is smaller. Proposals to establish a new health insurance option based on Medicare could also expand its coverage or restructure its cost-sharing requirements to make its value equivalent to that of a typical employment-based plan, but those steps would also raise its premium.

A related question that arises is whether enrollees in a Medicare-based option would be able to purchase a supplemental insurance policy. Most Medicare enrollees have some form of additional coverage that pays some or all of their cost-sharing requirements and limits their out-of- pocket costs. That added coverage raises Medicare's spending—an effect that is reflected in the program's current costs per enrollee. Prohibiting enrollees under a new Medicare option from purchasing such coverage would thus tend to reduce the premium for that option, holding other factors equal. Whether it would be less costly for the federal government to allow those enrollees to buy supplemental insurance or to reduce the cost-sharing requirements they face in the Medicare-based option would depend on the degree of supplemental coverage that was allowed, the extent of the reductions in cost sharing, and the manner in which the plan's premium was divided between the enrollee and the government.

Two additional issues would be deciding whether and to what extent any benefit-management techniques would be applied under the new option and determining what role the private insurers that currently offer Medicare benefits would play. The traditional fee-for-service Medicare program does relatively little to manage benefits, which tends to reduce its administrative costs but may raise its overall spending relative to a more tightly managed approach. In addition, most enrollees can obtain their Medicare benefits from a private health plan, including an HMO, so a proposal would need to specify whether that option was also available and how new enrollees would access it.

A further complication stems from the fact that Medicare's drug benefit has an unusual design and is delivered exclusively by private health insurers. To provide a drug benefit that is similar to the ones typically seen in private insurance plans would either require Medicare to select an exclusive contractor for that benefit (which could be more costly) or involve having Medicare's drug plans bid separately to provide the new drug benefit. Whether enrollees might choose not to purchase the drug benefit (as Medicare enrollees are allowed to do) and whether premium surcharges would be imposed for late enrollees (as is generally done in Medicare) would also need to be addressed.[152]

Payment Rates for Providers

In addition to the design of a plan's benefits, another key determinant of average costs per enrollee is the payment rates for doctors, hospitals, and other providers of health care. Medicare's payment rates are, on average, lower than private rates— nearly 20 percent lower for physicians' services and as much as 30 percent lower for hospital services in 2006. (See Chapter 5 for a more detailed comparison.) Using those payment rates would tend to make a Medicare- based health insurance plan less expensive than a comparable private plan, holding other factors equal. Providers, however, might be reluctant to accept those payment rates for new patients, which could limit enrollees' access to care. Because Medicare's fees for physicians are determined by a statutory formula that is intended to cap total payments to physicians, proposals would need to address whether and how payments made on behalf of new enrollees would factor into that calculation or be adjusted over time.

Administrative Costs

The Medicare program and private insurance plans have different administrative costs, and Medicare's costs are commonly cited as an example of low administrative spending for a large insured population. The share of costs in the fee-for-service Medicare program that are devoted to administration (about 1.5 percent) is lower than the share observed for large employers' plans, whose administrative costs average about 7 percent of premiums. (See Chapter 3 for a discussion of administrative costs for private insurers.) To some extent, those differences reflect both the characteristics of the Medicare population and the unique features of the program.

Differences in current administrative costs between Medicare and private insurers partly reflect differences in the tasks that each performs. Medicare has little need to advertise or seek out enrollees because eligible individuals are usually enrolled by default on the basis of Social Security records, which determine their eligibility. By contrast, private health plans need to establish and solidify their market presence and must compete with each other for enrollees and for employers as clients, generating costs for advertising, marketing, and sales. Further, Medicare does not employ many of the cost-management techniques used in the private sector, such as conducting utilization reviews or requiring prior administrative authorization for tests or procedures. (The use of such techniques is discussed more fully in Chapter 3.) At the same time, costs per enrollee for adjudicating and processing claims may be higher for Medicare because its enrollees use more services, on average. Medicare also takes steps upon which private insurers sometimes piggyback, such as making decisions about what treatments to cover or establishing and maintaining payment systems.

Another source of the difference in administrative costs between private insurers and Medicare is that private insurers retain profits. Those profits, which represent about 4 percent or 5 percent of the insurers' premium revenues on average, constitute a return on investment for the companies' owners or shareholders. A portion of that return compensates those investors for effectively lending funds to the company (rather than using them for their own consumption), and a portion constitutes a "risk premium" to compensate for the risk that insurers will incur financial losses (if, for example, the premium levels they specify in advance are not sufficient to cover the insured costs their enrollees actually generate). The Medicare program, by contrast, does not generate profits. The federal government bears financial risk for operating the program, but the economic costs of doing so are not reflected in the federal budget under current accounting practices.

One factor that complicates the comparison of administrative costs in Medicare and private health insurance plans is that Medicare enrollees are either elderly or disabled, so their average health care costs are much higher. As a result, the share of the premium accounted for by administrative costs is likely to be lower simply because the denominator for that calculation is larger. For the same reason, private insurers that offer Medicare's basic benefits (known as Medicare Advantage plans) report having lower administrative costs as a share of their total costs per enrollee—about half as high as for their enrollees under the age of 65 as a percentage of the premium.[153] Comparing administrative costs for Medicare and large private plans in terms of dollars spent per enrollee shows much smaller differences. In 2007, administrative costs per enrollee were on the order of $150 for Medicare and about $300 for large employment-based health plans.[154] By contrast, the administrative costs of policies purchased by smaller employers and individuals were much higher—roughly $1,000 per enrollee.

The amount of administrative costs that would be incurred per enrollee if a Medicare-based option was made more broadly available could differ from the program's current costs and would depend on the tasks involved. In particular, more effort would probably be required to seek out and process applications for enrollees than is the case for the current Medicare population, thereby raising average administrative costs. Any fixed costs of operating the program would be divided over a larger number of enrollees, however, which would tend to reduce the amount of administrative costs per enrollee.

Setting Premiums for Likely Enrollees

Another important consideration is the terms of the competition between a plan run by the federal government and plans that are privately run, especially with respect to how premiums for enrollees in the federal plan would be set. If the federal plan had to charge a community-rated premium that was designed to cover the full costs of expected enrollees but competing private plans did not face the same requirement, the federal plan would be most attractive to enrollees with health problems, and its premium would have to be correspondingly higher.

That effect could be attenuated if the premium for the government-run plan was adjusted so that it did not reflect the relative (and presumably higher) risk of its enrollees. Covering the difference between the plan's expected costs and those premium payments, however, would either generate federal costs or require some mechanism to recoup the difference from competing plans. Alternatively, providing a premium subsidy would make the government-run plan more attractive to a broader range of enrollees, but it might put the private-sector plans at a disadvantage in trying to compete with the government's plan. Even then, adverse selection into a Medicare-based plan could occur because Medicare currently provides broad access to doctors and hospitals and makes limited use of the benefit-management techniques commonly employed by private health plans—features that would make Medicare relatively attractive to people with health problems. The impact on the premium for a Medicare-based option would depend on how effectively any risk-adjustment mechanism could offset that impact.[155]

Range of Estimates

Depending on how those questions are resolved, the impact of adding a Medicare-based insurance option could vary substantially. Assuming, however, that such an option offered benefits comparable with those of private health plans, used Medicare's payment rates for providers, and based its premium on the costs of serving a broadly representative group of enrollees in the same region, that option would have lower premiums than those private plans in many parts of the country and would have comparable premiums in other areas. (In a few areas, Medicare's costs would be higher than those of private plans.) The primary basis for that assessment is the observation that many of the private plans now participating in

Medicare have average costs to deliver the same package of basic benefits that are higher than those in the fee-for-service program.[156]

The main reason for that disparity appears to be Medicare's lower payment rates, which in many areas of the country more than offset the effects on costs per enrollee of employing fewer benefit-management techniques in the fee-for-service program. Depending on the number of people expected to enroll in a Medicare-based option, the extent to which providers would accept those payment rates for a larger number of patients could require further analysis. The differences in payment rates and costs also vary geographically, however, and in some parts of the country the HMOs participating in Medicare are able to provide its benefits at costs comparable with those observed in the fee-for-service program.

Medicare-for-All

Many of the considerations that arise in designing a new option for individuals to enroll in Medicare would also affect the analysis of proposals to establish a single-payer system based on Medicare through which all U.S. residents could obtain their health insurance. In particular, the federal costs of such a proposal would depend primarily on the benefits that the system provided; the rates it used to pay doctors, hospitals, and other providers of health care; and the extent of any premium subsidies it offered to enrollees—all of which could differ from Medicare's current design. The rules and processes used to determine eligibility for the program and to enroll individuals who are eligible would also have significant implications.

Even under a single-payer system, individuals could have a choice of insurance plans or benefit designs, but the extent and nature of those options would also depend on the features of the proposal. If enrollees were allowed to choose a private health plan paid through Medicare or could purchase supplemental private insurance (as many Medicare enrollees currently do), the rules governing those choices and the possibility of adverse selection would remain important considerations. If, instead, the Medicare plan was the only option offered and all residents were required to enroll in it, then adverse selection would not occur. That approach could reduce the administrative costs that doctors and hospitals currently incur when dealing with multiple insurers. Some enrollees might prefer a different design, however, and the lack of competition from private health plans could take away a benchmark that is commonly used to assess the adequacy of Medicare's payments and the efficiency of its performance. More generally, that approach would raise important questions about the role of the government in managing the delivery of health care.

Providing Access to the Federal Employees Health Benefits Program

Some proposals would allow individuals and firms outside the federal government to purchase coverage through the Federal Employees Health Benefits program, which offers health benefits to current and former federal employees and their families. In 2008, FEHB included approximately 300 private health plans and about 8 million enrollees. Most of those plans are available only in a specific region of the country, but a few are available nationwide, so a given enrollee may have 10 to 20 plans from which to choose. The federal government makes a contribution (as an employer) that covers 75 percent of each plan's premium, subject to a cap set at 72 percent of the national average premium.[157]

The FEHB program thus incorporates some elements of managed competition, but not all of them. In particular, the formula for the federal subsidy provides relatively strong incentives for enrollees to consider whether a plan with above-average costs is worth the additional payment, but it gives enrollees only 25 percent of the savings when they choose a plan that has overall costs below the national average. Some plans therefore seem to compete for enrollees by providing additional benefits rather than by offering lower premiums. In addition, payments to the plans participating in FEHB are not risk-adjusted to account for the differing health status of their enrollees. As a result, over the years a few plans that offered more extensive coverage—and thus attracted relatively unhealthy enrollees—have seen their costs and premiums escalate because of adverse selection.

The effects of providing broader access to FEHB would largely depend on who was eligible to enroll in the program and how premiums for the new enrollees were set, which could be determined in various ways. For example, FEHB plans could be made available to the general public and the premiums could be set in the same way that they are currently set by other insurers in the individual and group markets; that is, those premiums could vary across individuals and firms to the extent that such variation was allowed in each state. Relative to current law, however, that approach would probably do little to expand insurance coverage. Insurers participating in FEHB could already have pursued that approach if they had wanted to (and some have). More important, the options available to individuals and firms under that approach would not differ substantially from those available in the individual and group markets today.

Alternatively, FEHB plans could be required to charge a community-rated premium reflecting only the costs of the new nonfederal enrollees. Assuming that FEHB plans could not deny coverage to applicants, that option would be most attractive to people who expected to have above- average costs for health care—those who currently face relatively high premiums or have been denied coverage in the individual market. As a result, the total premium charged to nonfederal enrollees would probably be substantially higher than those observed in the program today. Depending on the specific features of the proposal, an equilibrium could be reached in which a group of enrollees were willing to pay an above-average premium that covered their health care costs (and related administrative expenses for the insurers). But another possibility is that an adverse selection spiral could ensue, resulting in very high premiums and little or no enrollment under this option.[158] The fact that insurers participating in FEHB could offer community-rated policies in the individual market today—but generally do not do so—suggests that they would be reluctant to participate.

Providing access to FEHB would probably have a greater effect on insurance coverage rates if a proposal included some type of subsidy for new enrollees, either implicit or explicit; unlike the approaches discussed above, such alternatives would also generate some federal costs. An implicit subsidy could be provided if the premium charged to new nonfederal enrollees was the same as the one for federal enrollees. To the extent that nonfederal enrollees had higher average costs for health care (or generated higher administrative costs), the uniform premium would rise but the effect would be averaged across federal and nonfederal enrollees. (The implicit subsidy would then be the difference between the average cost of covering nonfederal enrollees and the uniform premium.) Compared with the previous alternatives, the lower premiums under this option would make it somewhat more attractive to nonfederal enrollees, but higher total premiums for FEHB plans would also mean higher payments for federal enrollees. To the extent that average premiums rose, the government's costs for its contribution on behalf of federal enrollees would increase.

Finally, providing access to FEHB plans would be most likely to attract enrollees if the federal government also provided an explicit premium subsidy. If that subsidy was available only to enrollees in an FEHB plan, however, people with individually purchased or employment-based coverage would have an incentive to drop that coverage and switch to the FEHB system; the strength of that incentive would depend on the size of the subsidy. Limiting eligibility for the FEHB option to people who had been uninsured for some period of time and did not have an offer of health insurance from their employer would constrain the potential number of enrollees somewhat but would still lead some individuals and employers to drop their existing coverage; limiting eligibility in that way might also be viewed as penalizing people who had purchased coverage or had sought out jobs that offered it. If, instead, subsidies for health insurance were not limited to FEHB plans, then enrollment in those plans would depend on their attractiveness relative to other options in the individual and group markets. (See Chapter 2 for a broader discussion of premium subsidies.)

Creating a Fallback Plan

To lessen the impact of potential errors in the design or implementation of a new insurance system or to guarantee broad access to new health insurance options, proposals to expand or restructure health insurance coverage could include provisions for fallback plans, in which the government would offer or support a plan of last resort. Such options can address concerns that private insurers might be unwilling to meet the terms of participation set for them or might be reluctant to participate because of uncertainty about who will enroll or the costs of providing the proposed benefits. As a result, provisions for fallback plans may entail having the government step in to bear some or all of the financial risk involved in providing insurance coverage, either by contracting with a private entity whose role is limited to administering the benefit or by having the government offer the benefit directly.

Both the role and the potential effects of fallback plans are illustrated by CBO's analysis of the provisions that were included under the Medicare drug benefit.[159] Because of the novelty of that benefit—stand-alone drug insurance—and uncertainty about its costs, there was a chance that the private insurers that were expected to deliver it would not participate, at least in some areas of the country. The legislation thus specified that a fallback plan would have to be made available if too few private insurers stepped forward, but it also placed restrictions on the organizations serving as fallback plans in an effort to prevent the prospect of low participation by insurers from becoming a self-fulfilling prophecy. After analyzing the overall incentives facing insurers, CBO assumed that the probability that fallback plans would be needed was relatively low and would decline over time. As it turned out, a large number of insurers chose to participate in the drug benefit and the fallback provisions were never triggered.

More generally, the effect of such provisions on the expected costs of a proposal would depend on two factors: the likelihood that the provisions would be triggered, and the relative cost of such plans if they were used. The likelihood that fallback plans would be needed depends largely on the attractiveness to private insurers of participating in the system, which in turn depends on the requirements they would face if they participated and on the risks they would face if they did not. The terms under which fallback plans would *cease* being offered would also affect the attractiveness of that option and thus the odds of triggering the fallback provisions in the first place.

The relative costs of such plans would depend on many of the same factors discussed above: the design of the benefit package, including the scope of the coverage and cost-sharing arrangements, the provisions or incentives for managing costs, the administrative costs involved, and the method for setting the enrollee's share of the premium. If the requirements for private insurers to participate in a revised system of health insurance were similar to those they currently face—or, as illustrated by the Medicare drug benefit, even if they were not—those insurers would be very likely to participate, so fallback provisions would probably not be triggered.

5. FACTORS AFFECTING THE SUPPLY AND PRICES OF HEALTH CARE SERVICES

The ultimate effects of proposals on access, spending, prices, and the amount of care received would depend not only on factors that affect the demand for health care services, such as the number of people who are insured and the scope of their coverage, but also on factors that affect the supply of those services. The methods of setting prices and paying for services affect the supply of health care services by influencing the decisions that providers make about how many patients to serve and which treatments their patients will receive. Because of the central role that doctors and hospitals play in providing health care, it is important to consider the incentives they face when making those decisions and whether a proposal would alter those incentives. In the longer term, those rates of payment also affect the number of doctors and hospitals.

To provide a basis for analyzing those issues, this chapter first presents an overview of factors that affect the supply of doctors, nurses, and hospitals in the United States. It then considers:

- The methods insurers use for paying providers— including fee-for-service payment, bundled or episode-based payment, capitated payment, and salary payment—and how the financial incentives stemming from those payment methods may affect the provision of health care services and spending per enrollee.
- How payment rates, or prices for services, are set (generally, by negotiation in the private sector and through administrative pricing for Medicare and Medicaid) and the relationship between how the rates are set and the level at which they are set.
- How providers, in response to changes in their payment rates or the demand for their services, might adjust the number or type of services they supply.
- Whether and to what extent the relatively low payment rates of public programs or the costs of providing uncompensated care for the uninsured yields higher payment rates for private insurers—a process known as cost shifting.

Although the focus of the analysis in this chapter is on doctors and hospitals, many other types of providers also deliver health care services. Those providers include dentists and other medical professionals as well as home health agencies, rehabilitation centers, and other types of facilities. Substantial shares of spending for health care also go to purchase goods, such as prescription drugs, medical devices, and durable and nondurable medical equipment. In some cases, the factors affecting supply, the methods of payment and rate setting, and the issues that arise are similar to those for doctors and hospitals. A full consideration of the supply and pricing issues involved in each of those sectors, however, is beyond the scope of this chapter.

Background on the Supply of Health Care Providers

Health care services are delivered to individuals by a combination of health care personnel (such as doctors, nurses, technicians, and aides) and facilities (such as hospitals, outpatient clinics, and clinical laboratories). Before considering the ways in which insurers pay providers for those services—or how changes in payments or in the demand for care affect the supply of services—it is useful to examine the supply of those providers.

In 2006, the health care industry in the United States employed about 14 million people, making health care the nation's largest industry, by employment.[160] That figure includes various types of health aides, therapists, and medical technicians as well as administrative and other support personnel employed at facilities where health care is provided. Although all may contribute to delivering services, focusing on the supply of physicians and nurses is useful because of the central role they play in determining the nature and amount of health care delivered. That focus also reflects the lead times that can be involved in changing the supply of practitioners—and concerns about current or projected shortages that have arisen—and highlights the increasing role played by physicians and nurses trained in other countries. Similarly, the hospital sector warrants particular attention because of its major role in treating patients and because of the large share of spending and employment in the health sector for which it accounts.

Physicians

The process of educating and training new physicians can be lengthy, reflecting the complexity of medical care. After obtaining a four-year college degree (usually with a "pre-med" or related major), prospective physicians generally spend four years training in medical schools and then enroll in residency programs that can last from three to seven years, depending on the medical specialty they are pursuing. U.S. medical schools graduate about 16,000 doctors of medicine per year, a figure that has held relatively steady over the past 20 years.[161] First-year residents numbered about 24,000 in 2006, up from about 18,000 in 1990 and about 22,000 in the late 1 990s. Almost three-quarters of the residency slots are filled by graduates of U.S. medical schools, and the rest go to graduates of foreign medical schools.

One important factor affecting the number of doctors in training is the subsidies that Medicare has provided for residency programs. Those subsidies have been estimated to exceed $70,000 per resident per year.[162] Before Medicare's creation, the federal government had also begun giving matching grants to medical schools to build or expand their capacity. Those policies—combined with the increase in demand for doctors brought on by Medicare's provision of near-universal coverage to the elderly—resulted in a doubling of the number of U.S.- trained medical school graduates between 1965 and 1985 and a substantial increase in the number of residency slots. Since 1997, however, Medicare has essentially capped the number of slots it subsidizes.

Roughly 800,000 physicians were practicing in the United States in 2006, up from about 560,000 in 1990. The number of doctors is expected to continue growing, but the rate of growth may slow until it is more in line with overall population growth. Reflecting that assessment, some organizations—including the Council on Graduate Medical Education, an advisory body to the Congress and the Department of Health and Human Services—have forecast that shortages of doctors will develop relative to the heightened demand for care of an aging society.[163] Whether those shortages materialize depends in part on whether changes are made to expand the domestic "pipeline" of new physicians, which can involve a lengthy process of approval and certification by provider associations.

Such projections of shortages raise a number of issues. One limitation is that such projections are based on assumptions about a required number of physicians per capita, with some adjustment for population characteristics such as age. In turn, those assumptions may be based on historical patterns in the use of services or on ratios of doctors to patients that are observed in an existing health plan that is treated as a model of efficient use. Whether historic ratios need to be maintained, however, or whether the ratios chosen by one health plan are the correct ones for the entire health sector in the future is not clear. Furthermore, any shortages that arise could be addressed not only by changes in the number of domestically trained physicians but also by changes in the number of hours that doctors work, in the use of ancillary personnel, in the productivity of existing doctors, or by other changes in medical practice. Moreover, to the extent that domestic training slots are limited, the supply of physicians could be augmented by having more foreign-trained doctors enter practice in the United States (which depends partly on immigration policy, because some graduates of foreign medical schools who seek to enter this country are foreign citizens). Finally, projections of requirements for the health workforce generally do not consider the role of prices or fees in determining the demand for or supply of physicians' services.

Nurses

Nurses constitute the largest health care profession; about 2.4 million registered nurses were employed in the United States in 2005.[164] A license to practice as a registered nurse can be obtained in several ways, including traditional four-year baccalaureate programs, accelerated programs for individuals who have related college degrees, and two-year associate's degree programs open to high school graduates. A small share of registered nurses has obtained additional education to become nurse practitioners, and recent reports indicate growing interest in that option. Nurse practitioners generally work with physicians in providing primary care, and in many states they have the authority to practice independently (for example, in most states they may diagnose patients' conditions, and they may also write prescriptions with the collaboration of a physician).

Concerns have arisen in recent years about shortages of nurses. One approach to address those shortages has been to recruit foreign-trained nurses. According to one study, about 14 percent of newly licensed registered nurses in the United States in 2003 were trained abroad, up from about 9 percent in 1995 and from a recent low of 5 percent in 1998.[165] Overall, the number of registered nurses practicing in the United States has increased steadily over the past few decades, but some analysts project that the nursing workforce will cease growing within the next 10 years, in part because of projected retirements—raising the prospect of nursing shortages.[166] Even without an inflow of foreign-trained nurses, however, it is not clear why a shortage of nurses would persist. If wages for nurses are free to adjust to market pressures, then short- term shortages would cause those wages to rise. That development would limit demand for nurses' services and would also increase supply—encouraging some nurses to work more hours and others to reenter the practice of nursing (for those who had been trained as nurses but had left the profession) and enticing new people to enter the field. In principle, those adjustments should continue until a wage is reached at which supply equals demand.[167]

Hospitals

Health care facilities vary widely in their size and scope, ranging from small medical clinics to large hospital complexes. Although hospitals retain a primary role in delivering care—accounting for about one-third of spending on health care services and about 40 percent of health care employment—changes in medical practice have allowed more services to be performed on an outpatient basis and have shortened recovery times from some surgeries, which in turn has reduced the need for lengthy hospitalizations and a large inpatient capacity. Even within the hospital sector, the share of revenue accounted for by inpatient care has fallen from 77 percent in 1990 to 62 percent in 2006 (with the remainder coming from the outpatient care that hospitals provide).

Reflecting those developments, the total number of hospitals in the United States dropped from 6,649 in 1990 to 5,764 in 2003—a 13 percent decline—and has remained at about that level since then. Hospital capacity, as measured by the total number of beds, decreased by about 20 percent during the same period. Community hospitals, which are open to the general public and provide acute care and which constitute the vast majority of hospitals, saw a somewhat smaller decline; the total number of those hospitals and of beds in them fell by about 12 percent during that period. Since 1990, hospitals' average occupancy rates have generally ranged between 65 percent and 70 percent (with slightly lower rates seen among community hospitals).

Payment Methods and Providers' Incentives

Health insurance plans pay doctors, hospitals, and other providers of health care in various ways. Common methods include fee-for-service payment, bundled payments for defined medical episodes, and "capitated" payment— a fixed amount for all services that a patient receives over a specified period. Some health plans, such as staff-model health maintenance organizations, own the hospitals that serve their enrollees and employ doctors as salaried workers. Providers' financial incentives vary greatly among those approaches, so a health plan's choice of payment method can exert a significant influence on the use of medical care and spending per enrollee.

Proposals could seek to change payment methods directly or indirectly. An example of a direct approach would be to require changes in how payments are made in the Medicare program. The effects of such changes would depend on their breadth and design (a full analysis of which is beyond the scope of this chapter). By contrast, an indirect approach would encourage shifts in enrollment toward private health insurance plans that use lower-cost payment methods. For example, if enrollees were required to pay the full additional cost of joining a more expensive health plan (an approach discussed in Chapter 4), they might join a plan that uses a less expensive payment method.

More generally, fee-for-service payments can give providers an incentive to deliver additional services and thus may yield greater levels of spending and higher premiums. Payment methods that give providers stronger incentives to control spending on health care would tend to yield lower premiums (holding other factors equal) but would also raise concerns about the degree of financial risk that providers face and about their incentives to limit the use of beneficial services. Some enrollees would be reluctant to switch to plans that use such methods, and the challenges involved in changing payment systems would be substantial both for a private health plan and for the Medicare program.

Fee-for-Service Payment

As the name implies, fee-for-service systems make separate payments to providers for each service they deliver, whether it is a medical procedure, an office visit, or an ancillary service (such as an X-ray). Fee schedules specify payment amounts for a broad set of clinical tasks. After seeing a patient, the provider is paid an amount that reflects all services performed, with each individual service adding to the total.

Compared with other methods, fee-for-service payments generally reward all efforts to provide care and create no financial incentive to limit the use of beneficial services. If the fees for the services exceed the costs of providing them, however, such payments can encourage providers to perform a greater number or more expensive mix of services, even though the clinical value of those services may be slight. For their part, cost-sharing requirements for insured patients generally cover only a portion of the providers' fees, so patients have incentives to receive services as long as the expected benefit exceeds the portion they have to pay.

In the United States, most care provided by doctors is paid for on a fee-for-service basis. The Medicare program pays doctors in that way and has established more than 7,000 different billing codes for the specific services that physicians provide. Fee-for-service payment is also common among private health plans. Preferred provider organizations, which are the most popular type of private plan, generally use that method. In addition, many health maintenance organizations contract with a network of independent doctors and pay them on a fee-for-service basis—at least for specialty care and, in many cases, for primary care too.

Bundled or Episode-Based Payment

An alternative approach is to make a single fixed payment for a bundle of related services or for an episode of care, such as a hospital admission. The most prominent example of that approach is the prospective payment system that Medicare adopted in 1983 to pay hospitals for acute inpatient care. Under that system, most hospitals generally receive a fixed amount per admission that is based either on the patient's diagnosis or on the treatment he or she receives. Several hundred payment rates (one for each diagnosis-related group, as they are known) have been established. If treatment costs are less than the payment, the hospital keeps the difference; if treatment costs exceed the payment, the hospital incurs a loss, though in certain cases Medicare makes additional payments for high-cost "outlier" patients. (Private health plans typically pay hospitals a fixed amount per admission or per day.)

Because a fixed payment shifts some financial risk from the insurer to the provider, episode-based payments can create a strong incentive for providers to economize on care for a given health episode. After the prospective payment system was implemented, the number of days that Medicare enrollees spent in the hospital declined sharply—reflecting the fact that hospitals were no longer being paid more for longer stays. The number of hospital admissions also fell, reversing the trend before 1983 when hospitals were paid on the basis of their reported costs.

Although fixed payments can encourage hospitals to limit the costs of a given admission, Medicare's system is not designed to encourage savings in other ways (such as taking steps to avoid or prevent hospital admissions). In addition, for more than 40 percent of the payment groupings, Medicare's payment depends not just on the diagnosis (for example, a heart attack) but also on what procedure is performed (for example, a bypass operation).[168] In those cases, hospitals may still have incentives to provide more expensive treatments during an admission—because they would be paid more—but would retain incentives to control other costs associated with that admission.

Bundled or episode-based payment is mainly used for financing hospital care and postoperative care, perhaps because it is relatively easy to define medical episodes that involve those services. Under Medicare, for example, skilled nursing facilities (which provide postoperative rehabilitation services) generally receive a fixed payment per day, and agencies that provide home health care generally receive a fixed payment for each 60-day episode of care. In both cases, the payment amounts are adjusted to reflect the severity of each patient's condition.

In principle, episode-based payment could be used more broadly to cover all of the services involved in treating a given health problem—including those performed by physicians, hospitals, and other providers and facilities. In practice, however, assigning control over a patient's care or allocating payments across settings may be difficult, particularly when the providers are not otherwise linked. Even in the case of hospital admissions, Medicare pays doctors separately for the services they provide during a patient's hospital stay; that is, the payments for physicians and hospitals are not bundled. Determining what services are part of an episode may also be challenging, particularly if patients have multiple health problems.

Capitated Payment

Capitated payment is similar in concept to bundled or episode-based payment but is far broader in scope. Unlike an episode-based payment, which covers costs arising from a specific health event, a capitated payment generally covers all of a patient's care for any health problems over a specified period. In capitated payment arrangements, insurers typically pay providers (or provider groups) fixed monthly amounts in exchange for an agreement to treat any health problems that arise during a patient's period of enrollment.

Capitated payment creates especially strong incentives for providers to limit the use of costly services and thus can yield substantial savings. Capitated payments may also encourage providers to invest in types of care that reduce the likelihood that a patient will need costlier treatments in the future. In order to take such steps, however, providers would have to expect to have long-term relationships with their patients; if turnover among patients is rapid, providers may find it unprofitable to devote resources to such services under capitation because they would not be able to capture the financial benefits.

Although capitation can provide strong incentives to control costs, it raises concerns about the possible under- provision of needed care. Capitation may also encourage providers to avoid treating very sick patients if payments are not sufficient to cover those patients' higher expected costs. In principle, "risk-adjusted" payments—higher capitated payments for sicker, costlier patients—can minimize providers' incentive to "cherry-pick" healthier enrollees. In practice, however, risk-adjustment methods have some limitations (as discussed in Chapter 4). As in the case of risk-adjusted payments to health plans, the key question is whether doctors could systematically predict the expected costs of potential patients more accurately than the risk-adjustment models and whether that information could be used in ways that affect the range of patients that doctors see.

Another concern that arises with capitated payments is that they effectively make providers of clinical care the primary bearers of financial risk—a role traditionally played by insurers. In comparison with insurers or large provider groups, smaller provider groups would face greater variability in their patients' expected costs just because of random fluctuations that are beyond the doctors' control. Some private health plans adopted capitated payment methods in the 1990s, but anecdotal evidence indicates that physicians had difficulty managing the financial risks involved and that the use of capitation has subsequently declined.

To mitigate potential problems, some health plans blend capitated payment—typically for primary care—with other methods, such as fee-for-service payment, for specialty care. Blended models have also been proposed for Medicare as a way to help balance the differing incentives that fee-for-service and capitated payments provide.[169] Even so, a challenge for those approaches is to find an organizational unit that would receive and distribute the blended payment when various providers that treat Medicare patients are not linked financially. The effects could also differ substantially depending on whether participation by doctors was made voluntary or mandatory. (A related approach, in which a patient's primary care provider would serve as a "medical home" and coordinate his or her care—possibly in return for a capitated payment or other financial incentives to limit the use of specialty care—is discussed in Chapter 7.)

Salary Payment

Some plans employ providers, including physicians, as salaried workers. In those settings, providers' incentives are like those of salaried workers in other fields. Monitoring aspects of a physician's performance, including quality of care and cost control, are management functions of the employing organization. Compensation may consist simply of a salary, or it may include bonus payments for good performance (as discussed below). Organizations that employ salaried physicians include staff-model HMOs and the Veterans Health Administration.

In general, determining the effects of various payment systems on expenditure levels can be problematic because of the difficulties that arise in accounting for other factors that might affect comparisons between different private health plans or between private health plans and Medicare. In the case of salary payments, however, a useful comparison comes from the RAND Health Insurance Experiment, a large study conducted from 1974 to 1982 to test the effects of various health insurance designs by randomly assigning participants to different plans. The RAND study included a staff-model HMO plan and estimated that total expenditures for its enrollees were about 30 percent lower than those for enrollees in a

comparable plan using fee-for-service payment.[170] In addition, various comparisons of enrollees' health did not show systematic differences, although the ability of statistical methods to detect differences in health among participants in the experiment may be limited.

One important factor that limits the applicability of the RAND comparison, however, is that the plans it analyzed do not resemble current offerings in other respects. In particular, neither the HMO nor the fee-for-service plan required any cost sharing, and the fee-for-service plan did not use any of the cost-management techniques commonly employed by health plans today (see Chapter 3 for a discussion of those techniques and their impact).

Performance-Based Incentives

Some health plans offer financial incentives to providers to encourage desired performance. For example, they may give bonuses to providers that meet targets for quality (such as performing appropriate tests on patients with diabetes) or reduce payments to providers that do not.

Those arrangements, known as "pay for performance" initiatives, could be incorporated into fee-for-service systems in an effort to encourage doctors to provide only treatments that are deemed appropriate; they could also be used with capitation or salary arrangements to encourage providers not to stint on care.

Designing an incentive system can be challenging, however, especially when the system is implemented outside a staff-model setting. (In such a setting, providers' actions may be more easily observed or supervised.) In particular, developing valid and meaningful measures of performance quality can be difficult because of the complexity of medical care. Medical outcomes such as mortality or avoidance of acute health problems are relatively easy to measure, but conclusions about quality of care that are based on those measures can be misleading if they do not properly account for differences in the severity of patients' illnesses or if the provider being measured does not perform a given procedure often enough to make a reliable comparison.

Reflecting those difficulties in assessing outcomes, many attempts to gauge performance focus on "process" measures for treating specific conditions. For example, providers may be required to report whether they have followed several widely accepted treatment guidelines, such as prescribing medicines called beta blockers for patients who have had a heart attack. The value of such approaches depends on whether a provider's performance on those metrics is correlated with the overall quality of the care he or she delivers. Determining an optimal structure of bonuses or penalties may also be difficult.

Payment Rates

Payment systems determine what is being paid for, but the financial incentives created by different payment systems—and the spending levels they yield—also depend on the level at which payment rates (or the prices for services) are set.[171] How those rates are set also plays a role in determining their level.

- Payment rates in the private sector are generally set by **negotiation**, reflecting the underlying costs of the services and the relative bargaining power of providers and health plans; in turn, bargaining power depends on factors such as the number of competing providers (or provider groups of a particular type or specialty) within a local market area.

- Fee-for-service payment rates in Medicare and Medicaid are set **administratively**. Although a common goal of administered pricing systems is to set rates that cover the costs of an efficient provider, keeping payments in line with providers' costs for each specific service can be difficult. In addition, annual updates to those prices may reflect statutory formulas or legislative responses to budgetary and other pressures that may deviate from the changes in providers' costs.

The level of administratively set prices and mechanisms for setting them are particularly important considerations for proposals that would expand their use. For example, proposals for a single-payer system could establish a government entity that would set payment rates, perhaps using methods similar to those employed in the traditional fee-for-service portion of the Medicare program. Alternatively, some proposals would create a new public program similar to Medicare as an additional option for the general population. The new program would compete against privately run plans and could use administered pricing to set its payment rates. Still other proposals might expand the role of Medicaid or shift Medicaid enrollees to private health plans. The available evidence indicates that payment rates for Medicare and Medicaid are, on average, lower than those of private payers—in some cases, substantially lower—but the difference is much smaller in some areas of the country than in others.

Determining Rates in the Private Sector

In general, payment rates and fees in the private sector are set through some process of negotiation between health plans and providers. In the case of large hospitals or physician groups, those negotiations may be explicit, involving face-to-face bargaining. In other cases, the bargaining may be tacit, with health plans setting a payment rate schedule and adjusting it as necessary so that a sufficient number of providers are willing to accept the terms.

Partly to enhance their bargaining leverage, private health plans generally establish a network of providers from which enrollees are encouraged or required to obtain covered services. For example, preferred provider organizations usually charge relatively small copayments for visits to providers within the plan's network but have much higher cost-sharing requirements for visits to other providers. HMO plans generally require enrollees to obtain services within the plan's network in order to receive coverage. Faced with the threat of being excluded from the network and thus seeing fewer patients, many providers are willing to accept lower fees. (Plans may seek to exclude certain providers for other reasons, such as having a particularly high-cost practice style or performing poorly on quality measures.)

The effect of establishing a network of providers on payment rates depends on local market conditions. Other factors held equal, large health plans can probably negotiate lower prices than small plans because large plans can have a greater effect on the number of patients a provider sees (although providers would not be willing to accept payments that were lower than their costs for providing services). Hospitals or physician groups with few local competitors, however, are better able to resist demands for price concessions.

Medicare's Approach to Setting Payment Rates

The process used to set payment rates in the Medicare program exemplifies the workings of and challenges facing an administered pricing system. Medicare generally pays doctors and hospitals a fixed amount per service or per admission. Although the scope of the payments differs substantially between those two payment systems, the mechanisms for setting payment rates have many similarities. In both cases, a base or average payment amount is multiplied by a factor that is designed to capture differences in the resources needed to provide various services or to treat different types of patients. The base payment amount is updated annually according to statutory formulas, but that update may be—and often is—modified by legislation.

For inpatient hospital care, Medicare pays a flat rate for each stay. That rate depends on the diagnosis-related group to which the stay is assigned (which is determined by the patient's diagnoses and whether or not certain surgical procedures were performed). Each group is assigned a weight that is intended to represent the expected costliness of stays in that group relative to the national average. Medicare's payment for a given stay is thus determined by multiplying the group's weight by the base payment rate.[172] The Centers for Medicare and Medicaid Services, the agency that administers Medicare, reviews the definitions of all groups annually to ensure that they continue to include cases with clinically similar conditions requiring comparable amounts of inpatient resources. The base payment rate's initial value reflects the historical costs used in constructing the rate in 1983 (when the prospective payment system was adopted) plus annual updates that have been made since then. In the absence of legislative changes, the annual update is based on projected increases in hospitals' input costs (such as staff wages and the prices of medical supplies), but the update has frequently been altered by legislation in response to budgetary pressures or other considerations.

For physicians' services, Medicare uses a fee schedule that is based on an assessment of the relative resources needed to provide those services (including the time, skill, and training required of the doctor). The payment rate for a particular service is determined by multiplying the relative value or weight that has been established for that service by a base payment amount, known as the "conversion factor." As with inpatient hospital care, the base payment amount for physicians' services reflects the average level of historical spending per service at the time the fee schedule was adopted and subsequent annual updates to that amount. The fee schedule's relative weights are also updated at least every five years, with input from the American Medical Association and physicians' specialty societies; the list of service codes and the conversion factor are updated annually.

Under current law, the annual update for physicians' payments is determined by the "sustainable growth rate" mechanism, which entails target levels of expenditures and a method for adjusting payment rates in an attempt to bring actual expenditures in line with the targets over time. In essence, the targets are set so that spending per Medicare enrollee will grow at about the same rate as per capita gross domestic product.[173] If expenditures on physicians' services are equal to the targets, the conversion factor is updated by the projected change in the average price of inputs—such as the costs of office space and support staff—that are used to produce those services; the update is then adjusted to reflect expected improvements in productivity. In recent years, however, spending per enrollee on physicians' services has grown more quickly than the economy as a whole—consistent with long-term trends in health care spending—and Medicare's expenditures have exceeded the targets.

That outcome would have led to cuts in physicians' payment rates, but legislation has generally prevented those reductions from taking effect. The most recent intervention canceled a 10.6 percent reduction in Medicare's payment rates that was scheduled to go into effect on July 1, 2008. Instead, the legislation froze those payment rates for the remainder of the year and will increase them by 1.1 percent in January 2009. In the absence of further legislation, however, future payment rates will revert to the levels that were specified under prior law, necessitating a 21 percent reduction in payment rates under the physicians' fee schedule in 2010 and additional cuts in later years.

Determining whether Medicare's payment rates are adequate is difficult, in part because of the challenges involved in estimating providers' costs. Among the relevant issues are questions like how to:

- Account for the costs of providers' training,
- Allocate overhead costs or account for the costs of equipment or facilities that are shared with the production of other services,
- Deal with economies of scale in production,
- Address geographic differences in costs, and
- Set payment rates for new treatments and technologies.

In the view of some experts, updates to administered price schedules tend to lag behind changes in medical technology and practice techniques that affect the costs of services and treatments, and such lags may in turn affect the pace of technological advance.[174] Accounting for the value of the services that enrollees receive or the quality of different providers may also be difficult.

Despite those challenges, the Medicare Payment Advisory Commission (MedPAC) assesses the program's rates and makes recommendations each year to the Congress about the update factor that should be applied for hospital and physicians' services. MedPAC's analysis seeks to determine whether payments are sufficient to cover the costs of efficient providers and takes into account available data on access to services by enrollees and the financial condition of providers. In its most recent report, MedPAC recommended that payments to hospitals and physicians receive a full update for inflation in input prices in 2009 (with an adjustment to the update for physicians' payments that is in line with productivity gains for workers observed in the economy as a whole).[175]

For both inpatient care and physicians' services, the Medicare program also faces a considerable challenge in setting payment weights that accurately reflect the relative costs of providing different services, particularly given the changes over time in medical practice and providers' productivity. Evidence indicates that because of limitations in the available data on providers' costs, the weights have unintentionally resulted in some types of inpatient admissions (such as those for cardiac surgery) and some types of physicians' services (such as imaging) being more profitable than others.[176] Such differences—which can also arise for private payments—create incentives that can cause providers to deliver too much of some types of care and too little of others; they also encourage investments in some types of facilities and equipment that would not have otherwise been made.

Comparison of Public and Private Payment Rates

Many private insurers and states' Medicaid programs pay for physicians' services using payment rates that are based on Medicare's fee schedule. In many cases, their rates differ substantially from Medicare's rates, however, because they use different conversion factors. In the case of private plans, those differences are negotiated to reflect local market conditions and may vary for different specialties.

How large are the differences? An analysis by MedPAC indicates that Medicare's payment rates for physicians were, on average, nearly 20 percent lower than private insurers' rates in 2006.[177] As for Medicaid, one study concluded that the program's rates for physicians in 2003 were about 30 percent lower than Medicare's rates.[178] Charges for physicians' services, which are the amounts that uninsured patients are expected to pay unless they make arrangements to receive charity care, were about 125 percent higher than Medicare's rates, on average.

Private insurers and public programs also vary in how they pay for inpatient hospital care, but comparing their payment rates is more difficult. Data compiled by the American Hospital Association (a trade group representing hospitals) indicate that Medicare's average payment rates for inpatient care were about 30 percent lower than those of private insurers in 2006, and that the payments by Medicaid were about 5 percent lower than those of Medicare.[179] Those calculations are not direct comparisons; rather, they reflect the relative "payment-to-cost" ratios that hospitals reported for each insurer and thus depend on how fixed costs are allocated to different types of patients. In particular, they reflect a calculation that, on average, Medicare's payments were about 9 percent below the costs of serving Medicare patients, whereas private payments were about 30 percent above costs. Alternatively, if a greater share of hospitals' fixed costs was allocated to private patients, then the payment-to-cost ratio would fall for private insurers and rise for Medicare.

The relationship between Medicare's payment rates and those of private insurers varies geographically. Medicare's rates are established nationally and are adjusted to account for geographic variation in providers' input costs. The rates that private insurers are able to negotiate also depend to some extent on the relative negotiating leverage of providers and insurers in local market areas. Private rates are noticeably higher than Medicare's rates in areas with less competition among providers, such as small cities and rural areas. According to one study, the rates paid to physicians by private insurance plans are an average of 30 percent higher than Medicare's rates in small metropolitan areas and rural areas, 10 percent higher in medium-sized metropolitan areas, and 1 percent higher in large metropolitan areas.[180] Proposals that would shift payments from private rates to Medicare's rates would therefore lead to a much greater reduction in payment rates in rural areas than in large metropolitan areas.

Responses to Changes in Payment Rates or Demand for Services

Changes in payment rates would clearly have a direct effect on health care spending and insurance premiums, but they could also have an indirect effect by changing the number of services that providers would be willing to supply. Similarly, the effects of covering currently uninsured individuals would depend not only on the resulting increase in their demand for care but also on how that increase would affect the supply and prices of services.

Whether and to what extent supply might be constrained depends on several factors, including the size of the increase in demand and the amount of time available for adjustments to occur. CBO's analysis indicates that providing coverage to the uninsured population that is similar to coverage under current employment-based health plans would initially increase total demand for physicians' services and hospital care by 2 percent to 5 percent (see Chapter 3). Although supply constraints could cause the total use of services to increase by a smaller percentage, the extent to which those constraints would arise is not clear.

Responses to Changes in Payment Rates

A decline in the amount that a provider is paid would generally be expected to result in fewer services being delivered. That type of response has been observed in skilled nursing facilities and home health agencies, and there is some evidence that it occurs in hospitals.[181]

In the case of physicians, however, payment cuts could lead them to increase the amount of services they provide to offset the effect of lower rates on their income. That possibility arises because doctors play a major role in determining how much and what types of care their patients receive—a situation that does not apply to most producers of goods or services. Doctors thus have some ability to induce demand for additional services, and the capacity of insurers to monitor such actions is limited. Researchers attempting to analyze such effects typically assume that doctors incur some "psychic" costs when they induce demand, but those costs are balanced against the gains from increasing their income.[182] Doctors could also respond to fee cuts by increasing the reported number or types of the services they provide, without actually increasing their activities, but many physicians might be unwilling to engage in such "up-coding," and others would be deterred from doing so by the risk of detection.

Previous studies of the effects of changes in Medicare's payment rates on the number and types of services that physicians provide yield mixed evidence of a behavioral response. Some studies have found that doctors respond according to the standard economic model, increasing their supply of services when payments rise and decreasing them when payments fall.[183] Other studies have found that physicians respond to reductions in payment rates by increasing the volume of their services so as to offset between 20 percent and 40 percent of the rate cut's impact on their total payments.[184] An analysis of Medicare payments conducted by CBO in 2007 is consistent with the latter studies; it found that physicians responded to recent reductions in those payment rates by increasing the reported volume and intensity of the services they deliver.[185] In particular, that study concluded that the response of physicians offsets about a quarter of the reduction in spending that would otherwise occur. The extent to which that response represented increases in the actual services provided or changes in the reporting of existing services could not be determined because it is not observable.

On the basis of that study, CBO would expect responses of that magnitude to changes in payments to physicians when those payments are in the range of Medicare's current rates. Substantially lower rates, however, such as those paid by Medicaid, may not be sufficient to cover some providers' costs. If that was the case, doctors would not have an incentive to induce demand for services because they would lose money on the added services; indeed, they might choose not to accept patients who were candidates for those services. Furthermore, over a prolonged period of time, lower average payment rates would be expected to yield fewer practicing physicians than otherwise.

More substantial changes in payment rates could have broader effects on the supply of health care services, depending on the share of patients involved. In particular, adopting Medicare's current rates under a single-payer proposal would cause a significant reduction in payments for the services provided to a substantial fraction of physicians' patients—particularly for physicians who practice in geographic areas with limited competition among providers. Such changes in payment rates could diminish the supply of physicians in areas that experienced more substantial declines in rates, which in turn could reduce access to care in those areas. Moreover, lowering payment rates for hospital services to the level of Medicare's rates could cause a significant decline in the financial condition of some hospitals, which over time could reduce access to hospital services in some geographic areas and lower the quality of care that those hospitals deliver.

Responses to Changes in Demand for Services

Proposals that expanded health insurance coverage would tend to increase the demand for health care services, but the extent to which the use of services and spending on them would increase is less clear. Particularly in the short run, the supply of U.S.-trained health care providers is largely fixed. Substantially expanding the capacity of medical schools and teaching hospitals can take many years, partly because of institutional barriers such as the need for approval and certification from various provider associations. Even if the capacity to train practitioners in the United States is changed, the training time required for new providers is substantial, especially for physicians.

In the interim, those constraints could be alleviated by changing the number of hours that providers work, improving their productivity, shifting responsibilities among providers, or increasing the flow of practitioners from other countries. Any remaining shortages in the supply of services would result in higher prices or greater difficulty in obtaining access to a provider (for example, longer lags in scheduling appointments).[186] Studies of how large-scale insurance expansions—both in the United States and in other countries—affect the use of services provide some evidence about the extent to which use of services and spending would increase as a result in the near term. Even so, determining in advance whether and how the impact of a particular proposal would be affected by supply considerations is difficult.

Potential Responses in the Near Term

If policy changes resulted in greater demand for health care services, the textbook response would involve some combination of a larger quantity supplied and higher payment rates to bring supply and demand back into balance. Supply might increase more quickly if payment rates were allowed to adjust; such adjustments would tend to be more rapid with negotiated payment rates than with administered prices. (Whether and how quickly demand adjusted to the new rates would also depend on how those rates affected patients' cost-sharing requirements.)

In the short run, one adjustment that could be made to expand the supply of services would be an increase in the hours worked by providers who are currently in practice. Physicians may be relatively unresponsive to changes in payment rates, however, either in terms of changing their total hours worked or their decisions about retirement. Some studies (including one by CBO) have suggested that when doctors receive higher fees, they actually tend to reduce the number or complexity of the services they provide.[187] Nevertheless, CBO's analysis also found that, after accounting for physicians' responses to changes in the level of Medicare fees, the average volume and intensity of physicians' services provided to each Medicare beneficiary has grown by about 4 percent annually in recent years—indicating that providing more services is feasible even if the number of providers or their work hours are relatively fixed.

Other adjustments that could be made include improving the productivity of physicians or shifting some of their responsibilities to nurses and other providers, thereby allowing more services to be provided without increasing doctors' hours. For example, steps such as using nurse "help lines" to triage medical problems, outsourcing other activities typically conducted in the physician's office, or opening primary care clinics at pharmacies and retail stores could enable the delivery of greater quantities (or different kinds) of medical services by a given number of health professionals. Other shifts in responsibility could require additional training. For example, registered nurses can obtain advanced training (typically two years are required) to become nurse practitioners or certified nurse midwives, so that they can perform many tasks performed by physicians. Lags in implementing new proposals would allow such adjustments in supply to begin in anticipation of the changes in demand. To the extent that additional services could be produced using lower- cost staff, the effect on payment rates and spending would also tend to be smaller.

Finally, graduates of foreign medical schools provide additional flexibility in the physicians' workforce. The share of practicing physicians who were trained abroad is currently about 25 percent, up from about 20 percent in 1985. Although several thousand graduates of foreign medical schools enter residency programs in the United States each year, options for increasing the supply of physicians through that route could be constrained by the number of residency slots. Alternatively, doctors who have completed residency programs or equivalent training abroad may also be able to enter directly into practice in this country, depending in part on the credentialing rules used in their state. The extent to which they would do so in response to greater demand for health care services in the United States depends on the attractiveness of their opportunities abroad and, for those who are not U.S. citizens, on immigration policy.

Evidence from Previous Insurance Expansions

Analyses of several relatively large-scale insurance expansions may shed light on how providers' responses would interact with changes in demand for services to determine the ultimate effect on health care spending. (Studies examining how smaller-scale coverage expansions, which are less likely to raise issues about supply, affect the demand for care by the formerly uninsured are examined in Chapter 3.) One limitation of such analyses, however, is that several factors—including payment mechanisms and rates—may have been changed at the same time, making it difficult to isolate the effects of each element.

One study examined the impact that Medicare's creation had on subsequent hospital admissions and spending in the United States.[188] Before 1965, about 25 percent of seniors had private health insurance coverage that was comparable with Medicare, and seniors accounted for about 10 percent of the total U.S. population; therefore, about 7.5 percent of the population gained extensive coverage because of Medicare. The resulting increase in the use of services by the elderly was found to be consistent with the impact that would be predicted using the findings of the RAND Health Insurance Experiment. Overall, however, the effect on hospital admissions—for the elderly and nonelderly combined—was several times larger than that, and by 1970, Medicare's introduction had led to an increase in hospital admissions of 30 percent to 45 percent. The author attributed that effect to the broader adoption of treatments and methods of providing care (such as those used in dedicated cardiac care units) that also had a dramatic impact on care for the nonelderly.

Those findings suggest that the supply of services can respond rather rapidly to an expansion of insurance coverage. Indeed, the results indicate that the overall effect on the use of services could be much larger than the increase in the use of services for people who had gained coverage under the new program. One factor that may have contributed to that response, however, was the relatively generous payment system that Medicare adopted. Following the common practice of private insurers at the time, Medicare initially paid hospitals on the basis of their incurred costs—an approach that gave hospitals little incentive to control those costs. The increase in hospital spending that resulted from Medicare's creation could well have been smaller under a less generous payment system.

Another example comes from the province of Quebec, which implemented Canada's universal health insurance plan for physicians' services in late 1970. That plan covered all costs for services that doctors provided in their offices, in clinics or hospitals, or during house calls. When researchers compared the use of physicians' services shortly before the change and two years later, they found that the number of office visits (which were covered) rose sharply but that the number of telephone contacts doctors had with patients (which were not reimbursed) declined. Overall, the number of face-to-face contacts in all settings increased modestly.[189]

The study also found that the average hours doctors worked fell by about 15 percent, primarily because of a decline in the average amount of time spent on each office visit. The study did not seek to account for the effects of any changes in physicians' payment rates that came with the adoption of a uniform fee schedule or for the impact on health care spending of the changing mix of doctors' activities. A survey of patients did find that waiting times to schedule an appointment roughly doubled, indicating that the supply of services did not increase as much as patients would have wanted when care became free to them. Moreover, total contacts with patients rose for lower-income families (whose demand for care increased most sharply) but fell for higher- income families—indicating that the overall supply of services was constrained, at least in the short run.

A more recent example comes from Taiwan, which implemented universal health insurance in 1995. One study examined the effects on services used by adults and found that among the one-quarter who were previously uninsured, the number of visits to physicians increased by about 70 percent and the number of hospital admissions more than doubled; use rates for people who had been insured previously were largely unchanged.[190] Another analysis found that the overall rate of hospital admissions in Taiwan grew by about 10 percent between 1994 and 1996.[191] Those figures would suggest that Taiwan's health care system was able to accommodate the increase in demand, but another factor was that payments to physicians working in primary care clinics were raised by about 20 percent. That change helps explain why the number of physicians working in such clinics, which had been increasing by about 5 percent per year, grew by 10 percent in 1995. (Whether those doctors shifted from the hospital sector, which accounted for about 60 percent of physicians' employment, or came from another source is not clear.)

Uncompensated Care and Cost Shifting

Another issue that arises when analyzing providers' payments is whether relatively low payments by public programs or the costs of providing uncompensated care to the uninsured result in higher payment rates for private insurers—a process known as cost shifting. In many cases, uninsured individuals pay much less than the costs of the care they receive, so doctors and hospitals might seek to make up those losses by charging more to private health plans. Similar pressures to raise private payment rates could occur if payments from public programs did not cover the average costs of their patients (which could be termed "undercompensated" care). To the extent that costs are being shifted, proposals that reduced the uninsured population or switched enrollees from public to private insurance plans would have ripple effects on private payment rates and thus on private insurance premiums.

The evidence indicating that private payment rates are higher than public rates—and that they also appear to exceed the costs of treating privately insured patients—is sometimes taken as proof of cost shifting. There are, however, other explanations. In general, a firm that has some monopoly power will be more profitable if it charges different prices to different sets of purchasers that reflect differences in the groups' willingness to pay (a practice known as price discrimination). The fact that hospitals receive different payment rates from public and private insurers may reflect that same behavior. Differences in payment rates across different types of insurers do not, however, mean that costs have been shifted from one type to another. The key question about cost shifting is whether an *increase* in the rates paid on behalf of some patients (including people who used to receive charity care but would now have insurance) would cause a *decline* in the rates paid by others (such as private insurers).

Whether and how such cost shifting would occur depends on several other factors, including the amount of uncompensated care that is provided, the adequacy of public payment rates, and the degree of competition facing hospitals and doctors. Recent estimates (discussed below) indicate that hospitals provided about $35 billion in uncompensated care in 2008, but the available evidence suggests that less than half of those costs—and probably much less—were shifted to private insurers. Estimates of uncompensated care provided by doctors are considerably smaller, and cost shifting does not appear to be a substantial factor affecting payment rates for physicians. Although assessing the adequacy of Medicare's payments to doctors and hospitals is more difficult, MedPAC's analysis indicates that those payments are sufficient to cover the costs of efficient providers in 2008; that finding suggests that Medicare's payments do not generate cost shifting in competitive markets. Medicaid's payment rates for doctors and hospitals probably fall below the costs of treating that program's enrollees, but whether the costs of those shortfalls are shifted is not clear.

The Potential for Cost Shifting

Cost shifting could occur only under certain conditions, so it is useful to review them carefully. There are two basic scenarios: one that involves a provider market with limited competition, and one that involves a competitive provider market.

An extreme example of **limited competition** would be an isolated community that is served by a single hospital. Because of its monopoly power, such a hospital could negotiate payment rates from private insurers that exceed its costs for those patients. In response to a reduction in payments from public insurance programs or an increase in the amount of uncompensated care that it provides, that hospital might be able to secure higher payments from private insurers to offset its losses. In order for such cost shifting to occur, however, the hospital would have to have been charging private insurers less than it could have; that is, the hospital would have to have had monopoly power that it had refrained from using fully.[192]

Whether some hospitals have market power that they have failed to exploit is unclear. One reason that many hospitals might not have fully used their market power is that most of them are nonprofit organizations. As a result, their goals of serving the community and the corresponding makeup of their governing boards may lead them to charge private insurers less than the profit- maximizing price (that is, the price a monopolist would charge).[193] In other respects, however, the behavior of nonprofit and for-profit hospitals can be difficult to distinguish. For example, a recent study by CBO found that nonprofit and for-profit hospitals provided similar amounts of uncompensated care.[194] Whether a hospital's goal is to maximize profits, serve the community, or some combination of the two, the key questions remain: Would hospitals (and other providers) that have market power lower private payment rates if proposals either reduced uncompensated care or raised the payments that providers receive for enrollees in public programs? Or would hospitals still seek to charge private insurers a profit-maximizing price, either as an end in itself or as a means of financing other efforts to serve their community?

Cost shifting could also occur in a **competitive provider market** in order to offset the costs of uncompensated care or to make up for losses that might arise from relatively low public payment rates. Why would they accept those rates in the first place? In general, providers have some operating costs that do not vary with their patient load (fixed costs) and some that do (variable costs). If public payment rates were high enough to cover the variable costs of serving those patients—but contributed little or nothing toward covering providers' fixed costs—it would still be worthwhile for providers to accept those payments, at least in the short run. Providers could try to make up for losses from undercompensated care by charging more to private insurers. If competing providers had roughly comparable burdens of uncompensated and undercompensated care, then those higher private rates could probably be sustained in a competitive market.[195]

Providers facing shortfalls in payments would also have alternatives, however, including the option of reducing their costs. That approach would yield higher paymentto-cost ratios and could reduce the quality of care that patients receive, but it would not raise private payment rates. Indeed, with a lower cost structure, hospitals may reduce their rates for private insurers. By the same token, a decline in uncompensated or undercompensated care might allow providers to offer care of higher quality (at a higher cost), but it might not yield a corresponding reduction in private payment rates and could even cause private rates to increase.

Estimates of Uncompensated Care and the Adequacy of Public Payments

Estimates of how much uncompensated care the uninsured receive vary depending on the data sources used and on how the concept is defined and measured. Analysts generally define uncompensated care as care for which the provider is not paid in full by the patient or a third party.[196] It includes both charity care (for which little or no payment is expected) and bad debt (for cases in which payment is sought but not collected). Studies differ, however, in how they define "full" payment, with some comparing the payments that are received to the list prices that providers post. A more useful comparison, however, is to the total payments that providers would receive for the same service when treating a privately insured patient, because that amount (which is generally much lower than the list price) more closely resembles their costs.

A recent study by Hadley and others, which used that analytic approach, examined a sample of medical claims for uninsured individuals and projected that they would receive about $28 billion in uncompensated care in 2008.[197] That study also examined cost reports from hospitals and a survey of doctors and generated a different estimate: The gross costs of providing uncompensated care would be about $43 billion in 2008, of which $35 billion would come from hospitals and $8 billion from doctors. Total spending on hospital care in 2008 is estimated to be about $750 billion, so those figures would imply that uncompensated care accounts for about 5 percent of hospital revenues, on average. Those findings are consistent with CBO's analysis of uncompensated hospital care (cited above), which found that a sample of for-profit and nonprofit hospitals incurred costs for such care that averaged between 4 percent and 5 percent of their operating revenues.

Another point on which analysts disagree is whether to consider only the gross costs of providing uncompensated care or to net out offsetting payments that providers receive from sources other than insurers. As the Hadley study noted, about half of hospitals' aggregate costs for uncompensated care may be offset by added payments under Medicare and Medicaid to hospitals that treat a disproportionate share of low-income patients.[198] Whether hospitals seek to recoup from private payers the gross costs they incur for providing uncompensated care or their net costs after accounting for those offsetting payments is not clear; the answer depends in part on how well the offsetting payments are targeted toward hospitals that provide uncompensated care.

As for physicians, the figures cited above indicate that they provide a relatively small amount of uncompensated care—representing about 1 percent of the roughly $500 billion spent on physicians' and clinical services in 2008. Another study found that, on net, uncompensated care provided by office-based physicians was close to zero after the higher payments made by some uninsured individuals were taken into account.[199] That study also found that if those offsetting payments were ignored, the gross amount of uncompensated care provided by physicians was about $3 billion per year in the 2004–2005 period. Either way, the uncompensated care that physicians provide seems unlikely to have a substantial effect on private payment rates.

As with estimates of uncompensated care, assessments of the adequacy of payments from Medicare and Medicaid vary depending on the data and the points of comparison that are used. The data from hospitals' cost reports compiled by the American Hospital Association indicate that Medicare's payments covered about 91 percent of costs for those patients in 2006 (whereas private payments were reported to average about 130 percent of the costs of treating those patients).[200] Correspondingly, the AHA estimated a shortfall in Medicare's payments to hospitals of about $19 billion in 2006. As noted above, however, those calculations depend partly on how hospitals' fixed costs are allocated.

MedPAC's most recent analysis indicates that Medicare's payments are sufficient to cover the costs of efficient hospitals. That assessment took into account hospitals' reported losses on Medicare patients, although MedPAC's calculations used a slightly different approach and found a smaller gap between payments and costs (about 5 percent in 2006, compared with AHA's estimate of 9 percent). That analysis also considered other indicators of whether payments were adequate, including beneficiaries' access to care, the volume of services provided to them, and hospitals' plans for expansion (a measure of financial health). Indeed, MedPAC's analysis suggests an alternative explanation: Instead of low Medicare payment rates causing private rates to be higher, high private payment rates at some hospitals may be leading them to relax their efforts to control costs. In turn, that tendency may have pushed up per-patient costs and thus caused payment-tocost ratios for Medicare (and private) patients at those hospitals to be lower than they would be at hospitals that have lower per-patient costs.

As for Medicaid, AHA's analysis of hospitals' cost reports indicates that the program's payments covered about 86 percent of costs, on average, in 2006 (with the added Medicaid payments to hospitals that treat a disproportionate share of low-income patients included in that analysis). That calculation translates into an estimated shortfall in payments of about $11 billion. Medicaid's payment rates appear to be lower than Medicare's, so even if AHA's calculation overstates the shortfall, it seems likely that Medicaid's payment rates fall somewhat below hospitals' average costs for those patients.

Because physician markets are generally competitive, individual doctors or group practices would be able to shift costs to private payers only to the extent that Medicare and Medicaid payments did not cover their costs (which can be difficult to estimate). Even so, MedPAC's conclusion that Medicare's 2008 rates for doctors are adequate indicates that little scope for cost shifting exists in that sector. As for Medicaid, the available evidence indicates that many doctors do not accept Medicaid patients, which implies that those payments, in many cases, fail to cover doctors' costs. The extent to which doctors who accept Medicaid payments are able to shift costs to private payers depends in part on whether their competitors have comparable numbers of Medicaid patients.

Evidence about Cost Shifting

How much cost shifting actually occurs? Differences in public and private payment rates are sometimes taken as proof that costs are being shifted, but those differences reflect several factors, and it is not obvious whether or to what extent private payment rates would change as a result of changes in uncompensated care or public payment rates. Researchers who have attempted to evaluate whether hospitals shift costs to private payers have generally focused not on payment levels but on changes in the prices paid by private insurers following increases or (more commonly) reductions in Medicare or Medicaid fees.

Those studies have produced varied results, depending on the period studied and the methods used. The evidence that some cost shifting had occurred was relatively strong when researchers examined periods of less vigorous competition in the medical marketplace, such as the early 1980s. For example, a 1988 study that examined how hospitals in Illinois responded to cuts in Medicaid payments found that hospitals raised private prices to offset about half of the revenue from Medicaid that had been lost.[201] Other studies from that period suggest that financial pressures led to a limited amount of cost shifting and also encouraged hospitals to adopt cost-containment measures.[202] The early 1980s were conducive to cost shifting because private insurers usually paid hospitals on the basis of their charges and engaged in little price negotiation or selective contracting. In such an environment, it may have been relatively easy for hospitals that faced a revenue shortfall on other patients to raise prices for private insurers.

After the mid-1980s, however, competitive pressures on hospitals intensified as private insurers became more aggressive in negotiating payments and establishing networks of preferred hospitals. Accordingly, the evidence of cost shifting generally became weaker.[203] For example, a study examining data from hospitals in California for the 1993–2001 period indicated that cost shifting in response to a 10 percent reduction in Medicare and Medicaid's fees increased the ratio of private payments to costs by 1.7 percent and 0.4 percent, respectively; that response for Medicare was generally lower than the effect that was estimated by applying a similar analytic approach to data from the 1980s.[204] In fact, one study suggested that cuts in public payment rates prompted hospitals with high numbers of Medicaid patients to *decrease* prices to private payers in an effort to attract more private patients.[205]

Overall, the impact of cost shifting on payment rates and premiums for private insurance seems likely to be relatively small. The available evidence indicates that hospitals shift less than half of the costs of reductions in public payment rates to private insurers—and in all probability, substantially less. Studies have not examined changes in uncompensated care as closely, but it seems reasonable to conclude that those costs are shifted to a comparable degree. Developments since the late 1990s— particularly consolidation of hospitals and pressure on private insurers to broaden their provider networks— appear to have strengthened hospitals' bargaining position, raising the possibility that more cost shifting will occur than was observed in the 1990s. Although payment-to-cost ratios for private insurers rose sharply between 2001 and 2004, it remains unclear whether hospitals have taken full advantage of their strengthened position or still have the degree of untapped market power that is necessary for cost shifting to occur in markets with limited competition.

6. Administrative Issues and Effects on Other Programs

Health care proposals that would substantially affect health insurance markets could have a number of important budgetary effects and other implications—for federal and state agencies as well as certain segments of the population—that are not discussed in the preceding chapters. In particular, the federal cost of such proposals and their impact on coverage rates would depend partly on the magnitude of the administrative costs and responsibilities that the proposals entail and partly on their interactions with other government programs.

Large-scale changes to the health insurance system would probably require the federal government to take on new administrative responsibilities. The extent and nature of those responsibilities, and the associated costs, would depend largely on the scope of a proposal—considerations that would also affect its timeline for implementation. In addition, proposals that established or expanded federally funded subsidies for health insurance might either shift costs from state governments and employers to the federal budget directly or create incentives for states and employers to reduce their current payments in ways that boost federal spending. Maintenance-of-effort requirements, under which states or firms must continue activities that they had performed before a new federal program was created, could discourage state governments and employers from cutting back on programs that provide similar health care benefits. Other types of maintenance-of-effort requirements could seek to recapture some or all of the states' savings resulting from a new federal program, thus reducing the net costs incurred by the federal government. In any case, the impact of such provisions would depend on how effectively they could be monitored and enforced.

The costs of proposals and their effects on coverage rates also depend on how the proposals would treat certain segments of the population and how they would interact with other federal programs. Proposals could affect the receipt of other federal benefits that are not directly related to health care in a number of ways. For example:

- Depending on how they are delivered, new subsidies for health insurance could be counted as income or assets when determining people's eligibility for a program; and
- Changes to the employment-based health insurance system could affect employees' cash wages and thus their eligibility for other federal benefits that are based on those earnings.

For certain segments of the population, such as military service members and veterans, eligibility and payment rules for new subsidies might need to be coordinated with rules under existing government programs. For other segments—in particular, unauthorized immigrants— decisions would need to be made as to whether to deny them federal assistance (as many current programs do). Whether and how proposals sought to include or exclude such populations would affect not only their costs but also their impact on the measured number of uninsured people—both directly and because enforcement provisions could affect enrollment more broadly. Other segments of the population are difficult to reach through existing programs and would present similar challenges to administrators of new subsidy programs or insurance mandates.

Implementation Issues and Timelines

Proposals that would significantly change health insurance markets and health care systems could create new administrative responsibilities for the federal government. How long it would take to implement such proposals— and how effectively they would be carried out—depends on their scope and on the funding that is made available for both start-up and operating costs. In assessing the ability of federal agencies to implement large-scale changes, the Congressional Budget Office would take into account the likelihood that adequate funding would be available. Even with sufficient funds, agencies might need several years to make a substantially new system operational and even more time to fully implement it. Various trade-offs would arise if proposals relied on state governments for implementation.

Administrative Responsibilities and Costs

Federal and state governments share responsibilities for the financing and regulation of health insurance and health care (see Table 6-1). Federal agencies perform tasks such as operating the Medicare program, administering tax provisions covering health care and health insurance, regulating the sale of drugs and medical devices, and overseeing employment-based health plans. Although Medicaid and the State Children's Health Insurance Program are jointly financed by the federal and state governments, state agencies largely administer the programs— determining eligibility and benefit levels and paying providers of health care and insurers. States also license and regulate physicians and health insurers, although many employment-based health plans are exempt from state regulation under terms of the Employee Retirement Income Security Act. (For further discussion of that law, see Box 1-1 on page 6.)

Major proposals affecting health insurance could assign new responsibilities to either an existing or a new agency, and current responsibilities could be shifted between federal and state agencies. Enacting a mandate that required individuals to obtain health insurance or employers to provide it would probably require one or more government agencies to monitor health insurance coverage (as discussed in Chapter 2). Federal and state agencies might also be called on to administer subsidies for health insurance to a broader population than existing programs cover. Proposals to create regional purchasing groups for health insurance might involve interstate collaboration or modify states' ability to regulate insurance markets.

Trade-offs are implicit in either starting a new agency or relying on existing agencies, and they could affect the costs and impact of implementing a health care proposal. A new agency might benefit from a focused mission and dedicated resources but would face the challenge of "starting from scratch." Creating a new agency could also entail substantial start-up costs. Some of those costs could be reduced by shifting employees from existing agencies to the new agency, but the new agency would then face the additional challenge of aligning the disparate responsibilities and corporate cultures of workers from different government offices. Existing agencies have staff members and other resources already in place but might find it difficult to expand their activities to include new tasks. Moreover, existing agencies might require significant investments in infrastructure if new programs differ substantially from their current responsibilities.

The Internal Revenue Service's administration of the health coverage tax credit (HCTC) provides an example of the difficulties inherent in implementing a new program. In managing the HCTC program, which assists workers displaced as a result of international trade, the IRS had to take on activities with which it had little previous experience. Typically, taxpayers claim tax benefits on their annual income tax returns and receive those benefits by having their income tax reduced or receiving a larger tax refund. Under the HCTC program, the IRS has to determine throughout the year whether individuals are eligible for benefits and then pay monthly premiums on their behalf to insurers. The program was enacted in 2002 and served about 45,000 people in 2005 (including workers, their spouses, and their dependents). For fiscal years 2003 and 2004, the IRS received a total of $81 million in administrative funds to start the program. As the agency has developed new systems and gained experience, administrative costs have fallen to about $15 million a year.[206]

CBO's analysis of the administrative costs for government agencies to implement a major initiative would reflect current agency budgets and an assessment of the effort required for the new activities. In 2003, the Centers for Medicare and Medicaid Services operated the Medicare Part A and Part B programs with an administrative budget of about $5 billion, or less than 2 percent of the programs' costs. To put into operation the Medicare drug benefit and carry out the other administrative responsibilities generated by the Medicare Prescription Drug Improvement and Modernization Act of 2003, legislation provided an additional $1.5 billion for CMS and the Social Security Administration in 2004 and 2005. Ongoing administrative costs for the drug benefit are about $900 million per year, or about 2 percent of program costs.

Table 6-1. Current Allocation of Major Administrative Responsibilities for Financing and Regulating Health Care

Agency	Current Responsibilities
	Federal Government
Social Security Administration	Administers enrollment in Medicare; collects premiums for Medicare enrollees.
Centers for Medicare and Medicaid Services	Pays claims under and administers Medicare; oversees Medicaid; issues regulations on payment and coverage.
Internal Revenue Service	Administers the tax code, including tax benefits for health insurance and health care.
Food and Drug Administration	Approves drugs and medical devices; monitors advertising.
Department of Labor	Oversees employment-based benefits, including health insurance, covered by the Employee Retirement Income Security Act.
Office of Personnel Management	Administers the Federal Employees Health Benefits program and the Federal Employees Dental and Vision Insurance Program.
Department of Defense	Provides health care to current and retired members of the armed forces, their family members, and other eligible beneficiaries through the TRICARE program.
Department of Veterans Affairs	Determines eligibility for veterans' health benefits; maintains and operates veterans' hospitals, outpatient clinics, nursing homes, and other facilities.
	State Governments
Medicaid Agencies	Determine eligibility for Medicaid and the State Program and administer payments to providers and insurers under those programs.
State Medical Boards	License physicians to practice medicine in state.
Insurance Departments	Regulate private health insurance (except for employment-based plans that are exempt from state regulation).

Source: Congressional Budget Office.

Implementation Timelines

The time required to implement a proposal would vary greatly depending on its nature and scope, but it seems likely that instituting major changes to the health insurance system would take several years. About two years elapsed between enactment of the Medicare drug benefit in December 2003 and the availability of that new benefit to enrollees in January 2006. Approximately half of that time was spent creating a regulatory framework for the program based on the enacted legislation. That framework involved several stages that are common to the regulatory process: First, policies were developed, with input from the public; next, proposed rulings were issued in the *Federal Register,* followed by a public comment period; and last, final rules were issued, which could take effect up to 60 days after publication in the *Federal Register*.

Once the regulatory framework was established, CMS solicited and reviewed bids from the private insurance plans that would deliver the benefit, provided information about those plans to enrollees, and processed their choice of plans. Even with that amount of lead time, some problems (regarding assignment of enrollees to plans, filling of prescriptions, and collection of premiums) occurred during the initial months after the drug benefit became available.

The schedule for implementing the Massachusetts health care mandate requiring adults to obtain health insurance coverage also provides insight into the time involved in implementing a major proposal. The legislation was enacted in April 2006, and it took about a year for the new private health insurance options mandated by that law to be delineated and become available. (An accompanying expansion of eligibility for Medicaid was accomplished more quickly.) As part of implementing the new program, the state needed to develop a system to report whether individuals have qualified insurance coverage— an important step because those who do not could be subject to financial penalties. (By design, those penalties are being phased in gradually and will be fully implemented in 2009.)

Implementing a health insurance proposal designed at the federal level could pose additional challenges for the states. Depending on the nature of the proposal, tradeoffs could arise between the role given to states and the time it takes to implement the changes involved. In some cases, implementation by each of the 50 states—as well as the District of Columbia and any affected territories— would take longer than action by the federal government. Six state legislatures meet only biennially, limiting their ability to respond quickly to new federal policies if conforming changes in state laws or additional state expenditures are necessary. Moreover, differences among states— in population, geography, or current insurance coverage rates—might generate unanticipated challenges and additional delays. Massachusetts was able to implement its health care mandate quickly because the share of that state's population that was uninsured was relatively low and because officials were motivated to do so. If other states had to implement a similar policy, they might not be able to move as quickly.

One way to ease implementation of a new federal program would be to build on existing state programs. Initial implementation of SCHIP—a program enacted in August 1997—was able to proceed relatively rapidly because it largely built on the existing infrastructure of Medicaid (a program that already served children in low- income families). As a result, about half of the states were able to have an SCHIP program operating within a year. But a few states took more than two years to begin their programs, and even among the states that acted early, a common approach was to pursue a modest coverage expansion first and then take additional steps in later years. (Another reason for taking a gradual approach may have been concern that the authorizing legislation reduced federal funding by 25 percent after four years.) Consequently, several years elapsed before some states were using the full amount of money available to them under the program.

Delegation Issues

A potential challenge in implementing major changes to the health care or health insurance systems is known in political science as the "agency" problem, which can arise when a principal (through legislation, for example) delegates authority to an agent (such as a government agency). The problem occurs if those agencies implement the legislation in a way that does not reflect the drafters' intentions.

Another agency problem can arise when states are given responsibility for spending federal dollars; they have less of an incentive to be fiscally prudent because they are not spending their "own" money. The Medicaid program attempts to limit agency problems by tying federal contributions to state spending and other requirements. Specifically, federal matching payments are structured so that each additional dollar in state spending is reimbursed at an average of 57 cents by the federal government. But experience with Medicaid indicates that the program's funding structure creates opportunities for states to maximize federal spending and minimize state spending. Even federally administered programs such as Medicare are not immune to agency problems—which may arise between federal legislators and program administrators or between federal and local administrators—but federal authorities may have more control over such programs.

Maintenance-of-Effort Requirements

When the federal government creates a new program that could reduce the financial obligations of other payers— particularly states or employers—interest may arise in establishing maintenance-of-effort (MOE) requirements.

New federal programs could substitute federal funds for payments now made by states or employers directly, or they could induce states or employers to scale back their activities in ways that would raise federal costs. As applied to states, maintenance-of-effort provisions, which aim to prevent that type of cost shifting, can be structured in two ways:

- By requiring states to maintain existing programs at historical eligibility or benefit levels, or
- By requiring them to continue spending funds at certain historical or projected levels or return some of their savings to the federal government.

The two approaches have many similarities and, in both cases, the effects on federal spending would depend heavily on how the requirements were defined and how effectively they could be enforced. Two examples of effective MOE provisions are the ones that were included with the enactment of S CHIP and the Medicare drug benefit. Applying similar MOE requirements to the private sector would be difficult, however, unless proposals specified new enforcement mechanisms and sufficient penalties for violations.

Maintaining Eligibility or Benefit Levels

One goal of provisions that require states to maintain existing programs at historical eligibility or benefit levels may be to prevent states from shifting the responsibility for funding to the federal government for populations or benefits that are already covered and partially subsidized by state funds. Another goal may be to guarantee that people who receive a certain level of services or benefits are not made worse off after the transition to a new system.

When the State Children's Health Insurance Program was enacted, certain maintenance-of-effort requirements were imposed. SCHIP was designed to cover uninsured children in families whose income is somewhat higher than the maximum allowed for children under Medicaid. SCHIP also provides a higher federal matching rate, covering about 70 percent of the program's health care costs, on average, compared with 57 percent under Medicaid.[207] The law froze Medicaid income-eligibility levels for children so that states could not reduce those levels, remove children from the Medicaid rolls, and then reenroll those same children under SCHIP in order to receive a greater federal financial contribution. In a large-scale proposal to change the health insurance system, a similar approach could require states to maintain eligibility levels for low- income people under existing programs.

Maintaining State Funding

Maintenance-of-effort provisions could be implemented that would require states to continue spending funds at certain historical or projected levels. That spending could take the form of reimbursements to the federal government. In that way, MOE provisions could seek to capture some or all of the state savings that might result from a new federal program, in effect offsetting the costs of the new program.

The prescription drug benefit under Medicare provides an example of that approach. The Medicare Modernization Act transferred responsibility for covering outpatient drug costs for people eligible for both Medicare and Medicaid (the "dual eligible" population) from Medicaid to Medicare. By itself, that transfer of responsibility would have substantially reduced states' costs for Medicaid. But the law also included an MOE provision that effectively requires states to transfer to Medicare most of the estimated funds that they would have spent on drug benefits in the absence of the new benefit. That provision is referred to as a "clawback" mechanism.

In general, requirements for states to maintain funding levels would need to specify several features in order for their effects to be estimated. First, they would have to specify the categories of spending that would be subject to the MOE provisions and establish the initial spending level that would have to be maintained. The MOE requirement for the Medicare drug benefit was a relatively well-defined target, including virtually all Medicaid spending on outpatient prescription drugs for dual- eligible enrollees.[208] If a new federal program would cover only a portion of enrollees' current Medicaid spending, however, disentangling the funding streams might be more difficult.

Another consideration would be whether and how MOE payments would be adjusted over time to approximate what states' costs would have been in the absence of the new federal program. The initial MOE payment could be indexed in later years to reflect changes over time, such as growth in the population eligible for the program or increases in health care costs. Possible indexes include general price inflation, nominal growth in the economy, or growth in overall health care costs; a faster-growing index would yield larger MOE payments. Even over a decade, the choice of an index could significantly affect the amount of the MOE payments; by CBO's estimates, general price levels (as measured by the consumer price index) are expected to increase by 21 percent between 2009 and 2018, total health expenditures are expected to grow by about 80 percent in nominal terms over that period, and Medicaid's costs will roughly double. What states' costs in the future would actually be in the absence of a new federal program is unknowable, however.

Complying with MOE Requirement

Maintenance-of-effort requirements would be less effective if states are able to take action to minimize their impact. States could minimize such requirements by limiting eligibility or benefit levels for the affected programs or by reducing financing amounts before the requirements could take effect. Lax enforcement of maintenance-of-effort requirements could weaken their effect.

A critical design issue is the date selected to freeze eligibility or benefit levels in existing programs or to establish the initial amount of funding subject to the MOE requirements. If that date fell after the proposal is enacted, states could minimize their costs—and boost federal payments—by scaling back the targeted programs in the interim period. States might even begin to modify programs earlier if they anticipated successful enactment of new subsidies. To limit those possibilities, the S CHIP statute set the date for freezing eligibility levels for Medicaid at a point several months before the law was enacted. Similarly, the Medicare drug benefit program used data from all of 2003 (after its enactment in December of that year) to establish the initial amount of funding subject to the MOE requirements.

Another issue is how the federal government would monitor and enforce the MOE provisions. Monitoring and enforcement would be easier if MOE requirements were applied to existing programs, like SCHIP and Medicaid, with established reporting systems. SCHIP and Medicaid already require federal approval before states can change eligibility levels or program benefits. Similarly, for MOE requirements that recapture state funds, the most effective enforcement mechanisms are those that allow the federal government to recoup any state MOE payments by adjusting downward the amount of funds it would otherwise send to the states to finance the overall program. Under the Medicare drug benefit's MOE provisions, for example, the federal government can recover any unpaid amounts by reducing its reimbursement to states for the remaining costs of Medicaid—costs that are substantially larger than the MOE payments. The issues of monitoring and enforcement become more complex, however, if the existing programs that are subject to MOE requirements lack established reporting and enforcement mechanisms or if new and untested systems have to be created.

The extent to which states take advantage of opportunities to minimize the effect of such obligations appears to be tempered by their concern about the impact on their residents of cutbacks in services and programs. Although states have frequently found ways to reduce their own expenditures while increasing federal Medicaid payments, the means for shifting responsibility for funding were legal at the time states used them—and states have generally complied with laws intended to prevent future occurrences. Furthermore, states have attempted to avoid reductions in eligibility and benefit levels. More than half of Medicaid spending goes to cover populations and services that are not required by federal law, and states have not taken significant action to reduce eligibility or limit benefits even in difficult economic circumstances.

When analyzing any new subsidy proposals, CBO will evaluate the opportunities available to state governments to minimize the impact of MOE provisions without significantly burdening their residents. States would be expected to fully comply with MOE requirements that are similar in design to those contained in the S CHIP and Medicare drug benefit programs, both of which appear to have been enforced effectively. Depending on the extent to which proposals differ from those provisions, CBO would assess the degree to which states would be likely to shift current expenditures to a new program.

Applying MOE Requirements to Employers

Because new federal subsidies for health insurance could replace payments made by employers—or induce employers to reduce contributions for employees' health plans or drop plans entirely—proposals might apply MOE requirements to the private sector.[209] One approach would be to require employers who previously offered health insurance to their employees to maintain prior eligibility rules, benefit amounts, or total contributions. That approach would be similar to the MOE requirements that now apply to state governments. Another approach would be to require employers to increase cash wages by the amounts previously spent on health insurance if their share of those costs declined because of the provision of health insurance from other sources. (In the latter instance, CBO would expect market forces to adjust employees' compensation, in the aggregate, even in the absence of a requirement on employers.)

For several reasons, however, maintenance-of-effort requirements for employers would be more difficult to implement in the private sector than in the public sector. The federal government does not mandate that employers offer health insurance, nor does it specify the level of benefits that must be provided (with certain limited exceptions) or the contribution that employers offering such coverage must make. Although employers deduct their aggregate contributions toward health insurance as a business expense when calculating their tax liabilities, they do not currently report contributions made on behalf of each employee. As a result, no established reporting or enforcement mechanisms exist that would allow the federal government to closely monitor whether employers were maintaining their effort. Separately identifying and monitoring eligibility, benefit levels, and contributions effectively would be an extremely complex undertaking. Furthermore, imposing a requirement on employers would create an incentive for businesses to reorganize or rename themselves in order to avoid the requirement (an option not available to states). Thus, unless proposals specified a significant new administrative structure and added sufficient penalties for violations, CBO would assume that many employers would not fully comply with MOE provisions regarding coverage or benefits.

Effects on Other Federal Programs

Legislative changes to the health insurance system could affect other federal benefits that are unrelated to health insurance, in a number of ways. For example:

- A new subsidy for health insurance premiums could be counted as income or assets for means-tested benefit programs (those that require recipients to have limited resources), thereby affecting eligibility and the amount of benefits received under those programs.
- Modifications to employment-based health insurance could shift compensation from wages to fringe benefits (or vice versa). That change would affect the amount of Social Security benefits as well as benefits under any other government programs for which eligibility or payments are based on a recipient's earned income.

To the extent possible, CBO would consider those interaction effects in its analysis of proposals.

Inclusion of Subsidy Payments in Income or Assets

A number of federal programs would treat tax credits for health insurance or other subsidies as income or assets under current laws and regulations. The programs examined below do not constitute an exhaustive list but rather illustrate how proposals to change the health insurance system might affect their enrollment or benefits.

Supplemental Security Income

The SSI program is a mandatory program, providing cash payments (based on income) to needy individuals who are aged, blind, or disabled. (In mandatory programs, spending levels are not subject to the annual appropriation process.) To be eligible, a person must have income and assets below certain limits. In most states, SSI recipients automatically qualify for Medicaid.

The SSI program defines **income** as any cash or in-kind payment that can be used to meet a person's needs for food or shelter. Needs-based assistance funded by state and local governments and refunds of income taxes are excluded from income. Refundable tax credits—other than the earned income tax credit and the child tax credit—are included in income. Although unspent tax refunds may be included in **assets,** the portion of income tax refunds that is attributable to the earned income tax credit and the child tax credit is excluded from countable assets for nine months following receipt. In addition, a person's living arrangements or use of institutional health care can affect SSI receipt. For example, monthly SSI benefits can be reduced if an individual is in a hospital or nursing home for the entire month and Medicaid pays more than half the bill.

A new program that subsidized enrollees' health insurance through payments to insurers or providers would generally not affect income as defined under SSI eligibility rules because the beneficiary cannot convert those payments (or the medical services received as a result) into food or shelter. But if a new subsidy was structured as a tax credit or other cash payment, it could be considered income or an asset—unless it was specifically excluded. Because SSI recipients have low income, however, they might not benefit from such a tax credit unless it was made refundable.

Supplemental Nutrition Assistance Program

Formerly known as the Food Stamp program, the Supplemental Nutrition Assistance Program provides low-income individuals and households with debit-like cards that can be used to purchase selected groceries. Many recipients of Temporary Assistance for Needy Families or SSI are also eligible for SNAP benefits. Other households must have cash income and assets below specified thresholds to receive those benefits, which decline as income rises. Both cash income and assets are defined broadly for the purpose of determining eligibility. By law, however, nonrecurring payments (such as tax refunds) and certain recurring payments (such as advance payments of the EITC) are excluded from income but are generally counted as assets. EITC payments are also excluded from countable assets for 12 months after receipt.

Whether new subsidies for health insurance would affect eligibility for SNAP benefits would depend, in part, on the subsidies' design. Programs that provided recipients with in-kind benefits—such as free or low-cost medical services—rather than cash would not directly affect SNAP eligibility or benefits. However, SNAP benefits could decline for disabled or elderly beneficiaries, who can deduct medical expenses from income when determining eligibility for nutrition assistance, if their out-of-pocket medical expenses fell as a consequence of new subsidies. In contrast, recurring cash payments (if not considered reimbursements) would generally be counted as cash income and assets unless explicitly excluded from the program's eligibility determination.

Temporary Assistance for Needy Families

Temporary Assistance for Needy Families is a mandatory program that primarily assists low-income households. Unlike SSI and SNAP, however, TANF is administered as a block grant provided by the federal government to the states— which then determine eligibility rules and benefit amounts for their residents. Depending on how each state defined income and assets, a new federal subsidy for health insurance could affect the amount of TANF benefits that people received. But those changes would not affect a state's entitlement to federal funding: Each state would continue to receive the same allotment as specified under federal law. As a result, CBO's cost estimates for new federal subsidies for health insurance would not reflect offsetting savings in the TANF program.

Changes in Workers' Earnings and Income

Employers' payments for health insurance premiums are exempt from income and payroll taxes; similarly, those premium payments are not counted as income to workers when determining eligibility for and the amount of certain transfers (such as Social Security benefits) and tax provisions, including the EITC. Changes to the employment-based health insurance system could affect Social Security benefits or the EITC in two ways. First, proposals that would repeal or limit the current exclusion of employers' contributions for health insurance would also cause those contributions to be counted as income to workers when determining their Social Security benefits or EITC—unless specifically excluded from income solely for those provisions. Second, any proposal that would induce changes in the allocation of workers' compensation between wages and health insurance benefits would affect Social Security benefits or the EITC. Offsetting the effects of such changes would present significant challenges.

Social Security

Unlike the programs discussed earlier, Social Security benefits are not means-tested, but the payments that a person receives are a function of his or her past earnings. To the extent that a proposal had an impact on taxable wages—as would happen if the current tax exclusion for employment-based health insurance was limited or eliminated—that outcome would affect not only payroll tax revenues but also future Social Security benefits.

Changes in the overall composition of compensation for workers could have other effects, both immediate and long lasting, on the benefits paid to all people filing new claims for Social Security benefits. The reason is that the calculation of an individual's initial benefit is based on his or her previous earnings, but all income earned in the years before attaining the age of 60 is indexed to that year according to average wage growth in the economy. As a result, proposals that substantially shifted employers' health insurance payments to cash compensation could increase measured wage growth sharply during the transition period and thus yield higher benefit payments for all new claimants. Proposals could seek to offset that impact by temporarily adjusting the benefit formula, but they would have to rely on an estimate of the impact because it would be difficult, in practice, to determine precisely what wage growth would have been otherwise.

Earned Income Tax Credit

Low-income people may be eligible for the earned income tax credit, which is refundable (that is, paid to them even if they do not have any income tax liability). To be eligible, individuals must have some wage or self-employment income. The amount of the EITC increases initially as earned income rises until it reaches a maximum credit amount; then, the credit declines gradually as income continues to rise. When income reaches a certain threshold—which varies with marital status and family size—the credit falls to zero.

The current exclusion of health insurance premiums from earned income reduces the credit for workers with very low wages (who are in the credit's phase-in range) and increases the credit for workers with somewhat higher income (who are in the phaseout range). Correspondingly, proposals that included employers' contributions for health insurance in earned income or caused workers' compensation to shift from employer- paid health insurance premiums to wages would increase EITC payments for workers in the phase-in range and reduce the credit for those in the phaseout range.

Proposals that reduced or eliminated the exclusion of employer-paid premiums could hold the EITC "harmless" by specifying that those premiums not affect the computation of the credit. Using a different definition of income to compute the EITC, however, would increase the program's complexity; workers, for example, would have to compute income two different ways when completing their tax returns—first to compute their income taxes and then to calculate the EITC.

Offsetting the effects of proposals that changed the composition of compensation in a way that held each worker harmless would be all but impossible, for two reasons. The amount spent by employers on health insurance for each worker is not monitored by the IRS, and there is no way to determine with certainty what workers' earnings otherwise would have been. Even so, an aggregate adjustment could be made to reduce the impact, on average.

Coverage of Certain Populations

Policymakers seeking to expand health care coverage need to decide whether and to what extent to cover certain populations. Those considerations may make the proposals more challenging to administer and may affect their net impact on the federal budget. Some populations, such as members of the military and veterans, receive health insurance or health care from the federal government, so the creation of new subsidy programs or mandates could require additional coordination and could influence the use of those benefits. Other groups, such as prison inmates and unauthorized immigrants, are not eligible for federal assistance for health insurance under current programs. Whether those groups were included or excluded by a proposal would affect its cost and would have an impact on coverage rates. Additional groups, such as the homeless, are difficult to reach through existing programs and would probably present administrative challenges to new efforts to expand coverage.

Military Families and Retirees

Many active-duty members of the military, their families, and military retirees receive health insurance benefits through the Department of Defense. In 2006, about 9 million people were eligible for benefits under DoD's collection of health plans known as TRICARE.[210]

Some TRICARE beneficiaries have access to other insurance, such as private employment-based coverage offered to a working spouse. If beneficiaries choose to use other insurance plans because they prefer the benefit structure of those plans or because access to TRICARE providers is limited in their area, TRICARE becomes the secondary payer to that other insurance. In 2006, about 12 percent of eligible family members of active-duty service members—400,000 people in total—also had other health insurance. The percentage of eligible military retirees under the age of 65 and their families enrolled in other health insurance plans has declined from 49 percent in 2001 to 33 percent in 2006 (for a total of about 1.1 million retirees under age 65 and family members). If legislation caused private employers or other insurers to provide benefits that were less comprehensive or more expensive, reliance on TRICARE could climb; conversely, more affordable or accessible health coverage options from other sources could cause reliance on TRICARE to fall, decreasing the program's discretionary spending requirements.

The TRICARE beneficiary population includes more than 200,000 families and military retirees and their families who are either temporarily or permanently living overseas. Most service members are stationed overseas at least once during their career, although not all family members accompany active-duty members who are deployed overseas. In addition, some military retirees choose to move overseas after retirement. Because Medicare does not cover services provided outside the United States, TRICARE is the primary payer for medical expenses incurred by military retirees over age 65 who are living overseas. Thus, legislation that changed TRICARE coverage in some way might affect TRI CARE beneficiaries living overseas differently than those residing in the United States.

Veterans

Legislative changes to the health care system might also affect beneficiaries of the Veterans Health Administration, which is part of the Department of Veterans Affairs (VA). Those who previously served in the military can apply to receive health care services from the VA. In fiscal year 2007, there were about 23.5 million veterans, 13.5 million of whom were eligible to enroll in the VA health care system. Of those 13.5 million eligible veterans, 7.8 million were enrolled with the VA (2.8 million of those enrollees did not seek care from the VA) and 5.7 million were not enrolled. Almost 80 percent of enrolled veterans report having some other type of health coverage.[211] On average, eligible individuals receive no more than half of their total health care through the VA system, even among the groups that rely on VA care most heavily (such as veterans with severe disabilities incurred while serving).

Veterans who apply for enrollment in the VA are assigned to one of eight priority groups on the basis of their service-connected disabilities, service-related exposures, income, assets, and other factors. Veterans with the most severe disabilities and lowest income and assets are placed in the highest-priority groups, and higher-income veterans without service-connected disabilities are placed in the lowest-priority groups. In an effort to reduce the growth in the VA's medical spending, a freeze on enrollment took effect in January 2003 for veterans assigned to the lowest priority group. About 10 million veterans are ineligible to enroll for the VA's services because of that freeze.

Legislation that provided alternative coverage for low- income people might draw patients away from the VA system. A substantial portion of the VA's enrollees have low income and may be going to the VA for medical services because they have limited access to other sources of care or face higher out-of-pocket costs if they seek care from other providers.

If alternative coverage allowed them to receive affordable medical services from other providers, they might rely less on the VA's care, thus opening up additional capacity for other patients, including those in the lowest-priority group. More generally, increases in the affordability of private health insurance might reduce the use of the VA's services. However, any legislation that required or encouraged veterans to increase their use of the VA's services would place pressure on existing resources unless it included an accompanying increase in appropriations. (Funding for the Veterans Health Administration is discretionary and thus is subject to annual appropriations.)

Populations Served by the Indian Health Service

The Indian Health Service (IHS) program, and the people it serves, might also be affected by proposals to modify the health care system. The IHS offers a broad range of health care services, including primary care, ancillary services (such as diagnostic laboratory and radiology services), specialty services, and inpatient care to an estimated 1.8 million American Indians and Alaska natives—about 55 percent of all American Indians and Alaska natives eligible to receive care in IHS facilities.[212] The IHS provides that care through 48 tribal hospitals and more than 600 primary care clinics. Because of staff shortages, limited facilities, and a capped budget, the IHS rarely provides benefits comparable with complete insurance coverage for the eligible population; as a result, estimates of the uninsured population in the United States do not treat the IHS as a source of insurance. As funds permit, the IHS contracts with outside providers to deliver services not available at its facilities.

Under current law, Medicaid, Medicare, and private insurance plans pay the IHS for services furnished to patients who have coverage under those plans. Approximately 17 percent of the program's total funding is attributable to insurance collections, with payments from Medicaid accounting for about 90 percent of all insurance collections. Proposals that would expand health insurance coverage might increase the funding available to the IHS indirectly through greater insurance recoveries. However, because IHS funding is discretionary, the budgetary effects of those changes would depend on provisions enacted in subsequent appropriation acts.

Children in Foster Care

Under current law, child welfare agencies are responsible for ensuring that children in foster care receive needed health care services. Foster children include those under age 18 living in a foster home, group home, or the home of a relative.

Proposals seeking to expand health care coverage would need to address several issues regarding children in foster care. First, changes in Medicaid's eligibility rules or benefits could significantly affect those children. Child welfare agencies usually ensure that foster children receive health care services by enrolling them in Medicaid. Of the approximately 800,000 children who received foster care services in 2001, more than 600,000 were enrolled in Medicaid.[213]

Second, the treatment of foster children under proposals mandating that parents or guardians obtain health insurance for children could lead to some confusion. Although child welfare agencies are responsible for ensuring that foster children receive needed health care services, children in foster care can be enrolled in the health plan of a birth parent or a foster family. A mandate requiring parents and guardians to provide health insurance could cause confusion among foster parents, birth parents, and state agencies over which party bears responsibility for ensuring that children are covered.

Third, applying a mandatory enrollment requirement for children of a certain age could affect children in foster care who have reached an age—typically, 18—when the state and their foster families are no longer required to give them assistance. In 2005, approximately 25,000 children were in that category. About half of the states have implemented federal options and waivers to extend Medicaid benefits to that population up to age 21.

Incarcerated Adults and Juveniles

Under current law, correctional authorities, including federal officials, are required to provide medical care to adults and juveniles in their custody. In 2006, an estimated 2.3 million adults and juveniles were in prisons, jails, and residential placement facilities. Proposals to expand coverage for health care could continue to make correctional authorities responsible for such care, or they could extend assistance to incarcerated adults and juveniles.[214]

State, local, and tribal governments do not receive federal matching funds under the Medicaid or IHS programs for care or services they provide to incarcerated individuals. Medicare payments made on behalf of beneficiaries in the custody of law enforcement agencies are also prohibited under federal law. Therefore, spending by state, local, and tribal governments for inmates' health care—estimated to total more than $6 billion in 2003—is supported predominantly by state and local funds and, to a lesser extent, by money collected from inmates.[215] At the federal level, the Bureau of Prisons estimates that health care costs to treat its approximately 200,000 inmates totaled about $740 million in fiscal year 2007. Those funds are discretionary and thus subject to annual appropriations.

Foreign-Born Residents

In 2006, roughly 37 million foreign-born individuals, representing about 12 percent of the U.S. population, resided in the United States. That category includes naturalized citizens, legal permanent residents, nonimmigrants (noncitizens who are in the country temporarily), refugees, and unauthorized immigrants. Regardless of their citizenship status, foreign-born residents are generally included in the counts of the insured and uninsured in the United States. For that reason, the treatment of foreign-born residents affects the impact that a health care proposal would have on overall rates of coverage. In particular, studies indicate that of the roughly 12 million unauthorized immigrants in this country, about half have health insurance and half are uninsured—so those 6 million uninsured people would account for more than 10 percent of the uninsured population.[216]

Under current law, naturalized citizens (about one-third of foreign-born residents) are eligible for federal health insurance benefits on the same terms as native-born citizens. However, for many of the remaining two-thirds of foreign-born residents, Medicare and Medicaid rules restrict eligibility.[217] For example, legal permanent residents who entered the country after August 1996 are not eligible to receive most services under Medicaid until they have resided in the United States for five years; similar restrictions apply to Part B of Medicare. Except for emergency care and immediate services for childbirth—which must be provided under federal law—nonimmigrants and unauthorized immigrants are generally prohibited from receiving federally funded services.[218] In contrast, some state and local governments provide additional services to noncitizens regardless of their immigration status.[219]

Depending on how applicants are required to demonstrate citizenship status, proposals that restrict immigrants' access to health insurance benefits could also affect receipt of benefits by U.S. citizens. Until July 2006, applicants for Medicaid were required to declare, under penalty of perjury, that they met the citizenship or immigration requirements to be eligible for coverage. Under the Deficit Reduction Act of 2005, however, individuals who apply for Medicaid and claim to be U.S. citizens are required to provide certain documents (such as a birth certificate or passport) to prove their citizenship. Following implementation of the new requirements, some states have reported a drop in enrollment, which appears to be concentrated among U.S. citizens who were unable to provide the requisite documentation. CBO has estimated that if states could, instead, verify an individual's name and Social Security number with the Social Security Administration, enrollment in Medicaid would initially increase by 500,000 and then grow by an additional 200,000 in subsequent years.[220]

Residents of U.S. Territories

The unique nature of the laws or economies of the five U.S. territories—Puerto Rico, American Samoa, Guam, the Commonwealth of the Northern Mariana Islands, and the U.S. Virgin Islands—raises several issues under proposals to expand health insurance coverage. Although residents of the U.S. territories are generally not included in counts of the insured and uninsured, the manner in which proposals treat them would have implications for federal spending and overall coverage rates.

One important distinction is that the roughly 4 million residents of the five territories generally do not pay federal income taxes, even though they are U.S. citizens. Instead, each territory has its own individual income tax. Therefore, proposals that sought to encourage participation in a health plan by imposing a federal tax penalty for noncompliance with a mandate or by offering a federal tax credit to offset the costs of insurance premiums would have an impact on territorial residents only to the extent that the territory's tax code "mirrored" the federal tax code. The U.S. territories with such mirrored provisions in their tax codes are Guam, the Commonwealth of the Northern Mariana Islands, and the U.S. Virgin Islands, which, in total, represent about 10 percent of the population in the five territories.

Individuals in the U.S. territories also are less likely to be insured by their employer than the population in the 50 states. In addition, individuals living in the territories face challenges in accessing health care services that are similar to those faced by residents of rural areas within the United States, including limited access to health care facilities and a shortage of primary care practitioners and other health care providers. Proposals that provided a subsidy for health insurance might therefore have a limited impact in the territories if the infrastructure and staffing of health care services remained at current levels.

Proposals that modified or expanded the Medicaid and SCHIP programs also would have a limited impact on the U.S. territories unless the proposals were specifically structured to apply to the territories. Although the territories participate in those programs, they operate them under rules different from those that are applied to the 50 states and the District of Columbia. For example, territories are not required to cover the same eligibility groups, and they are permitted to use different financial standards (regarding income and assets) in determining eligibility. The U.S. territories are also subject to overall spending caps for both programs and must provide matching funds up to the cap and pay all costs above the cap.

Individuals in Households Headed by an Unmarried Couple

In the United States, approximately 5.5 million households are headed by unmarried couples (including both opposite-sex and same-sex couples). More than 2.2 million of those households have children less than 18 years of age living with them. Many unmarried couples purchase multiple health insurance policies to cover household members, possibly in response to current tax laws. Under current law, an individual whose employer provides benefits for domestic partners generally would not be entitled to the same tax exclusion as his or her married coworker. Thus, any premiums paid by an employer on behalf of a domestic partner would be subject to income and payroll taxes.[221] Those considerations could affect the design of a proposal to expand health insurance coverage.

Homeless People

People who are homeless are more likely to suffer from mental illness, substance abuse, and other illnesses and disabilities. The homeless population has been estimated at approximately 670,000 on a given night and 1.6 million over the course of a year (in 2007). Most homeless people are uninsured and face financial and other barriers to obtaining health care services.[222] As many as 30 percent of the homeless receive Medicaid; although the remainder are poor, many do not qualify because they are not aged, disabled, or the caregivers of minor children. Others may be eligible but do not enroll in Medicaid—in some cases, because they are unaware of the program, lack documentation to confirm eligibility, or submit incomplete applications (some applications by the homeless may leave the address or phone number blank, even though Medicaid agencies allow applicants to designate a third party as a mailing address).

Homeless people who are not enrolled in Medicaid generally obtain care from "safety net" providers, such as federally funded health centers, local health departments, and public hospitals. The Health Care for the Homeless program, which is part of the federal health centers program, is specifically designed to deliver primary care and other services to the homeless. In 2007, 200 organizations received federal grants under the Health Care for the Homeless program and served approximately 700,000 patients.[223] No national estimates are available on the number of homeless people who use other types of health care providers or the services they receive.

Proposals that extended health insurance coverage to the homeless population could increase the funding available to safety net providers (through the greater insurance payments they would receive) and could also give homeless people the means to enroll in a private plan. Enrolling homeless people in an insurance plan would present administrative challenges, however, because many of them would probably lack the necessary documentation to verify their citizenship or their eligibility for subsidies.

Individuals Refusing Coverage for Religious Reasons

A segment of the population refuses medical treatment because of their religious faith. For example, the Church of Christ, Scientist, teaches that medical problems should be treated through prayer rather than through traditional medical care. Isolated cases have been reported in the media in which members of other churches, as well as people who are not affiliated with an organized religion, rely on prayer rather than medical treatment or do not consider it appropriate to purchase health insurance. A proposal that sought to achieve universal coverage would need to specify whether people who refuse medical treatment or insurance coverage for religious reasons would be excluded from the system (and whether that exclusion would apply only to adults or whether parents would have the right to exclude their children).

7. CHANGES IN HEALTH HABITS AND MEDICAL PRACTICES

Some proposals to modify the health insurance system would include provisions designed to change the behavior of individuals and medical providers. Certain provisions could:

- Encourage individuals to adopt healthier lifestyles or to get recommended vaccinations and screening tests.
- Induce changes in the ways that medical providers treat patients and diseases—with the goal of improving that care—by expanding the role of primary care physicians (as part of a "medical home" concept in which care is coordinated across settings); implementing programs to help manage care for chronic diseases; funding research on the comparative effectiveness of different treatment options; and making investments in health information technology.
- Focus on the ways in which patients and medical providers settle disputes about treatment, by modifying the system that determines liability for medical malpractice.

Each of those initiatives could improve people's health or the quality of care that they receive. For example, vaccines can prevent the spread of diseases, screening tests may be able to detect illnesses at an earlier and more treatable stage, and improvements in care coordination could ensure that treatments follow evidence-based guidelines and that patients avoid unnecessary or duplicative tests. A question that often arises is whether those initiatives would also reduce health care spending—and thus whether they would affect the budgetary costs of a broader proposal aimed at expanding health insurance coverage. A related question is whether initiatives that reduce certain types of health care spending can yield sufficient savings to offset the costs of the initiatives themselves.

Although such initiatives would, in many cases, result in better health, it is less clear that they would reduce total spending for health care. Many studies that have examined the impact of such initiatives do not indicate net savings, for several reasons. In some cases, the challenge is largely one of identifying and targeting those people whose participation in a health care initiative would result in net savings. Broad programs aimed at preventive medical care and disease management could reduce the need for expensive care for a portion of the population, but they could also provide additional services, and incur added costs, for individuals who would not have needed costly treatments anyway. In order to generate net reductions in spending, the savings such interventions generate for people who would have otherwise needed expensive care must therefore exceed the costs of vaccinating, screening, or coordinating care for much larger populations.

A related issue is that many individuals or health plans might already be taking the steps involved (or will do so in the future) even in the absence of a new requirement or incentive (such as a subsidy). The effect of any proposal would have to be measured against that trend, and a large share of any subsidies involved could simply go to people or plans who will take those steps without new requirements or incentives (sometimes referred to as "buying out the base"). Some doctors and hospitals have already adopted electronic medical recordkeeping, for example, and more will do so in the future under current law—so any subsidy payments those providers might receive under a proposal would add to its costs but would not affect its impact.

In other cases, doctors and patients may not have sufficient incentives to change their use of health care services. Even though research may indicate that a given treatment is no better clinically than a less expensive alternative—or that the incremental benefits of the more expensive treatment do not warrant its added costs—health care practitioners may continue to provide the more expensive treatment if the payments they receive or the share of costs paid by patients are not adjusted to reflect those findings. Similarly, proposals to establish "medical homes" may have little impact on spending if the primary care providers who would coordinate care do not receive financial incentives to limit their patients' use of specialists.

Other initiatives that would yield health benefits might not generate substantial savings—at least, not in the near term. Taxes on tobacco or junk food have been shown to be effective at reducing smoking and obesity (particularly among young people). However, the effects of such initiatives—particularly those that seek to prevent the onset of unhealthy behavior in childhood—on health care spending would probably take years to materialize. In the long term, spending on diseases caused by that unhealthy behavior could decline substantially, but the impact on federal costs would also have to account for people living longer and receiving Social Security and Medicare benefits for more years. Similar issues are raised by other initiatives (such as investments in health information technology) that might require substantial start-up costs; those costs can be difficult to recapture over the typical five- and ten-year budgetary time frames used to evaluate legislative proposals.

Demonstrating savings might also be difficult because of data limitations and other methodological concerns. Although analysis by the Congressional Budget Office found some evidence of links between tort limitations for medical malpractice cases and health care spending, the results are inconsistent and depend on the particular relationships and specifications tested. One reason for the mixed results may be the difficulty of disentangling the effect of certain changes to the medical malpractice system from other factors affecting medical costs. In other cases, studies that report savings may have methodological problems that raise questions about their results or whether those findings can be applied to broader populations. For example, many studies of disease management programs lack comparable treatment and control groups, making it difficult to determine whether the results reflect the impact of the programs themselves or differences between the patients who participated and the ones who did not.

Modifying Health Habits

Many people behave in ways that increase their risk for disease, disabilities, and death. They may smoke, consume too much alcohol, overeat, or drive without wearing a seat belt. Modifying those habits or replacing them with other, better habits (such as exercising and following a nutritious diet) could improve their health and extend their life span. Some researchers and policymakers have suggested that reducing the prevalence of risky behavior—through public awareness campaigns, financial incentives, or regulations—could also help restrain the growth in health care spending.

Achieving substantial savings in health care spending or federal outlays from such initiatives, however, presents several challenges. First, behavior modification may take years of costly intervention and a combination of approaches to succeed. Second, even if initiatives change people's behavior, the resulting health benefits may take a long time to emerge—so the immediate impact on health spending may be limited. Third, the long-term savings on health care from reductions in the incidence of illnesses and disabilities may be substantial, but any savings to the federal government could be at least partially offset by additional expenditures as healthier individuals live longer; for example, Medicare costs could rise for the treatment of other diseases and conditions during those extra years of life, and expenditures for programs that are not directly related to health (such as Social Security) could also increase as life spans are extended.

Trends in Obesity and Smoking

Among the health habits that are associated with higher morbidity and mortality in the United States, smoking and obesity are the most prevalent.[224] Each is also associated with higher-than-average use of health care services. In a 2008 report, CBO found that health care spending per person among the obese was 34 percent higher than spending by otherwise similar individuals of normal weight.[225] Among those with especially high rates of obesity (who are classified as "morbidly obese"), health care spending was 70 percent higher.[226] Another study found that average health care spending per person was 21 percent higher among current or past smokers than among people with similar characteristics who never smoked.[227]

Recent trends in obesity and smoking reveal the challenges and opportunities that policymakers will face if they mount new efforts to reduce the prevalence of poor health habits. Obesity rates among adults have more than doubled over the past 40 years (see Figure 7-1).[228] In addition, the share of children ages 6 to 11 who are overweight has quadrupled, climbing from about 4 percent to approximately 19 percent.[229] Overweight children have an increased likelihood of becoming obese as adults, and they are at risk for health conditions that were once considered exclusively adult illnesses, such as Type 2 diabetes, high blood pressure, and high cholesterol.[230] Conversely, smoking rates have fallen by roughly half over the past 40 years, at least partly as a result of policy initiatives. Even so, approximately one-fifth of adults and one-quarter of high school students continue to smoke.

Those trends could have far-reaching implications. Although average life expectancy has been steadily increasing in the United States over the past several decades, there has been a growing disparity in life expectancy between individuals with high and low income and those with more and less education.[231] Smoking, obesity, and unhealthy lifestyles may contribute to that disparity. One study estimates that differential trends in smoking- related diseases explain at least 20 percent of the increasing gap in life expectancy between groups with different levels of education.[232] The nationwide increase in obesity began among the less educated and could now explain part of the widening socioeconomic gap in mortality rates.[233]

Evidence about the Effects of Policies on Health Habits

Proposals to modify the health care system might seek to encourage healthier lifestyles through public awareness campaigns, financial incentives, or regulations. Much of the evidence about the impact of different approaches for changing people's behavior comes from policies that the U.S. government adopted to discourage tobacco use. Although single approaches might work for some people, reductions in tobacco use were most likely a result of the combined impact of various interventions.[234] Similar conclusions could be reached about strategies to prevent or reduce obesity. The timing and targeting of the initiatives—in particular, whether they are aimed at adults or children—could also play a role in determining their impact.

Information Campaigns

Some proposals would try to modify people's behavior by providing them with more information about the risks of that behavior. Examples of that approach include requirements to place warnings on products known to have adverse effects on health or mandates for restaurants to provide caloric and nutrition content for entrees on menus. Other proposals would restrict advertising and other promotions of products associated with behavior that increases health risks.

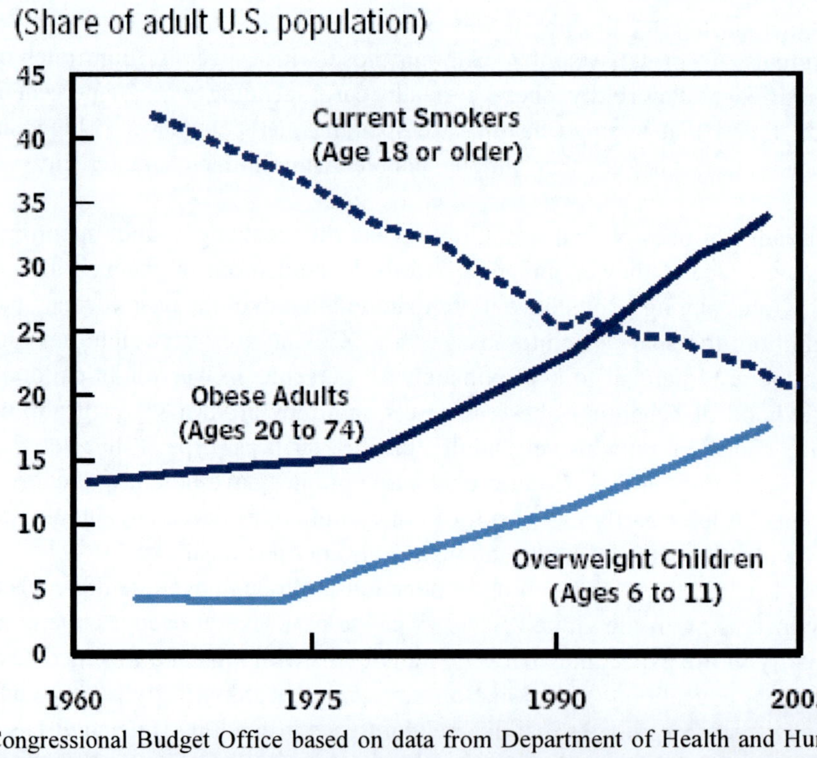

Source: Congressional Budget Office based on data from Department of Health and Human Services, National Center for Health Statistics, *Health, United States, 2007* (Hyattsville, Md., 2007).

Note: Estimates of the prevalence of smoking and obesity are adjusted for age. Estimates of obesity and overweight children reflect multiyear averages.

Figure 7-1. Trends in Smoking and Obesity

Perhaps the most prominent example of an information campaign involved smoking. The public release of the Surgeon General's report on smoking in 1964 drew much attention to the causal relationship between smoking and lung cancer, as well as possible links between smoking and other diseases (including emphysema and cardiovascular diseases). As a result of that report, the government implemented policies to limit tobacco advertising on television and radio and require warning labels on cigarette packages. Those policies appear to have measurably affected the population's beliefs about the risks associated with smoking.

The evidence is mixed, however, regarding the degree to which individuals change their behavior in response to the dissemination of information about health risks. A 2007 study found that individuals' beliefs regarding the health risks associated with tobacco affect their decisions to begin or quit smoking; in fact, smokers appear to *over-estimate*, rather than underestimate, the health and mortality risks from smoking.[235] Another study conducted in the early 1990s, however, found that a comprehensive community-based information campaign had no measurable impact on the overall prevalence of smoking or the share of heavy smokers who quit smoking.[236] Additional research from social psychology and behavioral economics on social norms—which generally finds that people's actions are based in part on their perceptions of how others might behave in similar circumstances—may provide insight into designing more effective information campaigns.

Financial Incentives

Some proposals would penalize people for behavior that is associated with health risks or reward people who adopt healthier lifestyles. Excise taxes imposed by the federal government (and many states as well) on tobacco and alcohol products could be increased, for example, or new taxes could be applied to items linked to potential health problems (such as sugar-sweetened beverages). Alternatively, eligibility for subsidies—through tax benefits or other means—could be expanded to include the costs of counseling and pharmaceutical therapies for smoking cessation or other clinical interventions that promote healthy behavior.[237]

Significant evidence shows that cigarette taxes reduce smoking. Studies have found that a 10 percent increase in the price of cigarettes decreases consumption among adults by between 4 percent and 6 percent (the effect may be larger for teenagers). Other studies have found that significant increases in taxes on unhealthy foods can diminish the consumption of those foods, lessen the prevalence of obesity, and reduce mortality rates.[238] Studies have also found that counseling and clinical interventions —including those with financial incentives—can be somewhat effective in changing people's behavior in the short term.[239] Most studies, however, do not show sustained changes in behavior, either because they do not test for it or because the interventions are not effective over longer periods.

Regulation

Some proposals would expand the regulatory functions of the government to restrict access to unhealthy products or to expand the availability of counseling or other clinical interventions aimed at encouraging healthy behavior. The federal government, for example, requires that schools serve meals that meet nutrition guidelines in return for receiving lunch subsidies. At the state and local level, governments have banned the sales of soft drinks in schools and the use of trans fats in restaurants and bakeries. Research shows that bans on smoking in the workplace are effective. A study from the 1990s found that such bans decrease smoking prevalence by 5 percentage points and average daily consumption of cigarettes by 10 percent.[240] As part of a broader legislative package, proposals that required health insurers to provide mandated benefits might also include clinical counseling and pharmaceutical therapies among those benefits.

Research from the field of behavioral economics may offer new insights about how to develop more effective regulatory strategies to reduce obesity. A recent review of the literature on behavioral economics and social psychology concluded that findings from those fields could help policymakers and analysts better understand how people make food choices.[241] For example, making healthy foods the default option in federal nutrition programs would, according to the study's authors, raise the perceived value of those foods. Many people have problems of self- control when choosing food, possibly because they shop for food when they are hungry or they place great value on immediate gratification. Allowing people to make food choices in advance—by letting students preselect menu options in the federal nutrition programs, for instance, or giving recipients of the Supplemental Nutrition Assistance Program (SNAP, formerly known as the Food Stamp program) the option to preorder groceries by telephone—might spur them to make healthier choices. Also, paying SNAP benefits more often than once a month might prevent food hoarding and bingeing among recipients who place a greater value on consumption today than on deferred gratification. The authors did not estimate the potential savings for those interventions and concluded that more research is needed to evaluate the costs and benefits of those types of strategies for reducing obesity.

Timing and Targeting of Interventions

Another factor that may affect the success of proposals to change people's health habits is the timing and targeting of interventions. Some experts suggest that policies that focus on preventing the onset of risky behavior might offer greater gains than those that attempt to change long-established habits. One justification for a focus on early intervention is the possibility that certain critical developmental stages during childhood play a disproportionate role in determining whether people become obese later in life.[242] Another justification for focusing on prevention is the relative lack of success with weight loss interventions among adults. Few successful interventions have been found for a general population over an extended time despite significant commercial investment in those weight loss programs.[243] Most participants in weight loss programs either quit the program or regain the weight afterward. At the same time—and notwithstanding the arguments for earlier intervention—research on attempts to reduce obesity among children generally has not produced promising results either.[244]

Impact of Proposals on Health Care Spending

The impact that proposals to modify people's behavior would have on health care spending depends on several factors in addition to their effects on health habits. Even if the proposals were effective in causing people to adopt healthier lifestyles, the effects on health and spending might not materialize for many years. Furthermore, proposals that focus on changing people's behavior might have a limited effect on their health. Although individuals who discontinued harmful habits would generally become healthier, they would probably not be as healthy as people who had never engaged in that behavior. In addition, proposals that seek to prevent the onset of unhealthy behavior in childhood, while having the greatest potential impact on health over the long term, would be very unlikely to have a substantial effect on health care spending over the five- and ten-year time frames typically used in budgetary analysis.

To the extent that the proposals successfully reduced risky behavior, however, long-term savings might be offset by other expenditures or budgetary effects. Reductions in smoking would decrease federal and state revenues from excise taxes on cigarettes, for instance. Many of the approaches to altering behavior—such as offering financial rewards to people who undergo weight loss or smoking cessation counseling—would have short-term direct costs that must be balanced against any savings from future health improvements. Behavioral interventions that are successful in improving health may extend people's life span and the quality of their life, but that impact could cause federal expenditures for retirement benefits and Medicare to increase in the longer term.

Notwithstanding those important caveats, CBO would consider persuasive evidence of budgetary savings in analyzing the effects of various proposals. For example, CBO has estimated that proposed regulation of tobacco products by the Food and Drug Administration would lessen the number of women on Medicaid who smoke during pregnancy; in turn, that outcome would yield modest program savings from reduced complications during pregnancy and a smaller likelihood of having babies with low birth weights. (Children with low birth weights have higher medical costs, particularly at birth, but also later in life.) The substantial difference in health care spending for obese and normal-weight individuals also suggests a potential for savings; the primary challenge appears to be identifying strategies that can effectively reduce rates of obesity.

Expanding the Use of Clinical Preventive Services

Clinical preventive services are delivered to patients in a medical setting—that is, by a doctor or other health care practitioner. Those services include immunizations and other interventions that prevent diseases from arising (known as primary prevention) and screening tests that can determine the presence of a disease before symptoms appear (known as secondary prevention).[245]

To the extent that clinical preventive services avert diseases or lead to their early treatment, they have the potential to reduce health care costs as well as improve the quality and length of patients' lives. For that reason, some proposals would seek to expand the federal government's role in encouraging the use of preventive services. However, the impact of specific preventive services on health care spending varies, depending on the disease being targeted and the population that receives the service. A preventive service can be clinically effective (that is, improve health) and cost-effective (meaning that the costs of the service are low relative to its health benefits) but not result in net savings to the health care system.[246] Targeting clinical preventive services to people who would benefit from them the most would increase the chances of obtaining long-term net savings, but—for many preventive services—more research is needed to evaluate who in the population would be best served by such treatments.

Coverage and Use of Preventive Services

Federal and state governments use a combination of subsidies, mandates, and outreach campaigns to encourage the use of certain preventive services. When the Medicare program was implemented in the 1960s, it did not include coverage for preventive services, but coverage has since been added for a number of specific services, such as cholesterol screenings, mammograms, and colonoscopies. For most children enrolled in the Medicaid program, the federal government requires that preventive services be covered through the Early and Periodic Screening, Diagnostic, and Treatment program. In addition, the Vaccines for Children program provides free vaccines to doctors for children who are uninsured, underinsured, or eligible for Medicaid.

Many states also require private health insurance plans to cover certain preventive services. In 2008, all states except Utah mandated coverage for breast cancer screening, and more than half required coverage for cervical cancer screening. Although private health insurance coverage provided by large employers is generally exempt from state mandates, most private insurers appear to cover immunizations and various screening tests, and almost all plans that require enrollees to pay a deductible exclude at least some preventive services from it.[247]

The share of the population that receives recommended preventive services varies widely, depending on the preventive service and the age group. In general, adherence to the recommended guidelines for childhood vaccinations is quite high—in 2006, the percentage of children between 19 and 35 months old who had received the recommended schedule of vaccinations was close to or above 90 percent. The share of adults receiving recommended vaccinations and screenings is much lower. For example, mammography is recommended every one to two years for all older women and is covered by Medicare without being subject to the normal deductible. According to claims data, however, only about half of the women enrolled in Medicare actually received a screening mammography in 2004 or 2005.[248] Similarly, an influenza vaccination is recommended each flu season for all older individuals, but fewer than half of Medicare beneficiaries had a claim submitted for an influenza vaccination in 2006.

The effects on health care spending of proposals to subsidize or mandate coverage of preventive services would depend, in part, on whether the initiatives successfully encouraged the targeted population to use those services. Because many preventive services are already covered by both private and public health insurance, the impact of any proposal on whether an insurance plan includes a preventive service in its benefit package would tend to be modest. Moreover, providing coverage for preventive services (even at a relatively low cost to enrollees) does not ensure that those services will be used. Research in behavioral economics and the role of default options could yield new approaches to encourage greater use of clinically beneficial and cost-effective preventive services.

Effects of Preventive Services on Health Care Spending

The net effect of preventive services on health care spending depends on several factors, in addition to whether people use such services. On the one hand, preventive services can lessen or eliminate the costs of treating a disease by lowering the incidence of the disease or detecting it in its initial stages. On the other hand, savings from preventive services would be offset by certain costs, which could more than offset the savings from prevention or early detection. Those costs include:

- The *direct cost* of the preventive service;
- The cost of treating any *adverse reactions* to the preventive service;
- The cost of *follow-up testing and treatment* for patients with positive screening tests; and
- The cost of treating unrelated diseases that occur because of an individual's *extended life span*.

If preventive services are clinically beneficial and extend an individual's life span, they could also increase federal spending on Medicare (for the treatment of other diseases and conditions during those extra years of life) as well as the costs of programs that are not directly related to health (such as Social Security).

Certain types of preventive services have been found to yield substantial net savings, largely because the initial costs are low and the long-term benefits are large. For example, physicians can quickly explain the benefits and harm of daily aspirin use for the prevention of cardiovascular events for middle-aged patients; the costs of that type of intervention are low, and the long-term health care savings are comparatively large. Similarly, medical providers can immunize children against a variety of potentially life-threatening and costly diseases in a single office visit.[249]

For many other types of preventive services, however, the net impact on spending for health care is less certain. The influenza vaccine provides one example of a preventive service with an uncertain impact on spending. The costs of respiratory disease among the elderly are high, the direct cost of the vaccine is modest (Medicare pays physicians roughly $25 to $40 per vaccination), and serious adverse reactions are very rare. Because the vaccine reduces the incidence of influenza and related respiratory diseases, it lowers the costs of treating them. The vaccine also lessens the risk that recipients will transmit the disease to others, a concern not only for influenza but also for other communicable diseases. Those considerations have led the Advisory Committee on Immunization Practices (a panel of experts established by the federal Department of Health and Human Services, or HHS) to recommend annual influenza vaccinations for certain segments of the population, including adults age 50 or older.

That recommendation primarily reflects the efficacy of the vaccine; however, the evidence regarding its impact on health spending is mixed. Although some studies found that the costs of providing influenza vaccinations for the elderly were more than offset by savings from avoiding illnesses, those studies typically lacked comparable treatment and control groups, making it difficult to determine whether the results reflect the impact of the vaccine itself or differences between the patients who were vaccinated and the ones who were not.[250] A 2006 study, guided by the National Commission on Prevention Priorities, concluded that the influenza vaccination for older adults—although highly cost-effective—does not reduce net health care spending.[251] Viewed from a broader perspective, achieving near-universal vaccination for influenza among the elderly could improve the length and quality of people's lives but nevertheless, on net, increase federal spending over the long term. Because the influenza vaccine appears to reduce mortality among the elderly, it increases both Medicare's costs and Social Security spending. Those additional costs could—if sufficiently large—more than offset the substantial savings from reduced treatment of influenza and related conditions within conventional budgetary time frames.

The prostate specific antigen (PSA) test for prostate cancer illustrates the potential for preventive services to have some adverse effects, both clinically and economically. The direct cost of a PSA blood test is modest. The bulk of the costs associated with PSA testing arise from the follow-up testing and treatment provided to patients with a positive result (that is, one that indicates possible cancer). More than 10 percent of previously unscreened men in their sixties who receive the PSA test have a positive result that would generally result in a recommendation for a follow-up biopsy. Among patients who receive follow-up biopsies, about 70 percent do not have prostate cancer—indicating that the PSA test generates many "false positive" results. Moreover, only a small minority of patients have a malignant condition that, if left untreated, would progress to the point of causing clinically significant symptoms. Therefore, researchers have expressed concern that prostate cancer is being "over-diagnosed" and that the aggressive treatment of prostate cancer can significantly reduce a patient's quality of life. In response to such concerns, the U.S. Preventive Services Task Force (another HHS panel) recently recommended that doctors stop screening men ages 75 and older for prostate cancer.

More generally, the challenge that arises in obtaining savings from the use of preventive care is that vaccinations and screening tests are typically given to a large number of people—only a fraction of whom would have the disease in question otherwise. Furthermore, the savings for that subgroup have to be large enough to offset the overall costs of the preventive services. To assess the extent of those competing considerations, researchers affiliated with the Tufts Medical Center recently reviewed hundreds of clinical studies on the health and economic effects of preventive services.[252] (The studies did not encompass all services, just those that had been rigorously evaluated.) The researchers found that only about 20 percent of the preventive services that had been assessed yielded savings. (For about 3 percent of the preventive services studied, the findings indicated that the intervention worsened health and increased costs. The remainder improved health but caused net spending to rise.)

In many other cases, the clinical and economic implications of preventive services are not well understood. The U.S. Preventive Services Task Force publishes recommendations based on its reviews of clinical evidence. In its 2006 guide, the task force neither recommended for or against approximately 40 percent of the preventive services it reviewed, because of a lack of clinical evidence. The federal government could expand the clinical evidence base and resolve at least some of those areas of uncertainty by funding and setting priorities for clinical research. Even if that happened, however, the impact on health costs would be highly uncertain and would depend on whether research findings tended to support the use of preventive services that would also result in an increase in total health spending or those that would decrease such spending.

Establishing a "Medical Home"

The concept of establishing a "medical home" has been promoted as a means to improve the coordination and quality of medical care and to give patients greater access to care. According to its proponents, medical homes would give patients ready access to a primary care provider who coordinates services across settings (specialists' offices, hospitals, and laboratories) and across types of care (acute, chronic, and preventive). The American Academy of Family Physicians describes the medical home concept as follows:

> At its core [the medical home] is an ongoing partnership between each person and a specially trained primary care physician. This new model provides modern conveniences, like e-mail communication and same-day appointments; quality ratings and pricing information; and secure online tools to help consumers manage their health information, review the latest medical findings and make informed decisions. Consumers receive reminders about necessary appointments and screenings, as well as other support to help them and their families manage chronic conditions such as diabetes or heart disease. The primary care physician helps each person assemble a team when he or she needs specialists and other health care providers such as nutritionists and physical trainers.[253]

The concept of a medical home combines several elements that would involve changes in current medical practice, including greater use of health information technology, disease management tools, and preventive services (all of which are discussed in this chapter). It also relies on an adequate supply of primary care physicians. (See Chapter 5 for further discussion of issues relating to the supply of physicians.) But the medical home concept has several elements that are not discussed elsewhere in this chapter:

- Assignment of patients to a primary care provider who may play a "gatekeeper" role (authorizing and managing referrals to specialists);
- Options to contact a primary care provider through means other than office visits (by e-mail or telephone, for instance); and
- Access to a primary care provider or a trained triage nurse outside of normal office hours.

Improving coordination in health care could provide patients with better care and might reduce their anxiety and confusion as they seek assistance from a broad assortment of medical professionals. Some proponents also believe that improvements in coordination would yield health care savings, and they have suggested that the federal government encourage more health plans to adopt medical homes (by requiring that subsidies for health insurance be used for plans that provide a medical home, for example, or by making new Medicare or Medicaid payments to physician practices qualifying as medical homes). The impact of medical homes on health care spending remains unclear, however. Medical homes could lead to increases in health care spending if patients responded by seeking more services—or if payments to primary care physicians were simply an add-on to current outlays. The available evidence suggests that medical homes would be most likely to reduce health care spending if the coordinating physician also had a financial incentive to limit the use of specialty care.

Summary of Evidence

Under one model of the medical home concept, the primary care provider would coordinate referrals for specialty care and be paid a capitated monthly amount for that service. The American Medical Association recently estimated the additional time and equipment required for physicians and nurses to provide the coordination of care, tracking of patients, and outreach involved in the medical home model.[254] Its estimates suggest that the annual monetary costs of providing a medical home (above and beyond standard primary care services) would be about $650 per Medicare beneficiary in 2009—an increase of more than 20 percent over the current amount of Medicare spending per beneficiary for physicians' services.

Other features of the medical home concept could also cause spending to rise, although some of the increases could be at least partially offset by savings. Improving patients' access to primary care providers through extended hours on evenings and weekends, "24/7" telephone triage, or "open access" scheduling (that is, same- or next-day appointments) would tend to increase use and spending. Those initiatives might result in some offsetting reductions in the use of specialist services or emergency room care, but the savings would probably be small unless proposals provided substantial financial incentives for care coordination. Paying primary care providers for responding to patients' telephone calls or e-mails could also cause health care spending to increase, but those costs could be offset either partially or fully by savings if visits to the doctor's office or emergency room declined as a consequence. (In addition, patients might benefit by avoiding the time and travel costs associated with in-office and emergency room visits.)

Improving the coordination of care could, in principle, reduce health care spending. Determining the precise impact of care coordination is challenging, though, especially when it is implemented along with other changes in care processes. One Medicaid pilot project that uses the medical home model—Community Care of North Carolina—has reported savings among beneficiaries with asthma and also among those with diabetes. However, it is difficult to determine whether those savings resulted from the gatekeeper element of the medical home model or from other key elements of that initiative, which include disease management, development of clinical guidelines, and patients' education.[255]

The effect of gatekeeper arrangements on the use of specialist care by patients depends critically on the health care delivery system and payment environment. In the context of fee-for-service payments to physicians operating independently, a gatekeeper arrangement does not appear to decrease referrals to specialists and may increase the number of visits to primary care providers by patients seeking referrals. Alternatively, approaches in which primary care providers play more of a "gateway" role than a "gatekeeper" role (by streamlining the referral process, employing referral coordinators who are not physicians, and offering telephone-based referrals) may limit the increase in payments for primary care but facilitate larger increases in specialty care.

The experience of Harvard Vanguard Medical Associates (HVMA), a Boston-based staff-model health maintenance organization, illustrates the key role of payment incentives. In 1998, that plan eliminated its requirement that patients receive a referral from a primary care provider before seeing a specialist.[256] Afterward, the number of specialist visits per member was unchanged, indicating that gatekeeping made little difference in the use of specialty care in that setting. One possible reason that elimination of the gatekeeping requirement had no impact on the number of visits to specialists was that primary care and most specialty care in HVMA was provided by a group practice of salaried physicians, so the elimination of gatekeeping did not create new incentives for them to increase or decrease the provision of care.

In contrast, there is evidence that gatekeeping arrangements can reduce the use of specialists in a fee-for-service setting when coupled with clear financial incentives for primary care providers. One older study describes an experiment conducted in 1979 in which enrollees in United Healthcare were randomly assigned to a plan either with or without a gatekeeper.[257] In the gatekeeper plan, patients were assigned to primary care providers who also received bonuses or "withholds" (reductions in payments) based on their patients' use of specialists' care, hospital care, prescription drugs, and other ancillary services. The number of visits to specialists in the gatekeeper plan was one-third lower than the number of visits in the plan without gatekeepers.

Factors Affecting the Adoption of the Medical Home Model

Proposals that make federal subsidies for health insurance to plans contingent on their use of medical homes could accelerate the adoption of that model, but the impact on health care spending would depend on several factors. Proposals that simply codified the definition of a medical home would probably have only very minor implications for medical practice. Likewise, proposals that encouraged plans to adopt a gatekeeper approach might have a limited impact if that change was not combined with financial incentives for primary care providers. Furthermore, to the extent that the medical home model improved care or reduced spending, it would most likely be adopted over time in a competitive insurance market regardless of whether it was a precondition for receiving federal subsidies. Thus, the incremental effect on health care spending of a proposal to link subsidies for insurance to a plan's adoption of the medical home model could be small.

At the same time, nationwide implementation of the medical home concept could be affected by constraints on both labor and capital resources. An inadequate supply of primary care providers and a lack of multispecialty group practices in many regions of the country could slow the spread of the medical home model. The ability of primary care physicians to coordinate care across settings could also be severely hampered by a lack of compatible information technology systems.

Adopting Disease Management Programs

Disease management programs can help patients manage the routine care of common chronic diseases, such as diabetes or coronary artery disease. Those programs could improve the quality of health care. Furthermore, some observers contend that they would help control costs. Interest in disease management programs is partly motivated by two concerns: the large share of health care costs attributable to chronic diseases; and potential problems with coordination and continuity of care in the current fee-for-service delivery system. To date, however, evidence about cost reductions in the private sector from plans that have implemented such programs has been inconclusive, and programs tested in the Medicare population have not shown cost reductions either. Nevertheless, CBO will continue to analyze new evidence about such programs as it becomes available.

Background

Although much of health care could be considered disease management in one form or another, structured programs to manage diseases typically incorporate some or all of the following elements: education of patients about their disease and how to treat it; monitoring of patients' symptoms and their adherence to evidence-based treatment plans; and efforts to coordinate care across providers and settings (after a hospital discharge, for instance) or to provide support and feedback to a patient's primary care physician. Although similar in some respects to medical homes, disease management programs are usually run by health plans or by outside vendors who specialize in those services (sometimes in collaboration with a patient's primary care physician).

Disease management programs are typically designed to address a specific chronic disease, although a vendor may provide a range of programs covering several diseases. The programs also vary in their target populations and the intensity of the services they provide; some programs seek to serve all enrollees with a given health condition (known as a population-based approach) but involve less interaction with each patient, whereas others target higher-risk cases (such as those patients deemed likely to require a hospital admission) and use more aggressive and more expensive interventions. Although they often have some components in common, specific interventions targeting the same disease may vary widely in their design.

Formal disease management programs are a relatively new phenomenon, but their use in the private health insurance market has grown substantially. According to industry surveys, nearly all large health plans offer some type of disease management service, and 83 percent of 500 major employers use such programs.[258] (Widespread adoption is sometimes seen as evidence that the programs reduce costs—and some insurers report such effects—but another possibility is that the programs generate health or other benefits that warrant a net increase in spending.) Such services are generally not available in the fee-for-service Medicare program, but various approaches for serving that population have been studied in demonstration projects. In addition, many states are experimenting with disease management programs for Medicaid beneficiaries, expanding the share of the population with access to those programs.

Summary of Evidence

In a 2004 letter, CBO reviewed a number of evaluations of disease management programs that had been published in peer-reviewed journals, focusing primarily on programs for diabetes, coronary artery disease, and congestive heart failure.[259] Some studies found net cost reductions for selected groups of patients, but it was not clear whether those targeting strategies could be replicated or if the results would hold up when applied to broader sets of patients. Overall, CBO found that the evidence was insufficient to conclude that disease management programs generally reduce health care spending, once the costs of the programs themselves are included in the analysis.

A more recent review of the literature by analysts at RAND examined studies of programs that encompassed a broader set of diseases. That analysis reached a similar conclusion: The evidence about cost savings is inconclusive.[260] Programs for congestive heart failure were generally successful in reducing hospital admission rates but not by enough to show clear savings net of the programs' costs. Programs for patients with depression improved the care that those patients received but also were found to increase health care costs. Programs for coronary artery disease and diabetes were found to increase adherence to evidence-based treatment guidelines and to improve some intermediate measures of patients' conditions (such as hemoglobin levels for diabetics, which measure control of blood sugar); still, evidence about improved long-term clinical outcomes or net savings was inconclusive.

Questions about the effectiveness of disease management programs for the Medicare population have led to demonstration and pilot projects designed to test those approaches. In general, those projects have not found cost reductions from disease management. One possible reason is the monthly fees paid to disease management vendors, which ranged from roughly $75 to $160 per enrollee in one of the Medicare demonstration projects. In some cases, there were no cost reductions, even before taking into account the payments made to the vendors. Offsetting those fees would require large reductions in health care spending, which have not yet been demonstrated.[261]

Challenges in Demonstrating Savings

Studies analyzing disease management programs may fail to demonstrate conclusive cost reductions for several reasons. The challenges that are involved in reducing health care costs vary somewhat with the type of program being used. A population-based approach that seeks to serve all enrollees with a given health condition may provide services to many enrollees who either are not sick enough to benefit (or are unlikely to generate high costs) or are too sick to benefit. Predicting which enrollees are most likely to benefit can also be difficult, however. Alternatively, waiting for enrollees to develop a more serious condition (or for an "index" event, like a hospitalization, to occur) could improve accuracy but might miss opportunities for savings. In the Medicare population, an additional challenge is that many patients have multiple chronic conditions. That complexity makes it more difficult to identify and treat those patients in a timely manner.

In addition, a number of methodological limitations may account for the studies' failure to demonstrate cost reductions. Many studies focus on disease management programs' effects on processes of care or intermediate outcomes instead of their effects on spending, so determining whether those changes will reduce health care costs is difficult. And some of the studies that do analyze effects on spending do not account for the cost of providing the disease management program itself. Furthermore, participation in disease management programs is voluntary in many cases—a consideration that raises the potential for selection bias. If participants in a study are healthier than nonparticipants or take a more active role in their care, then comparisons of costs for the two groups may be misleading. Conversely, if study participants were chosen on the basis of having particularly high costs in a previous period, their costs would be expected to fall regardless of whether they participated in a disease management program (following a statistical phenomenon known as regression to the mean). Finally, it may be difficult to apply the results from a demonstration project to a broader population or another setting. For example, programs undertaken by health maintenance organizations may not achieve the same results if used in a more loosely managed health plan.

For those reasons, the most reliable means of assessing disease management programs is to construct randomly assigned treatment and control groups and compare comprehensive measures of their spending. Such methods have been used effectively in the demonstration and pilot projects undertaken for Medicare, but they are much less common in assessments of programs in private-sector health plans. Some studies may seek to exploit differences in the timing or locations of program rollouts to identify their effects, but even then questions about their methodology may arise.[262] As the RAND review noted, those "vendor-run assessments typically do not meet the requirements of peer-reviewed research in terms of the comparison strategy, and adequate control for selection bias and regression to the mean."

Overall, CBO's assessment is that proposals requiring private health insurance plans to adopt disease management programs would be unlikely to yield lower premiums. One reason is that private plans have largely embraced disease management already, so the incremental effect of a proposal on adoption rates is likely to be small. Moreover, if new evidence emerged about particular programs that conclusively demonstrated net reductions in health care costs, private health plans would probably adopt those programs even in the absence of a requirement— both to limit their own costs and to remain competitive in the insurance market. In that case, the effects of a legislative proposal would be limited to people who would not have access to the disease management program under current law.

Adoption in the fee-for-service Medicare program, by contrast, would probably require changes in legislation.

Although evidence of savings in that setting is lacking, certain types of private-sector programs—particularly those that have been evaluated using a rigorous evidence base and demonstrated either partial offsets to spending or actual net savings—would have a greater potential to limit federal spending. However, a key consideration that remains is whether the findings of such studies can be replicated in Medicare. Programs that can be targeted more effectively toward the Medicare enrollees most likely to benefit from them or most likely to generate savings may also be more likely to reduce federal spending on health care. Finally, programs in which the organization providing the disease management services has a stronger financial stake in the outcome also seem more likely to limit federal spending; for example, Medicare payments to vendors could be tied to a comparison of spending between enrollees in the program and a reference group (as was done in some of the recent Medicare demonstration projects). Even then, calculating what enrollees' costs would have been in the absence of disease management programs is a challenge, especially as those programs move from the demonstration phase to broader application.

Comparing the Effectiveness of Medical Treatments

Concerns about the limited evidence that is available to determine which treatments are most effective for which patients has led to proposals that would seek to expand the supply and use of information that compares the effectiveness of treatment options.[263] Some proposals would fund a government agency or other entity to conduct additional research in that area; CBO estimates that such research would yield findings that reduce federal spending for certain types of health care, although not by enough to offset the costs of conducting that research over a 10-year budgetary time frame. Over the longer term, the federal costs and savings might be in rough balance. Other options would change payment rules or cost-sharing requirements under Medicare or Medicaid to encourage the use of more clinically effective or cost- effective services or discourage the use of other services. However, the extent to which savings could be realized from such approaches would depend greatly on the details of the proposal.

Availability of Evidence

The term comparative effectiveness refers to a rigorous evaluation of two or more alternatives available for treating a given medical condition for a particular set of patients.

The most rigorous type of evaluation is a clinical trial in which patients are randomly assigned to various treatment options. For example, one study from 2007 randomly assigned patients with stable coronary artery disease into one of two treatment protocols: an angioplasty with a metal stent combined with a drug regimen; or the drug regimen by itself. That study found no differences between the two groups of patients in survival rates or the occurrence of heart attacks over a five-year period. Angioplasty did, however, appear to reduce the prevalence of angina (chest pain).[264] Such results are not uncommon, and they do not definitively prove that a medical procedure (angioplasty, in this case) lacks value; instead, they show that, for a specific group of patients, the procedure has value in relieving symptoms but not in improving rates of survival or avoiding major complications.

Although clinical trials generally yield the most persuasive results, they are also the most expensive and time- consuming type of comparative analysis. Other approaches to research on comparative effectiveness include the use of medical claims data or systematic reviews of the available evidence on individual treatments in order to construct head-to-head comparisons. Such approaches are less costly, but using observational data to draw inferences about effectiveness is difficult. Because patients are not randomly assigned to different treatments, researchers may not be able to separate out the true effect of the treatment from other factors that might have led the individual or medical provider to select that approach. (For example, more intensive treatments might have been given to sicker patients.) Whatever data they use, such studies may limit their focus to clinical effectiveness or may also consider cost-effectiveness, weighing the additional costs of a more expensive procedure against any additional benefits it might provide.

Some information about the effectiveness of new drugs, medical devices, or procedures is available, but rigorous comparisons of different treatment options are less common. Even though drugs and devices must be certified as safe and effective before they can be marketed, the regulatory process for approving those products does not evaluate them relative to alternatives. (There are a few limited exceptions.) In addition, some evaluations have found that clinical trials sponsored by drug and device makers are more likely than independent studies to find favorable results. For example, a 2006 study of antipsychotic drugs found that in 90 percent of the firm-sponsored trials, the results favored the drug made by the sponsoring firm; that outcome led to conflicting results across studies when the findings of the same drugs from different sponsors were compared.[265] In addition, medical procedures— which account for a much larger share of total health care spending—can achieve widespread use without a systematic analysis of their impact. Estimates about the current situation vary widely, but some experts believe that less than half of all medical care is based on or supported by adequate evidence about its effectiveness.[266]

Factors constraining the supply of and demand for such research explain why the current evidence base is so limited. Although private insurers sponsor some research assessing and comparing treatments (because they have incentives to restrict coverage of ineffective care), the private sector, in general, will not produce as much of that research as society would value. The knowledge created by such studies is expensive to produce, and private insurers (and other organizations conducting such research) may capture only a portion of the resulting benefits. Because the knowledge can be disseminated at essentially no additional cost (and charging all users for access to that information is not always feasible), all parties end up benefiting from it. Private insurers, therefore, do not invest as much in those efforts as they would if they alone benefited from the knowledge or if they took into account the benefits to all parties. For its part, the Medicare program lacks clear legal authority to take costs into account in determining which services are covered and has made only limited use of the available data on relative clinical effectiveness; consequently, its demand for comparative assessments has been minimal.

Limited data on the comparative effectiveness of different medical approaches may help explain why the use of certain treatments and the types of care provided vary widely from one area of the country to another. Researchers at Dartmouth, for example, found about a fourfold variation in the share of Medicare beneficiaries receiving a coronary artery bypass graft in different regions of the country, and those differences were not correlated with rates of heart attacks in each region. In part, that variation may reflect differing views among doctors about the effectiveness of bypass surgery. Furthermore, some evidence suggests that the degree of geographic variation in treatment patterns is greater when less evidence is available about the best treatment to use. Surgery rates for joint replacements provide one example. There is relatively little geographic variation in admission rates for Medicare beneficiaries who have fractured a hip, a condition that requires hospitalization. For knee and hip replacements, however, more discretion is involved, and the surgery rates vary more widely. For back surgery (the benefits of which are often in dispute), geographic variation in rates is even greater.

Effects on Health Care Spending

To generate additional information on comparative effectiveness, some proposals would fund new research through a government agency or other entity. Other options would link both new and existing evidence to payment rules or cost-sharing requirements under Medicare or Medicaid so as to provide incentives for using more clinically effective or cost-effective services or to discourage the use of other services.

Generate Additional Information

Proposals generally specify how much research funding they would provide, so the main question that arises in determining their overall impact on the budget is whether that research would affect spending by federal health insurance programs. Predicting the impact that additional information about comparative effectiveness could have on health care spending is difficult because it is hard to know what that research will show. As a general rule, however, the fee-forservice payment system by which most health care in the United States is currently financed often provides financial incentives for doctors and hospitals to adopt new and more expensive treatments and procedures even if hard evidence about their effectiveness is not available. Furthermore, some analyses have found that clinical trials sponsored by drug and device makers are more likely than independent studies to find favorable results. Over the long term, therefore, generating additional objective information about the relative costs and benefits of treatments seems likely to offset those tendencies somewhat— and is thus more likely to reduce total health care spending than to raise it. Under current coverage and payment rules for Medicare and Medicaid, the resulting changes in medical practice (spurred in some cases by private insurers) would reduce spending under federal programs because doctors tend to treat their patients in a similar manner regardless of their source of insurance.

In some instances, comparative effectiveness research has already led to changes in patterns of medical practice, causing doctors and patients to pursue less invasive and less costly treatments. One example concerns patients with emphysema. A study initiated by Medicare examined the effects of surgery to reduce lung volume for patients with that condition. Although the study found that the procedure had medical benefits for some types of patients (and Medicare continued to provide coverage in those cases), the additional information about the treatment's risks apparently discouraged many doctors and patients from pursuing that option, and its use dropped as a result.[267] Similarly, the study of angioplasty cited earlier appears to have contributed to a decline in the use of stents.

Although new research into comparative effectiveness might lead to net cost savings over a long period of time, its effects during the conventional 10-year horizon for budgetary estimates would be limited. In addition to the time required to get the new activities under way, a lag would exist before results were generated—particularly if they depended on new clinical trials. Initially, the available results would probably address a relatively small number of medical treatments and procedures; additional time would have to elapse before a substantial body of results was amassed. For all of those reasons, it would probably take several years before new research on comparative effectiveness could reduce health care spending substantially. CBO has estimated that such approaches could eventually yield federal savings on health care that roughly equal the outlays for research, but the savings would not be large enough to offset the costs of the research within a 10-year budgetary time frame.

Some features of proposals to fund additional research on comparative effectiveness would affect their likely budgetary impact:

- Higher funding levels would tend to generate more studies and thus would yield greater savings (although the incremental effects would eventually decline because the capacity to conduct high-quality research in this area is not unlimited).
- Savings may be more likely to result from a research agenda that explicitly prioritizes assessments of costly technologies that are suspected of being overused.
- Assessing cost-effectiveness as well as clinical effectiveness would yield a somewhat larger effect on health care spending than would research focused only on clinical effectiveness—because it would help highlight cases in which the additional benefits of a more costly treatment are relatively small.
- Efforts to bolster comparative effectiveness research would be more likely to change medical practice patterns if the organization coordinating the research was respected and trusted by doctors and other professionals in the health care sector.

Other features regarding the organization and funding system for the new research—for example, whether to fund an existing government agency or create a new public/private partnership—would not affect the estimated budgetary impact of the research.

Provide Incentives for Implementation of Research Findings

Merely conducting comparative effectiveness research is unlikely to have major effects on clinical practice patterns. For the research to have a much larger impact, providers' financial incentives would need to be realigned accordingly. If changes in law were made, Medicare could use information about comparative effectiveness to promote the use of more effective care. The program could, for example, choose not to cover treatments that were found to be less clinically effective or less cost- effective. Alternatively, Medicare could tie its payments to providers to the cost of the most clinically effective or most cost-effective treatment, or enrollees could be required to pay for at least a portion of the additional costs of less clinically effective or less cost-effective procedures. To the extent that such approaches reduced the use of less effective services or shifted care to less expensive treatments, the potential impact on Medicare spending could be substantial. Similar approaches could be applied in the Medicaid program, although additional issues of coordination would arise because states generally set payment rates and coverage rules (subject to broad federal requirements) and jointly finance the program. Although such proposals could reduce federal spending in more substantial ways than would result from added research alone, the extent to which savings could be realized would depend greatly on the details of the proposal.

Adopting Health Information Technology

Health information technology (IT) could significantly increase the efficiency of the health care sector by helping providers manage information.[268] It could also improve the quality of health care and, ultimately, the outcomes of that care for patients. In particular, electronic health records—comprising electronic documentation of providers' medical notes, electronic viewing of laboratory and radiological results, electronic prescribing of medications, and an interoperable connection among providers of health care—could have a sizable impact on medical practices. When used effectively, electronic health records could reduce the duplication of diagnostic tests; remind physicians about appropriate preventive care; identify harmful drug interactions or possible allergic reactions to prescribed medications; and help physicians manage the care of patients who have complex chronic conditions.

The promise of those potential benefits has led many observers to suggest that the federal government should promote the nationwide adoption of health IT. Research indicates that, at least in certain settings, health IT facilitates reductions in health care spending—if other steps are also taken to alter incentives so as to promote savings. By itself, the adoption of more health IT offers many benefits, but it is generally not sufficient to produce substantial cost savings because the incentives for many providers to use that technology to control costs are not strong.

Summary of Evidence on Improvements in Efficiency from Adopting Health IT

The potential of health IT to reduce spending for health care largely depends on its ability to make care more efficient by cutting the cost of delivering services, avoiding redundant services, and improving providers' productivity. Evidence from the literature on health IT, however, does not uniformly support the possibility of such savings. The potential for savings appears to depend heavily on their source and whether that source is in a hospital or in an ambulatory care setting (such as a clinic or a physician's office). In addition, savings are difficult to assess because the trimming of costs in one area of a physician's practice, for example, may be offset by increased costs or reduced efficiency in another area.

Estimating the impact of some potential sources of savings—especially those arising from greater exchange of information among providers, insurers, and patients—is especially difficult because health IT networks are in an early stage of development. Furthermore, health care providers and hospitals that were early adopters of health IT may have been motivated by particular characteristics of their organizations or operations that made them more likely than nonadopters to achieve benefits from health IT—in which case the outcomes they have seen might not apply to a broader group. Evidence of savings in the health care sector as a whole from adopting health IT is also limited.

Although the evidence of savings regarding specific applications is mixed, savings could accrue in some areas.

- Research has shown that physicians' offices can realize savings from reducing the pulling of paper charts and the use of transcription services, although the extent of the savings will depend on the size of the practice and how well physicians use the new systems.[269]
- Most of the available evidence suggests that electronic health records have the potential to reduce duplicated or inappropriate laboratory tests.[270] However, a 2005 evaluation of laboratory services in outpatient facilities that adopted health IT systems did not find a difference in the number of duplications.[271]
- Two studies found that the adoption of health IT did not have any significant effect on whether or not a radiology test was ordered. However, it may have affected the type of test ordered.[272]
- Several studies have investigated whether electronic health records increase the productivity of nurses and physicians. Although the studies have shown mixed results, the measures of productivity that researchers have used in such studies are limited and do not exhaust the ways in which the use of health IT might affect productivity.[273]
- Some research suggests that health IT could reduce the length of hospital stays by speeding up certain hospital functions (such as ordering tests and medications) and by avoiding costly errors (such as adverse drug reactions that could lead to delays in discharging patients).[274] However, reductions in average lengths of stay may not result in comparable reductions in costs, because health IT may speed certain procedures but not eliminate them.

Incentives for and Barriers to Adoption

The most auspicious examples of health IT have tended to involve relatively integrated health care systems. In such systems, a hospital network or a health plan typically owns the hospitals that provide most care to enrollees, and doctors and other providers work exclusively for the organization (either for a salary or under contract). Because the systems are integrated, they are able to capture savings that are generated by health IT at most points in the process of delivering care.

For example, Kaiser Permanente is a large integrated system in which the health plan (primarily a health maintenance organization) and the providers (physicians and most hospitals and ancillary service providers) exclusively contract with one another to provide care to the health plan's enrollees. For such a system, reducing the number of unnecessary office visits, for example, benefits the providers, the health plan, and the patients: It may lower the plan's costs for providing health care while minimizing inconvenience for patients. Kaiser has implemented systemwide electronic health records in its facilities in some regions.

In those areas, physicians have used such consultations to reduce the number of unnecessary office visits (compared with the number in regions without electronic systems).

A number of other integrated health care systems— including Intermountain Healthcare, Geisinger Health System, and Partners HealthCare—have implemented electronic health records either across their organizations or in some regions, and administrators of those systems believe that the efficiency and quality of the care they provide have improved as a result. The Department of Veterans Affairs, which also has an integrated health care system, uses electronic health records to serve nearly 6 million patients in more than 1,400 hospitals, clinics, and nursing homes. According to the VA, its use of health IT has reduced its costs and improved the quality of the care it provides.[275]

For doctors and hospitals that are not part of integrated systems, however, the benefits of health IT are not as easy to capture, and perhaps not coincidentally, those physicians and facilities have adopted electronic health records much more slowly. Even though the use of health IT could generate savings for the health system as a whole that might offset the start-up and operating costs involved, many physicians might not be able to reduce their own office expenses or increase their own revenue sufficiently to pay for it. As a result, relatively few providers have adopted health information technology— according to recent estimates, about 5 percent of physicians.[276]

Costs of Implementing Health IT

The fixed costs of investing in health IT can be quite high; for small physician practices and small hospitals, those costs might be particularly high relative to their expected revenues. A few studies have examined the costs of implementing electronic health records and computerized physician order entry systems in hospitals. Such costs are difficult to measure, however, because hospitals vary widely in size and type, different health IT applications may be implemented, and there is a general lack of data on costs. For those same reasons, any single hospital's experience in implementing a health IT system cannot be applied more generally to all hospitals.

For integrated health care systems, the annual costs to develop and maintain a health IT system are around 4 percent of operating costs. That calculation would imply that the costs of a nationwide health IT system (including systems already in place) would be on the order of $50 billion per year (given that approximately $1.3 trillion is expected to be spent in 2009 on hospital and physicians' services in the United States). Some studies indicate that, in addition to any initial investments, annual costs to operate and maintain a physician's office can average anywhere from $3,000 to $9,000 per physician. But other studies indicate that the costs of health IT may be falling. In particular, some Internet-based applications require an annual subscription fee that could be as low as $2,000 per physician. In general, if prices for a given level of capability continue to fall over time, the quantity and quality of the health IT systems that are purchased should increase.[277] Because of the fixed costs involved in developing health IT systems, those prices may themselves depend on rates of adoption.

Limited Incentives to Adopt Health IT

Even if the price of a health IT system fell, limited incentives would still tend to constrain the rate of adoption and blunt the impact that greater adoption would have on the use of health care services. Office-based physicians in particular may see no benefit if they purchase such a product, and they may even suffer financial harm. The use of health IT could reduce the number of duplicate diagnostic tests, for example (because the results of past tests would be more readily available), but that improvement in efficiency would be unlikely to increase the income of many physicians. For physicians who perform certain diagnostic tests in the office, decreasing the number of tests would reduce their income. (For physicians who order tests from laboratories and imaging centers, their income would not drop because those groups are paid separately by health insurance plans.) As a result, the capacity to avoid duplicating tests might not spur many physicians to invest in and implement a health IT system. Indeed, physicians might have a more powerful financial incentive to purchase additional office diagnostic equipment than to purchase a health IT system. Nevertheless, some physicians might invest in health IT to improve the quality of their patients' care, even if those purchases resulted in little or no net monetary savings.

Health insurance companies that are not integrated may still have an incentive to help providers acquire health IT systems. The technology could help lower the companies' costs and could improve both the quality of the care that providers deliver and the health of the patients. For doctors or hospitals that contract with many health plans, however, any benefits of adopting health IT would be spread across those plans, so no one plan would want to subsidize the full cost of a provider's health IT system. In addition, a plan may be reluctant or unable to coordinate with other plans regarding the assistance they offer to providers to acquire health IT systems. As an alternative to upgrading their providers' technology, plans might be able to obtain some of the same benefits by making improvements to their own IT systems and relying primarily on claims data.

Effects of Proposals to Adopt Health IT

In considering the impact of legislative proposals relating to health information technology, it is important first to consider the projected rate of adoption under current law. In the near term, the adoption of health IT is expected to continue to grow, primarily among providers who are able to capture the benefits of health IT internally, such as integrated systems, bigger hospitals, and larger physician practices. CBO expects that about 40 percent of physicians will adopt health IT by 2019, with near- universal adoption anticipated over the next quarter- century. The next step is to evaluate whether a proposal affects the expected adoption of health IT—either its speed or its scope—and then whether that change would increase or decrease health care spending or federal budgetary outlays. In general, the effects of health IT on spending would depend on the incentive structure facing providers and patients. As with all analyses of the budgetary effects of proposals, the estimated impact would be limited to changes that occurred as the result of federal legislation as opposed to changes that would have naturally happened as the industry evolved over time.

If the federal government chose to intervene directly to promote the use of health IT, it could do so by subsidizing that use or by imposing a penalty for failing to use a health IT system. From a budgetary perspective, a penalty is more likely than subsidies to generate savings for the federal government because of the costs of the subsidies. Under the latter approach, payments would end up going to some providers who would have adopted a health IT system even without a subsidy as well as to providers for whom the subsidy made the difference in their decision to adopt a system. Conversely, penalties for providers who do not adopt a system would generate federal receipts. However, providers might respond differently to a subsidy or a penalty depending on how those interventions were presented and enforced.

In the context of a broader proposal to modify the health care system, expansions in the use of health IT would interact with other systemwide changes. For example, a proposal that would institute a system of bonuses paid to providers that reduced the total costs of patients who have chronic diseases might encourage providers to adopt health IT so that they could more effectively monitor and influence their use of care. Changes made to other components of the health care system could even increase the potential for savings from health IT by providing stronger incentives for providers and patients to focus on the cost and value of the health care they produce and consume.

One potential benefit of health IT that has not been examined carefully involves its role in research on the comparative effectiveness of medical treatments and practices. Widespread use of health IT could make available large amounts of data on patients' care and health, which could be used for empirical studies that might improve the quality of health care and help make the delivery of services more efficient. By making clinical data easier to collect and analyze, health IT systems could support rigorous studies to compare the effectiveness and costs of different treatments for a given disease or condition. Then, in response to the studies' findings, those systems could aid in implementing changes in the kinds of care provided and the way in which services were delivered, as well as track progress in carrying out the changes.

Modifying Laws about Medical Malpractice

Some proposals would seek to change medical practices by focusing on the ways in which patients and medical providers settle disputes about treatment. Such proposals would modify the system for determining liability for medical malpractice. (Medical malpractice claims are a class of common-law causes of action, known as torts.) State law allows individuals to sue physicians and other health care providers for breaches of duty that result in personal injury. The medical malpractice system has two basic objectives:

- Compensating injured patients for their losses (which can include medical costs, wages, and pain and suffering); and
- Deterring negligent behavior by medical providers.

Critics charge that the current system is subjective and too costly and that excessive damage awards have increased health care spending, both directly (through higher premiums for malpractice insurance) and indirectly (by leading doctors to order additional tests or procedures in an attempt to diminish their risk of being sued—so-called defensive medicine). Other charges are that legal fees consume too large a share of awards and that many patients and their families receive little or no compensation when malpractice occurs. Doctors and hospitals generally have malpractice insurance to protect against the financial risk of a lawsuit, but they have raised concerns about the rising costs of that insurance.

Some proposals would address concerns about the malpractice system by establishing tort limits, such as caps on damage awards. Although some studies have found that tort limits have substantial effects on health care spending, CBO's own analysis has yielded mixed results—partly reflecting the difficulty of disentangling the impact of those limits from other factors that affect spending. Overall, the analysis indicates that tort limits would reduce malpractice premiums but might not have a broader impact on the use of health care services.

Other approaches could be taken to address concerns about the malpractice system. Those approaches include subsidizing medical malpractice premiums or regulating their growth; creating alternative processes for dispute resolution; providing malpractice protection to physicians and hospitals in return for compliance with national guidelines for clinical practice; and establishing a "no- fault" system, which would provide compensation for all medical injuries regardless of whether any negligence was involved. Some states have already taken similar steps, but CBO has not yet analyzed their effects and would have to draw on those experiences as well as other research in evaluating any new federal proposals.

Background

In 2003, about 181,000 severe medical injuries occurred in U.S. hospitals (representing 0.5 percent of all hospital admissions) that were attributable to negligence (see Table 7-1). Only about 17 percent of affected patients chose to file a malpractice claim. Patients who did not file a claim may have been unaware that negligence had occurred, or they may have been discouraged from filing a lawsuit because of the time, effort, and expense involved.

From the point of view of many physicians and hospital officials, the medical malpractice system is a "lottery" in which being sued depends on factors beyond their control. To some extent, data on malpractice suits supports that perception. One study found that among the malpractice claims filed in 2003, only about half were associated with a severe negligent injury.[278] That study also estimated that about 12 percent of indemnity payments in medical malpractice cases went to claimants who did not suffer an injury because of negligence. Examined in another way, however, the same data indicate that the filing of malpractice claims and the payment of claims are not random. Hospital stays during which a severe negligent injury occurred were about 250 times as likely to result in a malpractice claim when compared with stays in which such an injury did not occur.[279] In addition, that study found that claimants in cases in which a negligent injury occurred were about two and a half times as likely to receive a payment compared with claimants in cases without such an injury.

In 2008, health care providers are likely to spend more than $30 billion to defend against and pay medical malpractice claims.[280] Although that amount of money is substantial, it represents about 1.5 percent of national health expenditures and less than 3 percent of total payments to doctors and hospitals. Administrative costs in the medical malpractice system—including legal fees, administrative costs for malpractice insurers, and court costs—have been found to account for about half of the total spending on malpractice claims.[281] That high percentage primarily reflects the current legal process of determining whether negligence occurred and what the compensatory payment should be.

In theory, new tort limits could lower overall spending for health care in two ways. (See Box 7-1 for a description of commonly proposed limits.) First, tort limits would reduce premiums for malpractice insurance by decreasing the size of the average award paid by malpractice insurers to claimants and perhaps also by reducing the probability that a medical provider would be sued for malpractice.[282] A drop in malpractice premiums would tend to reduce the prices that providers and insurers negotiate for health care services. (It would also decrease Medicare spending, because Medicare's payments rates for physicians' and hospitals' services include an amount to pay for malpractice premiums.) Second, changes in tort law could decrease health care spending by reducing the intensity and volume of health care services provided. The argument for such a utilization effect is built on two premises: that fear of litigation drives medical providers to deliver additional—and often unnecessary—medical services, and that the proposed tort limits would lessen that perceived threat among physicians and thereby reduce utilization and spending. Note, however, that imposing limits on malpractice torts could also constrain the ability of injured patients to collect compensation and might lead to more negligent care.

Summary of Evidence

Several studies have examined the experience of states that have implemented tort limits and found that various types of restrictions on malpractice liability can reduce total awards and thereby lead to lower premiums for malpractice insurance. The Office of Technology Assessment issued a report in 1993 summarizing the first wave of studies on the experience of states that set limits on malpractice liability in the 1970s and 1980s.[283] The report concluded that caps on damage awards consistently reduced the size of claims and, in turn, lowered rates for malpractice insurance premiums. Furthermore, it found that limits on the extent to which various parties could be held liable were also effective in slowing the growth of premiums. Similarly, a 2004 study that examined state data from 1993 to 2002 found that a cap on noneconomic damages reduced malpractice insurance premiums by more than 15 percent.[284]

In previous analyses, CBO considered the effects of limits on tort claims for medical malpractice at the state level and concluded that such limits decreased both malpractice awards and malpractice insurance premiums. In its 2008 report titled *Budget Options, Volume 1: Health Care*, CBO estimated that imposing limits on torts for medical malpractice cases would lower malpractice premiums nationwide by about 6 percent, on average, from the levels likely to occur under current law. (The savings in each state would depend in part on the restrictions already in effect.) Savings of that magnitude would have only a modest impact on total health care expenditures, however—reducing total health care spending by less than 0.2 percent.

Table 7-1. Medical Injuries, Negligence, and the Filing of Malpractice Claims, 2003

Did a Severe Medical Injury Occur?	Was the Severe Injury Due to Negligence?	Medical Encounters: Number (Thousands)	Medical Encounters: Percentage of Total	Number of Malpractice Claims Filed (Thousands)	Percentage of Medical Encounters That Result in a Malpractice Claim
No	Not Applicable	37,685	98.6	11	0.03
Yes	No	355	0.9	15	4.26
Yes	Yes	181	0.5	30	16.77
All Medical Encounters	Sometimes	38,221	100.0	57	0.15

Source: Congressional Budget Office adapted from David M. Studdert and others, "Disclosure of Medical Injury to Patients: An Improbable Risk Management Strategy," *Health Affairs*, vol. 26, no. 1 (January/February 2007), pp. 215–226.

Note: Medical encounters represent all inpatient hospital discharges in 2003.

Box 7-1. Types of Tort Reforms

Proposals to modify health care in the United States might place limitations on the system that governs tort claims for medical malpractice in a number of ways.[1] In general, those limits are of two types: limits on who can be found liable, and caps on the payments that can be made.

Limits on Liable Parties

The principle of joint-and-several liability allows a claimant to recover the entire amount of a damage award from any one of the parties found to be responsible for an injury, regardless of each party's degree of responsibility for that injury. Proposals to eliminate that principle could specify instead that each party is responsible only for the share of damages equal to its degree of responsibility for the injury. Proposals to modify joint-and-several liability might, for example, allow it to be applied only to the defendant found to be at least 50 percent responsible for an injury (so that only that party could be required to pay the full claim). Eliminating joint-and-several liability would reduce the awards that are actually paid in cases in which some of the defendants did not have adequate resources to pay their share of the award.

The statute of limitations specifies the period of time following an injury during which the injured party may file a claim for damages. Proposals affecting that statute generally would shorten the period of time available to file and thus would tend to reduce the number of lawsuits and awards. Two types of limits could be applied, the first based on the amount of time that had elapsed since the alleged injury occurred, and the second based on the amount of time that had elapsed since the alleged injury was discovered. One recent proposal would impose a filing deadline of three years after an alleged injury occurred or one year after it was discovered (whichever date was earlier).

Caps on Payments

Caps on payments can themselves take several forms. One common proposal would limit the amount of noneconomic damages that can be awarded. Economic damages cover medical costs and lost earnings; noneconomic damages compensate for pain and suffering and mental distress. Other proposals would place a cap on punitive damages. Punitive damages are not intended to compensate the injured party for losses but instead to punish the defendant for egregious behavior and deter other health care providers from similar behavior. Proposals could limit the situations in which plaintiffs might receive punitive damages, cap the amount of punitive damages that plaintiffs could receive, or do both. Finally, some proposals would cap the contingency fees that claimants' attorneys can collect as a percentage of the total damages recovered.

Proposals could also address the more complex issue of payments that are known as "collateral-source benefits." They constitute compensation for an injury from other sources, such as a health or disability insurance policy. Some proposals would reduce the amount of damages a plaintiff can receive by the amount of any collateral-source benefits the plaintiff had received (either on a mandatory basis or at the discretion of the court).

Other proposals would prevent those third parties from receiving any portion of a damage award.

[1] For a broader discussion of tort reform proposals and their implications for equity and economic efficiency, see Congressional Budget Office, *The Economics of U.S. Tort Liability: A Primer* (October 2003).

CBO and other researchers have also used the variation in state laws to assess whether tort limits on malpractice claims have broader effects on health care spending. One prominent set of studies examined the relationship between state tort limits and Medicare spending on hospital care for patients with heart disease and concluded that those limits would ultimately reduce such spending by between 4 percent and 9 percent.[285] Other studies have found much smaller effects.

After carefully considering the economic literature and conducting its own statistical analysis of the data, CBO has not found consistent evidence that changes in the medical malpractice environment would have a measurable impact on health care spending.[286] In part that is because the estimated effects of limits on malpractice torts vary substantially across different measures of health care spending and across different types of tort limits. In some cases, specific tort limits appear to be associated with reductions in health care spending; in other cases, there appears to be no relationship; and in still other cases, tort limits appear to be associated with higher spending (a finding that is counterintuitive). That data analysis also indicated the challenges involved in using statistical methods to separate the effects of tort reforms from the impact of other factors that might affect spending on health care.

CBO has not yet analyzed in detail other approaches to change the malpractice system or offset effects that are perceived to be adverse. Most of those approaches—such as restricting the increases in premiums made by medical malpractice insurance carriers or creating special courts for malpractice cases or processes for alternative dispute resolution—have already been adopted by one or more states. In addition, a no-fault compensation fund is in place for injuries related to vaccines.[287] CBO would consider the evidence from those examples in estimating the effect of enacting one or more of the approaches into federal law.

8. Effects on Total Health Care Spending, the Scope of the Federal Budget, and the Economy

Proposals that would substantially change the health insurance market and health care systems could affect total spending on health care, the flow of payments between various sectors of the U.S. economy, and the operation of the economy. The Congressional Budget Office will consider those effects in its analysis of major health care proposals.

CBO will use data from the national health expenditures (NHE) and other sources to estimate the impact of various proposals on total health care spending. Some proposals might contain provisions that explicitly limit the rate of growth in total health care spending; such proposals might impose a global budget or budgetary cap for all or a part of that spending. In analyzing the effectiveness of such strategies, CBO will consider several factors, including the scope of the global budget, the targets selected for different categories of spending, and the mechanisms used to enforce the caps.

Changes to the health care system could also affect revenues and—more generally—the flow of funds between households, employers, and federal and state governments. Proposals that would affect the flow of payments might raise several budgetary concerns that have not been examined in earlier chapters of this chapter. Some proposals might assign the federal government a more active role in the health insurance market. For example, the government could be required to disburse subsidies to cover the cost of health insurance, collect health insurance premiums from policyholders, or make payments to insurers. Any of those changes might raise questions regarding who—the government, the insured, or the insurer—bears financial responsibility for any shortfalls in payments that might occur. Other proposals might require that individuals or businesses make payments directly to nongovernmental entities. Depending on the specific features of a proposal, CBO might judge that payments resulting from federal mandates should be recorded as part of the federal budget, even if the funds did not flow through a federal account.

Proposals that would make large-scale changes to the provision and financing of health insurance could also affect the operation of the broader economy in various ways. Because most health insurance is currently provided through employers, proposals could affect labor markets by changing both individuals' decisions about whether and how much to work and employers' decisions to hire workers. Such effects could arise in several ways:

- Proposals that decreased the economic gains from an additional hour of work, through higher taxes or the phaseout of subsidies or credits for health insurance as income rises, could cause some people to work less or not at all.
- Proposals that made health insurance less dependent on employment status could induce some people to retire earlier and others to change jobs more often.
- Proposals that treated firms differently on the basis of characteristics such as size or average wages could affect the allocation of workers among firms.
- Proposals that required employers to provide health insurance could adversely affect the hiring of employees earning at or near the minimum wage because the total compensation of those workers could exceed their value to the firm.

Proposals could also affect the size of the nation's stock of productive capital, especially through their effects on government budgets. The net effect on the economy of a broad proposal to restructure the health care system would depend crucially on its details.

Effects on National Health Expenditures

Proposals that would significantly alter the health insurance market or the delivery of health care could also have a major impact on the amount and composition of overall spending on health care in the United States. CBO intends to include an estimate of the impact of major proposals on the total amount of national health expenditures in its analysis. For specific categories of spending, however, particularly by type of service, determining the likely impact presents greater challenges and may not be feasible.

Background on NHE Estimates and Projections

The Centers for Medicare and Medicaid Services produces estimates of total health spending in the United States—the national health expenditures—for current and future years. The largest component of the NHE is spending on health care goods and services, but the NHE also includes amounts spent on program administration, the net cost of private insurance (that is, the difference between benefits and premiums), public health activities, research, equipment, and structures. The estimates are sorted by the source of funding (private or public) and by the type of service (hospital, physician, pharmaceutical, and so forth).

CMS uses a variety of data and techniques to measure national health expenditures. For government programs like Medicare and Medicaid, CMS uses administrative records to determine current spending levels. Estimating spending on health care in the private sector presents a larger challenge because doctors, hospitals, and insurers are not required to report income to the federal government by type of service and sources of funding. To estimate that spending, therefore, CMS uses surveys from public and private sources, such as the Census Bureau, the National Center for Health Statistics, and private industry organizations (for instance, the American Hospital Association).

CMS also projects future health care spending by funding source and type of service. The projections are based on historical trends and observed relationships between health care spending and the economy. In its projections, CMS uses the same macroeconomic and demographic assumptions as those used in its annual report on the Medicare trust funds.[288] CMS estimates that national health expenditures will total $2.6 trillion in 2009 and will grow to $4.3 trillion by 2017. (See Table 1-4 in Chapter 1 for CMS's projections by funding source and type of service for 2009.)

The NHE estimates are especially useful for monitoring trends in total health care spending in the public and private sectors. They provide less insight into the impact of policy changes on particular segments of the population, however, mainly because the estimates are accounting measures of transactions and thus do not identify where the true responsibility for financing health care falls. The NHE accounts show the net cost of private insurance, for example, but they do not reveal who paid for the health insurance premiums, whether the premiums were initially paid by consumers or their employers, or whether employers' payments for premiums were ultimately passed on to their employees through reductions in wages or in other forms of compensation. Similarly, the NHE category for medical research does not show the total amounts expended by all parties on studies and evaluations. Instead, that category includes only the amounts invested by government agencies or nonprofit organizations. Furthermore, although drug manufacturers and other commercial entities fund research efforts using at least some of the profits they earn from sales of drugs and other items, those research funds are not separately identified in the NHE data. As a result, complete information about the distribution or incidence of health care costs is missing from the current presentations of NHE data.

CBO's Analysis of NHE Data

CBO uses CMS's estimates and projections of national health expenditures in its analyses of the effects of proposals on health care spending. When appropriate, CBO adjusts those estimates to reflect its own baseline assumptions of spending for federal programs, differences in the technical and economic assumptions used by the two agencies, and other relevant factors. For example, CBO substituted its own projections of growth rates for drug spending for those used by CMS when producing estimates of the costs of Medicare's drug benefit. As new information on health care spending becomes available, CBO might consider modifying the estimates from CMS in other ways.

Global Budgets for Health Care

Some proposals might try to restrain spending on health care by establishing a global budget. A global budget for health care applies the notion of a fixed payment for health care services to a health system, in whole or in part. In the same way that certain health plans cap aggregate payments to physicians, global budgets try to minimize incentives for providers to increase the volume of services in response to reduced fees. A global budget can function in a single-payer system (one in which a single entity—generally, a government agency—pays health care providers) or in a multipayer system (one in which individuals, employers, and the government jointly fund health care expenditures). A global budget could be constructed on a macro level, in which an overall spending target is set, or it could be devised on a per capita basis, with adjustments for age, sex, health status, and other determinants of health care spending.

The potential effects of such approaches, and the concerns and implementation challenges they raise, can be seen in Medicare's current payment system for physicians as well as in examples from other countries that have adopted global budgets. In many regards, the challenges associated with global budgeting are also analogous— albeit on a larger scale—to those presented by administered pricing systems (see Chapter 5). Those experiences suggest that whether global budgets are effective depends on their scope, the targets selected for future spending, and the methods by which they are monitored and enforced. One of the challenges of global budgeting is that there can be trade-offs between some of those parameters. Government officials, for example, might find it difficult to enforce budget caps on patients' out-of-pocket expenditures, but limiting global budgets to government programs might spur some patients and providers to move to or shift costs to the private sector, where spending was not constrained. Another challenge is selecting parameters for a global budget that would limit the growth in spending but not result in a misallocation of resources that could adversely affect patients' health.

Examples and Potential Challenges

In the United States, budget caps have been implemented at the national level for several federal health care programs and at the local level by some state governments and communities. Those experiences may have limited application to broader efforts to implement a global budget, though; when budget caps are limited to a specific program or community, patients and their providers may turn for care to other sectors in which spending is not as constrained. The experiences of other countries—including Canada, the United Kingdom, and Germany—may provide more insight into the effects of implementing a global budget that encompasses most or all of the population.

The most comprehensive example of a global budget in the United States is found in the Medicare program. Medicare's payment system for physicians—known as the sustainable growth rate mechanism—sets annual and cumulative spending targets for those payments.[289] Doctors are paid a fixed fee for each service they provide, but if total spending exceeds the target amounts, an across- the-board reduction is supposed to be made in future fees to bring spending back into line (on both an annual and cumulative basis). The SGR targets were initially set in 1998 to reflect spending on physicians' services at that time. For subsequent years, payments per enrollee are allowed to increase at about the same rate as growth in per capita gross domestic product and by an estimated change in fees for physicians' services (after adjusting for certain factors, such as changes in laws and regulations, which affect health care spending but are outside the control of providers and patients). Since 2002, actual and projected payments for physicians' services have consistently exceeded the target amounts, and as a result, substantial reductions in the nominal level of doctors' fees have been projected in order to meet the spending targets. After the Medicare program reduced physicians' fees by nearly 5 percent in 2002, legislation was enacted to limit or delay the impact of the scheduled reductions in each of the following years (which, in some cases, has meant that larger fee reductions will be needed in the future for spending to remain within the targets).

Another example of budget caps at the federal level is the health care system for military veterans. Because that system is funded through the annual appropriation process, the resources available in each fiscal year are capped. As a result, the Department of Veterans Affairs places veterans in different categories, weighing factors such as income and service-connected disability in determining which veterans will receive care. More than 10 million veterans who do not rank high enough on the VA's list are not eligible for VA-funded care (see Chapter 6 for further details).

Some states and communities have also tried to establish budgets for certain subsets of health care expenditures. In the early 1990s, Oregon sought to expand its Medicaid program to a broader population—all residents below the federal poverty level—while limiting the number of services that were covered to constrain the state's costs. Toward that end, the state developed a prioritized list of medical services and would cover only those services above a cutoff point; the list is updated every two years as part of Oregon's biennial budget process to reflect both new information on medical care and changes in the state's fiscal condition. Although the priority list has made decisionmaking about the allocation of public sources for health coverage more explicit, its impact on costs has been modest—partly because many of the more expensive types of treatments are included on the list. Nor has the state's Medicaid program been able to avoid cutbacks in enrollment: In 2004, tight budget resources led the state to freeze enrollment in its Medicaid program for some low-income adults.[290]

The experience of Rochester, New York, during the 1980s provides some insight into the effectiveness of a global budget that was not limited to a government program. In that community, the local hospitals voluntarily agreed to an overall cap on revenues from all insurers (including Blue Cross and Blue Shield, Medicare, and Medicaid). A prospective payment program was established and monitored by a nonprofit agency, whose board contained representatives of the local hospitals. According to one analysis, hospital costs in Rochester increased more slowly than the national average, and the hospital sector's share of health care costs fell from 55 percent to 38 percent over that decade. Rochester's experiment ended in the late 1980s, when a federal waiver of certain Medicare regulations was terminated.[291]

Other countries have also established global budgets of various types. In the United Kingdom, a health care budget is set nationally and then allocated to regional organizations. As with an integrated health plan, doctors generally receive a salary or a fixed payment per patient rather than per service, and hospitals receive a budget allocation. In Germany, the payment system for physicians is similar to Medicare's, with fee-for-service reimbursement of doctors and fee adjustments to meet spending targets. In Canada, expenditure caps have been applied in a number of provinces, both through hospital budgets and through global caps on physicians' expenditures.

One concern about such approaches is that they may discourage the use of effective (as well as ineffective) health care. Comparisons of health indicators across countries, however, do not show any definitive differences that are attributable to the existence of global health budgets. For example, the United States compares unfavorably with some countries that use global budgets in measures such as life expectancy or infant mortality rates, but survival rates for certain types of cancer are higher in the United States than in those countries. The role that global budgets play in affecting those health outcomes is unclear, however. Given the many factors that affect health status, it would be difficult to isolate the impact of global budgeting.

Key Parameters

The goal of a global budget is to limit total health care spending or certain types of health care spending to a predetermined amount. The experiences in the United States and other countries suggest that establishing and defining that amount would entail several steps:

- Defining the scope of the budget,
- Setting targets for future spending, and
- Establishing mechanisms to monitor and enforce the spending targets.

Those steps could be specified in law; alternatively, some or all of them could be delegated to a national board or federal agency.

Scope of the Budget

A first step in establishing a global budget would be to determine its scope—that is, what services and payments it would encompass. A global budget could cover all health-related services, including those that are elective (such as cosmetic surgery) or related to health indirectly (long-term care, for example), or its scope could be limited to services typically covered by a health insurance policy. A global budget could also seek to limit only insured costs or could address out-of-pocket costs as well. Similarly, the budget could include payments for health care from all sources (including private insurers, Medicare, and Medicaid) or could cover a narrower set of payers. In general, a broader scope would make a global budget more challenging to implement and monitor, especially if it encompassed out-of-pocket spending by individuals. However, a broader scope might also reduce the "leakage" of payments from covered to exempted sectors—which could arise in an effort to circumvent the budget cap.

Targets for Spending

A second step would be to set an initial level for the global budget and a formula or process for updating it over time. One key issue is whether the initial spending target would reflect current spending levels or a lower level that was set as a policy goal. A closely related issue is how the budget target would be updated from year to year; to the extent that a growth rate was specified that was lower than projected growth in health care spending, the budgetary constraint would become more binding over time.

A similar issue is how to allocate the overall budget targets—by geographic areas (such as states), across provider types (such as hospitals and physicians), or both. In setting targets on the basis of geography, a key issue would be whether to accommodate current differences in spending among regions—which are substantial—or to seek reductions in those differentials. In setting targets by provider type, a key issue would be how to make trade-offs across those sectors or to accommodate underlying changes in medical practices over time.

In general, assigning budgets to specific hospitals or providers might increase accountability but would also raise concerns about potential misallocations of those limits. Allocating budgets on the basis of individual hospitals' historical operating costs, for example, would in effect reward relatively inefficient hospitals and penalize relatively efficient ones. In addition, more uniform budgets could require that high-cost hospitals make difficult adjustments, particularly if those higher costs reflected having sicker patients or providing higher quality care. Proposals might also need to address the scope of services to which the budget applied, and whether and how any adjustments might be made for emergencies.

Monitoring and Enforcement Mechanisms

Choices about the scope of any global budget would not only help determine the challenges involved in monitoring and enforcing it but also shape what mechanisms might be needed to do so. In general, the less effective the monitoring and enforcement mechanisms, the more likely it is that actual spending would stay at the level projected in the absence of a global budget.

One challenge in implementing a global budget might be the lack of accurate and timely data with which to monitor spending. Although the national health expenditures include information on private health care spending, the data are estimated by CMS using surveys from public and private sources. No other agency currently monitors private spending. Even for a large public program like Medicare that receives data from actual claims, it takes several years to reconcile and settle payments. That long span highlights the difficulty of measuring health care spending in real time.

Another key question regarding implementation of a global budget is how payments would be adjusted if they exceeded the spending targets. Total payments could be adjusted prospectively, by capping the amount of premiums paid to insurers, for example, or by allocating fixed amounts to different types of providers (hospitals, for instance). Alternatively, retrospective adjustments might be needed to bring actual spending into line with the targets. Retrospective adjustment mechanisms could include penalties for insurers that have excess spending or reductions in fee-for-service payment rates for providers if total costs exceeded spending targets.

Each approach presents substantial challenges in implementation. If providers continued to receive fee-for-service reimbursement, global budgets would not create incentives for them to restrict spending; indeed, they could partly offset the effects of a reduction in fees by increasing the volume or intensity of the services they provide. Over time, the resulting increase in volume would cause further reductions in fees, which might ultimately cause some providers to cut back on services. A global budget would have more binding effects if it was combined with a system of capitation in which provider- or plan-level incentives and systemwide incentives were aligned to encourage the efficient provision of care. The challenge with a global budget based on capitation, however, is bringing the demand for services in line with the resources that are available.

Factors Affecting CBO's Estimates

Key considerations in CBO's analysis of any proposal for a global budget would be its scope, the severity of its limits, and the monitoring and enforcement mechanisms it includes. In particular, new monitoring systems would be needed in order to impose an effective budgetary constraint on spending that is not currently financed by the federal government. Without such a system, it is unlikely that an effective and binding budget could be devised to encompass all spending on health care—inevitably, some private spending would occur outside the scope of the cap, and it would be difficult to detect such spending. Proposals with weaker monitoring and lax enforcement mechanisms would be less likely to actually reduce spending below currently projected levels in the categories that are subject to the budget.

Impact of Proposals on the Composition of Compensation and Tax Revenues

Many proposals to modify the health insurance system could affect revenues by causing a shift between taxable and nontaxable forms of compensation. For example, capping the current exclusion for employment-based health insurance would increase revenues (including payments to the Social Security and Medicare trust funds) because premiums above the cap would be subject to individual income taxes and payroll taxes. A tax cap— that is, a limit on the amount of health insurance premiums that may be excluded from taxable income—would also raise revenues if, as a result, employers' contributions for health insurance plans were lower than what they otherwise would be and workers received higher wages or other taxable benefits instead.[292] Similarly, a tax credit for individually purchased health insurance could cause some employers to drop existing plans and instead boost other forms of taxable compensation.

Even proposals that would not amend the Internal Revenue Code would affect revenues if they caused a change in the allocation between taxable and nontaxable forms of compensation. A proposal requiring firms to provide health insurance coverage could increase employers' contributions for health insurance, causing wages and thus revenues to fall. Conversely, a proposal to impose a global budget could constrain health care costs, lowering employers' payments for health insurance and thus increasing wages and revenues.

Changing the tax treatment of health insurance would affect revenues not only by subjecting more wages to income and payroll taxes but also through interactions with a number of other tax provisions. For example, policies that caused changes in earned income would affect the amount that taxpayers could contribute to individual retirement accounts or claim as earned income tax credits and refundable child tax credits.

CBO will include in its analyses the effects of proposals on revenues. Estimates of proposals that change the Internal Revenue Code will be prepared by the staff of the Joint Committee on Taxation.

Flow of Payments and Budgetary Treatment

Major health insurance proposals could have a substantial influence on the flow of payments for health insurance and health care among government agencies, employers, individuals, insurers, and health care providers. If a proposal affected the flow of payments to or from the federal government, CBO would account for the timing of the outlays and receipts when estimating the net impact on the federal budget. In its analysis, CBO would also consider the effects on the budget of any federal mandates on individuals, other private entities, and state governments.

If legislation imposed a federal mandate to purchase or pay for health insurance, some revenues and costs could be reflected in the federal budget—even if the money was not collected or disbursed by federal agencies.

Timing of Payments

One consideration in analyzing the effects of proposals to expand health insurance coverage would be the impact on the timing of outlays and receipts to the federal government. Another consideration would be who would bear financial responsibility for any shortfalls in funding for insurance and health care.

The various payment arrangements used in Medicare illustrate different strategies for allocating risk between health care providers and the federal government. Hospitals and doctors participating in the fee-for-service Medicare program submit claims to local intermediaries or carriers after the services have been provided. The intermediaries process the claims, verifying that they are for covered services and actual beneficiaries. Only after that adjudication has occurred does the federal government make payments. (Additional processes exist for appeals and fraud detection.) For private health plans providing Medicare's basic and drug benefits (Medicare Advantage plans), however, the federal government makes a fixed payment per enrollee at the beginning of each month, and the plans then arrange payments to hospitals, doctors, pharmacies, and other providers. Although that approach accelerates the payments to private health plans, the plans bear the risk that the payments from the government might not be sufficient to cover their costs; conversely, the federal government bears the risk that the payments are too high. For the drug benefit, the federal government takes an additional step, reconciling federal payments with plans' actual expenditures at the end of each year. That reconciliation could result in the plans owing the government money or vice versa, but it also causes administrative costs—such as collection costs—to increase.

Similar issues would arise if a proposal required the Internal Revenue Service to collect premiums for health insurance. One approach would build on the system used for the health coverage tax credit (described further in Chapter 2). Under that program, individuals can send the amount of the premium that they owe directly to the IRS, which bundles that payment with the appropriate federal subsidy payments and sends the total sum to insurers.[293] Under an alternative approach, people would pay their portion of the premiums during the year through wage withholding and estimated quarterly payments. However, the IRS would not know until a taxpayer filed a return at the end of the year whether he or she had paid the full amount owed. In the interim, the Treasury Department would make monthly payments to insurers whether or not the payments from enrollees had been received. After the tax return was filed, the IRS would reconcile the amounts received from individuals with the payments owed and seek to collect or refund any discrepancies.

The advantage of the first approach to using the IRS is that it would limit federal exposure for unpaid premiums. The disadvantage is that it would require the IRS to actively collect and track taxpayers' payments throughout the year. An advantage of the second approach is that the IRS would not have to create a new large-scale infrastructure to collect premiums; its disadvantages are that it would involve potentially large temporary transfers of general revenue and that the IRS would have to determine whether any collection activities related to unpaid premiums were worth the expense.

Budgetary Treatment of Federal Mandates

When proposals would affect the outlays made or receipts collected by federal agencies, CBO would account for those effects in estimating the proposals' costs. When proposals would establish federal mandates that would not result in payments to or from the federal government, however, the issue of their budgetary impact would be less clear. In some cases, CBO would treat any resulting payments as part of the federal budget; in other cases, it would not. The extent of federal control and compulsion is a critical element in determining budgetary treatment. To assess whether transactions should be reflected in the federal budget, CBO would consider whether a proposal included these factors:

- Payments by individuals or employers that are the result of a federal mandate;
- Any required government payments (for example, subsidized premiums for low-income individuals);
- Oversight activities by federal agencies; and
- Restrictions on the amount of discretion allowed to entities that collect or pay premiums.

In general, CBO believes that federally mandated collections—those resulting from the exercise of sovereign power—should be recorded in the budget as federal revenues, even if such amounts are not paid to a federal agency. Similarly, a mandated transfer of any such collections to others should be recorded as a budget outlay. An example of such transactions is the existing Universal Service Fund, which collects money from telecommunications carriers and spends it to subsidize telecommunication services to high-cost areas, to low-income consumers, and to schools, libraries, and rural health care providers.

In its 1994 analysis of the Clinton Administration's health care proposal, CBO concluded that payments to and from the "health alliances" should be included in the accounts of the federal government but that they should be distinguished from other federal operations and shown separately—as is the practice for the Social Security program.[294] (Although those alliances would have collected and paid health insurance premiums, they might not have been considered federal agencies because they would have been established by states and other entities.) At that time, CBO based its view primarily on the judgment that the proposal would establish a federal entitlement to health benefits and that the mandatory premiums used to finance the new entitlement would constitute an exercise of the federal government's sovereign power.

Throughout this volume, CBO has used the term "mandate" when discussing certain types of proposals that would include new federal requirements for health insurance. The use of that term should not be interpreted to indicate a CBO conclusion that such requirements would meet the definition of "mandate" under the Unfunded Mandates Reform Act (UMRA). When analyzing specific legislative proposals, CBO assesses whether they would impose a mandate on state, local, or tribal governments or the private sector—an analysis that is required by UMRA. To the extent that a proposal would require state, local, or tribal governments or private entities to undertake some activity that they would not otherwise take on—or prohibit them from activities that they would otherwise pursue—it could constitute a mandate under UMRA. The discussions of proposals in this volume, however, do not consider the costs of potential mandates as defined in UMRA, nor do they attempt to quantify the impact of those proposals on states' spending.[295]

Macroeconomic Effects

Given that health care constitutes roughly one-sixth of the U.S. economy, any changes to the health care system could affect the operation of the broader economy. This section reviews possible effects of proposals to expand health insurance coverage on labor markets, the capital stock, and international competitiveness.

The overall economic effects of comprehensive changes to the health care system are difficult to predict. Although economic theory and experience provide some guidance about the effects of specific provisions, large-scale proposals to restructure the health insurance system may contain numerous pieces that could interact—affecting labor supply, the capital stock, and productivity in complex and possibly offsetting ways. Depending on the nature of those interactions, a comprehensive proposal might yield results that differ from those examined in this analysis.

Effects on Labor Markets

Large-scale changes to the health insurance system could affect labor markets by changing people's incentives to work and employers' decisions to hire workers. The availability of health insurance options can affect people's incentives to enter the labor force, work fewer or more hours, retire, change jobs, or even prefer certain types of firms or jobs. In addition, some proposals—such as employer mandates—could affect firms' decisions to hire workers.

Changing Incentives to Work

Changes in health care policy that affected taxes or subsidies could have an impact on the economic gains from work. For example, proposals that would increase government spending on health care might be financed in part by additional taxes. Taxes levied as a percentage of labor income have two opposing effects on how much people choose to work. On the one hand, those taxes reduce the amount of after-tax wages earned for each additional hour worked, which tends to diminish the incentive to work. Economists refer to that as the "substitution effect" of tax rates on the number of hours worked. On the other hand, by decreasing the amount of after-tax income earned for any given amount of work, taxes tend to encourage people to work more to make up the difference. Economists refer to that as the "income effect." Most studies conclude that for simple changes in tax rates on labor income, the substitution effect typically outweighs the income effect—on average, due largely to the response of secondary earners. (Secondary earners are generally the spouse of the main earner in a household.) Therefore, increases in marginal tax rates generally reduce the number of hours worked.[296]

The precise impact that tax financing had on hours worked would depend on the details of the tax changes. Some tax provisions that would increase revenue would reduce after-tax income but have little or no corresponding effect on the return from an additional hour's work. For example, a proposal to reduce the dollar amount of a flat tax credit (say, from $5,000 to $4,000) would affect after-tax income but have no impact on the after-tax hourly wage. Tax increases of that type would probably increase the number of hours worked.

Other types of proposals could have the opposite effect on people's incentives to work. For example, some proposals would include subsidies to help low-income people pay for health insurance. A subsidy could be provided through the transfer system (possibly as a voucher) or through the tax system (as an exclusion from income, a tax deduction, or a tax credit). A subsidy represents an increase in income, which might discourage work effort, all other things being equal.

To limit costs, subsidies are often phased out as a beneficiary's income rises. Over the phaseout range, a worker receives less compensation for each additional hour worked, because each dollar earned reduces the subsidy. That effect is sometimes referred to as an "implicit tax." That implicit tax can lead people to work fewer hours than they otherwise would, in the same way that income and payroll tax rates do.

Policymakers face a trade-off in deciding how to phase out subsidies. If subsidies are phased out quickly, the implicit tax rates, and thus the negative impact on work incentives, can be quite high. Implicit tax rates can be reduced by expanding the range over which the subsidy is phased out, but doing so increases the number of people subject to the implicit tax and, if the range is extended by raising the income level at which it is completely phased out, also boosts the total cost of the subsidy. In the extreme, a subsidy can be granted to everyone, which eliminates any effect on the economic gains from work but substantially increases costs. By contrast, a subsidy can be eliminated all at once at a certain income level (creating a "cliff" in the relationship between the subsidy and income), which eliminates the cost of phasing out the subsidy but significantly increases the disincentives to work for people whose potential income is in the neighborhood of the cliff.

Some aspects of the current health care system create work disincentives, so changes to that system could curtail or eliminate those effects. One program that creates work disincentives for its recipients is Medicaid. That program is structured so that eligibility for benefits is completely eliminated at specified income levels (a cliff).[297] For individuals with income close to those thresholds, working more and earning a higher income can lead to the loss of all Medicaid benefits, creating a powerful disincentive to work. A system that made health insurance coverage independent of income would eliminate that disincentive for current Medicaid recipients. As an example of the potential effects on labor supply, one study found that a series of increases in the income limit for Medicaid eligibility in the late 1980s and 1990s increased the labor force participation of working-age single mothers by 1.4 percent.[298]

Some proposals would limit current tax subsidies for health insurance by reducing or eliminating the tax exclusion for employment-based health insurance. Eliminating that exclusion would make a larger share of compensation taxable. By itself, that change would reduce after-tax income, encouraging people to work more to make up for their lost earnings.[299] Capping the exclusion would also affect the relative prices of goods: The effective price of health insurance would rise, making other goods appear less expensive. One such good would be "leisure"—which people "purchase" in forgone earnings by choosing to work less. Assuming there were no other changes, an increase in the price of health insurance would tend to boost the consumption of other goods— including leisure. As a result, labor supply would decline. CBO has estimated that the proposals in the President's budgets for fiscal years 2008 and 2009 to make employment-based health insurance taxable and create capped tax deductions for individuals with health insurance would reduce the supply of labor.[300]

Reducing the Link between Employment and Insurance

Proposals that would make insurance less dependent on employment status (for example, by substituting public programs or individually purchased insurance for employment-based health benefits) could induce more workers to retire earlier and could reduce the participation of younger workers in the labor force as well. (Proposals that strengthened the link between employment and health insurance—for example, by requiring coverage of employees—could have the opposite effects.)

Employment-based insurance offers a number of advantages (including lower administrative costs, favorable tax treatment, and coverage of existing conditions) that may be difficult or impossible for workers to obtain by purchasing insurance individually. For that reason, its availability can play an important role in people's decisions to enter or remain in the workforce—especially if they are nearing retirement. People who are insured through their employer but are not offered health benefits after retirement have an additional incentive to remain employed until they qualify for Medicare at age 65. Proposals that include some kind of "bridge" coverage for early retirees would remove that incentive and increase the likelihood of retirement before age 65, thereby decreasing the supply of labor.

A review of the literature found that workers whose health insurance covers them in retirement are more likely to retire at any given age and tend to retire earlier, on average, than those without such benefits.[301] Some studies found that the availability of health benefits during retirement increases the probability of retirement before age 65 by 30 percent to 80 percent.[302] Studies using other estimating techniques generally found smaller effects, and a few found little or no effect. However, the weight of the evidence indicates that retirees' health coverage probably leads to earlier retirement. Such findings suggest that proposals that would substitute other forms of coverage for employment-based insurance could cause some people to retire earlier than they would under the current system.

Increasing the availability of health insurance outside the workforce could also reduce the labor force participation of younger workers, although there is less evidence supporting that effect. The impact on participation would probably be highest among secondary earners because they tend to be more responsive to changes in compensation than are primary earners. Currently, if primary earners are not offered family coverage through their employer, other members of their household may enter the workforce in order to get the benefits of employment- based insurance. Some research indicates that spouses not covered under primary earners' insurance are more likely to be employed than spouses who are covered through such a plan. Expanding access to health insurance could cause some of those secondary earners to stop working.

Changing the Degree of Job Lock

Some of the same advantages of employment-based health insurance that may keep more people in the labor force can also affect how often workers change jobs. People who have medical problems (or have family members with medical problems) can have an incentive to stay in a job that provides health insurance benefits in order to cover those preexisting conditions, even if more productive opportunities exist elsewhere. (Those opportunities could include working for a different employer or becoming an independent entrepreneur.) That phenomenon is sometimes referred to as "job lock."

The evidence is mixed regarding the effects of employment-based health insurance on job turnover. Although some empirical studies find that workers are less likely to change jobs when faced with the potential loss of health insurance, others find little or no effect.[303] Much of that evidence is difficult to interpret, however, because many jobs that provide health insurance have other attributes that discourage turnover. Moreover, most studies to date rely on data collected before enactment of the Health Insurance Portability and Accountability Act in 1996. That law placed some constraints on the ability of employment-based plans to deny coverage for preexisting conditions, especially for workers who were previously covered under other plans, and therefore has most likely reduced the importance of job lock.

To the extent that employment-based insurance affects turnover, it can have both beneficial and adverse effects on the economy. Firms may have a greater incentive to invest in their workers (by providing training or increasing their skills or knowledge) if the probability of retaining those workers is increased. However, workers may also choose to stay in their current positions solely to retain their current health coverage rather than move to other jobs in which they could be more productive.

Mandating Insurance Coverage

Some proposals would require employers to offer health insurance to their employees. Because employees largely bear the cost of health benefits in the form of lower wages, the effects of those proposals on employment and hours worked could be relatively minor.[304] However, an employer mandate could affect the amount of work available for certain categories of workers.

In particular, a plan that mandated that employers offer health insurance could reduce the hiring of low-wage workers. In a competitive market, the demand for and the supply of labor determine the total compensation— including both wages and benefits—that employees earn. If employers were required to provide health insurance benefits, their employees' wages and other forms of compensation would be lower than what they otherwise would be by the amount of the cost of the insurance. However, wages and other forms of compensation for employees earning amounts at or near the minimum wage might not be able to fall by the full cost of the health insurance coverage required by law. That constraint could lead employers to hire fewer of those workers, increasing unemployment, although that effect is likely to be small. One study estimates that 224,000 workers (or about 0.2 percent of all private-sector workers) could become unemployed if firms were required to provide health insurance costing $2 per hour worked, on average.[305] In contrast, a study of the state-level employer mandate in Hawaii found that the rate of employment grew faster in Hawaii than in the rest of the United States after the mandate was instituted (perhaps because of factors other than the mandate).[306]

Affecting Workers' Choices of Firms

Some proposals to provide subsidies for health insurance or require employers to offer health insurance coverage would differentiate between firms on the basis of criteria such as the number of workers, revenues, or salary levels. That differentiation could create incentives for certain types of workers to work for certain types of firms.

The responses to those types of incentives could take several forms—some involving actions of workers, some involving actions of firms, and some involving actions of both parties. For example, new workers in the labor force could choose jobs with certain firms rather than others. Or those already in the workforce could quit their jobs and move to different firms. Firms could "outsource"— that is, lay off employees and contract with other companies for the same services. Alternatively, firms could divide themselves into subsidiaries with low and high average wages.

For example, the Clinton Administration's health proposal included subsidies to firms with low average wages to help offset the costs of mandated health benefits. Those subsidies would have created incentives for low- wage workers to work for firms with low wages, on average, and high-wage workers to work for firms with higher average wages.[307] In its analysis of the 1993 plan, CBO found that the resulting shift of workers among firms would increase the net budgetary cost of the proposal (because the shifts would reduce tax payments or increase subsidies) and also could decrease the efficiency of the allocation of workers to firms.[307]

Effects on the Nation's Capital Stock

Health care proposals would affect the nation's stock of productive capital through their impact on saving, because the amount of national saving determines the resources available for domestically owned investment. (National saving is the sum of private saving by households and businesses and government saving—federal, state, and local budget surpluses.) If a health care proposal increased government budget deficits, or reduced surpluses, it could decrease the resources available for investment and, therefore, the capital stock.

The effects of health care proposals on private saving are more ambiguous and partly depend on the specific provisions of any proposal. Proposals that expanded access to health insurance and medical care could reduce private saving, whereas those that reduced consumption of health care could increase private saving.

People who are not currently covered by insurance have an incentive to save more to guard against unforeseen medical expenses. Covering more people could reduce that motive for saving, which would lower private saving and result in a smaller capital stock. However, because many people who currently lack coverage are in low- income households, which tend to save very little regardless of whether they have insurance, the effect of expanding coverage on private saving may not be large. Furthermore, increasing the number of people with insurance would lessen their risk of incurring uninsured medical expenses, even if it reduced their saving.

Proposals that include an "asset test" for receiving subsidies or other benefits could also decrease saving. If receipt of benefits is dependent on a person's or household's assets being below a certain level, people may refrain from saving in order to stay below the limit. Such proposals could have an opposite effect on Medicaid recipients, however. Because the current Medicaid system includes asset tests, proposals that eliminated those tests could increase saving, particularly among households that have assets slightly below the current thresholds.[309]

Proposals might affect consumption, and therefore the capital stock, through their impact on income and on consumption of health care. Subsidies or other provisions that increase the after-tax income of recipients would probably increase consumption, all other things being equal, which would reduce the resources available for investment. More generally, proposals that resulted in an increase in consumption of health services would tend to reduce saving and investment unless other types of consumption fell by corresponding amounts. Conversely, proposals that reduced consumption of health services would probably boost saving and investment.

Productivity

To the extent that changes in the health insurance system led to improved health status among workers, the nation's economic productivity could be enhanced. Some research has also suggested that improved health status might increase the growth rate of productivity.

Studies have found that healthier workers work more hours and earn higher wages than those who are less healthy.[310] That relationship suggests that changes to the health insurance market that lead to better health outcomes could both increase the labor supply and raise productivity (presumably, workers earn higher wages when they are healthy because they are more productive).

Other studies compare the economic output of different countries and how that output is related to various measures of health status within each country.[311] Those studies generally find that countries with better health outcomes grow faster than other countries. The results must be interpreted with caution, however. Because higher income may lead to better health, the direction of causation is not clear. Greater growth may lead to healthier citizens, rather than vice versa. Moreover, those studies are based on the very wide range of health outcomes—for example, life expectancy—observed when developing countries are compared with industrialized nations. The implications for marginal advances in health outcomes in already fairly healthy countries are, therefore, unclear.

Because the impact on health outcomes from major changes to the health care system is uncertain, it is not clear whether such changes would have a substantial impact on overall economic output or productivity.

International Competitiveness

Some observers have asserted that domestic producers that provide health insurance to their workers face higher costs for compensation than competitors based in countries where insurance is not employment based and that fundamental changes to the health insurance system could reduce or eliminate that disadvantage. However, such a cost reduction is unlikely to occur, except in the short run.

The equilibrium level of overall compensation in the economy is determined by the supply of and the demand for labor. Fringe benefits (such as health insurance) are just part of that compensation. Consequently, the costs of fringe benefits are borne by workers largely in the form of lower cash wages than they would receive if no such benefits were provided by their employer.

Replacing employment-based health care with a government-run system could reduce employers' payments for their workers' insurance, but the amount that they would have to pay in overall compensation would remain essentially unchanged. Even though changes to the health care system could have various effects on the supply of labor, the underlying amount of labor supplied at any given level of compensation would hardly be affected by a change in the health care system. As a result, cash wages and other forms of compensation would have to rise by roughly the amount of the reduction in health benefits for firms to be able to attract the same number and types of workers.

Compensation could take some time to adjust to its market-clearing level (the point at which supply and demand are equal). During that time, firms that formerly provided health benefits—especially firms that employ workers under multiyear contracts—could experience substantial reductions in labor costs, which would boost their profits temporarily.[312] But those firms would experience no permanent change in their competitive status.

End Notes

[1] Those figures are CBO estimates and differ somewhat from the estimates of the uninsured population released annually by the Census Bureau (the most recent of which indicated that about 46 million people were uninsured at any given point in 2007). Like other estimates, CBO's figures represent the civilian, non-institutionalized population; they therefore include unauthorized immigrants but exclude residents of nursing homes, people who are incarcerated, and U.S. citizens living abroad. See Chapter 6 for further discussion of such populations.

[2] The issue of whether a policy proposal would be considered a mandate for purposes of the Unfunded Mandates Reform Act and related questions regarding the contents of a formal cost estimate are discussed in Chapter 8.

[3] Estimates of health insurance coverage presented in this chapter are derived from a simulation model that the Congressional Budget Office (CBO) developed in order to analyze the effects of various policy options on coverage and spending for health care. For a detailed description of that model and the data and evidence on which it is based, see *CBO's Health Insurance Simulation Model: A Technical Description,* Background Paper (October 2007).

[4] Henry J. Kaiser Family Foundation and Health Research and Educational Trust (Kaiser/HRET), *Employer Health Benefits: 2008 Annual Survey* (Washington, D.C.: Kaiser/HRET, September 2008).

[5] Even if a given labor market was not competitive, firms operating in that market would still be expected to hold total compensation fixed, so that other forms of compensation would be reduced to offset the costs of providing health insurance. The allocation of compensation among wages, health insurance, and other fringe benefits would reflect the preferences of workers and the firms' efforts to attract employees.

[6] For a discussion of that evidence, see Jonathan Gruber, "Health Insurance and the Labor Market," in A.J. Culyer and J.P. Newhouse, eds., *Handbook of Health Economics,* vol. 1 (Amsterdam: North Holland, 2006), pp. 645–706.

[7] One study examined the impact of a state mandate to cover maternity benefits and found that reductions in the wages of women of child-bearing age and their spouses roughly offset the average costs of providing those

benefits. See Jonathan Gruber, "The Incidence of Mandated Maternity Benefits," *American Economic Review,* vol. 84, no. 3 (June 1994), pp. 622–641.

[8] Jeff Liebman and Richard Zeckhauser, *Simple Humans, Complex Insurance, Subtle Subsidies,* Working Paper No. 14330 (Cambridge, Mass.: National Bureau of Economic Research, September 2008).

[9] Among firms that have similar numbers of workers, the share of firms reporting that they offer coverage to their employees is generally larger than the share of employees reporting that they have an offer, but that discrepancy simply reflects the fact that some workers at firms that offer coverage are not eligible to enroll in it. For example, many part-time workers are ineligible.

[10] Kaiser/HRET, *Employer Health Benefits: 2008 Annual Survey*; and *Employer Health Benefits: 1999 Annual Survey* (October 1999).

[11] For more information, see Mark Merlis, "The Federal Employees Health Benefits Program: Program Design, Recent Performance, and Implications for Medicare Reform" (briefing prepared for the Henry J. Kaiser Family Foundation, May 30, 2003).

[12] Workers who previously held employment-based insurance may seek coverage in the individual insurance market, and insurers must generally offer them a policy if they apply, but some workers may find the terms of that coverage unattractive. See Chapter 4 for additional discussion.

[13] Exceptions include self-employed individuals, who may deduct the costs of their health insurance from their taxable income, and individuals who claim itemized medical deductions in excess of 7.5 percent of their adjusted gross income. See Chapter 2 for additional discussion.

[14] According to the most recent estimates from the Census Bureau, about 700,000 elderly people, or roughly 2 percent of individuals age 65 or older, were uninsured in 2007.

[15] That figure includes retirees who continue to receive drug coverage from a former employer if that employer receives a subsidy payment from Medicare on their behalf.

[16] That figure represents average enrollment and excludes nonelderly individuals living in institutions (such as nursing homes) and people living in U.S. territories. CBO has also projected that the total number of individuals enrolled in Medicaid at any point during 2009 (including elderly and institutionalized enrollees and residents of territories) will be 65 million, of which about 59 million will be nonelderly. Many of those individuals will be enrolled in the program for only part of the year.

[17] According to one estimate, total spending on optional populations and benefits accounted for about 60 percent of the program's expenditures in 2001. Of that total, 30 percent was spent to provide optional benefits to mandatory groups; 50 percent, to provide mandatory benefits to optional groups; and 20 percent, to provide optional benefits to optional groups. See Kaiser Commission on Medicaid and the Uninsured, *Medicaid Enrollment and Spending by "Mandatory" and "Optional" Eligibility and Benefit Categories* (Washington, D.C.: Henry J. Kaiser Family Foundation, June 2005), p. 11.

[18] For additional information, see Congressional Budget Office, *The State Children's Health Insurance Program* (May 2007).

[19] Congressional Budget Office, *How Many People Lack Health Insurance and For How Long?* (May 2003).

[20] U.S. Census Bureau, *Income, Poverty, and Health Insurance Coverage in the United States: 2007,* P60-235 (August 2008).

[21] For a discussion, see Congressional Budget Office, *Nonprofit Hospitals and the Provision of Community Benefits* (December 2006).

[22] Jack Hadley and others, "Covering the Uninsured in 2008: Current Costs, Sources of Payment, and Incremental Costs," *Health Affairs,* Web Exclusive (August 25, 2008), pp. W399–W415. That study also reported that uncompensated care would total about $56 billion in 2008 if all costs not paid out of pocket by the uninsured were included in the tally. But that amount would seem to be an overestimate because the study found that, even though no payments were made by insurers, about half of those costs were directly compensated by various third parties (such as workers' compensation programs).

[23] Jonathan Gruber and David Rodriguez, *How Much Uncompensated Care Do Doctors Provide?* Working Paper No. 13585 (Cambridge, Mass.: National Bureau of Economic Research, November 2007).

[24] If the study by Hadley and others underestimated the number of services used by uninsured individuals, its estimate of uncompensated care could also be correspondingly low. (That factor could account for the higher estimate of uncompensated care that study derived using reports by doctors and hospitals.) If, instead, the study overestimated the number of services used by insured individuals, that would not necessarily affect the estimate of uncompensated care.

[25] For a summary of those studies, see Institute of Medicine, *Care Without Coverage: Too Little, Too Late* (Washington, D.C.: National Academy Press, 2002), www.iom.edu.

[26] Helen Levy and David Meltzer, "The Impact of Health Insurance on Health," *Annual Review of Public Health,* vol. 29 (April 2008), pp. 399–409. One study that sheds some light on the impact of health insurance on health is the RAND Health Insurance Experiment, which randomly assigned large groups of nonelderly individuals to different health insurance plans and tracked their experience over several years. In general, the study found that participants who faced cost sharing did not have worse health than those who got all of their care for free; one exception was lower- income participants with prior health problems, who did not control their blood

pressure as effectively when they faced cost sharing. An important limitation of the study, however, is that no participants lacked insurance. For additional discussion of those findings, see Congressional Budget Office, *Consumer-Directed Health Plans: Potential Effects on Health Care Spending and Outcomes* (December 2006), pp. 54–55.

27 Amy Finkelstein and Robin McKnight, "What Did Medicare Do? The Initial Impact of Medicare on Mortality and Out of Pocket Medical Spending," *Journal of Public Economics,* vol. 92, no. 7 (July 2008), pp. 1644–1668.

28 Kaiser/HRET, *Employer Health Benefits: 2008 Annual Survey.*

29 For additional discussion of those plans, see Congressional Budget Office, *Consumer-Directed Health Plans.*

30 Mercer Human Resource Consulting, *National Survey of Employer-Sponsored Health Plans 2004* (New York: Mercer, 2004).

31 AHIP Center for Policy Research, *Individual Health Insurance 2006–2007: A Comprehensive Survey of Premiums, Availability, and Benefits* (Washington, D.C.: America's Health Insurance Plans, December 2007).

32 If the cost of the tax expenditure from excluding premiums for employment-based insurance (estimated to be roughly $250 billion at the federal level in 2007) was included in public spending rather than private spending, then the public share of spending would be about 57 percent. See Chapter 2 for additional discussion.

33 Organisation for Economic Co-operation and Development, *OECD Health Data 2008*, www.oecd.org. Adjusting for differences in income would reduce that disparity somewhat because income in the United States is higher than the OECD average and higher income is correlated with higher spending on health care.

34 Chapin White, "Health Care Spending Growth: How Different Is the United States from the Rest of the OECD?" *Health Affairs,* vol. 26, no. 1 (January/February 2007), pp. 154–161.

35 Congressional Budget Office, *The Long-Term Outlook for Health Care Spending* (November 2007). The figure for per capita cost growth reflects the projected rate of growth after accounting for the aging of the population, referred to as "excess" cost growth. Those projections assume that no changes are made in federal policies.

36 For a discussion, see Congressional Budget Office, *The Long-Term Budget Outlook* (December 2007).

37 See Congressional Budget Office, *Technological Change and the Growth of Health Care Spending* (January 2008).

38 Joseph P. Newhouse, "Medical Care Costs: How Much Welfare Loss?" *Journal of Economic Perspectives,* vol. 6, no. 3 (Summer 1992), pp. 3–21.

39 See Alan M. Garber, "Cost-Effectiveness and Evidence Evaluation as Criteria for Coverage Policy," *Health Affairs,* Web Exclusive (May 19, 2004), pp. W4-284 to W4-296.

40 A more precise description would label the residual as the effect of changes in medical technology that are not attributed to other observed forces. For example, increases in income can account for some growth in health care spending, and the mechanism through which that growth occurs might also be the greater use of medical technology.

41 See Congressional Budget Office, *Accounting for Sources of Projected Growth in Federal Spending on Medicare and Medicaid*, Issue Brief (May 28, 2008).

42 Amy Finkelstein, "The Aggregate Effects of Health Insurance: Evidence from the Introduction of Medicare," *Quarterly Journal of Economics,* vol. 122, no. 1 (February 2007), pp. 1–37.

43 Kaiser/HRET, *Employer Health Benefits: 2008 Annual Survey*; and *Employer Health Benefits: 2000 Annual Survey* (September 2000).

44 See Cathy Schoen and others, "How Many Are Underinsured? Trends Among U.S. Adults, 2003 and 2007," *Health Affairs,* Web Exclusive (June 10, 2008), pp. W298–W309. The study relied on self-reported income and out-of-pocket health care costs of survey respondents; it defined individuals as underinsured if their health plan's deductible exceeded 5 percent of their income or if their out-of-pocket costs exceeded either 10 percent of their income (for those with family income above 200 percent of the poverty level) or 5 percent of their income (for those with family income below 200 percent of the poverty level).

45 Joseph P. Newhouse and others, "Are Fee-for-Service Costs Increasing Faster Than HMO Costs?" *Medical Care,* vol. 23, no. 8 (1985), pp. 960–966.

46 National Center for Health Statistics, *Health, United States, 2007,* DHHS Publication No. 2007-1232 (November 2007). Recent data on obesity rates suggest that those rates may have leveled off, but it is probably too early to tell whether that development is temporary or is likely to endure.

47 See Congressional Budget Office, *Technological Change and the Growth of Health Care Spending*, Box 1, p. 10.

48 National Center for Health Statistics, *Health, United States, 2007.* About 3 percent of the population was estimated to have undiagnosed diabetes in both years (which was determined by conducting medical tests on survey participants).

49 Kenneth E. Thorpe and others, "The Rising Prevalence of Treated Disease: Effects on Private Health Insurance Spending," *Health Affairs,* Web Exclusive (June 27, 2005), pp. W5-317 to W5-325.

50 Congressional Budget Office, *High-Cost Medicare Beneficiaries* (May 2005).

51 Matthew J. Eichner, Mark B. McClellan, and David A. Wise, *Insurance or Self-Insurance? Variation, Persistence, and Individual Health Accounts*, Working Paper No. 5640 (Cambridge, Mass.: National Bureau of Economic Research, June 1996).

[52] Elliott S. Fisher and others, "The Implications of Regional Variations in Medicare Spending, Part 2: Health Outcomes and Satisfaction with Care," *Annals of Internal Medicine,* vol. 138, no. 4 (February 18, 2003), pp. 288–298.

[53] See John E. Wennberg, Elliott S. Fisher, and Jonathan S. Skinner, "Geography and the Debate Over Medicare Reform," *Health Affairs,* Web Exclusive (February 13, 2002), pp. W96–W114; and Center for the Evaluative Clinical Sciences, Dartmouth Medical School, *The Dartmouth Atlas of Health Care 1999* (Lebanon, N.H.: Health Forum, Inc., 1999), pp. 22–23.

[54] For a more extensive discussion of this topic, see Congressional Budget Office, *Geographic Variation in Health Care Spending* (February 2008).

[55] This chapter focuses on subsidies to individuals or their employers. Another approach would be a federal reinsurance program that would seek to reduce premiums by covering a portion of the spending insurers incur for their high-cost cases.

[56] See Chapter 1 for further discussion of the incidence of employers' contributions for health insurance.

[57] Employees of a firm that does not offer cafeteria plans cannot exclude their share of health insurance premiums from taxable income for income and payroll tax purposes. However, they may be able to claim those premiums as an itemized deduction on their income tax return if their total medical expenses exceed 7.5 percent of adjusted gross income.

[58] Although considered part of compensation, employers' contributions for payroll taxes are not subject to income taxes or the employees' portion of payroll taxes.

[59] An offsetting consideration is that excluding health insurance premiums from taxable wages reduces future Social Security benefits, which are based on average earnings, at the same time that it reduces payroll tax payments (see Chapter 6 for further discussion).

[60] Joint Committee on Taxation, *Tax Expenditures for Health Care*, JCX-66-08 (July 30, 2008).

[61] The estimate of the tax expenditure includes the amounts (or outlays) paid to taxpayers in excess of their income tax liability, which result from the refundable nature of the health coverage tax credit.

[62] In its 2008 and 2009 fiscal year budgets, the Bush Administration proposed a deduction that applied to both the individual income and payroll tax bases. However, exempting premiums for individually purchased health insurance from payroll taxes presents administrative challenges; employers cannot easily adjust withholding for such premiums because they do not have independent information regarding how much each of their workers paid for health insurance in the individual market.

[63] See Chapter 8 for a discussion of the impact of asset tests on savings.

[64] Such a change in coverage need not result from previously insured individuals dropping their current policies to enroll in public plans, although that is one possibility. Another possibility, for example, is for people who lost their coverage to decline coverage at a new job if they now qualify for a public program.

[65] Efforts to minimize crowd-out become even more challenging over time, as some firms go out of business and other firms are created. A new firm, which previously might have offered its employees health insurance, may decide not to offer coverage, knowing that many of its workers can obtain public subsidies instead. The likelihood of that effect goes up as the share of the firm's workforce that qualifies for subsidies increases.

[66] Congressional Budget Office, *The State Children's Health Insurance Program* (May 2007), pp. 11–12.

[67] Janet Holtzblatt and Janet McCubbin, "Issues Affecting Low- Income Filers," in Henry J. Aaron and Joel Slemrod, eds., *The Crisis in Tax Administration* (Washington, D.C.: Brookings Institution, 2004), pp. 148–200.

[68] Michael Ponza and others, *NSLP/SBP Access, Participation, Eligibility, and Certification Study: Erroneous Payments in the NSLP and SBP,* vol. 1, *Study Findings* (Report No. CN-07-APEC, submitted by Mathematica Policy Research, Inc., to the Department of Agriculture, November 2007).

[69] See Jennifer Stuber and others, *Beyond Stigma: What Barriers Actually Affect the Decisions of Low-Income Families to Enroll in Medicaid?* George Washington University Medical Center Issue Brief (July 2000); Janet M. Currie and Jeffrey Grogger, "Explaining Recent Declines in Food Stamp Program Participation," in William G. Gale and Janet Rothenberg-Pack, eds., *Brookings- Wharton Papers on Urban Affairs, 2001* (2001), pp. 203–244; and Marianne P. Bitler, Janet Currie, and John Karl Scholz, "WIC Eligibility and Participation," *Journal of Human Resources*, vol. 38 (Supplement 2003), pp. 1139–1179.

[70] The counts of the insured population, however, do not reflect those who have such "provisional" insurance.

[71] A more complete description of the model, the key parameters and assumptions it uses, and the academic literature on which it is based can be found in Congressional Budget Office, *CBO's Health Insurance Simulation Model: A Technical Description*, Background Paper (October 2007).

[72] See Jonathan Gruber and Michael Lettau, "How Elastic Is the Firm's Demand for Health Insurance?" *Journal of Public Economics,* vol. 88, nos. 7–8 (2004), pp. 1273–1293; Jack Hadley and James D. Reschovsky, "Small Firms' Demand for Health Insurance: The Decision to Offer Insurance," *Inquiry,* vol. 39, no. 2 (2002), pp. 118–137; and Len Nichols and Linda J. Blumberg, "Estimating Employer Elasticity of Demand for Health Insurance" (paper presented at Academy Health Annual Research Meeting, Washington, D.C., 1999).

[73] CBO generally assumes a "linear" relationship between the change in the price of insurance and the elasticity of offer; that is, the elasticity of offer does not vary with the magnitude of the price change.

74 For a more extensive discussion, see Congressional Budget Office, *The State Children's Health Insurance Program.*

75 See Thomas Buchmueller and others, "The Effect of SCHIP Expansions on Health Insurance Decisions by Employers," *Inquiry*, vol. 42, no. 3 (2005), pp. 218–231; and M. Susan Marquis, "The Role of the Safety Net in Employer Health Benefit Decisions," *Medical Care Research and Review*, vol. 62, no. 4 (2005), pp. 435–457.

76 See Linda J. Blumberg, Jessica Banthin, and Len Nichols, "Worker Decisions to Purchase Health Insurance," *Journal of Health Care Finance and Economics*, vol. 1, nos. 3–4 (2001), pp. 305–325; and Jonathan Gruber and Ebonya Washington, "Subsidies to Employee Health Insurance Premiums and the Health Insurance Market," *Journal of Health Economics*, vol. 24, no. 2 (2005), pp. 253–276.

77 For further discussion of that option, see Congressional Budget Office, *Budget Options, Volume 1: Health Care* (December 2008).

78 Andrew Dick, "Will Employer Mandates Really Work? Another Look at Hawaii," *Health Affairs*, vol. 13, no. 1 (1994), pp. 343–349.

79 See Norman Thurston, "Labor Market Effects of Hawaii's Mandatory Employer-Provided Health Insurance," *Industrial and Labor Relations Review*, vol. 51, no. 1 (1997), pp. 117–135; and SangHyop Lee and others, *The Effect of Mandatory Employer-Sponsored Insurance (ESI) on Health Insurance Coverage and Labor Force Utilization in Hawaii: Evidence from the Current Population Survey (CPS) 1994–2004*, Working Paper No. 05-12 (Honolulu, Hawaii: University of Hawaii at Manoa, Department of Economics, July 6, 2005), www.economics WP_05-12.pdf.

80 Sharon K. Long, "On the Road to Universal Coverage: Impacts of Reform in Massachusetts at One Year," *Health Affairs*, vol. 27, no. 4 (July/August 2008), pp. W270–W284 (published online as a Web Exclusive, June 3, 2008).

81 Massachusetts's affordability standards use information from tax returns to verify eligibility for income-related exemptions and also take into account the cost of premiums. In 2008, individuals with annual income of up to $52,500 were exempt from the mandate if they could not find health insurance with a premium of less than $330 a month. For families, the corresponding income and premium amounts were, respectively, $110,000 and $792.

82 For individual income tax returns, the audit rate is about 1 percent, with audit rates somewhat higher for returns reporting business income.

83 James Andreoni, "Criminal Deterrence in the Reduced Form: A New Perspective on Ehrlich's Seminal Study," *Economic Inquiry*, vol. 33, no. 3 (July 1995), pp. 476–483.

84 Janet G. McCubbin, *Optimal Tax Enforcement: A Review of the Literature and Practical Implications,* Working Paper 90 (Washington D.C.: Department of the Treasury, Office of Tax Analysis, December 2004).

85 Studies find conflicting evidence regarding the impact of perceptions of fairness on tax compliance. In one experiment, participants were more likely to engage in tax evasion when told that their tax burden was high relative to that of others; compliance improved if, instead, they were told that their tax burden was relatively small. See Michael W. Spicer and Lee A. Becker, "Fiscal Inequity and Tax Evasion: An Experimental Approach," *National Tax Journal*, vol. 33, no. 2 (June 1980), pp. 171–175. However, a second study found that perceptions of fairness had no impact on compliance. See Paul Webley and others, *Tax Evasion: An Experimental Approach* (Cambridge, England: Cambridge University Press, 1991).

86 Robert B. Cialdini, "Crafting Normative Messages to Protect the Environment," *Current Directions in Psychological Science*, vol. 12, no. 4 (2003), pp. 105–109.

87 Leighton Ku and Bowen Garrett, *How Welfare Reform and Economic Factors Affected Medicaid Participation: 1984–96*, Assessing the New Federalism Discussion Papers 00-0 1 (Washington, D.C.: Urban Institute, February 2000); Currie and Grogger, "Explaining Recent Declines in Food Stamp Program Participation."

88 Brigitte C. Madrian and Dennis F. Shea, "The Power of Suggestion: Inertia in 401(k) Participation and Savings Behavior," *Quarterly Journal of Economics*, vol. 116, no. 4 (November 2001), pp. 1149–1187.

89 James Choi and others, "For Better or For Worse: Default Effects and 401(k) Savings Behavior," in David A. Wise, ed., *Perspectives in the Economics of Aging* (Chicago.: University of Chicago Press, 2004).

90 John Beshears and others, *The Importance of Default Options for Retirement Saving Outcomes: Evidence from the United States*, Working Paper No. 12009 (Cambridge, Mass.: National Bureau of Economic Research, January 2006).

91 See Didem Bernard and Jessica Banthin, *Premiums in the Individual Insurance Market for Policyholders Under Age 65: 2002 and 2005,* AHRQ Statistical Brief No. 2002 (Agency for Healthcare Research and Quality, April 2008); AHIP Center for Policy Research, *Individual Health Insurance, 2006–2007: A Comprehensive Survey of Premiums, Availability, and Benefits* (Washington, D.C.: America's Health Insurance Plans, December 2007); and the Kaiser Family Foundation and Health Research and Educational Trust, *Employer Health Benefits: 2005 Annual Survey* (Washington, D.C.: Kaiser/HRET, September 2005) and *Employer Health Benefits: 2007 Annual Survey* (September 2007).

92 Actuarially equivalent plans cover the same share of health care spending for a given population; see Box 3-1 on page 64 for a more detailed explanation.

[93] Maryland Health Care Commission, *Study of Mandated Health Insurance Services: A Comparative Evaluation* (January 1, 2008), http://mhcc.maryland.gov/health. pdf.

[94] For evidence on the extent to which insurers would cover mandated benefits in the absence of the mandates, see Maryland Health Care Commission, *Study of Mandated Health Insurance Services;* and Jonathan Gruber, "State-Mandated Benefits and Employer-Provided Health Insurance," *Journal of Public Economics,* vol. 55 (1994), pp. 433–464.

[95] For a description of the RAND experiment, see Joseph P. Newhouse and the Insurance Experiment Group, *Free for All?: Lessons from the RAND Health Insurance Experiment* (Cambridge, Mass.: Harvard University Press, 1993).

[96] The plans that required coinsurance also featured an annual limit on enrollees' out-of-pocket costs that was equal to the lesser of $1,000 (in nominal dollars) or a percentage of family income.

[97] The standard drug benefit also specifies an initial coverage limit; enrollees who do not have additional coverage are responsible for all of their drug costs between that point and the catastrophic threshold (in the so-called doughnut hole).

[98] The Kaiser Family Foundation and Health Research and Educational Trust, *Employer Health Benefits: 2008 Annual Survey.* Only about 2 percent of workers are enrolled in indemnity plans that do not use managed care tools.

[99] See Justin S. White, Robert E. Hurley, and Bradley C. Strunk, *Getting Along or Going Along? Health Plan-Provider Contract Showdowns Subside*, Issue Brief No. 74 (Washington, D.C.: Center for Studying Health System Change, January 2004).

[100] Glen P. Mays, Gary Claxton, and Justin White, "Managed Care Rebound? Recent Changes in Health Plans' Cost Containment Strategies," *Health Affairs*, Web Exclusive (August 11, 2004), pp. W4-427 to W4-436.

[101] Plans use various methods to pay providers, some of which are designed to give providers incentives to limit spending. The payment methods that plans use and their effects are examined in Chapter 5.

[102] See Robert H. Miller and Harold S. Luft, "HMO Plan Performance Update: An Analysis of the Literature, 1997–2001," *Health Affairs,* vol. 21, no. 4 (July/August 2002), pp. 63–86.

[103] See the Congressional Budget Office's cost estimates for S. 6, Patients' Bill of Rights Act of 1999 (June 16, 1999); for H.R. 2315, Patients' Bill of Rights Act of 2001 (July 20, 2001); for S. 1052, Bipartisan Patients' Bill of Rights Act (July 20, 2001); and for H.R. 2563, Bipartisan Patient Protection Act (July 26, 2001). All of CBO's estimates reflect the marginal effect of the federal legislation on costs. That is, they compare the projected costs under the new law with the estimated costs that would have prevailed in the absence of the new law (recognizing that some health plans may have made the proposed changes even without the new law).

[104] See Diana Farrell and others, *Accounting for the Cost of U.S. Health Care, 2008: A New Look at Why Americans Spend More* (San Francisco: McKinsey Global Institute, December 2008). National health expenditure data show a comparable estimate of about $89 billion for 2006.

[105] For a discussion, see James C. Robinson, "Use and Abuse of the Medical Loss Ratio to Measure Health Plan Performance," *Health Affairs*, vol. 16, no. 4 (July/August 1997), pp. 176–187.

[106] Lower estimates of administrative costs for large-employer groups may reflect only the fees paid to insurers who act as third-party administrators but who do not assume financial risk for operating an employer's plan; when the employer is acting as the insurer, some administrative costs are borne by the employer but may not be included in the estimates.

[107] For example, see M. Susan Marquis and Stephen H. Long, "The Uninsured Access Gap and the Cost of Universal Coverage," *Health Affairs* (Spring 1994), pp. 211–220; and Brenda C. Spillman, Stephen Zuckerman, and Bowen Garrett, *Does the Health Care Safety Net Narrow the Access Gap?* Discussion Paper 03-02 (Washington, D.C.: Urban Institute, April 2003).

[108] Joan L. Buchanan and others, "Simulating Health Expenditures Under Alternative Insurance Plans," *Management Science,* vol. 37, no. 9 (September 1991), pp. 1067–1090.

[109] Janet Currie and Jonathan Gruber, "Health Insurance Eligibility, Utilization of Medical Care, and Child Health," *Quarterly Journal of Economics,* vol. 111, no. 2 (May 1996), pp. 431–466. Because actual enrollment in Medicaid reflects preferences about insurance and may be triggered by a health problem, the study compared groups who gained eligibility for the program (regardless of whether they actually enrolled) to groups whose eligibility did not change.

[110] Jessica S. Banthin and Thomas M. Selden, "The ABCs of Children's Health Care: How the Medicaid Expansions Affected Access, Burdens, and Coverage Between 1987 and 1996," *Inquiry,* vol. 40, no. 2 (Summer 2003), pp. 133–145.

[111] J. Michael McWilliams and others, "Impact of Medicare Coverage on Basic Clinical Services for Previously Uninsured Adults," *Journal of the American Medical Association,* vol. 290, no. 6 (August 13, 2003), pp. 757–764.

[112] J. Michael McWilliams and others, "Use of Health Services by Previously Uninsured Medicare Beneficiaries," *New England Journal of Medicine,* vol. 357, no. 2 (July 12, 2007), pp. 143–153.

[113] Jack Hadley and others, "Covering the Uninsured in 2008: Current Costs, Sources of Payment, and Incremental Costs," *Health Affairs,* Web Exclusive (August 25, 2008), pp. W399–W415.

[114] Lisa Ward and Peter Franks, "Changes in Health Care Expenditure Associated with Gaining or Losing Health Insurance," *Annals of Internal Medicine*, vol. 146, no. 11 (June 2007), pp. 768–774. That study also found that individuals who lost insurance coverage had expenditures while uninsured that were comparable with those of continuously uninsured individuals.

[115] CBO used MEPS data for 1997 to 2005 rather than data for a single two-year period to expand the size of the samples and thus increase the precision of the estimates. The data were adjusted for age, sex, health status, education, and income so that the analysis compared individuals who appear similar in observed characteristics other than insurance status.

[116] CBO measured the use of health care services using a single index that reflected the use of physicians' and hospital services, weighted by average expenditures for each kind of use. Thus, reported payments for individual services did not affect the comparisons between insured and uninsured individuals.

[117] Thomas C. Buchmueller and others, "The Effect of Health Insurance on Medical Care Utilization and Implications for Insurance Expansion: A Review of the Literature," *Medical Care Research and Review*, vol. 62, no. 1 (February 2005), pp. 3–30.

[118] The uninsured currently account for about 8 percent of health care use nationwide; a 25 percent increase in their use of services would thus translate into a 2 percent increase for the country as a whole, and a 60 percent increase would translate into a rise of nearly 5 percent in total use.

[119] For additional analysis of issues related to the regulation of insurance markets, see Congressional Budget Office, *CBO's Health Insurance Simulation Model: A Technical Description* (October 2007); and *The Price Sensitivity of Demand for Nongroup Health Insurance* (August 2005).

[120] That challenge is not unique to health insurance; the likelihood of an automobile accident or a homeowners' insurance claim can also vary across policyholders in predictable and observable ways. See Chapter 1 for additional discussion about the predictability of health care spending.

[121] Catherine Hoffman and Karyn Schwartz, "Eroding Access Among Nonelderly U.S. Adults with Chronic Conditions: Ten Years of Change," *Health Affairs*, Web Exclusive (July 22, 2008), pp. W340–W348. The other chronic conditions examined were stroke, emphysema, and cancer.

[122] Kenneth E. Thorpe and others, "The Rising Prevalence of Treated Disease: Effects on Private Health Insurance Spending," *Health Affairs*, Web Exclusive (June 27, 2005), pp. W5-317 to W5-325.

[123] Joseph P. Newhouse, Melinda Beeuwkes Buntin, and John D. Chapman, "Risk Adjustment and Medicare: Taking a Closer Look," *Health Affairs*, vol. 16, no. 5 (September/October 1997), pp. 26–43.

[124] Many other laws and regulations govern health insurance but are beyond the scope of this chapter. State insurance agencies are generally charged with monitoring the financial health of insurance firms to ensure that they will be able to meet their promises to pay claims. Furthermore, many of those agencies regulate the sales practices of insurers. Federal law also establishes reporting and disclosure requirements and fiduciary standards for the plans' administrators. All of those regulations can also affect insurance premiums and coverage.

[125] See Mark Merlis, *Fundamentals of Underwriting in the Nongroup Health Insurance Market: Access to Coverage and Options for Reform*, NHPF Background Paper (Washington, D.C.: National Health Policy Forum, April 13, 2005). In principle, insurers could charge a higher premium to applicants who have very high expected costs, but in practice they appear to assume that individuals who would be willing to pay premiums exceeding twice the standard rate would be likely to have even higher covered costs for health care—so rather than charge a very high premium, insurers generally deny coverage to such applicants instead.

[126] Ibid. A recent analysis also found that in three states, a dominant insurer used community rating even though the state did not require all insurers to adopt that practice; see Congressional Budget Office, *The Price Sensitivity of Demand for Nongroup Health Insurance*, Background Paper (August 2005).

[127] General Accounting Office, *Private Health Insurance: Federal and State Requirements Affecting Coverage Offered by Small Businesses,* GAO-03-1 133 (September 2003).

[128] See M. Susan Marquis and Stephen H. Long, "Effects of 'Second Generation' Small Group Health Insurance Market Reforms, 1993 to 1997," *Inquiry*, vol. 38, no. 4 (Winter 2001/2002), pp. 365–380; and Amy Davidoff, Linda Blumberg, and Len Nichols, "State Health Insurance Market Reforms and Access to Insurance for High Risk Employees," *Journal of Health Economics*, vol. 24, no. 4 (July 2005), pp. 725–750.

[129] Information on the status of high-risk pools comes from www.statehealthfacts.org. See also Bernadette Fernandez, *Health Insurance: State High-Risk Pools*, RL3 1745 (Congressional Research Service, October 1, 2008).

[130] Congressional Budget Office, cost estimate for S. 1955, the Health Insurance Marketplace Modernization and Affordability Act of 2006 (May 3, 2006).

[131] A similar approach would facilitate the formation of association health plans, which can be offered by trade, industry, or professional associations to their member firms. That option would be attractive for smaller firms with relatively healthy workers that are located in states that regulate premiums more extensively or have more extensive benefit mandates. For an analysis of a recent legislative proposal, see Congressional Budget Office, cost estimate for H.R. 525, Small Business Health Fairness Act of 2005 (April 8, 2005).

[132] Congressional Budget Office, cost estimate for H.R. 2355, Health Care Choice Act of 2005 (September 12, 2005).

[133] See Statement of Joseph Antos, Assistant Director for Health and Human Resources, Congressional Budget Office, before the Subcommittee on Civil Service, House Committee on Government Reform and Oversight, October 8, 1997.

[134] Joint Committee on Taxation, *Tax Expenditures for Health Care*, JCX-66-08 (July 30, 2008).

[135] One offsetting consideration is that excluding health insurance premiums from taxable wages reduces future Social Security benefits, which are based on average earnings, at the same time that it reduces payroll tax payments.

[136] Assume, for example, that an insurance policy has a total premium of $5,000. Someone receiving a 20 percent tax subsidy would thus pay $4,000 on net. If the tax subsidy was eliminated, that person would pay $5,000, or 25 percent more. Someone receiving a 40 percent tax subsidy would currently pay $3,000 for that policy. If the tax subsidy was eliminated, that person would pay $5,000, or 67 percent more.

[137] Jonathan Gruber and Michael Lettau, "How Elastic Is the Firm's Demand for Health Insurance?" *Journal of Public Economics*, vol. 88, no. 7 (July 2004), pp. 1273–1294.

[138] Bradley T. Heim and Ithai Lurie, "Do Increased Premium Subsidies Affect How Much Health Insurance Is Purchased? Evidence from the Self-Employed" (draft, Department of Treasury, Office of Tax Analysis, January 7, 2008).

[139] See Alain C. Enthoven, "The History and Principles of Managed Competition," *Health Affairs*, vol. 12 (Supplement 1993), pp. 24–48.

[140] James Maxwell and Peter Temin, "Managed Competition Versus Industrial Purchasing of Health Care Among the Fortune 500," *Journal of Health Politics, Policy, and Law*, vol. 27, no. 1 (2002), pp. 5–30.

[141] For a discussion of this issue, see Mark McClellan and Sontine Kalba, "Benefit Diversity in Medicare: Choice, Competition, and Selection," in Richard Kronick and Joy de Beyer, eds., *Medicare HMOs: Making Them Work for the Chronically Ill* (Chicago: Health Administration Press, 1999), pp. 133–160.

[142] Under a managed competition system, insurers could be allowed to vary individuals' premiums so that the premiums reflected each enrollee's expected costs for health care, in which case those premiums would already be adjusted for risk. In many respects, such an arrangement would resemble the current market for individually purchased insurance.

[143] David M. Cutler and Sarah J. Reber, "Paying for Health Insurance: The Trade-Off Between Competition and Adverse Selection," *Quarterly Journal of Economics*, vol. 113, no. 2 (May 1998), pp. 433–466.

[144] Newhouse, Buntin, and Chapman, "Risk Adjustment and Medicare." Studies finding that at least 20 percent to 25 percent of health care spending is predictable largely reflect comparisons of individuals' average spending over several years and thus account for any reason that one person's spending is higher than another's. Risk-adjustment models, by contrast, generally adjust payments using information only about individuals' age and sex and the diseases or health conditions with which they have been diagnosed. Those models thus do not take into account other differences among individuals (such as their preferences about health care) that affect their spending. Those features reflect an apparent reluctance to assign different adjustment factors to people who have the same demographic characteristics and health problems.

[145] For a discussion of that evidence, see Congressional Budget Office, *Designing a Premium Support System for Medicare* (December 2006), pp. 31–35.

[146] For a discussion of those challenges, see Elliot K. Wicks, *Health Insurance Purchasing Cooperatives*, Commonwealth Fund Issue Brief No. 567 (November 2002), www.commonwealthfund.org.

[147] A plan's actuarial value reflects the share or amount of health care costs that it would cover for a given population; see Box 3-1 on page 64 for additional discussion.

[148] Jeff Liebman and Richard Zeckhauser, *Simple Humans, Complex Insurance, Subtle Subsidies,* Working Paper No. 14330 (Cambridge, Mass.: National Bureau of Economic Research, September 2008).

[149] Raj Chetty, Adam Looney, and Kory Kroft, *Salience and Taxation: Theory and Evidence*, Working Paper No. 13330 (Cambridge, Mass.: National Bureau of Economic Research, August 2007).

[150] Amy Finkelstein, *E-ZTax: Tax Salience and Tax Rates,* Working Paper No. 12924 (Cambridge, Mass.: National Bureau of Economic Research, February 2007).

[151] Many of the same issues are raised by proposals to establish a "premium support" system within Medicare, under which private health plans and the fee-for-service program would compete for enrollees. For a discussion, see Congressional Budget Office, *Designing a Premium Support System for Medicare*.

[152] For a discussion of those issues, see Congressional Budget Office, *Issues in Designing a Prescription Drug Benefit for Medicare* (October 2002).

[153] James G. Kahn and others, "The Cost of Health Insurance Administration in California: Estimates for Insurers, Physicians, and Hospitals," *Health Affairs,* vol. 24, no. 6 (November/ December 2005), pp. 1629–1639.

[154] Administrative costs for Medicare borne by the Centers for Medicare and Medicaid Services were $6.5 billion in calendar year 2007 (including both mandatory and discretionary funds); that figure includes payments to the Social Security Administration to cover its costs related to administering the Medicare program. Total program expenditures for that year were about $441 billion. About 44 million people were enrolled in Part A, Part B, or

both in that year (including about 8 million enrollees in private health plans providing those Medicare benefits).

155 For an illustration of how inadequate risk adjustment could lead to higher premiums for beneficiaries in the traditional Medicare program, see Thomas Rice and Katherine A. Desmond, "The Distributional Consequences of a Medicare Premium Support Proposal," *Journal of Health Politics, Policy, and Law*, vol. 29, no. 6 (December 2004), pp. 1187–1226.

156 That analysis reflects the bids that those private plans submit and not the payments they receive, which are generally higher than the bids. Plans' bids reflect their expected costs for providing Medicare benefits in the service area where the plan is offered (generally, a county or a multicounty region). In 2008, about half of the enrollees in Medicare Advantage plans are in plans whose bid exceeds the average cost of Medicare enrollees in the fee-forservice program who live in the plan's service area.

157 For more information, see Mark Merlis, "The Federal Employees Health Benefits Program: Program Design, Recent Performance, and Implications for Medicare Reform" (briefing prepared for the Henry J. Kaiser Family Foundation, May 30, 2003).

158 For additional discussion, see Mark Merlis, *Opening the Federal Employees Health Benefits Program to Individual Purchasers* (report prepared for the Department of Health and Human Services, Office of the Assistant Secretary for Planning and Evaluation, July 31, 2001), www.markmerlis.com.

159 For a more extensive discussion, see Congressional Budget Office, *A Detailed Description of CBO's Cost Estimate for the Medicare Prescription Drug Benefit* (July 2004), pp. 8–11.

160 Unless specified otherwise, data used in this section on health care employment and facilities come from National Center for Health Statistics, *Health, United States, 2007* (Hyattsville, Md., 2007), www.cdc.gov/nchs/hus.htm.

161 In addition, U.S. schools of osteopathic medicine produced nearly 3,000 doctors of osteopathy in 2005. Those doctors generally enter residency programs in the United States.

162 See Sean Nicholson and David Song, "The Incentive Effects of the Medicare Indirect Medical Education Policy," *Journal of Health Economics*, vol. 20, no. 6 (November 2001), pp. 909–933; and Congressional Budget Office, *Medicare and Graduate Medical Education* (September 1995).

163 The Council on Graduate Medical Education had forecast excesses of physicians in the 1980s and 1990s, partly on the basis of projections that the spread of managed care plans during that period would reduce demand for all physicians (and for specialists in particular).

164 That figure does not include about 700,000 licensed practical nurses and licensed vocational nurses, who have less training and responsibility than registered nurses.

165 See Barbara L. Brush, Julie Sochalski, and Anne M. Berger, "Imported Care: Recruiting Foreign Nurses to U.S. Health Care Facilities," *Health Affairs*, vol. 23, no. 3 (May/June 2004), pp. 78–87. That study found that the overall share of the nursing workforce that was trained abroad was below 5 percent but was rising because of the recent influx of foreign-trained nurses.

166 David I. Auerbach, Peter I. Buerhaus, and Douglas O. Staiger, "Better Late Than Never: Workforce Supply Implications of Later Entry Into Nursing," *Health Affairs*, vol. 26, no. 1 (January/ February 2007), pp. 178–185.

167 For additional discussion of issues regarding nursing shortages, see Charles E. Phelps, *Health Economics*, 3rd ed. (Boston: Addison Wesley, 2003), pp. 308–311.

168 Mark McClellan, "Hospital Reimbursement Incentives: An Empirical Analysis," *Journal of Economics and Management Strategy*, vol. 6, no. 6 (Spring 1997), pp. 91–128.

169 For a specific proposal, see Elliott S. Fisher and others, "Creating Accountable Care Organizations: The Extended Hospital Medical Staff," *Health Affairs*, Web Exclusive (December 5, 2006), pp. W44–W57. For a more general discussion, see Joseph P. Newhouse, *Pricing the Priceless: A Health Care Conundrum* (Cambridge, Mass.: MIT Press, September 2002).

170 See Joseph P. Newhouse and the Insurance Experiment Group, *Free for All? Lessons from the RAND Health Insurance Experiment* (Cambridge, Mass.: Harvard University Press, 1993). The RAND analysts did not have data on actual spending per enrollee in the HMO, which can be difficult to calculate for staff-model plans because a separate payment is not made for each service provided. Instead, analysts had data on the use of services by HMO enrollees and imputed their spending. Thus, the difference in spending between the HMO and other plans did not generally reflect differences in the prices paid for or average costs of specific services.

171 The discussion in this section primarily describes issues regarding fee-for-service or episode-based payment rates, but many of the same considerations would apply in setting capitation rates or salary levels.

172 The payment amounts are adjusted to reflect geographic variation in hospitals' input prices and to account for the presence of other health problems (known as comorbidities) or complications that arise during treatment; additional payments are made for extraordinarily costly "outlier" cases. A variety of other adjustments are also made; for example, payments are modified for rural hospitals and for teaching hospitals.

173 For additional information, see Congressional Budget Office, *The Sustainable Growth Rate Formula for Setting Medicare's Physician Payment Rates*, Issue Brief (September 6, 2006).

[174] For example, see Joseph P. Newhouse, *Pricing the Priceless;* or Newhouse, "An Iconoclastic View of Health Cost Containment," *Health Affairs*, vol. 12 (Supplement 1993), pp. 153–171.

[175] See Medicare Payment Advisory Commission, *Report to the Congress: Medicare Payment Policy* (March 2008). The commission also recommended adopting a payment incentive program for hospitals to encourage higher quality of care and a process for measuring and reporting physicians' use of resources on a confidential basis.

[176] See Kevin J. Hayes, Julian Pettengill, and Jeffrey Stensland, "Getting the Price Right: Medicare Payment Rates for Cardiovascular Services," *Health Affairs*, vol. 26, no. 1 (January/February 2007), pp. 124–136; and Paul B. Ginsburg and Joy M. Grossman, "When the Price Isn't Right: How Inadvertent Payment Incentives Drive Medical Care," *Health Affairs,* Web Exclusive (August 9, 2005), pp. W5-376 to W5-384.

[177] See Medicare Payment Advisory Commission, *Report to the Congress*, p. 89.

[178] See Stephen Zuckerman and others, "Changes in Medicaid Physician Fees, 1998–2003: Implications for Physician Participation," *Health Affairs*, Web Exclusive (June 23, 2004), pp. W4-374 to W4-384.

[179] See Appendix 4 of American Hospital Association, *Trendwatch Chartbook 2008: Trends Affecting Hospitals and Health Systems* (prepared by Avalere Health for the American Hospital Association, Spring 2008), p. A-35, www.aha.org.

[180] Dyckman & Associates, *Survey of Health Plans Concerning Physician Fees and Payment Methodology* (report prepared for the Medicare Payment Advisory Commission, August 2003).

[181] Congressional Budget Office, *The Impact of Medicare's Payment Rates on the Volume of Services Provided by Skilled Nursing Facilities*, Background Paper (July 2007).

[182] For a discussion of the economic principles involved, see Thomas G. McGuire and Mark V. Pauly, "Physician Response to Fee Changes with Multiple Payers," *Journal of Health Economics*, vol. 10, no. 4 (1991), pp. 385–410.

[183] See, for example, Jack Hadley and James D. Reschovsky, "Medicare Fees and Physicians' Medicare Service Volume: Beneficiaries Treated and Services per Beneficiary," *International Journal of Health Care Finance Economics*, vol. 6, no. 2 (June 2006), pp. 131–150.

[184] See, for example, Nguyen Xuan Nguyen and Frederick William Derrick, "Physician Behavioral Response to a Medicare Price Reduction," *Health Services Research*, vol. 32, no. 3 (August 1997), pp. 283–298.

[185] Congressional Budget Office, *Factors Underlying the Growth in Medicare's Spending for Physicians' Services*, Background Paper (June 2007). "Intensity" refers to the complexity of services used in delivering patient care. For example, use of a computerized axial tomography (CAT) scan rather than an X-ray would represent an increase in intensity—and would result in a higher payment from Medicare to reflect the greater cost of providing the more complex service.

[186] According to press reports, the recent expansion of insurance coverage in Massachusetts has caused demand for visits to primary care physicians to exceed supply, making it difficult to obtain appointments. For a discussion of the key features of that expansion, see Chapter 2.

[187] Congressional Budget Office, *Factors Underlying the Growth in Medicare's Spending for Physicians' Services.*

[188] Amy Finkelstein, "The Aggregate Effects of Health Insurance: Evidence from the Introduction of Medicare," *Quarterly Journal of Economics*, vol. 122, no. 1 (February 2007), pp. 1–37.

[189] See Philip E. Enterline and others, "Effects of 'Free' Medical Care on Medical Practice—The Quebec Experience," *New England Journal of Medicine*, vol. 288, no. 2 (May 31, 1973), pp. 1152– 1155; Philip E. Enterline and others, "The Distribution of Medical Services Before and After 'Free' Medical Care—The Quebec Experience," *New England Journal of Medicine*, vol. 289, no. 22 (November 29, 1973), pp. 1174–1178; and the discussion of the results of those studies in Thomas C. Buchmueller and others, "The Effect of Health Insurance on Medical Care Utilization and Implications for Insurance Expansion: A Review of the Literature," *Medical Care Research and Review*, vol. 62, no. 1 (February 2005), pp. 3–30.

[190] Shou-Hsia Cheng and Tung-Liang Chiang, "The Effect of Universal Health Insurance on Health Care Utilization in Taiwan: Results from a Natural Experiment," *Journal of the American Medical Association*, vol. 278, no. 2 (July 9, 1997), pp. 89–93.

[191] Jui-Fen Rachel Lu and William C. Hsiao, "Does Universal Health Insurance Make Health Care Unaffordable? Lessons from Taiwan," *Health Affairs*, vol. 22, no. 3 (May/June 2003), pp. 77–8 8. That study also found that subsequent efforts by the government to institute a global budget for health care services helped control the growth of spending in that country. For a discussion of such global budgets, see Chapter 8 of this chapter.

[192] To the extent that a hospital with market power charges prices that exceed its costs, the question of why competing hospitals have not entered those markets arises. The apparent persistence of limited competition among hospitals in many areas, however, indicates that some barriers to entering the market exist, at least in some areas of the country.

[193] See Paul B. Ginsburg, "Can Hospitals and Physicians Shift the Effects of Cuts in Medicare Reimbursement to Private Payers?" *Health Affairs*, Web Exclusive (October 8, 2003), pp. W3-472 to W3-479.

[195] See Congressional Budget Office, *Nonprofit Hospitals and the Provision of Community Benefits* (December 2006).

[196] In the strict sense of the term, such markets might not be considered fully competitive because hospitals would have to feel compelled to continue serving patients for which they were under- compensated. Without that

constraint, some hospitals would probably stop accepting those patients; those hospitals could then lower their fees to private payers and take private business away from competing hospitals (to the extent that they had sufficient capacity). Hospitals that continued to be undercompensated would suffer financial losses and would either have to receive outside assistance or eventually exit the market.

196 By definition, no payments are received from insurers, but some care provided to uninsured individuals is paid for by other third- party sources, such as workers' compensation programs (for on- the-job injuries) or veterans' benefits.

197 Jack Hadley and others, "Covering the Uninsured in 2008: Current Costs, Sources of Payment, and Incremental Costs," *Health Affairs*, Web Exclusive (August 25, 2008), pp. W399–W415. As discussed in Chapter 1, that study estimated that people who are uninsured for all of 2008 receive about $540 in uncompensated care, on average, and that people who are uninsured for part of that year receive about $150 in uncompensated care.

198 Conversely, a reduction in uncompensated care could provide a policy rationale to reduce those payments from Medicare and Medicaid.

199 Jonathan Gruber and David Rodriguez, *How Much Uncompensated Care Do Doctors Provide?* Working Paper No. 13585 (Cambridge, Mass.: National Bureau of Economic Research, November 2007).

200 American Hospital Association, *Trendwatch Chartbook 2008*.

201 See David Dranove, "Pricing by Non-Profit Institutions: The Case of Hospital Cost-Shifting," *Journal of Health Economics*, vol. 7, no. 1 (1988), pp. 47–57.

202 Stephen Zuckerman, "Commercial Insurers and All-Payer Regulation: Evidence on Hospitals' Responses to Financial Need," *Journal of Health Economics*, vol. 6, no. 3 (September 1987), pp. 165–187, and Jack Hadley and Judith Feder, "Hospital Cost Shifting and Care for the Uninsured," *Health Affairs*, vol. 4, no. 3 (Fall 1985), pp. 67–80.

203 Michael A. Morrisey, *Cost Shifting in Health Care: Separating Evidence from Rhetoric* (Washington, D.C.: AEI Press, 1994); and Jack Hadley, Stephen Zuckerman, and Lisa I. Iezzoni, "Financial Pressure and Competition: Changes in Hospital Efficiency and Cost-Shifting Behavior," *Medical Care*, vol. 34, no. 3 (1996), pp. 205–219.

204 See Jack Zwanziger, Glenn A. Melnick, and Anil Bamezai, "Can Cost Shifting Continue in a Price Competitive Environment?" *Health Economics*, vol. 9, no. 3 (April 2000), pp. 211–226; and Jack Zwanziger and Anil Bamezai, "Evidence of Cost Shifting in California Hospitals," *Health Affairs*, vol. 25, no. 1 (January/ February 2006), pp. 197–203. Although Zwanziger and colleagues concluded that the strength of cost shifting had not diminished by 1991, the 2006 paper generally finds less cost shifting in the more recent period. The estimated effect of a cut in Medicaid's fees was low in both periods.

205 See David Dranove and William D. White, "Medicaid- Dependent Hospitals and Their Patients: How Have They Fared?" *Health Services Research*, vol. 33, no. 2, pt. 1 (June 1998), pp. 163–185.

206 The program's relatively high administrative costs—roughly $300 per enrollee each year—partly reflect the fact that certain ongoing expenses are spread across a relatively small number of participants.

207 Federal matching rates under both programs vary across states and cover a higher percentage of medical costs in states with lower income per capita. The minimum matching rate is 50 percent for Medicaid and 65 percent for SCHIP. Different rates may apply for administrative costs.

208 States' Medicaid programs may continue to cover and receive federal matching funds for a few classes of drugs that were excluded from the Medicare drug benefit.

209 As noted in Chapter 1, economists generally agree that cash wages and other forms of compensation would increase as payments for health insurance declined, but it is less clear how that adjustment would apply to individual workers within a firm.

210 The TRICARE program is available to current military service members, their families, and those who qualify for military retirement by serving at least 20 years in uniform or by receiving a disability retirement. Service members who separate before achieving military retirement do not receive TRICARE coverage but instead can apply for enrollment with the Department of Veterans Affairs.

211 In 2007, most had some type of non-VA coverage, including Medicare Part A (39 percent), Medicare Part B (37 percent), Medicare Part D (19 percent), medigap (22 percent), Medicaid (8 percent), TRICARE (17 percent), and private insurance (51 percent).

212 Eligibility for IHS services is limited to individuals who are members of a federally recognized tribe and who live in the service area of an IHS facility. Thus, not all of the estimated 3.3 million American Indians and Alaska natives living in the United States are eligible to receive health care services through the IHS.

213 All children for whom federal foster care payments are made— approximately 50 percent of children in foster care—are eligible for Medicaid. The remaining 50 percent are generally eligible for Medicaid under guidelines established by state Medicaid programs.

214 Incarcerated adults and juveniles are not included in most counts of the insured and uninsured. Those counts generally exclude the institutionalized population.

215 That estimate is based on data from the Census Bureau on local government expenditures and the *2002–2003 State Health Expenditure Report* copublished by the Milbank Memorial Fund, the National Association of State Budget Officers, and the Reforming States Group in June 2005.

[216] Karina Fortuny, Randy Capps, and Jeffrey S. Passel, *The Characteristics of Unauthorized Immigrants in California, Los Angeles County, and the United States* (Washington, D.C.: Urban Institute, March 2007); and Jeffrey S. Passel, *Unauthorized Migrants: Numbers and Characteristics* (Washington, D.C.: Pew Hispanic Center, June 14, 2005).

[217] Refugees and individuals who have been granted asylum are eligible to receive most federal benefits for the first seven years they are in the United States.

[218] Unauthorized immigrants may receive care through Medicaid under the following circumstances: if they meet certain income requirements and are pregnant; if they are under the age of 19 or at least 65 years old; if they are disabled; or if they are the caregiver of a child under the age of 18. However, such "emergency" Medicaid coverage pays for only those services that are necessary to stabilize a patient.

[219] Section 1011 of the Medicare Modernization Act made $1 billion available to states between fiscal years 2005 and 2008 for the health care costs of their unauthorized immigrants.

[220] Congressional Budget Office, letter to the Honorable Nancy Pelosi regarding the budgetary impact of section 211 of H.R. 3963 (October 25, 2007).

[221] If the worker could claim his or her domestic partner as a dependent, then the tax exclusion might apply. However, an individual must have low income and meet other support and residency tests to be claimed as a dependent.

[222] Department of Housing and Urban Development, Office of Community Planning and Development, *The 2007 Annual Homeless Assessment Report* (July 2008); and Patricia A. Post, *Casualties of Complexity: Why Eligible Homeless People Are Not Enrolled in Medicaid* (Nashville, Tenn.: National Health Care for the Homeless Council, May 2001).

[223] Department of Health and Human Services, Health Resources and Services Administration, "Health Care for the Homeless Program Marks 20th Anniversary" (July 2007).

[224] Ali H. Mokdad and others, "Actual Causes of Death in the United States, 2000," *Journal of the American Medical Association,* vol. 291, no. 10 (March 10, 2004).

[225] Congressional Budget Office, *Technological Change and the Growth of Health Care Spending* (January 2008).

[226] Obesity is defined on the basis of body mass index (BMI), which equals weight (in kilograms) divided by height squared (in meters). Among adults, normal weight is defined as a BMI between 18.5 and 25, overweight is defined as a BMI between 25 and 30, and obesity is defined as a BMI of 30 or greater. Morbid obesity—also known as clinically severe obesity—is defined as a BMI of 40 or more. Children are defined as overweight if they exceed the 95th percentile of the Centers for Disease Control and Prevention's 2000 growth charts for their age and sex.

[227] Roland Sturm, "The Effects of Obesity, Smoking, and Drinking on Medicaid Problems and Costs," *Health Affairs* (March/April 2002).

[228] Department of Health and Human Services, National Center for Health Statistics, *Health, United States, 2007* (Hyattsville, Md., 2007), Figure 13.

[229] Ibid.

[230] See, for example, R. Whitaker and others, "Predicting Obesity in Young Adulthood from Childhood and Parental Obesity," *New England Journal of Medicine,* vol. 337, no. 13 (September 25, 1997), pp. 869–873; and M. K. Serdula and others, "Do Obese Children Become Obese Adults? A Review of the Literature," *Preventive Medicine,* vol. 22, no. 2 (1993), pp. 167–177.

[231] Congressional Budget Office, *Growing Disparities in Life Expectancy,* Issue Brief (April 17, 2008).

[232] Ellen R. Meara, Seth Richards, and David M. Cutler, "The Gap Gets Bigger: Changes in Mortality and Life Expectancy, by Education, 198 1–2000," *Health Affairs*, vol. 27, no. 2 (2008), pp. 350–360.

[233] Charles L. Baum and Christopher J. Ruhm, *Age, Socioeconomic Status, and Obesity Growth,* Working Paper No. 13289 (Cambridge, Mass.: National Bureau of Economic Research, August 2007).

[234] David Mechanic and others, eds., *Policy Challenges in Modern Health Care* (Piscataway, N.J.: Rutgers University Press, 2005).

[235] W. Kip Viscusi and Jahn Karl Hakes, "Risk Beliefs and Smoking Behavior," *Economic Inquiry,* vol. 46, no. 1 (January 2008), pp. 45–59.

[236] However, the share of light-to-moderate smokers who quit was 3 percentage points higher in the intervention group than in the control group. See COMMIT Research Group, "Community Intervention Trial for Smoking Cessation (COMMIT): I. Cohort Results from a Four-Year Community Intervention," *American Journal of Public Health,* vol. 85, no. 2 (February 1995), pp. 183–192.

[237] Current law allows individuals to deduct from their taxable income the costs of smoking cessation programs and, if the treatment is for a specific disease diagnosed by a physician, fees for membership in a weight reduction group, but taxpayers must have total medical expenses in excess of 7.5 percent of their adjusted gross income to qualify for such deductions. Overall, less than 8 percent of tax filers claim the deduction for itemized medical expenses. The share of filers who deduct costs related to the prevention of smoking or obesity is probably much smaller.

[238] Jason M. Fletcher, David Frisvold, and Nathan Tefft, *Can Soft Drink Taxes Reduce Population Weight?* University of Michigan Working Paper (August 18, 2007), http://sitemaker.umich.edu/ frisvold/files/

soda_taxes_and_obesity_20070817web.pdf; and Oliver Mytton and others, "Could Targeted Food Taxes Improve Health?" *Journal of Epidemiology and Community Health,* vol. 61, no. 8 (2007), pp. 689–694.

239 Anjali Jain, *What Works for Obesity?: A Summary of the Research Behind Obesity Interventions*, paper prepared for United Health Foundation (London: BMJ Publishing Group, April 30, 2004), www.unitedhealthfoundation.org/obesity. Institute of Medicine, *Health and Behavior: The Interplay of Biological, Behavioral, and Societal Influences* (Washington, D.C.: National Academy Press, 2001); and Kim Sutherland, Sheila Leatherman, and Jon Christianson, *Paying the Patient, Does it Work?* (London: Health Foundation, October 2008), http://health research_reports/paying_the_patient.html.

240 William N. Evans, Matthew C. Farrelly, and Edward Montgomery, "Do Workplace Smoking Bans Reduce Smoking?" *American Economic Review*, vol. 89, no. 4 (September 1999), pp. 728–747.

241 David R. Just, Lisa Mancino, and Brian Wansink, *Could Behavioral Economics Help Improve Diet Quality for Nutrition Assistance Program Participants?* Economic Research Report No. ERR-43 (Department of Agriculture, Economic Research Service, June 2007).

242 Debbie A. Lawlor and Nish Chaturvedi, "Treatment and Prevention of Obesity—Are There Critical Periods for Intervention?" *International Journal of Epidemiology,* vol. 35, no. 1 (2006), pp. 3–9.

243 Adam Gilden Tsai and Thomas A. Wadden, "Systematic Review: An Evaluation of Major Commercial Weight Loss Programs in the United States," *Annals of Internal Medicine,* vol. 142, no. 1 (January 4, 2005), pp. 56–66; and Jerome P. Kassirer and Marcia Angell, "Losing Weight—An Ill-Fated New Year's Resolution," *New England Journal of Medicine,* vol. 338, no. 1 (January 1, 1998), pp. 52–54.

244 Evelyn P. Whitlock and others, *Effectiveness of Weight Management Programs in Children and Adolescents,* Evidence Report/ Technology Assessment No. 170 (prepared by the Oregon Evidence-Based Practice Center, Portland, Ore., for the Agency for Healthcare Research and Quality, September 2008).

245 Counseling to encourage healthy behavior or discourage unhealthy habits is also considered a preventive service. Public health measures, such as wastewater treatment, play an important role in preventing disease but are beyond the scope of this chapter.

246 Cost-effectiveness is measured by comparing the net cost of a service (measured in discounted, or current year, dollars) to the net health benefits (typically measured in quality-adjusted life years, or QALYs). QALYs take into account both an individual's life expectancy and his or her health status over the remaining life span. A year of perfect health is worth 1 QALY, and a year of less than perfect health is given a weight that is less than 1. A preventive service, or a medical service more generally, is regarded as cost-effective if the cost per QALY falls below a given threshold.

247 See Eileen Salinsky, *Clinical Preventive Services: When Is the Juice Worth the Squeeze?* Issue Brief No. 806 (Washington, D.C.: National Health Policy Forum, August 24, 2005); and Kaiser Family Foundation and Health Research and Educational Trust, *Employer Health Benefits: 2008 Annual Survey* (Washington, D.C.: Kaiser/HRET, September 2008).

248 J. P. Bynum and others, "The Influence of Health Status, Age, and Race on Screening Mammography in Elderly Women," *Archives of Internal Medicine,* vol. 165, no. 18 (October 10, 2005), pp. 2083– 2088.

249 See Michael Maciosek and others, "Priorities Among Effective Clinical Preventive Services: Results of a Systemic Review and Analysis," *American Journal of Preventive Medicine*, vol. 31, no. 1 (2006), pp. 52–61.

250 John P. Mullooly and others, "Influenza Vaccination Programs for Elderly Persons: Cost-Effectiveness in a Health Maintenance Organization," *Annals of Internal Medicine,* vol. 121, no. 12 (December 15, 1994), pp. 947–952; and Kristin L. Nichol and others, "Benefits of Influenza Vaccination for Low-, Intermediate-, and High-Risk Senior Citizens," *Archives of Internal Medicine,* vol. 158, no. 16 (September 14, 1998), pp. 1769–1776. For a recent critique of the methodology used on those studies, see L. Simonsen and others, "Mortality Benefits of Influenza Vaccination in Elderly People: An Ongoing Controversy," *Lancet Infectious Diseases,* vol. 7, no. 10 (October 2007), pp. 658–666.

251 Maciosek and others, "Priorities Among Effective Clinical Preventive Services."

252 Joshua T. Cohen and others, "Does Preventive Care Save Money? Health Economics and the Presidential Candidates," *New England Journal of Medicine,* vol. 358, no. 7 (February 14, 2008), pp. 661– 663.

253 American Academy of Family Physicians, fact sheet on patient- centered medical home, www.aafp.org/online/etc/medialib/ aafp_org/documents/policy/fed/medicalhome.Par.0001 .File.tmp/ PC-MHfactsheet.doc (accessed June 25, 2008).

254 American Medical Association, Specialty Society RVS Update Committee, "Medicare Medical Home Demonstration Project," letter to Kerry N. Weems, administrator of the Centers for Medicare and Medicaid Services (April 29, 2008). The $650 estimate is based on the "Tier III" medical home, as defined in the AMA letter.

255 Stephan Wilhide and Tim Henderson, *Community Care of North Carolina: A Provider-Led Strategy for Delivering Cost-Effective Primary Care to Medicaid Beneficiaries* (June 2006), www.aafp.org/ online/etc/medialib/aafp_org/documents/policy/state/medicaid/ ncfull.Par. 0001 .File.tmp/ncfullreport.pdf.

256 Timothy G. Ferris and others, "Leaving Gatekeeping Behind— Effects of Opening Access to Specialists for Adults in a Health Maintenance Organization," *New England Journal of Medicine,* vol. 345, no. 18 (November 1, 2001), pp. 1312–1317.

[257] Diane P. Martin and others, "Effect of a Gatekeeper Plan on Health Services Use and Charges: A Randomized Trial," *American Journal of Public Health,* vol. 79, no. 12 (December 1, 1989), pp. 1628–1632.

[258] David Matheson and others, *Realizing the Promise of Disease Management: Payer Trends and Opportunities in the United States* (Boston: Boston Consulting Group, February 2006).

[259] Congressional Budget Office, "An Analysis of the Literature on Disease Management Programs," letter to the Honorable Don Nickles (October 13, 2004).

[260] Soeren Mattke, Michael Seid, and Sai Ma, "Evidence for the Effect of Disease Management: Is $1 Billion a Year a Good Investment?"*American Journal of Managed Care*, vol. 13, no. 12 (December 2007), pp. 670–676.

[261] Randall Brown and others, *The Evaluation of the Medicare Coordinated Care Demonstration: Findings for the First Two Years* (Princeton, N.J.: Mathematica Policy Research, March 2007).

[262] Victor Villarga and Tamin Ahmet, "Effectiveness of a Disease Management Program for Diabetes," *Health Affairs*, vol. 23, no. 4 (July/August 2004), pp. 255–266. For responses to Villarga and Ahmet, see Thomas Wilson and Ariel Linden, "Measuring Diabetes Management," and Joe Selby and K.M. Narayan, "Lowering Diabetes Costs," both in *Health Affairs,* vol. 23, no. 6 (November/ December 2004), pp. 277–278.

[263] For additional discussion of this topic, see Congressional Budget Office, *Research on the Comparative Effectiveness of Medical Treatments: Issues and Options for an Expanded Federal Role* (December 2007).

[264] William E. Boden and others, "Optimal Medical Therapy With or Without PCI for Stable Coronary Disease," *New England Journal of Medicine,* vol. 356, no. 15 (April 12, 2007), pp. 1503–1516.

[265] Stephan Heres and others, "Why Olanzapine Beats Risperidone, Risperidone Beats Quetiapine, and Quetiapine Beats Olanzapine: An Exploration of Head-to-Head Comparison Studies of Second Generation Antipsychotics," *American Journal of Psychiatry,* vol. 163, no. 2 (February 2006), pp. 185–194.

[266] See Institute of Medicine, *Learning What Works Best: The Nation's Need for Evidence on Comparative Effectiveness in Health Care* (September 2007), p. 2, www.iom.edu/ebmeffectiveness.

[267] National Emphysema Treatment Trial Research Group, "A Randomized Trial Comparing Lung-Volume-Reduction Surgery with Medical Therapy for Severe Emphysema," *New England Journal of Medicine,* vol. 348, no. 21 (May 22, 2003), pp. 2059–2073.

[268] For more extensive discussion, see Congressional Budget Office, *Evidence on the Costs and Benefits of Health Information Technology* (May 2008).

[269] Samuel J. Wang and others, "A Cost-Benefit Analysis of Electronic Medical Records in Primary Care," *American Journal of Medicine,* vol. 114, no. 5 (April 1, 2003), pp. 397–403.

[270] David W. Bates and others, "A Randomized Trial of a Computer- Based Intervention to Reduce Utilization of Redundant Laboratory Tests," *American Journal of Medicine,* vol. 106, no. 2 (February 1999), pp. 144–150; David W. Bates and others, "What Proportion of Diagnostic Tests Appear Redundant?" *American Journal of Medicine*, vol. 104, no. 4 (April 1998), pp. 361–368; William M. Tierney and others, "Computerized Display of Past Test Results: Effects on Outpatient Testing," *Annals of Internal Medicine,* vol. 107, no. 4 (October 1987), pp. 569–574; and William M. Tierney and others, "Computer Predictions of Abnormal Test Results: Effects on Outpatient Testing,"*Journal of the American Medical Association*, vol. 259, no. 8 (February 26, 1988), pp. 1194–1198.

[271] Terhilda Garrido and others, "Effect of Electronic Health Records in Ambulatory Care: Retrospective, Serial, Cross Sectional Study," *British Medical Journal,* vol. 330, no. 7491 (March 12, 2005), pp. 581–585.

[272] Ibid.; and Linda H. Harpole and others, "Automated Evidence- Based Critiquing of Orders for Abdominal Radiographs: Impact on Utilization and Appropriateness," *Journal of the American Medical Informatics Association*, vol. 4, no. 6 (November/ December 1997), pp. 511–521.

[273] Lise Poissant and others, "The Impact of Electronic Health Records on Time Efficiency of Physicians and Nurses: A Systemic Review," *Journal of the American Medical Informatics Association,* vol. 12, no. 5 (September/October 2005), pp. 505–516; Lisa Pizziferri and others, "Primary Care Physician Time Utilization Before and After Implementation of an Electronic Health Record: A Time-Motion Study," *Journal of Biomedical Informatics,* vol. 38, no. 3 (June 2005), pp. 176–188; J. Marc Overhage and others, "Controlled Trial of Direct Physician Order Entry: Effects on Physicians' Time Utilization in Ambulatory Primary Care Internal Medicine Practices," *Journal of the American Medical Informatics Association,* vol. 8, no. 4 (July/August 2001), pp. 361–371; and David Gans and others, "Medical Groups' Adoption of Electronic Health Records and Information Systems," *Health Affairs,* vol. 24, no. 5 (September/October 2005), pp. 1323–1333.

[274] Hagop S. Mekhjian and others, "Immediate Benefits Realized Following Implementation of Physician Order Entry at an Academic Medical Center," *Journal of the American Medical Informatics Association,* vol. 9, no. 5 (September/October 2002), pp. 529–539.

[275] A recent Congressional Budget Office report discusses the VA system in greater detail; see Congressional Budget Office, *The Health Care System for Veterans: An Interim Report* (December 2007).

[276] Rates of adoption vary by the definition of health IT used in a particular survey. The rates provided in this analysis are based on the adoption of health IT systems that include all or most recommended capabilities—such as electronic documentation of providers' notes, electronic viewing of laboratory and radiological results, electronic prescribing, computerized physician order entry, clinical decision support, and interoperability with

other systems. See Catherine M. DesRoches and others, "Electronic Health Records in Ambulatory Care—A National Survey of Physicians," *New England Journal of Medicine,* vol. 359, no. 1 (July 3, 2008), pp. 50–60.

[277] Extremely low prices, however, might signal that a product has lower quality and fewer components or features.

[278] David M. Studdert and others, "Claims, Errors, and Compensation Payments in Medical Malpractice Litigation," *New England Journal of Medicine,* vol. 354, no. 19 (May 11, 2006), pp. 2024– 2033.

[279] Among hospital stays during which a patient experienced a severe negligent injury, the probability of the hospital being sued was about 17 percent. Among hospital stays during which a patient either did not experience a severe medical injury or experienced a severe medical injury that was not due to negligence, the probability of the hospital being sued was about 0.07 percent. The ratio of those probabilities (17 percent/ 0.07 percent) is about 250.

[280] Congressional Budget Office calculations based on data from Towers Perrin, *2007 Update on U.S. Tort Cost Trends* (December 2007).

[281] Studdert and others, "Claims, Errors, and Compensation Payments in Medical Malpractice Litigation." Tillinghast-Towers Perrin examines tort costs more broadly, including nonmedical torts, and estimates that payments to claimants (net of attorneys' fees) represent about 46 percent of insured tort costs. See Tillinghast-Towers Perrin, *U.S. Tort Costs: 2003 Update* (December 2003).

[282] The proposed limits could reduce the probability that claims would be filed if they affected the decisionmaking process of potential plaintiffs and their attorneys. Generally, plaintiffs' attorneys receive payment in the form of a contingency fee, meaning they receive a percentage of any award or settlement. Plaintiffs' attorneys, in choosing which cases to take on and which cases to pursue, assess each case to determine the likelihood of receiving an award and the probable amount of any resulting fee. If caps on awards and on attorneys' fees reduced contingency payments, plaintiffs' attorneys would be less likely to take on certain cases, and, in the longer run, fewer attorneys might practice that branch of the law.

[283] Office of Technology Assessment, *Impact of Legal Reforms on Medical Malpractice Costs,* OTA-BP-H-1 19 (September 1993).

[284] Kenneth E. Thorpe, "The Medical Malpractice 'Crisis': Recent Trends and the Impact of State Tort Reforms, *Health Tracking Trends*, Web Exclusive (January 21, 2004).

[285] See these articles by Daniel P. Kessler and Mark B. McClellan: "Malpractice Law and Health Care Reform: Optimal Liability Policy in an Era of Managed Care," *Journal of Public Economics,* vol. 84, no. 2 (May 2002), pp. 175–197; *How Liability Law Affects Medical Productivity,* Working Paper No. 7533 (Cambridge, Mass.: National Bureau of Economic Research, February 2000); and "Do Doctors Practice Defensive Medicine?" *Quarterly Journal of Economics,* vol. 111, no. 2 (May 1996), pp. 353–390.

[286] The details of that research and CBO's synopsis of other studies examining defensive medicine can be found in Congressional Budget Office, *Medical Malpractice Tort Limits and Health Care Spending,* Background Paper (April 2006).

[287] See Health Resources and Services Administration, National Vaccine Injury Compensation Program (VICP), www.hrsa. gov/ vaccinecompensation.

[288] Background information on the derivation of the national health expenditures can be found at www.cms.hhs.gov/ NationalHealthExpendData/downloads/dsm-06.pdf and www.cms.hhs. gov/NationalHealthExpendData/ downloads/ projections-methodology.pdf.

[289] The Balanced Budget Act of 1997 established the sustainable growth rate system, replacing the volume performance standard that had linked payments to the overall growth in the number and mix of services since 1992. Before 1992, Medicare paid physicians on the basis of the lowest of three charges: the physician's actual charge, the customary charge (the amount the physician usually charged for the service), or the prevailing charge (the amount that similar doctors charged).

[290] Oregon Health Services Commission, Office for Oregon Health Policy and Research, *Prioritization of Health Services: A Report to the Governor and the 74th Oregon Legislative Assembly* (Salem, Ore., 2007).

[291] For additional description and details, see Institute of Medicine, *Changing the Health Care System: Models from Here and Abroad* (Washington, D.C.: National Academy Press, 1994), www.nap.edu/catalog.php?record_id=9218#toc; and William J. Hall and Paul F. Griner, "Cost-Effective Health Care: The Rochester Experience," *Health Affairs,* vol. 12, no. 1 (1993), pp. 58–69.

[292] Some nontaxable benefits—such as employers' contributions for social insurance (payroll) taxes—are linked by law to wages and thus automatically change as wages rise or fall.

[293] Individuals also have the option of paying the full amount of the premium directly to the insurer during the year. If they choose that option, they claim the credit on their tax return, thus lowering the amount they owe or increasing their tax refund. Most HCTC claimants, however, opt to pay their share of the premiums to the IRS and thus receive the benefits of the subsidy sooner.

[294] For a discussion of this issue, see Congressional Budget Office, *An Analysis of the Administration's Health Proposal* (February 1994), pp. 41–50.

[295] For more information on UMRA, see Congressional Budget Office, *Identifying Intergovernmental Mandates,* Issue Brief (January 2005).

[296] See Congressional Budget Office, *Labor Supply and Taxes* (January 1996).

[297] Although eligibility for Medicaid varies by state, all states are required to cover pregnant women and children under age 6 whose family income is at or below 133 percent of the federal poverty level, as well as children who are at least 6 and under 19 with family income of up to 100 percent of the federal poverty level.

[298] For estimates of the size of the effect on labor supply, see Aaron S. Yelowitz, "The Medicaid Notch, Labor Supply, and Welfare Participation: Evidence from Eligibility Expansions," *Quarterly Journal of Economics,* vol. 110, no. 4 (November 1995), pp. 909–939.

[299] Proposals might include provisions that offset the impact on after- tax income; for example, the measure included in the President's budgetary proposals for fiscal year 2008 included increases in other deductions to roughly eliminate, on average, the effect on after-tax income. See Congressional Budget Office, *An Analysis of the President's Budgetary Proposals for Fiscal Year 2008* (March 2007).

[300] Ibid.

[301] See Jonathan Gruber and Brigitte C. Madrian, *Health Insurance, Labor Supply, and Job Mobility: A Critical Review of the Literature,* Working Paper No. 8817 (Cambridge, Mass.: National Bureau of Economic Research, March 2002).

[302] Those studies sought to examine the correlation between health benefits and the probability of retirement, controlling for other factors.

[303] For a discussion of those studies, see Brigitte C. Madrian, *The U.S. Health Care System and Labor Markets,* Working Paper No. 11980 (Cambridge, Mass.: National Bureau of Economic Research, January 2006), p. 19.

[304] See Lawrence H. Summers, "Some Simple Economics of Mandated Benefits," *American Economic Review,* vol. 79, no. 2 (May 1989), pp. 177–183.

[305] Katherine Baicker and Helen Levy, *Employer Health Insurance Mandates and the Risk of Unemployment,* Working Paper No. 13528 (Cambridge, Mass.: National Bureau of Economic Research, October 2007).

[306] Norman K. Thurston, "Labor Market Effects of Hawaii's Mandatory Employer-Provided Health Insurance," *Industrial and Labor Relations Review,* vol. 51, no. 1 (October 1997), pp. 117–135.

[307] That plan included subsidies to firms with low average wages to help them pay for the mandated health benefits (because for firms paying low wages, the health benefits represent a higher fraction of the wage bill). That means low-wage workers would effectively have their wages subsidized if they worked at a low-wage firm but not if they worked at a high-wage firm. Smaller firms also would have received higher subsidies under the plan. See Congressional Budget Office, *An Analysis of the Administration's Health Proposal.*

[308] Ibid. For example, CBO estimated that the shifting of employees would have raised the cost of the Clinton Administration's 1993 health care proposal by $12 billion per year once the shifting was complete. In addition, differential treatment based on firms' size could also lead to an inefficient allocation of capital and could change the structure and distribution of firms. For example, subsidies to small firms could encourage large firms to break up into small ones, even if that form of organization was not the most efficient.

[309] Jonathan Gruber and Aaron Yelowitz, "Public Health Insurance and Private Savings," *Journal of Political Economy,* vol. 107, no. 6 (1999), pp. 1249–1274; and Alex Maynard and Jiaping Qiu, "Public Insurance and Private Savings: Who Is Affected and by How Much," Internet draft, October 31, 2005, www.carleton.ca/ economics/seminar%20papers/Alex%20Maynard-April21% 202006.pdf.

[310] See, for example, Robert Haveman and others, "Market Work, Wages, and Men's Health," *Journal of Health Economics,* vol. 13, no. 2 (1994), pp. 163–182.

[311] For a review of such studies, see David E. Bloom, David Canning, and Jaypee Sevilla, "The Effect of Health on Economic Growth: A Production Function Approach," *World Development,* vol. 32, no. 1 (2004), pp. 1–13.

[312] For purposes of estimating the impact of proposed legislation, CBO makes the simplifying assumption that total compensation is fixed and that changes in health insurance costs translate immediately into offsetting changes in wages and other forms of compensation.

CHAPTER SOURCES

The following chapters have been previously published:

Chapter 1 – This is an edited, excerpted and augmented edition of a United States Congressional Research Service publication, Report Order Code RL32237, dated January 28, 2008.

Chapter 2 – This is an edited, excerpted and augmented edition of a United States Congressional Budget Office publication, Pub. No. 3102, dated December 2008.

INDEX

D

E

F

G

H

I

O

P

Q

R

S